Of Walls and Bridges

OF WALLS AND BRIDGES

The United States and Eastern Europe

Bennett Kovrig

A Twentieth Century Fund Book

NEW YORK UNIVERSITY PRESS
New York and London

Copyright © 1991 by the Twentieth Century Fund, Inc.
All rights reserved
Manufactured in the United States of America

p 10 9 8 7 6 5 4 3 2

Library of Congress Cataloging-in-Publication Data
Kovrig, Bennett.
Of walls and bridges : the United States and Eastern Europe /
Bennett Kovrig.
p. cm.
"A Twentieth Century Fund book."
Includes bibliographical references and index.
ISBN 0-8147-4612-8 (acid-free paper)—ISBN
0-8147-4613-6 (pbk. : acid-free paper)
1. Europe, Eastern—Foreign relations—United States.   2. United
States—Foreign relations—Europe, Eastern.   3. United States—
Foreign relations—1945– . I. Title.
DJK45.U5K69   1991
327.73047—dc20   91-2181
                                                            CIP

New York University Press books are printed on acid-free paper
and their binding materials are chosen for strength and durability.

Book design by Ken Venezio

For Michael, Ariana, and Alexander

The Twentieth Century Fund is a research foundation undertaking timely analyses of economic, political, and social issues. Not-for-profit and nonpartisan, the Fund was founded in 1919 and endowed by Edward A. Filene.

Foreword

In the years since World War II, America's policies toward the nations of Eastern Europe were overwhelmingly influenced by global competition between the United States and the USSR. It is tempting to say that the apparent ending of that struggle may result in an even more limited American role in that part of the world. This work, by Bennett Kovrig of Trinity College in Toronto, significantly enriches our understanding of the complexity and nuance of past U.S. policy and of the stakes and possibilities for future American relations with the region.

Hegel's assertion that men and nations learn nothing from history may be right, although not for lack of edifying material. Surely the story of the past forty-five years of U.S. policy toward Eastern Europe offers lessons to current American leaders. There is much to be said, for example, for patience and consistency, underground liberation operations notwithstanding.

The objectives of policy should be realistic, avoiding promises that simply cannot be kept. In addition, we must keep in mind that success is often terribly expensive. The victory over communism in Eastern Europe required billions of Western dollars and a steadfast American will. Realizing the full fruits of that achievement and setting the stage for a long peace likewise may be costly.

Kovrig's book could not be more timely. It may keep many of us from closing the door on our thinking about the cold war in Eastern Europe before we fully understand what happened during those decades of tension, hope, and, finally, triumph. Moreover, Kovrig's study, which was completed during a time of rapid change, continues the Twentieth Century Fund's tradition of supporting research that influences American foreign policy.

RICHARD C. LEONE, Director
The Twentieth Century Fund

Contents

Interest. Kohl's Drive for Unity. Two Plus Four Make One. Europeanism and Regionalism. Finlandization and Beyond. America and the Architecture of Europe.

Acknowledgments

The original impetus for the undertaking came from the Twentieth Century Fund's late director, Murray Rossant, and Scott McConnell. The Fund's current director, Richard C. Leone, and publications director, Beverly Goldberg, and their staff, especially Nina Massen, John Samples, Carol Kahn, Susan K. Hess, and Steven Greenfield, gave generously of their advice and support. Every author should have such good shepherds. To them, and to Niko Pfund of New York University Press, my heartfelt thanks. I'm also indebted to the staff of Radio Free Europe, where I served as Director of Research and Analysis in 1987–88, for the unique expertise and documentation that they have accumulated and continue to offer to students of Eastern Europe.

Introduction

If consistency of purpose and flexibility in tactics are the inseparable hallmarks of a sound foreign policy, America's engagement in the affairs of Eastern Europe has stood the test of history. Only a nation possessed of ideological certainty and the attendant sense of mission could persevere so doggedly in championing the cause of democratic self-determination in a distant region vulnerable to the imperial ambitions of more proximate great powers.

To be sure, pursuit of that goal was fraught with frustration and compromises dictated by other strategic priorities and the limits of American power. Liberation rhetoric could not stop the tanks in Budapest. For all the gradualism of the diplomacy of peaceful engagement, the Brezhnev doctrine prevailed over "socialism with a human face" in Prague. America's differentiation policy nurtured the seeds of Solidarity but did not prevent its temporary demise. The United States dared not jeopardize the West's immediate security by a more aggressive pursuit of its objectives in Eastern Europe, but those objectives were never sacrificed to expedient appeasement of the Soviet Union.

While these tactical adjustments all failed to undo Soviet hegemony, the broad strategy of containment was exerting a steady erosive effect on the Eastern empire. A secure and prospering West set the example.

Economic warfare aggravated the imbalances in the militarized command economies of the Soviet bloc. The ideological war, culminating in the human rights crusade of the 1970s, stiffened internal opposition and drove Communist regimes into a hopeless quest for domestic legitimacy. In retrospect, the struggle was an uneven one, pitting historically irresistible claims to individual freedom, national dignity, and material progress against the self-serving schemes of tyrannical oligarchies. By promising utopia and delivering misery, the latter fanned expectations that they could not fulfill, thus sealing their own fate. The architects and agents of containment anticipated this outcome and strove to speed its arrival.

America's refusal to countenance the legitimacy and permanence of Soviet domination and Communist dictatorship in Eastern Europe found vindication in the exhilarating wind of freedom that swept the cold war into history in 1989. Historians will long debate the causes of the erosion of Soviet power and hegemonic will. But who can doubt that the sustained pressure of containment contributed materially to the chronic instability and ultimate collapse of that empire?

This book aims to trace the historical elements of continuity and flexibility in the pursuit of America's interests in Eastern Europe. The first three chapters give a chronological overview of relevant policies and actions from the Roosevelt to the Bush administrations. Some of this ground was covered in a book I wrote almost twenty years ago, *The Myth of Liberation*. The origins of the cold war have been exhaustively analyzed by an army of statesmen and scholars, and only the essential aspects bearing on Eastern Europe are related here. The account of America's responses to Titoism and the succeeding convulsions that shook the region benefits from more recent revelations.

The remaining three chapters focus more narrowly on the themes of human rights and democratization, the application of economic leverage, and European security, looking back to prior experiences with these issues and forward to the new tasks that face Washington's policymakers. Chapters four and five assess the intent and result of ideological and economic warfare and consider the new necessities of economic and political rehabilitation. Readers familiar with the circumstances of the 1989 revolutions and the shortcomings of socialist economics can skip the relevant sections in chapters four and five, but others might find the brief accounts helpful.

Chapter six investigates, from the perspective of East European policy, the salient issues of European security, from the rigidities of the cold war to the contemporary challenge of devising a new and stable architecture for Europe. As the East Europeans reach westward, as Germany is unified, and as the Soviet Union retrenches and undergoes its own revolution, the balance of power in Europe is being inexorably transformed. The chapter therefore ranges beyond Eastern Europe proper to address historical and current issues of German policy and America's European policy, and to broach the problems of broader European integration.

Eastern Europe is a ramshackle and wobbly wing, greatly in need of reinforcement by the architects of a new European house. It remains vulnerable to the influence, benign or otherwise, of more powerful neighbors, and to its own internal divisions as well. The stimulus of the cold war is gone, but America's commitment to a stable and secure European order must endure. Creative engagement in the affairs of Eastern Europe is an essential component of that commitment and responsibility.

What began as an orderly reassessment of Washington's approaches to Eastern Europe became a chase after a moving target. The exercise brought unexpected rewards, for it came to encompass a historic transformation as the outlines of a new Europe began to take shape.

1

Promises to Keep

After forty years of political and economic exile, the East Europeans are beginning their journey home. Notwithstanding occasional miscalculations and mishaps, the United States has been steadfast in pursuit of this goal. It would be ironic if America's principled commitment flagged just when at long last there looms the prospect of success. Indeed, the promise of self-determination has kept the U.S.-East European relationship alive.

In World War I, the United States contributed the Wilsonian vision of national self-determination to legitimate its participation and forge a more peaceful and democratic order in Europe. But neither its commercial nor its security interests were great enough to warrant active engagement in the affairs of that troublesome region. America's interest in Eastern Europe remained minimal until its global confrontation with the Soviet Union.

Some East European nations, notably Poland and Hungary, gloried in memories of past greatness, but all had fallen prey to Austro-German, Russian, and Ottoman imperial ambitions. Nationalism got its reward at the end of World War I, though Wilson's promise was easier to proclaim than to apply evenhandedly in the ethnic mosaic of Eastern Europe. The compromises reached at Versailles left perhaps only the

5

Czechs fully satisfied. The redrawing of the map at Versailles created an unstable collection of weak states, divided by historic and irredentist animosities. The resulting power vacuum invited foreign manipulation and influence. Predominantly conservative regimes dreaded the new Bolshevik virus and succeeded in repelling it, but the renascent Germany's economic and military power proved irresistible.

Left defenseless by Western appeasement of Hitler, the East Europeans succumbed piecemeal to the Nazi *Gleichschaltung*. Democratic Czechoslovakia was truncated, partitioned, and subjugated, as was Poland in concert with the Soviet Union. Hungary was lured into the Axis by partial satisfaction of its territorial revisionism at the expense of Czechoslovakia and Romania, and the latter was similarly recruited with the bait of regaining Bessarabia from the Soviets. Military force temporarily secured a more compliant regime in Yugoslavia, though the Germans never succeeded in fully pacifying that country. By 1941, German power was preponderant in the region, and Bulgaria, Hungary, Romania, as well as the puppet states of Slovakia and Croatia, were allied to Hitler.

Washington had exhorted the East Europeans to resist German pressure, without offering concrete support. Yugoslavia's Prince Paul protested to the U.S. ambassador, Arthur Bliss Lane, "You big nations are hard. You talk of our honor but you are far away."[1] The United States did not accept the subjugation of Poland, Czechoslovakia, and Yugoslavia, and granted recognition to their exile regimes in London. But American interest in the fate of these countries was not sufficient to overcome isolationism, and there were no commitments such as that to Poland which finally impelled Britain and France to challenge Hitler. When Roosevelt in June 1942 reciprocated declarations of war by the three Axis satellites, he observed that they had taken that step "not upon their own initiative or in response to the wishes of their own peoples but as instruments of Hitler."[2] Regarded by the great powers with a mixture of sympathy and condescension as pawns and victims, the East Europeans could only hope that the war would produce a more benign constellation of forces on the continent.

In historical perspective, the war in Europe may be seen as the continuation of German and Russian rivalry, a contest that neither the feeble efforts of the West Europeans nor the hamstrung League of Nations could attenuate. Although the contest had acquired an ideological dimension, the fundamental stakes remained national power and influence. For most Americans, fascism (with its virulent Nazi variant) and communism were equally abhorrent, but the struggle for predominance in East-Central Europe did not appear to involve crucial U.S. interests. To be sure, Tocqueville's prophecy of American and Russian greatness and competition began to materialize in the twentieth century. The Bolshevik Revolution challenged American values but did not palpably endanger American security and commerce.

Only when Hitler's war had brought Russian power and Communist ideology into the heart of Europe did the United States confront what it perceived to be a direct challenge to its interests. Only then did Eastern Europe assume crucial importance for American foreign policy, as a testimony to Soviet duplicity and aggressiveness and a stimulus for rallying the democracies. The Soviet domination of Eastern Europe not only made a mockery of America's professed war aims but also ostensibly threatened the remaining bastions of liberal democracy and capitalism. Although Washington soon adjusted its challenge to Soviet imperialism to coincide with the limits of its power, its refusal to condone the subjugation of the East Europeans became a doctrine that endures to this day.

Misfortunes of War and Diplomacy. The Grand Alliance came into being to roll back the drive by Germany and Japan for world power, and not for the sake of a few suppressed nations such as the East Europeans.[3] The primary objective was military victory, but political advantage in the peaceful world to come was clearly a secondary aim from the start. Separate and joint political calculations informed Allied tactics and strategy, encompassing both realistic expectations and idealistic hopes regarding the future of Eastern Europe. While there was some realization that these interests might not be fully reconcilable, until Yalta such concerns were subordinated to the requisites of Allied unity. The acrimony that erupted when the time came for peacemaking had its roots in the compromises and misperceptions that accompanied the conduct of total war.

Stalin's Postwar Plans. There is no evidence that Stalin had a blueprint for a postwar order, and until Stalingrad his battle for survival overshadowed longer-term objectives. Initially, the Soviet Union disclaimed any intention of exporting its version of socialism to the prospective liberated areas, but doubtless Stalin already held the view later expressed to the Yugoslav partisan leader Milovan Djilas that in this war "whoever occupies a territory also imposes on it his own social system."[4] He had already demonstrated his readiness to seize opportunities for extending Soviet power, to realize old tsarist ambitions for territorial expansion. His pact with Hitler in 1939 was inspired partly by disappointment at British and French reluctance to challenge Germany, but it brought the USSR tangible gain at the expense of the Baltic states, Finland, Poland, and Romania.

Although the Comintern was nominally dissolved, Communist parties throughout Europe were mobilized by Moscow to lead the resistance, and Stalin anticipated that the political credits thus earned would serve Communists well after the defeat of the Axis. The parties professed a "national front" version of the Comintern's earlier popular front tactic in order to rally anti-Nazi resistance in both Eastern Europe (where, apart from Yugoslavia, the Communist underground was negligible) and Western Europe, where only Charles de Gaulle's Free French emerged as a serious competitor. All of them presented a soothing democratic image that belied their unwavering dedication to eventual Communist revolution.

Thus, in July 1943, an exile "National Committee for a Free Germany" was set up under Soviet auspices, with the future leader Walter Ulbricht playing a prominent role.[5] As the fortunes of war turned against Hitler, and particularly after the opening of the second front, a more confident Stalin proceeded to develop political strategies. A proto-government, the Lublin Committee of Polish Communists, was established in July 1944, and when the Warsaw uprising broke out the following month, the Red Army stood by while the Germans conveniently massacred the anti-Communist Home Army. Also in August, Stalin launched a major offensive on the Romanian front and declared war on Bulgaria, where, within days, a Communist coup followed.

Although Stalin was perfectly aware that the majority of East Europeans abhorred communism, the question was not whether but how Communists and fellow travelers would secure a predominant political role in the liberated areas and ensure governments "friendly" to the Soviet Union on its western approaches. To all appearances, until Yalta Stalin genuinely hoped that he could both obtain a sphere of influence in

Eastern Europe and retain the cooperation and support of the Western Allies.[6] This expectation was due to mutual misperceptions as well as to expedient self-deceptions that can be traced back to the beginnings of the Grand Alliance.

The Atlantic Charter. In August 1941, four months before Pearl Harbor and America's entry into war, Roosevelt and Churchill issued a joint declaration of common principles that would guide their foreign policies. This "Atlantic Charter" proclaimed that they sought no territorial or other aggrandizement nor frontier changes that did not accord with the freely expressed wishes of the peoples concerned, their respect for the "right of all peoples to choose the form of government under which they will live," and their "wish to see sovereign rights and self government restored to those who have been forcibly deprived of them."[7] These principles embodied the American vision for postwar peace, in Eastern Europe and elsewhere, but they were not followed up with concrete planning based on feasibility and the interests of the other Allies. How the principles of the Atlantic Charter could be reconciled with the Soviet Union's "legitimate security interests" was a problem to be amicably resolved by the "Four Policemen" or by the planned United Nations. Indeed, Washington remained wedded to the principle of no predetermination of specific details of the postwar political and territorial settlement until victory was in hand.

Stalin perceived the problem and tried to secure Allied legitimation of the territorial gains he had won by the Molotov-Ribbentrop Pact. Churchill was disposed to compromise, but Washington demurred. In arguing against acceptance, the State Department's European division noted that "there is no doubt that the Soviet Government has tremendous ambitions with regard to Europe" and that "it is preferable to take a firm attitude now" in defence of the Atlantic Charter principles.[8] Occasionally, Roosevelt himself privately anticipated that the Soviet Union would become predominant in East-Central Europe, but more typically he would wax optimistic about his ability to handle Stalin so that the latter "won't try to annex anything and will work with me for a world of democracy and peace."[9]

The U.S.-Soviet Alliance. The axiom that my enemy's enemy is my friend has produced few odder couples than Roosevelt and Stalin, but the United States behaved as the most loyal of allies. Washington's domestic propaganda depicted the man who perfected totalitarianism, created the Gulag, and eliminated millions of his subjects as the benevolent Uncle Joe, agrarian reformer and soldier of freedom. Immense quantities of war materiel and relief supplies were shipped to the USSR under the Lend-Lease program. Comradely loyalty ruled in military circles as well. Even after Stalin's flouting of the Yalta agreements became apparent, Eisenhower stuck to earlier understandings in holding back his advance to allow the Soviets to capture Berlin, Vienna, and Prague and withdrawing his forces to prearranged demarcation lines. Years later, Churchill would lament privately that with Eisenhower elected president he could not in his chronicle of World War II "tell the story of how the United States gave away, to please Russia, vast tracts of Europe they had occupied." [10]

The Office of Strategic Services, under its colorful head, "Wild Bill" Donovan, was not above deceiving allies. In August 1943, Donovan had urged secret talks with Hitler's Balkan satellites to induce them to turn against the Germans and form "relatively stable non-Communist but not anti-Russian governments." Although there were doubts about the feasibility of the project, on September 7 the Joint Chiefs of Staff instructed the OSS to proceed and inform the British and the Soviets but "not consult with the Soviets on the political phase of the proposed operations." Preliminary secret talks were held with the Hungarians and the Bulgarians in neutral capitals, and special operations missions were dispatched to those countries, but since the Americans could not promise to send troops to the Soviet sphere of operations, the separate peace feelers proved fruitless. Hungary, Bulgaria, and Romania would have no choice but to seek armistice terms from Moscow. By September 1944, Donovan was reporting to the president that the USSR clearly intended to dominate the Balkans. Yet the OSS also cooperated extensively with the NKVD, and as late as December of that year, when Moscow had already imposed in Bucharest the first of a series of leftward reorganizations of the government, Donovan betrayed an anti-Soviet plot by Romanian military officers to his Soviet counterparts. [11]

To be sure, no amount of cooperation could fully allay Stalin's chronic suspicions. Despite the Allied agreement on unconditional surrender, he professed outrage at "Operation Sunrise," the secret negotiation conducted by Allen Dulles's OSS team in Bern for the surrender of German forces in Italy, although the Soviets themselves had engaged in tentative contacts with the Germans in the spring and summer of 1943.[12] But Roosevelt's flattery, ingenuous complaints about the need to pacify Polish-American voters, and gentle mockery of Churchill for being an imperialist hardly prepared Stalin for a rigid application of the Atlantic Charter principles at war's end. He had little reason to anticipate that serious objections would be raised to the consolidation of a sphere of influence he considered to be the rightful spoils of war and essential for Soviet security.

Churchill, like Stalin, was more concerned than the president about the political implications of military strategy. In the course of 1943 he repeatedly advocated an Anglo-American thrust into the Balkans, with the obvious aim of preempting the Soviets. But Stalin, who had the psychological advantage of bearing the brunt of the German onslaught and was already suspicious about Anglo-American procrastination in relieving the pressure, insisted on confirmation of Operation Overlord (the assault in northern France), which was also preferred by the U.S. Joint Chiefs of Staff. At the Teheran conference in December 1943, Roosevelt concurred with Stalin, remarking that he saw "no reason for putting the lives of American soldiers in jeopardy in order to protect real or fancied British interests on the continent."[13] The following June, after the Normandy landing, Churchill revived the option of an Anglo-American offensive from northern Italy through the Ljubljana Gap into Central Europe. The president conceded that the attendant political considerations were important but refused to alter existing strategy. The Soviet Union's responsibility for the eastern front would not be diluted in the interest of Western political advantage, though in retrospect such advantage could have dramatically altered the postwar order in Europe.

The East Europeans who observed Allied diplomacy saw that Stalin would hold the trump card in the postwar settlement of their countries' fate, but they adopted divergent tactics. The pro-Soviet exile government of Czechoslovakia's Edvard Benes took the initiative of negotiating a separate mutual defense treaty with the Russians in December 1943 involving the restoration of prewar frontiers and the inclusion of Communists in postwar government. Britain and the United States deplored the treaty as premature, while the Soviets regarded it as a political commitment giving them a *droit de regard* over Czechoslovakia's future political life.

Allied solidarity was tested most sorely by the dilemma of Poland, whose people and leaders were generally Russophobic. The Poles had gallantly if hopelessly resisted the Soviet-German onslaught, and they were making a solid contribution to the war effort on several fronts. General Wladyslaw Sikorski's London government had the allegiance of most Poles, including a sizable underground "Home Army." Polish-Americans were not a negligible factor in U.S. electoral politics. But history had taught the Poles that both Germany and Russia were a threat to their national survival, a lesson confirmed by the Molotov-Ribbentrop Pact. The Soviets nominally conceded in 1941 that the pact had lost its validity, but they registered their wish to retain the new frontier. This corresponded roughly to the Curzon line, which had been proposed by the World War I allies at Versailles; in the Treaty of Riga (1921) ending the Polish-Russian war, the actual frontier was extended eastward by some 150 miles. The ethnic mix of Poles, Ukrainians, and Byelorussians in the disputed region offered little guidance. Much to Churchill's and Roosevelt's discomfort, the Poles adamantly demanded restoration of the Riga frontier.

Stalin perceived that the Central European confederation promoted by the London Poles was directed as much against the Soviet Union as against Germany, and when in April 1943 Sikorski implied (accurately) that the Soviets and not the Germans were guilty of the massacre at Katyn of several thousand Polish officers, Moscow severed relations with the government-in-exile. Irritated by the Poles' obduracy, and reluctant to jeopardize relations with the USSR, Churchill and Roosevelt at Teheran agreed in principle to Stalin's demand for the Curzon line and territorial compensation for Poland at the expense of Germany. The deal not only flouted the Atlantic Charter but also made a future Poland vulnerable to German irredentism and dependent on great power guarantees, in practice on Soviet protection. The furious Poles urged the Americans to reconsider, but the opening of the second front drew near, and Cordell Hull observed that the United States "could not afford to become partisan in the Polish question to the extent of alienating Russia at that crucial moment." [14]

Having written off the exile Poles, Stalin in August-September 1944 proceeded to use the Warsaw uprising to eliminate much of the anti-communist leadership in Poland and discredit the London exile regime. Ambassador Averell Harriman was appalled at Stalin's refusal to allow

American aircraft carrying supplies for the insurgents to use Soviet bases, but Churchill and Roosevelt refrained from pressing the issue. The Germans eventually crushed the uprising and razed Warsaw. This was the moment, reflected George Kennan later, "when, if ever, there should have been a full-fledged and realistic showdown with the Soviet leaders: when they should have been confronted with the choice between changing their policy completely and agreeing to collaborate in the establishment of truly independent countries in Eastern Europe or forfeiting Western-Allied support and sponsorship for the remaining phases of their war effort."[15] But the immediate enemy was Hitler, and loyalty to the Soviet ally prevailed over more sophisticated and long-term calculations.

Spheres of Influence. Increasingly anxious about the spread of Soviet and Communist influence into areas of traditional British interest in the Balkans, Churchill sought Roosevelt's concurrence in a spheres of influence agreement with Moscow. Predetermination and spheres of influence were anathema to Secretary of State Hull, leaving the president to privately give limited assent to Churchill. The latter proceeded in October 1944 to conclude the notorious percentage agreement with Stalin. The division of influence favored the Soviet Union 90–10 in Romania and 75–25 in Bulgaria; Britain secured a 90–10 edge in Greece; influence in Yugoslavia and Hungary was divided 50–50. The deal, insisted Churchill, was purely provisional and did not commit the United States, though Ambassador Harriman had participated as an observer.

At the Moscow embassy, George Kennan wrote to the like-minded Harriman that "as far as the border states are concerned the Soviet Government has never ceased to think in terms of spheres of interest" and expected the United States to be sympathetic.[16] But in Washington the proposed new international organization had planning precedence, and little progress was made in defining political priorities in Eastern Europe. Stalin probably drew encouragement from American passivity and the percentage deal, which, given foreseeable military outcomes, left him with carte blanche in all but Greece. In the event, he (unlike his Yugoslav, Bulgarian, and Albanian associates) refrained from directly assisting the Communists in the ensuing Greek civil war, and he evidently expected his allies to behave with equal restraint in respect to the other countries.

This assumption of Soviet primacy was reflected in the armistice agreements with the three minor Axis allies. They were negotiated in Moscow and signed in September 1944 for Bulgaria and Romania and in January 1945 for Hungary. Despite some Western objections, British and American participation in the Allied Control Commissions was clearly subordinated to the Soviet Union; the Italian model, in which the Soviets were given only token representation, was for Stalin a convenient precedent for linking political predominance to military occupation. The Americans tried to mitigate Moscow's reparations demands and its disposition to favor Romania's claim to Transylvania over that of Hungary, but in the end could only reserve their right to reopen contentious issues at the eventual peace conference.

By the beginning of 1945, coalition governments had been formed under Soviet auspices in the three satellites, and the Communists were reaching for power from above and below with the material assistance of the occupying power. In Yugoslavia, Tito was consolidating his power as the London exile government faded into irrelevance. The British had pragmatically shifted their support away from the less effective forces of the royalist Dragoljub Mihajlovic, while the Americans remained hostile to Tito and suspicious of Russian and British schemes. A British agent who was in Albania at the critical moment in the autumn of 1944 when the Germans pulled out believed that with a "very small British or American intervention we could have saved Albania for the West," but the tiny country fell into the hands of Enver Hoxha's Communists.[17] As for Poland, Stalin's intent to designate the Lublin Committee of National Liberation as the provisional government drew the objections of a "disturbed and deeply disappointed" Roosevelt, but the act was nevertheless consummated on January 5.[18] The political consequences of military strategy and Soviet liberation were becoming manifest.

In November 1944, Secretary of State Edward R. Stettinius summed up for the president America's major interests in Eastern Europe: free choice of political, social, and economic systems, non-restrictive trade and communications policies, freedom of access for American philanthropic and educational organizations, the protection of American property, and settlement of territorial disputes only after the cessation of hostilities.[19] The State Department briefing books Roosevelt took with him to the Yalta Conference in February 1945 accurately depicted the political mood of East Europeans as being "to the left and strongly in favor of far-reaching economic and social reforms, but not, however, in favor of a left-wing totalitarian regime to achieve these reforms." [20] Since "it now seems clear that the Soviet Union will exert predominant political influence over the areas in question," the United States "probably would not want to oppose itself to such a political configuration," but "neither would it desire to see American influence in this part of the world completely nullified." [21] There were less ambivalent hypothetical alternatives, such as Kennan's private advice to Charles Bohlen that the United States bite the bullet and "divide frankly Europe into spheres of influence," writing off Eastern Europe unless it was willing to "go whole hog" in opposing the Soviet domination; but this, in Bohlen's more representative view, "instead of relieving us of responsibility, would compound the felony." [22]

The Declaration on Liberated Europe. The State Department had drafted for the president a four-power declaration of policy governing provisional administrations, early free elections, and economic aid, all to be supervised by an "Emergency High Commission." At the final pre-conference briefing session, Roosevelt rejected the last component mainly on the grounds that the United States "would be loath to assume the responsibilities in regard to the internal problems of the liberated countries that such a standing high commission would unavoidably entail." [23] Shorn of its enforcing mechanism, the proposal issued from the conference as the Declaration on Liberated Europe, essentially a restatement of Atlantic Charter principles. As Churchill observed, the Charter was not "a law but a star." [24] Stalin was no doubt undisturbed by such a purely exhortative proclamation and reassured by Roosevelt's expressed intent to withdraw American troops from the continent within a maximum of two years.

If the Declaration on Liberated Europe nominally confirmed adherence to Atlantic Charter principles, the same could not be said of the agreements on Poland. Roosevelt and Churchill could secure only marginal modification of the Curzon line in favor of Poland and agreed to "substantial" compensation in the form of German territory. Lengthy debates produced only a weak agreement on the reorganization of the Communist provisional government "on a more democratic basis," to be followed by free elections. [25] American public opinion was little exercised by the Soviet Union's territorial demands but sensitive about democratic proprieties, and Roosevelt pleaded with Stalin that the elections be "beyond question, like Caesar's wife." [26]

It did not augur well for Poland that these fateful decisions were taken with scant regard for the views of the Polish government-in-exile, which promptly denounced them. Harriman, among others, has reflected that Roosevelt should have held out for better guarantees of democracy in Poland.[27] But the Poles had not cooperated with the Soviet Union against Nazi Germany in the 1930s, and Stalin was bound to be reluctant to expose his military lines of communication to Germany to a fully independent Polish government. Nor did the token inclusion of some exile politicians in a new Yugoslav assembly offer much prospect of democratic self-determination for that country. In Roosevelt's priorities at Yalta, East European issues were overshadowed by his proposed new international organization and the coordination of the final battle against Japan. His subsequent assurance to Congress, that the Allies would jointly help the East Europeans to "solve their problems through firmly established democratic processes," soon rang hollow even to the American public.[28] Washington's belated planning for peacetime rested on the preservation of a political consensus that was rapidly eroding.

With victory in hand in Europe, the divergent political interests of the Allies inexorably resurfaced. Lip service to the Atlantic Charter would no longer suffice for the concrete tasks of political and economic reconstruction. That Roosevelt's generous spirit and Churchill's pragmatic concessions in defense of the defensible produced an impression of fatalism and weakness with regard to Eastern Europe did not escape such concerned observers as Harriman, who warned from his Moscow vantage point: "It may be difficult for us to believe, but it still may be true that Stalin and Molotov considered at Yalta that . . . we understood and were ready to accept Soviet policies already known to us." [29]

Truman's Hard Line.   Poland remained the major source of discord, and Stalin's intent to allow only token participation by London politicians in the new provisional government drove the dying Roosevelt to protest that this would lead Americans to regard the Yalta agreements as having failed. As the State Department informed the incoming President Truman, since Yalta the Soviets had "taken a firm and uncompromising position on nearly every major question that has arisen in our relations," in particular on Poland.[30] Harriman told Truman on April

20 that "in effect what we were faced with was a 'barbarian invasion of Europe,' that Soviet control over any foreign country did not mean merely influence on their foreign relations but the extension of the Soviet system with secret police, extinction of freedom of speech, etc. and that we had to decide what should be our attitude in the face of these unpleasant facts."[31] After meeting in the White House with his top advisers on April 23, Truman adopted a hard line that he immediately conveyed to a stunned Molotov.

Far from turning conciliatory, Stalin proceeded to derive maximum political benefits from his military advantage, and Truman was not ready to accede to Churchill's urgings that Anglo-American forces should press forward and hold their positions regardless of predetermined occupation lines to gain some leverage over Soviet behavior in Eastern Europe; in July, they began to withdraw from the Soviet zone.[32] Truman sent Harry Hopkins to Moscow ("to see," recalls Kennan, "what could be salvaged from the wreckage of FDR's policy with relation to Russia and Poland"), but Stalin proved impervious to warnings about an increasingly hostile American public opinion and won agreement to a predominantly Communist provisional government.[33] On the understanding that free elections would follow, this regime was grudgingly granted recognition by the United States and Britain on July 5.

The Failure of Economic Leverage.   Indeed, as Washington's anger at Soviet actions in Eastern Europe mounted, the pullbacks followed by demobilization weakened its potential military leverage, and economic leverage was never seriously attempted. The abrupt termination of Lend-Lease shipments immediately after V-E day, though more a bureaucratic fumble than a calculated sanction, only reinforced Stalin's belief that the contest with Western imperialism was entering a new phase. The Soviets had earlier requested a $6 billion loan, but after visiting the Soviet Union, the House Select Committee on Postwar Economic Policy and Planning made its consent conditional on sweeping political reform in that country as well as on strict fulfillment of the Yalta and Potsdam undertakings with respect to Eastern Europe. Anticipating that Moscow would not accept such conditions, the State Department fatalistically gave up active consideration of a loan.[34]

The ravages of war had left most of the East European countries in desperate need of aid for immediate relief and reconstruction. The United

States provided credits for the purchase of American war surplus materiel, but the prospect of substantial loans soon waned as the Soviet
Union proceeded to reorient the region's economies eastward. American-
Polish negotiations on a loan were broken off in May 1946 when the
Warsaw government refused to provide information on its economic and
commercial policies and agreements. Tito was so unpopular in Washington that his request for an Export-Import Bank loan was rejected and he
did not even get credits for surplus. In March 1946, Washington protested to the Soviet Union that its exclusive trade agreement with Hungary violated the spirit of Yalta, and it deplored the "over-burdening
[of] the country with reparations, requisitions, and the cost of maintaining large occupation forces." It proposed a joint program of economic
rehabilitation, which had in fact been invited by the (non-Communist)
Hungarian finance minister, but Moscow rebuffed the initiative.[35] All
the United States could do was to return the gold reserve removed by the
retreating Nazis and grant a $15 million credit for surplus goods.

Economic leverage failed even in the case of relatively autonomous
Czechoslovakia. Prague asked for a $300 million loan in September
1945, then dropped the request, presumably because of Soviet pressure.
Talks were resumed in February, when Washington set a $50 million
limit, but they were marked by disagreements over the settlement of
American claims and the issue of disclosure of Czechoslovak economic
and trade policy. When at the Paris peace conference in August 1946 the
Czechoslovak delegation ostentatiously applauded a Soviet diatribe about
American economic imperialism, James F. Byrnes promptly ordered the
suspension of surplus deliveries, and the loan negotiations were suspended.[36] President Benes and other non-Communists privately approved
Washington's pressure, hoping that their country could retain economic
links with both East and West. That hope was definitively dashed only
when Moscow prevented Prague from enrolling in the European Recovery Program. But even in late 1945 the East European regimes were not
free enough to accept the reasonable conditions for American aid.[37]

Idealism vs. Reality.   Truman remained wedded to the diplomatic pursuit of Atlantic Charter principles not because the United States had
discovered crucial security or economic interests in Eastern Europe but
simply because the American people would not readily surrender the
democratic ideals for which the war had been fought. Through 1945

congressional attitudes became increasingly hostile to the Soviet Union and in favor of a tougher American stance. The United States accepted Soviet primacy of influence in Eastern Europe as long as it accommodated freely elected governments, whereas Stalin anticipated that such governments would not be sufficiently compliant to Soviet interests. That was the unbridgeable gap, and to condone a Soviet order that manifestly did not enjoy popular support in Eastern Europe was not a politically feasible option for the United States. On the other hand, as the president records in his memoirs, "I did not want to become involved in the Balkans in a way that could lead us into another world conflict."[38] Thus, from the start, the principled refusal to accept the Stalinist version of a sphere of influence was adjusted to the higher priorities of American power. The illusions inspired by the Atlantic Charter among ordinary Americans and East Europeans became the casualty of this asymmetry between idealism and harsh reality.

Peacemaking after Yalta consisted of piecemeal diplomatic efforts to salvage some minimal Western influence and a semblance of democracy in Eastern Europe. A prudent Stalin instructed East European Communists to pursue a coalition strategy while securing the key levers of power, notably the interior ministries. In 1945 he even allowed relatively free elections in Austria (which the Allies had agreed during the war to treat with undeserved charity as Hitler's first victim) and Hungary, but they resulted in humiliating defeat for the Communists. In Poland, despite Stalin's promise of early and unfettered elections, a fraudulent constitutional referendum was followed in January 1947 by an even more fraudulent election claimed by the Communists to give their bloc an overwhelming mandate. Only in unoccupied Czechoslovakia did the Communists in May 1946 win a substantial plurality, some 38 percent of the national vote, although their popular support subsequently waned. In Czechoslovakia as elsewhere the Communists' road to power depended more on unconventional methods (what the Hungarian party chief Matyas Rakosi called "salami tactics") than on parliamentarianism. When wartime harmony gave way to Western protests, the Soviets professed surprise. The veteran diplomat Maxim Litvinov complained off the record to a private visitor in mid-1945: "Why did you Americans wait until now to begin opposing us in the Balkans and Eastern Europe? . . . You should have done this three years ago. Now it's too late and your complaints only arouse suspicion here."[39]

Potsdam and the Cold War.   At the Potsdam Conference in July 1945, the deadlock over Eastern Europe remained unresolved. Despite Soviet urgings, the United States withheld recognition of the Bulgarian, Hungarian, and Romanian regimes and requested internationally supervised elections; the result, in the words of a participant, was "a complete impasse and might be said to have been the beginning of the cold war."[40] Nor could the West obtain more than token influence in the Allied Control Commissions, the Soviets again pointing to Western practice in Italy and reluctance to include them in the postwar supervision of Japan. With regard to Poland, Stalin presented the conference with the fait accompli of Polish administration in German territory east of the Oder-Neisse line and precipitous expulsion of the inhabitants. After securing a compromise on German reparations, Truman gave his assent subject to final determination at a peace conference (which never materialized). Nevertheless, two weeks later the Soviet Union concluded a treaty with Poland guaranteeing the new frontier.

The successful test of an atomic device at Alamogordo during the Potsdam Conference potentially shifted the global balance of military power in favor of the United States. Its immediate utility, which no one, including Stalin, questioned at the time, was to secure early victory over Japan. Truman did hope that it would be an asset in persuading the USSR to be more conciliatory with regard to Eastern Europe, and after the Japanese surrender he promoted the idea of an international authority for atomic energy. To the extent that this was intended as a bargaining chip, the effect was imperceptible, for while the Soviets eventually accepted the American proposal for a United Nations Atomic Energy Commission, they made only token political concessions in Eastern Europe in late 1945 and 1946.

Postdam was dominated by the problem of Germany. The division into occupation zones had been determined in rather casual fashion in early 1944 by the European Advisory Commission. It was now decided that the country (reduced by Soviet and Polish territorial acquisitions) would be treated as a single economic unit for all purposes, including reparations. Stalin was initially intent on extending his influence over a united Germany, instructing the German Communists in his zone to work within an embryonic multiparty system. The reparations compromise, on the other hand, enhanced the role of the zonal authorities at the expense of the Allied Control Council; the Soviets would take their due from their own zone and in addition receive 10 percent of industrial capital equipment deemed unnecessary for the German peace economy from the other zones as well as a further 15 percent in exchange for food and other commodities from the Soviet zone.[41]

The American approach was formally defined in JCS 1067, itself inspired by the harshly punitive Morgenthau Plan, and involved demilitarization, denazification, and deindustrialization. It soon became apparent, however, that starvation, collapse, and prolonged dependence on American relief aid could only be averted by promoting economic revival. Common Allied policy was necessary to achieve this on the basis of economic unity, but agreement was hampered both by Soviet unilateralism and by de Gaulle's resistance to unification and the restoration of central German administration. And American fears were mounting, as recorded by Kennan in March 1946, about the prospect of a Germany "nominally united but extensively vulnerable to Soviet political penetration and influence."[42] In the Soviet zone, Moscow-imposed economic reforms and the forced merger of the Social Democratic Party with the Communist Socialist Unity Party (SED) suggested that if Stalin was keeping his options open on unification, he would only condone it on his terms.

The Division of Europe. As the threat of a divided Europe loomed, Undersecretary of State Dean Acheson and Assistant Secretary for Economic Affairs Will Clayton presented Secretary of State Byrnes with a draft proposal (endorsed by the father of West European integration, Jean Monnet) for a European settlement on an all-European basis. Designed to forestall the consolidation of a Soviet sphere and to provide a secure framework for a disarmed and reunited Germany, the plan called for a regional UN security council to oversee the peace settlements and an all-European economic organization backed by American aid. "We believed," recalls Walt Rostow, one of the plan's authors, "that acceptance of the split was a weak, not a strong policy," and that this scheme would be a better test of Soviet intentions; Byrnes dismissed the plan; Truman never saw it; and Rostow himself concedes that the probability of Soviet concurrence was low.[43]

Byrnes in April 1946 proposed a four-power treaty guaranteeing the disarmament of Germany for twenty-five years. However, mounting disagreements with Moscow over reparations and implementation of a common export-import program drove the American zonal commander, General Lucius Clay, to suspend on May 3 further deliveries to the Soviet zone. Two months later, Molotov declared that in light of the reparations problem Byrnes's demilitarization guarantees were meaningless.

The fundamental reappraisal in early 1946 of American policy toward the Soviet Union was reflected in Byrnes's Stuttgart speech of September 6. The United States still favored unification and guaranteed demilitarization, but it would not let Germany become a Soviet satellite, and "if complete unification cannot be secured, we shall do everything in our power to secure maximum possible unification."[44] Three months later, the British and American zones were fused into the economic unit of Bizonia, to be joined in 1948 by the French zone. Secretary of State George C. Marshall made another futile effort, at Moscow in the spring of 1947, to secure an all-German peace settlement acceptable to the West, but the division of Germany and of Europe was only confirmed. The West would henceforth direct its efforts toward reconstructing its share of Germany and preserving its foothold in Berlin. To the extent that Stalin's quest for a sphere of dominance in Eastern Europe had been motivated by the fear of a resurgent Germany, the failure of the erstwhile allies to come to terms on that country's future only reinforced the strategic necessity of such a sphere for the Soviet Union.

The deterioration in Soviet-American relations had gathered speed in early 1946. In a speech on February 9, Stalin reminded Soviet citizens of the ineluctable conflict between communism and capitalism. A week later came the revelation in Canada of a Soviet espionage operation to obtain atomic secrets. Soviet policies in Iran, which Stalin appeared unwilling to evacuate, the Far East, the Middle East, as well as in Europe were appraised as inimical to American interests. In Congress, Republican criticism of the administration's alleged disposition to appease the Soviets became strident, notably on the part of Senator Vandenberg, who regarded Byrnes as a dangerous compromiser; and in November the Republicans for the first time since 1930 gained control of both houses. By March, an opinion poll suggested that 71 percent of the American people disapproved of Soviet foreign policy, and 60 percent felt the United States was too soft in its response.[45]

Less Patience, More Firmness. These perceptions of being "soft on communism" were reinforced by the famous "long cable" that the charge d'affaires in Moscow, George Kennan, sent to Byrnes on February 22, 1946. In his analysis, Kennan opined that the Soviet dictatorship was wedded to a rigid ideological doctrine denying the possibility of coexisting peacefully with the West and impelling it to expand power and influence. The United States, concluded Kennan, had to resist Communist expansion while waiting for internal changes to alter Soviet policy.[46] This intellectual rationalization of a "get tough" policy fitted perfectly the mood in Washington. Within two weeks, after consulting with Truman, Churchill delivered his historic "iron curtain" speech in Fulton, Missouri. The Soviets, he warned, wanted "the fruits of war and the indefinite expansion of their power and doctrines" and had contempt for military weakness. Only Western resolve, manifested through the United Nations by Anglo-American collaboration, could preserve peace.[47] In September, the President's special counsel, Clark Clifford, presented Truman with a report on U.S.-Soviet relations that went beyond the Kennan thesis in arguing that the USSR was preparing for an inevitable war with capitalist states. American concessions would be viewed as a sign of weakness and encourage it to increase its demands. Only the language of military power could dissuade the Soviet leaders.[48]

If the necessity of a policy of "patience with firmness" was rapidly becoming the conventional wisdom in Washington, the attainable objective according to Clifford's report was "to confine Soviet influence to its present area." The implication of the iron curtain metaphor was that Eastern Europe had slipped irretrievably into the Soviet sphere. As the new American ambassador, Walter Bedell Smith, reported from Moscow at the end of May, the common British and American view was that the Soviet Union "is determined to continue domination over these states and is prepared to go to almost any length and employ almost any measures to achieve this end." Therefore, "the facts of the situation compel us to view Europe not as a whole, but as divided essentially into two zones."[49] In the same spirit, a Joint Chiefs of Staff report in July concluded that the "chief European problem area in the postwar relations of the USSR and the Western powers will be in the zone lying between the belt of small countries on the USSR's western frontiers where Soviet influence will be predominant and the countries of Western Europe." That zone comprised Germany and Austria, for even Hungary and Czechoslovakia "appear to be in the Soviet sphere."[50] "The fact of the matter," observed Kennan at about the same time, "is that we do not have power in Eastern Europe really to do anything but talk."[51]

There was plenty of talk, most of it acrimonious and unproductive, for Washington persevered in its diplomatic efforts to secure reasonably representative governments in the countries liberated by the Soviet Union. In September 1945, at the first meeting of the Council of Foreign Ministers (created at Potsdam to work out the details of the peace treaties), Byrnes agreed to recognize the provisional Hungarian government upon receiving a pledge of free elections. But the Russians would make no similar concession regarding Bulgaria and Romania, where Soviet-Communist control was more advanced. A fact-finding mission headed by the Louisville publisher Mark Ethridge was dispatched by Byrnes to Sofia and Bucharest, and reported on December 3 on the authoritarian and unrepresentative character of those regimes. At the foreign ministers' meeting in Moscow later that month, Byrnes caved in and agreed to recognize the regimes, subject to inclusion of a few opposition politicians and elections. Truman was incensed at the compromise, asserting that he was "tired of babying the Soviets," but despite ritualistic American diplomatic protests the consolidation of Communist power proceeded complete with pseudoelections and the persecution of political opponents.[52] As for Yugoslavia, when the American ambassador arrived in Belgrade in December, he conveyed Washington's view that the recent elections there had not been free and that diplomatic relations were not to be construed as approval of the Tito regime.[53]

As negotiation over the peace treaties dragged on through 1946, it was apparent that in the case of Hitler's former allies in Eastern Europe the Soviet Union would call the shots. The Western powers championed Italy (securing over Yugoslav opposition an interim "free territory" solution for Trieste) and unoccupied Finland (which, being of marginal strategic importance, occasioned little controversy) but were fatalistic about the rest.

In the case of Hungary, where despite growing Communist pressure pro-Western elements still held a majority in the coalition government, the political stakes included the status of territories, inhabited in the majority by Hungarians, that had been reannexed from Czechoslovakia and Romania early in the war. Czechoslovakia wished to expel the Hungarians, Romania to recover all of Transylvania. The American minister to Budapest, H.F.A. Schoenfeld, had argued in March that it was "more important for us to consider the effect of a frontier revision on Hungarian internal politics than on Rumanian internal politics inasmuch as Hungary is still a twilight zone in respect to Soviet expansion whereas the shadows falling on Rumania are already of a deeper hue."[54] Although the Americans and British made a token effort to secure a territorial adjustment in favor of Hungary, the Soviet preference for rewarding Romania (which, however, had to cede Bessarabia to the Soviet Union) prevailed. Nor could Hungary be effectively aided by the West at the expense of Czechoslovakia, an Allied country, and the minority question was left to the two parties to resolve.[55] Only in the case of Bulgarian territorial claims against Greece did Western opposition succeed.

The resulting peace treaties, signed on February 10, 1947, in Paris, bound the various governments to respect human rights and fundamental freedoms and assigned supervision of their execution to the three great powers acting in concert. Despite an American attempt to reduce Hungary's reparations burden, the Soviets prevailed, as they did in trimming their Bulgarian client's reparations to Greece and Yugoslavia. The treaties limited the size of armed forces and specified the withdrawal within ninety days from ratification of occupation troops—apart from those required to guard lines of communication. Since the Soviet Union was blocking progress on German and Austrian peace treaties, that qualification legitimated its continued military presence. Truman reported lamely to Congress that he did "not regard the treaties as completely satisfactory. Whatever their defects, however, I am convinced that they are as good as we can hope to obtain by agreement among the principal wartime Allies. Further dispute and delay would gravely jeopardize political stability in the countries concerned for many years."[56] No one doubted that the conditions of that stability would be set by the Soviet Union. The treaties, observed Kennan, "contain numerous clauses which we know full well will never be implemented."[57] They would provide a legal basis for American protests, and nothing more.

American Policy Alternatives.   Could alternative American approaches have secured the realization of the Atlantic Charter's promise in Eastern Europe? The most plausible answer was Litvinov's, who, when asked in November 1945 by Harriman what the United States could do to satisfy the Soviet Union, replied: "Nothing."[58] A stronger formula might have been negotiated at Yalta, and the extent of Anglo-American military occupation maximized and exploited as a bargaining counter. But once the Red Army was entrenched in the region, only superior strength could have induced its withdrawal, and in 1945 the American public yearned for demobilization and tax cuts. Nor did the desirability of democracy in faraway countries warrant serious consideration of atomic blackmail. Washington could have reciprocated Soviet procrastination on the German and Austrian treaties, but that would have totally paralyzed the process and blocked the Finnish and Italian settlements without any likelihood of halting the Communist grab for power in Eastern Europe. As for a more comprehensive scheme of the Acheson-Clayton variety, it would have required a degree of mutual trust and compatibility of values that was absent even at the moment of greatest wartime harmony. In the final analysis, Eastern Europe was lost to democracy not in peace but in war.

The criticism that by pursuing democracy in Eastern Europe Washington rode roughshod over legitimate Soviet security interests and only accelerated the process of Sovietization is as fanciful as the notion that it was driven fundamentally by capitalist ambition. In fact, America's economic interest in the region was marginal. Exports in 1937 ranged from $147,000 for Albania to a still paltry $26 million for Poland; they added up to barely 2 percent of total U.S. exports. American assets amounted to some $560 million, 4 percent of global foreign investments, and of that only $278,600,000 were investments in American-controlled enterprises.[59] Protests at the alleged conversion of Eastern Europe into a Soviet colony and advocacy of nondiscriminatory commercial and economic policies were the reflection of a general American approach to world trade and finance that only the Communists found objectionable. That U.S. economic security needs informed the Marshall Plan and containment policy is self-evident and axiomatic, since such needs are inseparable from national security.[60]

Nor does the balance of evidence indicate that American political advocacy was counterproductive. The popular front tactics in the various countries appeared to be marginally calibrated to Soviet priorities and Western sensibilities. Poland was crucial to Soviet security, Bulgaria and Romania conceded by Churchill, Yugoslavia secured by Tito. In these countries Stalin took no risk of holding back Communist ascendancy. A greater concession to pluralistic democracy was afforded in Hungary, perhaps partly to compensate in Western eyes for the subjugation of Allied Poland; but there, too, the Communists were steadily advancing to a position of political predominance. And even in Czechoslovakia the Communists were maneuvering to undermine an already pro-Soviet regime. To the extent that Western action influenced the pace of domestic political change, it served to prolong rather than eliminate the token tributes to democratic practice paid by Stalin's servants.

Stalin's intention to secure Communist-dominated regimes was clear from the start, and the fact that this process was accompanied by some objectively beneficial social and economic policies, such as land reform, hardly made it democratic. It might as well be argued that rural electrification justified the eventual imposition of integral Stalinism. To be sure, as Kennan observed in October 1946, no East European regime was a perfect replica of the Stalinist model or professed to aim at a classic "dictatorship of the proletariat," but the superficial form was less significant than the emerging substance.[61] The early experiments with free elections had taught the Communists that there was no clean road to power. Communist rule, whatever its precise form, could not be reconciled with the requisites of democratic self-determination, and the United States jeopardized no higher national interest by its ultimately fruitless defense of principle.

The Policy of Containment. Master at long last of its western approaches, the USSR could have rested content; driven by the momentum of power and Marxist determinism, Stalin did not. Through 1947 and 1948 a fateful spiral of action and reaction confirmed the split between the Soviet Union and the West, and American policy regarding Eastern Europe became a function of this hardening confrontation. The term containment, coined by George Kennan (who had been appointed by Secretary of State Marshall to head the department's new Policy Planning Staff) in his famous "X" article in the July 1947 issue of *Foreign Affairs,* came to denote the complex and evolving response of the United States to the perceived Soviet threat.[62] In Kennan's view, the Soviet-directed Communist movement was impelled by a structure and ideology impervious to the influence of traditional diplomacy. Since this force threatened American values and ultimately American security interests, the United States had to bolster resistance, more by economic than by military means, in key areas, first and foremost in Western Europe. Thus contained, the Soviet threat could eventually be undermined by the system's internal stresses and contradictions, allowing for the resumption of more civilized dialogue and negotiation. In this essentially evolutionary approach, Eastern Europe's subjugation would add to the burdens of empire and hasten that empire's natural dissolution.

On March 12, 1947, the president announced that in response to an urgent appeal from London he had committed the United States to give military and economic assistance to the embattled anti-Communist regimes in Greece and Turkey. Avoiding the term communism, Truman declared that "totalitarian regimes imposed on free peoples, by direct or indirect aggression, undermine the foundations of international peace and hence the security of the United States," and that Washington would therefore take preventive steps. The administration subsequently made clear that this did not aim at countries already under Soviet control.[63] Convinced after his meeting with Stalin that the latter would not cooperate on the German and other European problems, Marshall turned to unilateral initiatives. Kennan's staff developed a proposal for stimulating European economic recovery which, revealed by the secretary of state on June 5, came to be known as the Marshall Plan. Ostensibly the offer did not exclude the Soviet sphere. The East Europeans, argued Kennan, should "either exclude themselves by unwillingness to accept the proposed conditions or agree to abandon the exclusive orientation of their economies," and in this way "we would not ourselves draw a line of division through Europe."[64]

But an earlier report by the Joint Strategic Survey Committee to the Joint Chiefs of Staff had already concluded that "no country under Soviet control should receive assistance from the United States until every vestige of Soviet control had been removed therefrom." It identified Germany as potentially the strongest military power in Western Europe and argued that its economic revival was of "primary importance" to American security. Therefore, although the State Department had included Hungary, Czechoslovakia, and Poland in its list of eighteen countries urgently needing American assistance, the JSSC report argued that because of security priorities no aid be given them.[65]

To the extent that the Marshall Plan was intended to test East European autonomy, the results confirmed Washington's expectations. The Soviets walked out of the preparatory conference, rejecting the conditions as interference in their internal affairs. Among the East Europeans, only the Czechoslovaks were bold enough to accept the invitation, and they were promptly ordered by Stalin to withdraw, on the grounds that the plan was anti-Soviet. Jan Masaryk commented bitterly: "It is a new Munich. I left for Moscow as Minister of Foreign Affairs of a sovereign state. I am returning as Stalin's stooge." [66]

American largesse was intended to expedite the economic revival and political consolidation of Western Europe, as well as to promote its integration, the first step being the creation of the European Coal and Steel Community. Covert funding was also given to anti-Communist parties and trade unions, notably in France and Italy. (In the case of the latter the CIA took some credit for the victory of the Christian Democrats in the 1948 elections.) In Eastern Europe, by the end of the 1947 the U.S. administration had approved export controls that increased its economic isolation; within a year, American exports were less than a quarter of the postwar high reached in 1946.[67] By 1952 American exports to the region (excluding Yugoslavia) had dwindled to less than $6 million. Although this strategic embargo was not expected to alter the satellites' status, it took its place in the general strategy of weakening Soviet military might (see chapter 5).

The Sovietization of Eastern Europe. Concurrently, the Sovietization of Eastern Europe gathered speed. Although Washington had few illusions about its remaining influence in the region, the Central Intelligence Agency anticipated that at least in Poland socialist and other democratic parties would retain a measure of independence for a long time.[68] But Stalin was impatient, and at a secret conference hastily convened by the Russians in September 1947 at Szklarska Poreba near the Polish city of Wroclaw, Andrei Zhdanov confirmed the division of the world into two antagonistic camps. In a carefully staged crescendo, the "democratic road to socialism" was roundly denounced. The Americans, with their Marshall Plan, were the immediate peril, and prompt adoption of the Soviet and Yugoslav models of Communist dictatorship (or, in the case of the French and Italian parties, uncompromising opposition) was the only acceptable tactic. A new institution, the Cominform, would help to coordinate the imposition of Stalinist uniformity.[69]

Within a few months, the more backward East European Communist parties had forcibly absorbed the social democrats, their main competitor for the allegiance of the working class. By the end of 1948 the elimination or neutralization of all institutionalized opposition, including the churches, was accomplished. The Americans, apart from delivering diplomatic protests, were reduced to facilitating the escape of a few politicians and scientists. Czechoslovakia had the longest road to travel, but by the autumn of 1947 Kennan foresaw the imminence of a Communist coup.[70] Washington's last-minute offer of a $25 million credit, designed to bolster democratic elements, arrived only days before President Benes caved in to Soviet and domestic Communist pressure and appointed, on February 25, 1948, a Communist government. The last domino had fallen.

The Militarization of Containment.   The Prague coup, combined with Soviet pressures over Berlin and Communist activism in Western Europe, created an atmosphere of crisis that hastened the militarization of containment. War, reported General Clay from Frankfurt in March (perhaps less out of anxiety than to provide the administration with political ammunition), "may come with dramatic suddenness."[71] The response to these alarums took the form of the Brussels Treaty, a West European collective defense agreement signed in March 1948, followed by the Senate's endorsement of the Vandenberg resolution, which called for an expansion of U.S. military strength and military as well as economic assistance programs. Stalin ordered the shift to a "war economy" throughout his domain, and by 1949 the satellite armies were being built up beyond treaty limits. There was no clear evidence to show that Stalin intended to use military force beyond his perimeter in Europe (with the possible exception of Yugoslavia)—he was cautious as well as opportunistic—but the West girded for war.

The perception of Soviet aggressiveness, not to say war hysteria, led to an emphasis on collective security, which in turn required quick resolution of the German impasse. When the Council of Foreign Ministers failed to make progress at its December 1947 meeting, the Western powers developed the "London Program" for the creation of an independent West Germany. Stalin responded in June 1948 by blockading Berlin. Rejecting more forceful options, Truman resorted to an air-bridge to sustain the city. When the Russians lifted the blockade in May 1949, Truman decided that the West had to keep rearming to prevent Stalin from exploiting weakness.[72] Kennan's Policy Planning Staff earlier had developed an alternative proposal for all-German elections and a phased withdrawal of occupation forces leading to a reunited and demilitarized Germany, but Dean Acheson (who took over as secretary of state in January 1949) recalls that "we soon came to believe that our chief concern should be the future of Europe, and that the reunification of Germany should not be regarded as the chief end in itself." [73]

What followed was the proclamation of the Federal Republic of Germany in the Western zone and the Soviet transfer of administration of its zone to a Communist-dominated provisional government. Moscow persisted with proposals to reunify Germany; the West persistently rebuffed them. It is conceivable that even if he could not attain his primary objective of a Communist-dominated reunited Germany, Stalin would have genuinely preferred a demilitarization and reunification to a militarized NATO (hurriedly founded in April 1949) that incorporated a majority of the Germans. But he had lost all credibility in the West, and Washington would not break the momentum of alliance-building for the sake of uncertain negotiation. Nor would compromise on Germany have eliminated the traditional Russian desire for influence in Eastern Europe, but it might have attenuated Soviet insecurity and the imposition of Stalinism. [74] In the event, the Marshall Plan and NATO dashed Stalin's hopes for a weak and vulnerable Western Europe and reinforced his determination to consolidate his domain in the East.

FDR's universalist vision of a peaceful world patrolled by the benevolent Four Policemen gave way to the reality of a tough and moralistic sheriff leading two cranky invalids and a hastily paroled mass murderer in a global battle for turf against a paranoid red bully. Just as the Soviet Union in 1941 was converted by American propaganda from godless pariah to stalwart ally, so West Germany was now hailed as an essential partner in the league for liberty and decency. The American public adjusted readily to this reversal of images; nazism had been a malignant tumor, but communism was a deadly global virus. And if for the Soviet Union Eastern Europe became an indispensable strategic and ideological asset, for Washington it became a reason to stiffen the West's resolve.

Fostering Anti-Communism. While a secure Western Europe was America's first priority, containment encompassed more aggressive tactics as well. On the premise that "the defeat of the forces of Soviet-directed communism is vital to the security of the United States," a

National Security Council (NSC) report in March 1948 recommended that the U.S. "develop, and at the appropriate time carry out, a coordinated campaign to support underground resistance movements in countries behind the iron curtain, including the Soviet Union." [75] The first full elaboration of American objectives came that August in NSC 20/1, prepared by the Policy Planning Staff on the request of Defense Secretary James V. Forrestal. A peacetime aim of the United States was "to encourage and promote by means short of war the gradual retraction of undue Russian power and influence from the present satellite area," to be accomplished "by skillful use of our economic power; by direct or indirect informational activity, by placing the greatest strain possible on the maintenance of the iron curtain," and by the attraction of a prosperous and free Western Europe. However, there was need for flexibility and prudence in order to "make possible a liberation of the satellite countries in ways which do not create an unanswerable challenge to Soviet prestige" and raise the risk of war.[76] By November 1948, the administration had convinced itself that "the ultimate objective of the leaders of the USSR is the domination of the world." American intelligence estimated that the Soviets could overrun continental Europe and the Near East as far as Cairo in six months. The Stalin-Tito schism raised expectations, however, that "if the United States were to exploit the potentialities of psychological warfare and subversive activity within the Soviet orbit, the USSR would be faced with increasing disaffection, discontent, and underground opposition." The United States therefore had to "place the maximum strain on the Soviet structure of power and particularly on the relationships between Moscow and the satellite countries." [77]

The fullest exposition of American policy regarding Eastern Europe came in NSC 58/2, approved by Truman on December 13, 1949. With Western Europe politically stabilized and on the road to economic recovery, "the time is now ripe for us to place greater emphasis on the offensive to consider whether we cannot do more to cause the elimination or at least a reduction of predominant Soviet influence . . . because [the satellites] are in varying degrees politico-military adjuncts of Soviet power." A war initiated by the United States was not a practical alternative. Less forceful tactics included the encouragement of Communist heretics and nationalists, of "non-Stalinist regimes as temporary administration," all without impairing the potential emergence of fully non-

Communist regimes; diplomatic pressure to attack Soviet-satellite ties; and measures to "jolt" the economic structure of the Soviet bloc, since "it is probably in the economic realm that we can most concretely make our influence felt."

Stressing the centrality of psychological warfare, NSC 58/2 recommended that the United States should "do what it can . . . particularly through covert operations and propaganda, to keep alive the anti-communist sentiment . . . in the satellite countries. To do less would be to sacrifice the moral basis of United States leadership of free peoples." That the proposed measures might not be up to the task was conceded in the final conclusion: "The United States should, in developing its plans and programs, bear in mind the possibility that the USSR might resort to a war susceptible of becoming global rather than suffer loss of the Eastern European satellite states."[78]

By the time the critical redefinition of American security objectives, NSC 68/2, was approved in September 1950, Communists had taken over China, the Soviets had tested their atomic bomb, and the North Koreans had launched their offensive against the South. According to intelligence estimates, the West's military buildup made "any major deferment of the Soviet program to attain world domination" unlikely, implying a definite danger of global war. The danger peaked in 1953.[79] On the other hand, the State Department considered that although the Kremlin was behind the Korean attack and would likely "probe the firmness of our purpose and our nerves at other sensitive points," it did not intend to set off a general war.[80] What Stalin's real plans were, and what the West knew of them, remains unclear. By one account, he had a scheme to move into West Germany and deliver an ultimatum to the United States to leave Europe within seven days, and he set off the Korean War to divert America's energies. Other sources have reported that at a top-level bloc meeting in January 1951 Stalin unveiled a plan to invade Western Europe. The Soviet bloc could only retain its military superiority for a few years, he said. It should therefore seize the opportunity and mobilize all its resources to extend socialism to the rest of Europe.[81]

Despite the uncertainties regarding Stalin's intentions, the key policymakers opted for decisive action. As the distinguished historian John Lewis Gaddis observed, a "cost-minimizing" strategy was superseded by a "risk-minimizing" strategy.[82] Containment began as a long-term policy with limited security objectives; as elaborated by Acheson and the new Policy Planning Staff director, Paul Nitze, in NSC 68/2, it became a call to arms to resist Communist expansion at all points of the compass: "The cold war is in fact a real war in which the survival of the free world is at stake."[83] Since the option of preventive war "would be repugnant to many Americans," and since atomic threat would not likely obtain Soviet capitulation, the feasible alternative was "a rapid buildup of political, economic and military strength."

This virtual state of war demanded offensive as well as defensive measures. The United States, recommended NSC 68/2,

should take dynamic steps to reduce the power and influence of the Kremlin inside the Soviet Union and other areas under its control. The objective would be the establishment of friendly regimes not under Kremlin domination. Such action is essential to engage the Kremlin's attention, keep it off balance and force an increased expenditure of Soviet resources in counteraction. In other words, it would be the current Soviet cold war technique used against the Soviet Union.

Appropriate techniques would include "intensification of affirmative and timely measures and operations by covert means in the fields of economic warfare and political and psychological warfare with a view to fomenting unrest and revolt in selected strategic satellite countries."

The prospect of change through negotiation had hardly been entertained in NSC 58, and in NSC 68/2 it was considered necessary only as a tactic to win support for the military buildup and the recruitment of Germans and Austrians to the cause. Another State Department report observed that while it was premature for the United States to publicly press for German rearmament, "our present German and European policies are designed to create with the maximum speed possible the conditions under which Germany can be completely aligned with the West."[84] That this was no time for real negotiation was confirmed by NSC 68/2:

The present world situation [. . .] is one which militates against successful negotiations with the Kremlin—for the terms of agreements on important pending issues would reflect present realities and would therefore be unacceptable, if not disastrous, to the United States and the rest of the free world. After a decision and a start on building up the strength of the free world has been made, it might then be desirable for the United States to take an initiative in seeking negotiations in the hope that it might facilitate the process of accommodation by the Kremlin to the new situation.

Indeed, Washington's priorities remained unaltered when in March 1952 Stalin called for quadripartite discussions on a peace treaty creating a reunited, neutral, but not necessarily demilitarized Germany. Stimulated presumably by NATO plans to boost military capacity with West German help, he appeared prepared to sacrifice the East German Communists; Ulbricht later admitted that a positive Western response would have "greatly endangered" the SED's position in the GDR.[85] But Acheson was not about to have three years of "colossal effort" to build a powerful alliance spoiled.[86] The allies proceeded to conclude in May "Contractual Agreements" with Bonn that allowed for West Germany's rearmament and eventual participation in the alliance. They agreed, as did West German Chancellor Adenauer, that the Soviet initiative threatened to delay ratification of the European Defense Community agreement (which was designed to integrate West German military forces with NATO) and devised a dilatory response in which they objected to the neutrality clause.[87]

Subsequent policy reviews reaffirmed the basic thrust of NSC 58/2 and NSC 68/2 on the subject of Eastern Europe, although they indicated growing pessimism regarding the ability of the United States to achieve its ultimate objective of detaching the satellites. The State Department noted in mid-1951 that the Communists were in total political control, and "popular discontent, though widespread, has no outlets sufficient to threaten the stability of the regimes, owing to the effectiveness of the police system and to the popular conviction that nothing can shake Soviet control short of a US victory over the USSR in war."[88] War, on the other hand, had to be avoided, and the NSC warned against overestimating America's ability to foster peaceful change.[89]

The Special Case of Yugoslavia. If the architects of the invigorated version of containment tempered their disposition to make trouble in Stalin's backyard with prudence, their reaction to the Stalin-Tito split was enthusiastic and secretly led to the inclusion of Yugoslavia in the perimeter to be defended by the West. Until late 1947 Tito was regarded in the East as a model Communist. But by pursuing independent plans for a Balkan federation, rebuffing Russian advice, and eventually purging his party of Stalin's agents, he brought down on his head the full wrath of the Soviet dictator. Stalin confidently expected that threats and subversion would soon bring a chastened Yugoslavia back to the fold, and on June 28, 1948, the Cominform formally expelled the "Tito clique." Instead, Tito's defiance of Stalin aroused wide popular support. Despite Washington's dislike of Tito, the split was immediately recognized by the CIA as "the most significant development in international communism in twenty years."[90] Kennan's initial report to the National Security Council cautioned that it would be "a frivolous and undignified error on our part to assume that because Tito had fallen out with Stalin he could now be considered our 'friend.'" Still, realpolitik dictated that a distinction be made between the Soviet threat and communism, and although Tito's regime was "deeply distasteful," the United States should "recognize that if Yugoslavia is not to be subservient to an outside power its internal regime is basically its own business." The West therefore should neither fawn on Tito nor repel his advances but sustain the demonstration effect of a successful defection from Moscow.[91]

By February 1949 Tito had come to be regarded as "perhaps our most precious asset in the struggle to contain and weaken Russian expansion," and an active policy was formulated to bolster his resistance to Stalin. Pressure to liberalize his regime would be suspended. Instead, the controls on exports, including munitions, would be lifted and economic aid coordinated with the allies. The only quid pro quo would be Tito's abandonment of assistance to the Communist guerrillas in Greece.[92] Over the next few years, American and other Western economic aid flowed to Yugoslavia (see chapter 5), but it was recognized that such limited assistance could not by itself sustain Tito if Stalin was determined to crush the heresy.

A year after the historic schism, indications were that direct Soviet attack on Yugoslavia was unlikely. This was one of the products of "Operation Silver," a CIA eavesdropping facility in Vienna.[93] By November the NSC calculated that, although Moscow appeared to be contemplating more drastic action, this was probably a war of nerves, for the Soviet Union was not likely to risk a direct military attack that could develop into a general conflict. However, the satellite armies in Bulgaria and Hungary began to make ominous preparations aimed at Yugoslavia.[94] The NSC estimated that the Yugoslavs could cope with Soviet-directed guerrilla operations and even with a satellite attack as long as it did not have substantial Soviet support. In any event, the United States had to give Tito assurances that it would provide "limited military supplies" in the event of an attack.[95]

The modalities of logistical assistance were worked out with the NATO allies, principally with Britain, and in consultation with the Yugoslavs. This was done amid great secrecy because of the "extreme sensitivity" of Belgrade to questions of Western military aid. But matters did not stop at contingency planning. As Frank Lindsay, the CIA's East European chief, recalls, "Tito told us that he wanted weapons badly, but not overtly, because this would give the Soviet Union a pretext for attacking him. We sent him five shiploads of weapons."[96] The links then established by American military and intelligence would be exploited long after the crisis had passed.

Reviewing the Soviet threat after the outbreak of the Korean War, the NSC doubted that the Soviet bloc would tie up its forces in a peripheral area such as Yugoslavia and regarded the continuing military deployments as designed for "intimidation, deception, or desire to be able to neutralize Tito in the event that a world war should ensue by inadvertence in the near future." The reestablishment of control over Yugoslavia would bring definite military advantages to the Soviet Union, but it could also have a disruptive effect on other Communist regimes and parties. There remained, however, the serious possibility of an attack by satellite forces, which the Yugoslavs might be able to repel if substantial military supplies from the West reached them in time. Were the Soviet Union nevertheless to attack Tito, the plan was to keep the United States out of direct involvement but to "support Tito to the extent possible by supplying arms and other forms of indirect assistance as well as participating in appropriate UN action." The NSC considered it "doubtful whether the Kremlin concludes that we would go to war if Yugoslavia were to be attacked either by its satellite neighbors alone or by the USSR and the satellites."[97]

In fact, the administration had decided to go to the limit in protecting Tito. Yugoslavia was perceived in Washington to be a significant asset, the loss of which would represent a serious strategic and political reverse for the West. A Soviet-dominated Yugoslavia would make NATO vulnerable in the eastern Mediterranean. Armed with the Korean experience, U.S. policy in the event of a military move against Yugoslavia was to obtain and support United Nations involvement in defense of that country's independence. It was anticipated that after the predictable Russian veto of Security Council action, the General Assembly would be called into emergency session under the freshly minted "Uniting for

Peace" Resolution to authorize the appropriate measures. The contingency plans coordinated between Washington and London envisaged the provision of strategic and tactical air support, and Acheson and Nitze also evoked the possibility of resorting to atomic weapons to quickly "localize and abort" aggression against Yugoslavia.[98]

It appears, then, that in the tense period of late 1950–51 the Truman administration committed itself to full military containment of Soviet expansion in the Balkans. It is not known whether this policy was fully conveyed to Tito, nor whether Stalin got wind of it through diplomatic or covert channels. In any case, the West's decisive response over Korea must have had a cautionary effect on the Soviet dictator. The fact is that the threat to Yugoslavia gradually receded, then vanished as Stalin's heirs made their peace with Tito. An overt American military aid program was inaugurated in 1951, and there were even some tentative overtures made to draw Tito into the Western alliance, but he remained steadfast in a nonalignment posture that granted few concessions to Western sensibilities. That, in the end, was sufficient if not optimal from Washington's point of view, for it preserved a model of national communism that with the aid of political warfare other East Europeans might be impelled to emulate. The subversion of Soviet power was a more immediate priority than the eradication of communism and full self-determination.

America's Propaganda Offensive.   America's relations with the governments of Eastern Europe reached their nadir in the early 1950s. A great totalitarian experiment in social engineering was under way behind the impenetrable iron curtain. Police terror, deportations and internment, and show trials, such as that of Hungary's Cardinal Mindszenty, suppressed all overt opposition. Diplomatic protests in 1949 at the "persecution of all political leaders and parties not amenable to the dictates of the minority ruling groups and denial of free expression" and at violations of the peace treaties' demilitarization clause were summarily rejected by Bulgaria, Hungary, and Romania as intrusions into spheres of domestic jurisdiction.[99] Nor did American-sponsored resolutions at the United Nations and an advisory opinion by the International Court of Justice deflect the regimes from their path. The United States blocked the admission of these three countries to the United Nations but clung to its diplomatic outposts despite recurring expulsions and charges of espionage.

"Nothing," declared Acheson at Berkeley in March 1950, "could so alter the international climate as the holding of elections in the satellite states in which the will of the people could be expressed."[100] Such public appeals and diplomatic demarches served psychological warfare as well as the domestic political need to generate acceptance of the burdens of containment. Washington was at war, against the Communist regimes and for the hearts and minds of the East European peoples. The principal weapons in this war, apart from economic sanctions, were propaganda and covert operations as the United States mounted a sustained campaign to undermine Soviet power in Eastern Europe.

In June 1948, following the CIA's success in the Italian elections, the National Security Council authorized the establishment of an Office of Special Operations, linked to the CIA and charged with the conduct of covert operations. Based on a proposal by Kennan, the project had the strong support of the President as well as George Marshall and Dean Acheson. The mandate of the soon-renamed Office of Policy Coordination (OPC) included "propaganda, economic warfare; preventive direct action, including sabotage, anti-sabotage, demolition and evacuation measures; subversion against hostile states, including assistance to underground resistance movements, guerrillas and refugee liberation groups." The only proviso was that such operations had to be conducted in such a way that the government could "plausibly disclaim" responsibility.[101]

The man chosen to head the OPC was Frank Wisner, a New York lawyer and former OSS operative in Romania and Germany, and he remained in charge when the OPC was converted into the CIA's Directorate for Plans in August 1952. Liberally funded and staffed by such OSS veterans as Frank Lindsay, who had spent nine months with Tito in 1944, the OPC became a major actor in the East European theater in collaboration with the British. One notable asset, inherited from the Nazis, was the German intelligence operative Reinhard Gehlen, whose new spy organization successfully penetrated East Germany. The OPC and the CIA were galvanized by the mandates in NSC 58/2 and 68/2 for a covert offensive against Eastern Europe. There was new sense of urgency, and policy directives called for intensified covert operations and the encouragement of individual defections from the Soviet bloc.[102]

In the realm of psychological warfare, the peoples of the Soviet Union and the satellites were soon identified as the primary target. Already in early 1946 George Kennan had asked the retired diplomat Joseph C. Grew to organize a private group for the task of aiding and employing East European refugee politicians, and soon there arose the idea of helping them to communicate with their homelands. There was a successful precedent in RIAS, the Radio in the American Sector of Berlin, created in February 1946 and oriented increasingly to an East German audience. On June 1, 1949, the National Committee for a Free Europe came into being, including such notables as Allen Dulles and Dwight D. Eisenhower. One of its tasks was to ride herd over East European emigre organizations, but a broadcasting facility became its concrete objective. General Clay was put in charge of the fund-raising campaign Crusade for Freedom; a replica of the original Liberty Bell was cast in England, and this "Freedom Bell" toured the United States to help raise money for Radio Free Europe. Crusade for Freedom was designed as much to raise public consciousness as to generate donations, for most of the funding for Radio Free Europe came from the CIA.

Radio Free Europe, based in Munich and staffed largely by emigres, began transmitting on July 4, 1950. Bulgaria, Czechoslovakia, Hungary, Poland, Romania, and, for a time, Albania were its targets. Radio Liberation (later Radio Liberty), similarly organized and funded, went on the air in 1953 with broadcasts in Russian and later other languages of the Soviet Union. The purpose of RFE, in Clay's words, was to "help those trapped behind the curtain to prepare for the day of liberation." The Free Europe Committee's president, C. D. Jackson, put it in the language of psychological warfare: to "create conditions of turmoil" in the satellites.[103] At the CIA, first Thomas Braden, then Cord Meyer, was put in charge of exercising policy control over RFE "on the basis of State Department guidance."[104] To raise the morale of the "captive peoples" and to foment unrest were both consistent with the policy of aggressive containment, though such crusading propaganda was bound to arouse unrealistic hope of Western aid. From the point of view of the CIA and the OPC, propaganda and other subversive operations were all part of a strategy to weaken enemy regimes, but there was little expectation that unaided internal opposition could bring about a Titoist, let alone Western-oriented, secession. The military, on the other hand, looked upon propaganda as a useful weapon in case of war with the Soviet Union. The Joint Intelligence Committee advised the Joint Chiefs of Staff in

September 1951 that while the East European peoples and armies were vulnerable to psychological warfare, "until assured of effective Allied support, they would show little defiance to the Soviets beyond slow-downs and minor covert assistance":

Among the present Satellites, the most effective results from psychological warfare probably could be developed in Poland. Strong, popular underground movements could be organized which might be able to undertake localized armed action against the Soviets. Effective resistance movements could also be expected with the Polish Armed Forces.

The Hungarians, observed the JIC, were a "traditionally passive people [who] consider themselves as pawns in the East-West struggle and expect the West to liberate them." [105] An earlier State Department plan for psychological warfare in the event of war observed similarly that many East Europeans "would welcome war in the hope of eventual liberation." [106]

Since the doctrine of containment not only ruled out the initiation of war by the United States but also aimed to forestall a Soviet attack, such calculations amounted to contingency plans and did not address the problem of propaganda means and objectives in a time of cold peace. Although the need to coordinate policy won some recognition in the creation in April 1951 of a Psychological Strategy Board, which included the under secretary of state, the deputy secretary of defense, and the CIA director, it took a revolution in Hungary to impose a sober reappraisal of the political costs and benefits of psychological warfare.

Beginning in 1949, the CIA resorted to secret flights over Eastern Europe to gather intelligence and, until the inception of Radio Free Europe, to drop propaganda to incite dissidence. In August 1951, the first balloon launch was made in West Germany in an operation that over the years would deliver several hundred million propaganda leaflets to Eastern Europe. The CIA's Vienna station placed on trains going into Hungary toilet paper bearing the picture of the hated dictator Rakosi. Such tactics were a measure of the impermeability of the iron curtain, for the OPC had only limited success in infiltrating agents into the tightly controlled police states of Eastern Europe. It did take over some of the networks of the British Secret Intelligence Service (SIS), and one of the assets acquired was Lt. Col. Jozef Swiatlo, a disillusioned official of the Polish UB secret police. He became a key figure in an extraordinary game of deception.

The story of "Operation Splinter Factor" rests on both corroborated evidence and investigations by an English journalist, who describes it as "probably the foremost intelligence battle of the Cold War."[107] The facts are that the Soviet secret services began in 1949 to orchestrate a massive purge of alleged Titoists and Western agents involving leading figures in the East European Communist parties; and that in the same year the American Noel Field, a Communist fellow traveler who had worked in refugee relief and for the OSS, defected to Prague and was soon arrested and used to implicate Communist traitors. Allen Dulles, at that time a senior consultant to the CIA, had been involved in East European intelligence operations after the war, mainly to help the escape of leading anti-Communists; soon he was appointed deputy director for plans and, in January 1951, deputy director of the agency. When Swiatlo proposed to implicate the Polish security chief, Jakub Berman, by branding Field a CIA agent, Dulles conceived of a plan that reportedly he later claimed became his "biggest success ever": to persuade Lavrenti Beria, the Soviet secret police boss, with contrived evidence that the CIA was orchestrating a regionwide conspiracy of Titoists with a huge army of agents and that Field was the linchpin of this conspiracy.[108]

Though already in full swing, Stalin's anti-Tito campaign acquired a new ferocity after the arrest of Field and his wife, Herta, and brother Hermann, who had followed him to Prague. The Soviet MVD's chief for southeastern Europe, Lt. Gen. Fedor Bielkin, was given carte blanche to extirpate traitors, and he began in Hungary, where the leading home Communist, Laszlo Rajk, was put on trial with two associates in September 1949 and subsequently executed. Testimony extracted from Field implicated Rajk in an American espionage network, and torture as well as false promises drove him to confess to a litany of crimes and betrayals. The purges spread to every other satellite, leading notably to the imprisonment of the Romanian Lucretiu Patrascanu, the execution of the Bulgarian Traicho Kostov and the Albanian Koci Xoxe, and the arrest (by Swiatlo!) in July 1951 of the already disgraced Stanislaw Gomulka. The purge in Czechoslovakia began only in late 1950, and it ended two years later with the trial and execution of Rudolf Slansky and other alleged conspirators; they, too, were linked to Allen Dulles and the Fields.[109] The obsessive search for traitors came to an end only with Stalin's death. Most East European parties ultimately acknowledged that these purges had been based on fabrications, and many of the victims, including Rajk, were posthumously rehabilitated. (Field and his wife were also eventually released and given $40,000 in compensation, and they remained in Budapest.) For Stalin, this terrifying charade had served to impose iron discipline at a time when he was contemplating offensive action against a still relatively weak Western Europe. If, as the British source describes, Allen Dulles and the CIA mounted a massive exercise in disinformation to feed Stalin's paranoia, the immediate result was not division and disaffection but consolidation. Only after Stalin's death did the disintegrative aftereffects of the purges begin to be felt, principally in Hungary, where the party's demoralization materially contributed to the outbreak of revolution.

The Promotion of Insurgency. Policy also called for the encouragement of insurgency, and America's campaign to destabilize Soviet power in Eastern Europe went beyond deception and psychological warfare. The Lodge bill, passed by Congress in June 1950 (Public Law 587), provided for military recruitment of East European emigres, but the army's response was slow and token. Of the handful actually enlisted, twenty-two were assigned in 1952 to the newly created Special Forces; in September 1953, some of the Special Forces were redeployed to West Germany to train for partisan action in Eastern Europe in time of war. Meanwhile, on the advice of the joint chiefs of staff, the OPC was given responsibility for paramilitary operations.[110]

The OPC collaborated with the SIS in aiding nationalist partisans in the Baltic states and the Ukraine, but by the early 1950s the resistance movements had been effectively quelled, and the program ended in failure. The prospects were apparently better in Poland, where scattered partisan activity by remnants of the Home Army persisted for several years after the war. The emigre "Freedom and Independence" movement (WIN by its Polish initials) claimed to have extensive human resources and organization in Poland, and beginning in 1950 the OPC responded with airdrops of arms, radios, and money. Verification of WIN's claims was hampered by the prompt apprehension of agents dispatched by the CIA. The operation continued until December 1952 when Warsaw radio proudly announced that for years the local end of WIN had been run by the secret police and had been making fools of the American cold warriors and of unwitting Polish dissidents.

Albania was the target of the most daring operation, the only one that aimed directly to overthrow a Communist regime. Washington and London had given provisional recognition to the Hoxha regime in November 1945, but instead of the promised free elections Hoxha imposed rule by terror. He also aided the Communists in the Greek civil war. A year later, after two British destroyers hit mines in the Corfu channel, all Americans were evacuated from Albania. Though isolated by Tito's defection, Albania remained a Soviet outpost, and the Soviets were installing at Valona Bay a submarine base that could control access to the Adriatic. In London, a secret "Russia Committee" reached the same conclusions as the American architects of containment—that promotion of unrest and the liberation of satellites by any means short of war could mitigate the Soviet threat. In February 1949, Foreign Secretary Ernest Bevin approved a plan to "detach Albania from the Soviet orbit."[111]

The operation had to be coordinated with the Americans, who, recalls the OPC's James McCargar, were equally optimistic that "we had only to shake the trees and the ripe plums would fall."[112] Albania, anticipated Wisner, would be "a clinical experiment to see whether larger rollback operations would be feasible elsewhere."[113] The Joint Chiefs of Staff concurred, as did the State Department, which in NSC 74 judged that Albania, "by virtue of its exposed geographical position and the relative instability of the present regime, is the most vulnerable of the Satellite States to Western efforts to loosen the Soviet grip in Eastern Europe."[114] The operation was cloaked in the utmost secrecy, and President Truman gave only oral approval to preserve the option of "plausible denial."

The idea was that infiltrated agents would lead a revolt to topple Hoxha. A CIA report in December 1949 found that while the overwhelming majority of Albanians were opposed to the regime, the security forces were strong and Stalin determined to keep his outpost.[115] Nor was there hope of help from Tito, who feared provoking the Soviets. But the SIS and the OPC proceeded to cobble together an "Albanian National Committee" from various emigre groups, mostly followers of the exiled King Zog, and the paramilitary training of recruits began on Malta. In October 1949, the British landed two parties of Albanian partisans on the Karaburun peninsula. Inauspiciously, they walked into an ambush; four were killed and the rest had to flee to Greece.

The OPC, originally the junior partner in the exercise, intensified its involvement in 1950, training a "labor battalion" of Albanians designated "Company 4000" in West Germany and beginning airdrops of combatants in November. The Soviet and Albanian security forces showed uncanny skill in capturing one mission after another. In fact, what was apparently called "Operation Valuable" was foredoomed. The SIS's liaison man in Washington, H.A.R. "Kim" Philby, had come under suspicion as early as May 1951 after the defection of two other Soviet spies, Donald Maclean and Guy Burgess, but he was simply retired. From him, from agents among free Albanians, and from the interrogation of captured partisans, Hoxha and Moscow discovered all about the operation by the end of 1951. The British terminated their involvement in early 1952, but the OPC, driven by bureaucratic momentum as well as the public calls for liberation in 1952, persevered for two more years before throwing in the towel and disbanding Company 4000. The balance sheet was grim. Several hundred Albanians had lost their lives, and the Communists had scored a propaganda victory.

In sum, though covert operations to destabilize Eastern Europe and roll back Soviet power kept the Communists on their toes, they brought few positive results. Such disappointments did not alter the conviction of Americans and emigres engaged in the covert war that they were fighting for a just cause. Psychological warfare, meanwhile, exploited the alienation of East Europeans from their masters and assured them of the continuing sympathy of the West. To the peoples sealed off by the hermetic iron curtain from normal contact with the West, the broadcasts that could penetrate jamming brought spiritual comfort and some hope of liberation.

Politics and Liberation. The requisites of domestic politics had played a part in the genesis of the Atlantic Charter, for the American people needed an ideological goal beyond the immediate necessities of national security to shoulder the burden of total war. Containment as well was wrapped in the ringing rhetoric of American democratic values. But this was a new type of war, with shifting frontlines and no prospect of early victory. The temptation to seek new formulas grew strong.

The bipartisan consensus exemplified by the Vandenberg resolution soon began to fray as the Communists triumphed in China and taxed America's endurance in the bloody and protracted Korean War. Partisan attacks multiplied on Roosevelt's and Truman's alleged sellout of Eastern Europe at the wartime conferences and on the policy of containment for being too costly and purely defensive. Senator McCarthy led a witch-hunt for Communist fellow travelers in the State Department and else-where who were responsible for the loss of China and other setbacks, and the trial of Alger Hiss persuaded many that America's interests had been betrayed by the Democratic administrations. While General MacArthur was lionized for his willingness to wage atomic war against China, Truman and Dean Acheson came to be depicted absurdly as soft on communism.

Authentic frustration as well as political partisanship fueled what became a great debate over foreign policy.[116] The Republican party's right wing led the attack on containment, which was described by Sena-tor Alexander Wiley as passive, "pantywaist" diplomacy.[117] The prof-fered alternative was at once aggressive and isolationist, calling for tougher action, including fomenting revolutions behind the iron curtain, which would lead to the defeat of communism and the trimming of America's military and economic sacrifice and commitments.

The belligerent mood in Congress was reflected by the passage in October 1951 of the Kersten amendment to the Mutual Security Act (Public Law 164, sec. 101[a]). It allocated $100 million "for any selected persons who are residing in or escapees from [the Soviet Union and the satellites] either to form such persons into elements of the military forces supporting the North Atlantic Treaty Organization or for other pur-poses." The United States, said the Republican congressman from Wis-consin, should assure the East Europeans that "we will do everything we can to work for their eventual liberation" and, at the opportune time, "actually assist" them in liberating themselves.[118] Moscow reacted an-grily, in diplomatic notes and at the United Nations, at the interference in domestic affairs suggested by the "residing in" clause, but the more lasting impact of the Kersten amendment lay in the realm of psycho-logical warfare, in inducing East European misapprehensions about America's intent.

By early 1952, the notion that there existed a dynamic alternative to the policy of containment had become widespread; as Paul Nitze put it, "the evolution of our policy had outrun public understanding and sup-port."[119] The stalemate in Korea was the most immediate issue, but much of the debate focused on Eastern Europe. James Burnham, the author of an influential book entitled *Containment or Liberation*, de-fined a policy of liberation as "the view that the key to the situation is what happens and what can be made to happen in Eastern Europe." Commitment to the goal of liberation, in his analysis, meant "all-sided political warfare; auxiliary military and para-military actions where called for; adequate preparation for whatever military action may be required in the future." [120] The critics of containment were presumably ignorant of secret commitments and covert measures, for what they denounced was a travesty of the operational policy. Dissatisfied with the results, they blamed the policy for the constraints of the global alignment of forces.

The most prominent exponent of liberation was John Foster Dulles, whose long experience in foreign affairs (including serving as an adviser to Truman) made him a leading contender for the post of secretary of state in a Republican administration. He had been advocating a more offensive strategy of liberation ever since 1949. In its fullest formulation, published in May 1952, Dulles's alternative called for the dynamic use of ideas based on moral principles. By making it "publicly known that it wants and expects liberation to occur," the United States could galvanize the captive peoples and "create new opportunities for liberation." The concrete means to that end proposed by Dulles differed little from existing tactics of psychological and economic warfare, and he disclaimed any intention of sparking off "bloody uprisings and reprisals." But he averred, citing Tito's defection, that "enslavement can be made so unprofitable that the master will let go his grip." [121]

In the spring of 1952, Dulles submitted to General Eisenhower, the putative leader of the GOP's internationalist wing, a policy proposal that included both liberation and the creation of a military deterrent capable of massive retaliation. Ike found the latter more attractive than the former, and indeed liberation was more in tune with the belligerence of Senator Robert Taft's nationalist-isolationist wing. Dulles nevertheless threw his support to the general and proceeded to draft a Republican foreign policy plank that could reconcile the two wings. It promised to "repudiate all commitments contained in secret understandings such as those of Yalta which aid Communist enslavements" and replace the "negative, futile and immoral" policy of containment with a message of liberation that would "set up strains and stresses within the captive world which will make the rulers impotent to continue in their monstrous ways and mark the beginning of the end." [122]

In the election campaign, notably in his American Legion convention address on August 25, Eisenhower paid lipservice to liberation with circumlocutions about peaceful instruments to aid those who yearn for freedom.[123] Two days later, at the American Political Science Association convention in Buffalo, Dulles was more forthcoming in outlining a strategy for stirring up and aiding resistance movements, but he righteously dismissed Averell Harriman's warning about provoking premature revolts and his evocation of the Warsaw massacre.[124] Reproved by Eisenhower, who cultivated the image of a peacemaker and was sensitive to the alarm liberation had caused among the European allies, a chastened Dulles stressed reliance on peaceful means and Titoism. Excessive rhetoric was curbed, and Eisenhower's promise to end the war in Korea overshadowed the issue of Eastern Europe, but as late as October Eisenhower reiterated his commitment to a "more dynamic foreign policy which, by peaceful means, will endeavor to bring about the liberation of the enslaved peoples." [125]

Sensitive to the popular appeal of liberation particularly among ethnic voters, the Democrats were reduced to arguing that the promise of liberation without external military support was irresponsible and that all peaceful efforts were already being exerted, though Adlai Stevenson evoked the additional option of negotiation. The apparent inconsistency between the advocacy of liberation and of budgetary stringency also drew unfavorable comment. But even if the salience of liberation as a major campaign issue was reduced by Eisenhower's ambivalence, the GOP exploited it and assigned the former ambassador to Poland, Arthur Bliss Lane, to the task of winning over ethnic voters. Polish-Americans and other East European "hyphenates" (who numbered some 11 million in all, not including Germans) were not unreceptive to allegations of a Yalta sellout (one GOP pamphlet was entitled *Betrayal! Over 100,000,000 East Europeans by the Democratic Administration*) and the promise of rollback. In the end, these tactics did stimulate defections from a traditionally Democratic constituency, reducing that party's Polish vote from 70 to around 50 percent, but they contributed only marginally to Eisenhower's landslide victory.[126]

This was the only American election in which policy regarding Eastern Europe occasioned significant debate. While it would be unfair to Dulles and other moralistic crusaders to dismiss liberation as merely a cynical electoral tactic, they cannot escape responsibility for arousing unrealistic expectations at home and abroad. Liberation had a lasting effect on the outside world and in Congress, where its superficial belligerence overshadowed its lack of distinctive substance. Closer scrutiny revealed that it offered no new American commitment to free the satellites. But the European allies, being on the frontline, apprehended the threat of violent confrontation, while the satellite peoples heard the promise of a crusade for their release.

In Congress, by the end of January 1953 five separate resolutions had been introduced calling for disavowal of the sinister deals made at wartime conferences at the expense of the East Europeans. The road from the Atlantic Charter had been rough, and not all the pitfalls were avoided by America's leaders. The clamor for repudiation of Teheran, Yalta, and Potsdam indicated the distance left to travel before purpose and power were finally reconciled.

2

Rebellion Too Far

The ambiguities of liberation did not disappear with Eisenhower's triumph. A succession struggle in the Kremlin presented the West with new opportunities as well as uncertainties. Stalinism's oppressive weight drove East Europeans to confront their masters, first in Czechoslovakia and East Germany, then in Poland and Hungary. The prospect of revising the division of Europe flickered briefly, then died out. The security priorities of Washington and Moscow remained unaltered, and the permanence of Soviet rule over Eastern Europe was reconfirmed. This was a dismal outcome for an administration whose election campaign had been marked by sonorous promises to restore freedom to the oppressed.

The impact of liberation on American politics waned rapidly after Eisenhower's election, but a crusading spirit continued to inspire true believers in the CIA and in Congress. America's message of hope to the East Europeans was ritualistically reiterated by the president and his secretary of state and by the propaganda organs, what the CIA's Frank Wisner called his "mighty Wurlitzer." "We shall never acquiesce in the enslavement of any people in order to purchase fancied gain for ourselves," said Eisenhower in his first State of the Union message.[1] But he also observed privately that he "always thought Foster was a bit too optimistic" about changes or upheavals in the satellites.[2]

At the Foreign Relations Committee hearings on his nomination, Foster Dulles used his favorite metaphor in predicting that if the United States kept alive the East Europeans' hope of liberation the Soviet Union's "indigestion will become so acute that it might be fatal."[3] Dulles insisted that those who doubted that this could be accomplished by moral pressure didn't know what they were talking about. Tito's rule, however reprehensible, was an example of successful heresy.

In Congress, the backwash of liberation produced a series of Republican resolutions demanding repudiation of Yalta. The trouble was that the State Department's files produced no evidence to support the popular allegation that Roosevelt had secretly sold out the East Europeans. Seeking bipartisan support, the administration introduced a moderate "Captive Peoples Resolution" that called for self-determination and, in deference to the sensibilities of Democrats, simply blamed the Soviets for flouting the terms of Allied agreements such as the Declaration on Liberated Europe. Speaking in its defense, Dulles insisted that the resolution was "no call to bloody and senseless revolution" but was necessary to reassure the East Europeans and generate a "spiritual power" that would ultimately overcome Soviet dictatorship.[4] Neither conservative Republicans nor liberal Democrats were satisfied with the resolution, and the resulting, bitter political wrangling was mercifully brought to an end by news of Stalin's death on March 5, 1953, much to the relief of Eisenhower and Dulles. To persist with the resolution "would be difficult now because it would look as if we were rejecting the peace bids," explained Dulles.[5]

Rollback through Negotiation? The death of the great dictator was unforeseen, and the president complained at a cabinet meeting three days later about the State Department's unpreparedness: "We have no plan. We are not even sure what difference his death makes."[6] The difference depended, of course, as much on Washington as on Moscow. Stalin's unexpected note of March 10, 1952, inviting talks on German reunification and his subsequent offer to meet with Eisenhower had been summarily rebuffed. The CIA's estimate regarding the consequences of his demise forecast continuity in Soviet domestic and foreign policy while the successors avoided difficult decisions and struggled for supremacy.[7] The new leader appeared to be Georgi Malenkov, who did display a disposition to talk with the West. In a speech at Stalin's funeral

Malenkov called for peaceful coexistence, and later he told the Supreme Soviet that he was ready to negotiate on all disputed or undecided questions.

These overtures, probably reinforced by confidential messages, arrived at a time when West Germany's integration into the Western military alliance was reaching its final phase. The signing in May 1952 of the European Defense Community Treaty appeared to settle the matter. However, while consensus reigned among the allies over the need to consolidate the security of free Europe, not all of them saw clearly or fully condoned the fateful significance of this step. If West Germany became a full-fledged member of the Western Alliance, its status would no longer be open to East-West negotiation, and the division of Europe could only be undone by unilateral concessions on the part of the Soviet Union. Such a prospect did not disturb Adenauer or Dulles. For both of them, the stability and security promised by the EDC far outweighed the loss of negotiating flexibility on the question of German reunification. The French, though secretly fearful of a reunified Germany, were too insecure to welcome fundamental reconsideration of the principles of Western security. They were, therefore, more ambivalent about the EDC.

Doctrinal adherence to the priority of alliance building required that Stalin's and Malenkov's overtures be interpreted as spoiling tactics designed to delay the West's military integration and as offering no genuine opportunity for negotiation. This pessimistic estimate of Soviet intentions drew strength from the sorry record of postwar diplomacy, but it also reflected an element of convenient fatalism that ruled out the very possibility of change and compromise in the Kremlin's calculations of Soviet interests.

Eisenhower and Dulles vs. Churchill.   While Dulles's predisposition was to construe the Soviet peace bids as phony and a trap, Churchill yearned for one last attempt at ending the cold war and tried to persuade Washington to seize the opportunity. If Eisenhower was elected, he observed in June 1952, he would "have another shot at peace by means of a meeting of the Big Three."[8] The secretary of state's first reaction was to keep up the pressure on Moscow, but Frank Wisner warned against provocative statements. The satellites, he reported, were a tinderbox, and the CIA needed time to prepare for exploitation of a revolt.[9]

Eisenhower opted for what he regarded as a conciliatory gesture.

"The slate is clean," he told his chief speechwriter, Emmet Hughes; "Now let us begin talking to each other."[10] In a speech delivered on April 16 before the American Society of Newspaper Editors, entitled "The Chance for Peace," the president invited the Soviets to negotiate "universal disarmament." Armistice in Korea, an Austrian peace treaty, the reunification of Germany by free elections, and freedom for other nations—"including those of Eastern Europe"—to choose their form of government would be appropriate demonstrations of Soviet sincerity.[11] This unexceptionable shopping list elicited an offended response from Moscow, notably regarding the reference to Eastern Europe. Dulles, meanwhile, felt compelled to reassert publicly the importance of assuring the East Europeans that "we do not accept their captivity as a permanent fact of history."[12]

Churchill, who disliked and distrusted Dulles, ignored the advice of the Foreign Office and much of his cabinet and continued to advocate negotiation. On May 11, in a foreign policy speech in the House of Commons, he called for an early summit meeting without preconditions. In the event, the mistrust of the Russians and single-minded pursuit of the EDC exemplified by Dulles and Adenauer prevailed over Churchill's boldness and Eisenhower's more tentative disposition to negotiate. On Dulles's recommendation the summit proposal was simply put on the agenda of an American-British-French conference, which—because of a stroke Churchill suffered in June and a French change of government— was postponed until December. Thus Malenkov's (and, apparently, Beria's) willingness to negotiate was not tested, and Churchill privately expressed disappointment in a "weak and stupid" Ike.[13]

It is difficult to avoid the conclusion that the West missed a rare opportunity in the spring and summer of 1953 to renegotiate the division of Europe. The stakes were immense; the risks appeared manageable. Stalin's uncertain successors could not have been expected to compromise Soviet security, but with Western incentives they might have been induced to redefine the conditions of that security. Their fear of Germany was historically well-founded, and the specter of West German rearmament haunted them. The threat of such rearmament was a bargaining chip of tremendous value in the West's diplomatic arsenal. The EDC proposal made the threat tangible and apparently immediate. Western security would hardly have been damaged by simply putting German rearmament on the agenda of a summit conference. America's strategic military supremacy remained an adequate guarantee of Western Europe's security, although the Soviet Union's successful test of a thermonuclear device in August 1953 served as a warning that the advantage would not last long.

As for the risk to Western unity, Churchill's advocacy of a summit without preconditions was itself a departure from alliance orthodoxy, while the French were divided on the desirability of the EDC and would eventually scuttle the scheme. The military integration of West Germany into the alliance came two years later by including the Germans in the Western European Union, and subsequent summitry no longer had a realistic chance of forging an East-West compromise attenuating Europe's division into blocs.

The Issue of German Unification.   Even this tangible risk was arguably outweighed by the potential benefits of negotiation. Unification still had vast support among East and West Germans, and while Adenauer and his party placed Western integration ahead of unification, the prospect of a reunited and neutralized Germany would in all likelihood have proven politically irresistible. A State Department report in July found "mounting conviction that the static foreign policy of the present government has become obsolescent and that eventual reunification might be brought about by means short of complete integration with the West."[14] As late as 1955, a confidential State Department estimate concluded that a neutralized Germany would incline as far as possible to the West and "would seek to equip and deploy its forces so that they might best complement NATO strength in Europe and improve the West's strategic position. They might even attempt limited covert contacts with the NATO powers in order to work out informal understandings concerning Western strategic planning."[15] Still, from a Western perspective, relinquishing West Germany as a military base and ally would have been a major concession, necessitating fundamental reconsideration of security conditions for the rest of Western Europe.

For at least some of the Soviet leaders, the prospect of a neutralized, largely disarmed, united Germany might plausibly have appeared to represent the lesser threat. To be sure, the plans to extend Soviet influence by the Red Army and the intermediary of Communist parties had been hatched before war's end and implemented systematically throughout Eastern Europe. But these plans were driven more by security considerations than by purely ideological imperatives. The former always over-rode the latter in Soviet foreign policy. Stalin and his successors remained uncertain about the viability of East Germany. Stripped of its industrial plant and hemorrhaging through the open sore of Berlin, it was at least in the short run a questionable economic asset. Soviet control was total (and was brutally asserted at the time of the June 1953 riots), yet the zone was not fully integrated into the bloc. In sum, it appears that Moscow was keeping its German options open and might have bargained at a time when it was still weaker strategically than the United States.

Negotiation on the future of Germany would have necessarily addressed a related Soviet idea, that of a new European security regime guaranteeing postwar borders. This scheme, which in the event reached fruition only in the 1970s with the Helsinki conference, sought Western (and therefore German) acquiescence in the Oder-Neisse boundary between Germany and Poland, enhancement of the Soviet Union's status as a major European power, and attenuation of the West Europeans' perceived need for an American-led military alliance. The West would have had to weigh carefully the form and implications of such a security regime, which it had previously dismissed as a propaganda ploy. Yet in September 1953, Dulles himself raised with Eisenhower the possibility of a "spectacular effort" to negotiate a mutual withdrawal of Soviet and American forces from Europe as well as an arms control agreement: "The present is a propitious time for such a move, if it is ever to be made, because we will be speaking from strength rather than weakness." The president expressed "emphatic agreement" with the need for an initiative to reduce tensions, but there is no evidence that the secretary of state's uncharacteristic flight of fancy went further.[16]

Negotiated resolution of the German question would inevitably have had a profound impact on the rest of Eastern Europe. The various Stalinist regimes justified their harsh rule at least in part with constant reminders of the threat of German revanchism and the unremitting hostility of the West. Malenkov's readiness to talk did not guarantee that the political status of the satellites was open to negotiation, but the creation of a unified and neutralized Germany and a new European security regime would have radically altered the perceptions of East Europeans. The new leaders in the Kremlin were already intent on alleviating Stalinism in their satellite domain, and a more settled international environment would have reinforced the pressures for domestic liberalization. Whether this process of decompression could have proceeded smoothly enough to forestall eruptions such as that which occurred in Hungary in 1956 is a question that lies at the limits of speculation.

The ailing Churchill persevered in his quest for a meeting with the Soviets, much to the irritation of his foreign secretary, Anthony Eden, who like Dulles regarded the strengthening of NATO as the priority that overrode all other considerations. When his proposal to meet Eisenhower in October in the Azores was rejected, he concluded (according to his secretary) that the president did not want to be confronted with a demand for a conference with the Soviets that he was unwilling to accept. Yet Churchill still thought that an exploratory visit to Malenkov "might do good and could do no harm." At the Bermuda conference in December, the president dismissed Churchill's "double-dealing" approach of strength and conciliation with the remark that Russia was just the same whore in a new dress.[17]

In February 1954, at the Berlin conference of foreign ministers, Vyacheslav Molotov advanced a "Draft General European Treaty of Collective Security in Europe," which aimed to unite all European states (including the two Germanys) in common defense, relegating the United States and Canada to the role of observers in the process. On the question of a German peace treaty, the Soviet proposal for German representation at a peace conference by a coalition government in which West and East Germans would have equal status was countered by Western insistence on a freely elected, all-German government. In March, the Soviet Union agreed to American participation in the treaty and made the novel suggestion that NATO could be preserved if it was expanded to include the USSR and the East Europeans. The Western powers, embroiled in disputes over ratification of the ill-fated EDC, dismissed these overtures as unrealistic, particularly in light of Soviet objections to free elections as a prelude to German unification.

The following June, during a visit to Washington, Churchill found Eisenhower more favorably disposed to the idea of a summit. After Dulles cooled the president's ardor, Churchill decided to go to the USSR without the Americans and "ask for freedom for Austria as an earnest of better relations." Eden and the cabinet were appalled at the prime minister's initiative, and in the event the telegram to Molotov evinced a cool reply.[18] It is tempting but wrong to dismiss Churchill's single-minded pursuit of negotiations as the mania of an old and vain man past his peak. He was all that, but he also perceived the necessity of attempting to break a deadlock not of his creation much as he had felt compelled in 1944 to reach a separate agreement with Stalin on influence in the Balkans. With his departure from office in April 1955 the West lost its wisest leader. His had been a lone voice in allied councils during the brief moment when summitry might have produced more than empty phrases.

Later, others regretted the missed opportunity. "I think I made a mistake in not taking the initiative and recommending such a meeting," records Charles Bohlen, then U.S. ambassador to Moscow.[19] Prudence and conservatism prevailed; consolidation of the West's security apparatus proceeded; and the division of Europe remained the subject of pious and ineffectual condemnation.

The prospects for successful negotiation on the German question had altered dramatically by the time a summit conference was finally convened in Geneva in July 1955. The leadership struggle in the Kremlin had been resolved in favor of Nikita Khrushchev, who took initiatives to stabilize his empire, pacify Tito, and explore opportunities in the third world. When, in October 1954 in Paris, the Western powers overcame the EDC fiasco and devised a new formula to bring West Germany into NATO, the Russians resorted to last-ditch attempts to forestall German rearmament. They convened in late November an Eastern bloc "European Security Conference" that warned that a countervailing alliance would be formed if the Paris agreements were confirmed. They also professed a new willingness to consider free, all-German elections. The West, as before, saw only destructive motives behind these maneuvers.

In a spectacular volte-face, Molotov in March 1955 unilaterally offered the Austrians a peace treaty with neutralization. Consummated by the four occupying powers on May 15 in Vienna amidst great rejoicing, the deal was presumably intended by the Russians as an incentive to those Germans tempted by neutrality. The previous day, however, the Soviet Union had staged the signing of the Warsaw Treaty, binding the satellites ever closer to their mentor. Dulles chose to construe the Austrian treaty as a Soviet retreat and opined on television that Austria's neighbors, Czechoslovakia and Hungary, "may find freedom contagious."[20] He also considered that Moscow had paid the price for a summit meeting and relaxed his previous opposition to such a conference.

At the summit, the Soviet leaders demanded the disbandment of the two alliances and the withdrawal of foreign troops from Europe as the precondition to any discussion of German reunification. At the subsequent meeting of foreign ministers, the West countered with Eden's proposal for all-German free elections, reunification, mutual security guarantees, and a demilitarized strip along Germany's eastern frontier. Neither side was disposed to compromise, and Dulles reported to the Senate Foreign Relations Committee that the Geneva meetings at least had the salutary effect of reconciling the West Germans to the practical impossibility of reunification.[21] Peaceful coexistence, hailed in the press as the "spirit of Geneva," rested on mutual and tacit acceptance of two exclusive spheres of influence in Europe.

Rollback by Other Means.   If the most propitious moment for negotiation was not seized by the United States, what remained of the revisionist impulse behind the slogans of liberation and rollback? During the summer of 1953 the administration conducted a planning exercise, "Operation Solarium," to consider broad foreign policy options. Separate study groups at the National War College reviewed the merits of containment, deterrence, and liberation, as well as of negotiation with the Soviets within a two-year time limit. George Kennan, though out of favor with the new secretary of state, participated in the exercise and had the satisfaction of winning the president's approval for a modified version of the containment strategy.[22] In fact, the "New Look" strategic concept, adopted in October 1953 as NSC 162/2, evoked NSC 68 and encompassed elements of all the options. Greater reliance on the nuclear deterrent and on alliances would, it was argued, help the United States regain the initiative in meeting Soviet challenges selectively, with superior force, and at lower cost ("more bang for the buck," as Secretary of Defense Wilson put it). Covert action and psychological warfare would be economical instruments of liberation, although NSC 162/2 concluded that "the detachment of any major European satellite from the Soviet bloc does not now appear feasible except by Soviet acquiescence or war." The same strategic directive allowed for the possibility of negotiation as long as this did not "delay or reduce efforts to develop and maintain adequate free world strength."[23]

The New Look was yet to be formulated when events in Eastern Europe took a violent turn. On June 1, 1953, a day after the Czechoslovak regime announced new economic austerity measures, workers at the Skoda factory in Pilsen rioted and stormed party and government offices. The riots were quickly quelled and thousands placed under arrest, but the message to both East and West was clear. Stalinist economics was not working, and totalitarian controls could not prevent spontaneous outbursts against Communist rule.

East German Uprising. Similar economic grievances sparked off an even more dramatic confrontation in East Germany. Party boss Walter Ulbricht's desperate attempt in May to raise industrial output by increasing production norms had already caused labor unrest and work stoppages. The new leadership in the Kremlin was ready to admit past economic mistakes and advised the East Germans to give greater emphasis to the production of consumer goods and to relax other unpopular strictures. Unfortunately, the reforms announced on June 11 did not prevent the elite brigade working on the Stalinallee construction project in East Berlin from taking its grievances to the seat of government on June 16. The demonstration called for a general strike and free elections. "This is a people's rising," declared one of the workers.[24] By the time even larger masses of demonstrators gathered the next morning, Soviet armored troops and special Volkspolizei units were ready for action. The spark spread rapidly through the zone, but the Soviet High Command promptly imposed martial law in East Berlin and other cities. Within a day some twenty-two demonstrators were killed and the uprising was effectively quelled.

The CIA station chief in West Berlin cabled headquarters for permission to distribute arms to the demonstrators. The head of the CIA's Eastern European Division, John A. Bross, consulted Frank Wisner, and in the absence of the new CIA director Allen Dulles, they decided to offer the rebels sympathy and asylum but no arms. When informed, Allen Dulles was reportedly unhappy with this prudent response. Eisenhower's recently appointed psychological warfare advisor, former Free Europe Committee president C. D. Jackson, was furious. The "blood of martyrs," he told Bross, would have helped to discredit the Soviet Union.[25] Jackson argued for a more forceful response in the spirit of liberation, evoking the possibility of similar uprisings in Czechoslovakia and elsewhere. To force the Red Army to take repressive measures in his view would give the West an important propaganda victory.

In a telephone conversation with Jackson on the afternoon of June 17, Foster Dulles averred that "these breaking-out incidents were symptomatic and we should do something about it." Jackson agreed.[26] The Psychological Strategy Board met to discuss the issue later that day, and it was put on the agenda of the following day's National Security Council meeting as an emergency item. Meanwhile, the White House refrained from public comment on the situation.

On the whole, official West German reaction was low-keyed, although Ernst Reuter, West Berlin's mayor, broadcast on June 18 an anguished plea to the world to heed the call of the East German workers for a different political system. That same day the allied commanders in West Berlin and the mayor sent a joint note to the Soviet military command deploring the use of force. When the U.S. high commissioner to Bonn, James B. Conant, visited Berlin three days after the uprising, he issued a protest at the Soviet closing of all crossing points. Washington, he recalls, "would have vetoed anything more drastic. A three-power statement was out of the question. London and Paris had little sympathy with the uprising."[27] The Americans distributed food to East Berliners and, a few weeks later, made the offer (in Moscow) of $15 million worth of foodstuffs to alleviate the evident shortages in East Germany. The offer was contemptuously dismissed.

Ulbricht and the Kremlin soon indulged in accusations that Western agents had fomented the uprising. Berlin was indeed the cockpit of the cold war, swarming with spies and agents; the Gehlen spy organization was well represented in the Eastern zone, and according to one Western account some arrested rioters were Western agents carrying sabotage instructions.[28] "The less we put our label on this, the better," reflected the secretary of state privately on the first anniversary of the uprising; such outbreaks are "wonderful if they appear to be wholly spontaneous."[29] Still, no conclusive evidence has surfaced to indicate that Western covert action helped set off the uprising.

It nonetheless remains true that the language of liberation was inherently inflammatory, and Western propaganda was instrumental in turning the riot into a nationwide uprising. One of the "national tasks" of psychological strategy was:

to reduce the effectiveness of the Soviet and communist administrative and control apparatus by conducting in a non-attributable manner psychological, political, and economic harassment activities in the Soviet Zone, and to prepare, under controlled conditions, for such more active forms of resistance as may later be authorized.

Propaganda was to include "information calculated to help create a climate conducive to disaffection in the Soviet Zone and East Berlin." The military was instructed to give support to CIA covert operations in pursuit of these objectives.[30]

America's intent was clearly to destabilize East Germany, and for years the U.S.-sponsored "Radio in the American Sector" (RIAS) had been broadcasting to a broad and receptive audience. A delegation of East Berlin workers presented itself at the RIAS on the afternoon of June 16 with the request that they be allowed to broadcast their demands. The station's political director, Gordon Ewing, claims that he had no instructions from Washington when he decided to air the demands as well as the message of a West Berlin union leader calling for a general strike in the Eastern zone. He was aware that RIAS would thereby be "pouring gasoline on the flames," and the radio's commentators did warn their listeners that they were at the mercy of the "Russian occupiers."[31] By June 17 new directives had gone out from the CIA to the propaganda radio in Europe.

This was to be a recurring dilemma for the agents of psychological warfare. Reinforcement of the East Europeans' abhorrence of their regimes and desire for freedom was an easy task and one that presumably enhanced the security of the West by sustaining political instability in the East. But what was the proper role of the propaganda organs in the event of rebellion? To cold-bloodedly continue with incitement? To belatedly warn their listeners that they faced hopeless odds? In resorting to both encouragement and caution, RIAS responded as best it could given the apparent lack of contingency planning. For East Germans, the very existence of RIAS was a symbol of Western concern for their fate, and its active role in spreading news of the uprising undoubtedly encouraged speculation in the East that American help was on the way. Such help was, of course, out of the question, not only because of the absence of political will but also because of the overwhelming superiority of Soviet forces in Central Europe.

The uprising played a part in the concurrent power struggle in the Kremlin. Stalin's sinister secret police chief, Lavrenti Beria, apparently chose to dabble in grand strategy after his mentor's death. Both Ulbricht and Khrushchev subsequently alleged that he had been plotting to make a deal with the West allowing for German reunification. Beria's grab for power met with the combined opposition of the party and military elites, which in July engineered his arrest. Ulbricht thereupon purged two alleged coconspirators, Wilhelm Zaisser (minister of state security) and Rudolf Herrnstadt (editor of the party paper). They were accused of having plotted a coup with Beria aiming at reversing the process of socialization in East Germany in order to facilitate reunification.[32] If Beria was in fact scheming to secure a compromise settlement of the German question, his elimination probably signified the ascendancy of a more cautious tendency in the Kremlin. That this was the conclusion reached in the West's chancelleries is suggested by Eden's reflection that Beria's fall was a defeat for moderation in Moscow.[33] More characteristic of the psychological warfare mentality was C. D. Jackson's report to the Eisenhower cabinet on July 10 to the effect that Beria's ouster offered a great opportunity for developing passive resistance in the satellites.[34]

What Happened to Liberation Policy?   Once order was restored in East Germany, Washington and its allies could safely indulge in confident postmortems. Dulles told his British and French counterparts in Washington on July 10 that the uprising had demonstrated the inherent weakness of the Soviet empire, and he extracted from them a public wish to see "true liberty restored" in Eastern Europe—the first time, he observed privately, that London and Paris had been willing to "embrace this principle." Eisenhower, for his part, sent a reassuring message to Chancellor Adenauer predicting that the contrast between democratic and prosperous West Germany and East Germany would "in the long run produce conditions which should make possible the liquidation of the present Communist dictatorship and of the Soviet occupation," and pledging America's political, diplomatic, and moral support.[35]

A concurrent resolution adopted by Congress in August lauded the heroic resistance of the East Europeans and expressed confidence that their sacrifices would advance the cause of freedom. This confidence was not shared by those who, like Bohlen, saw the opportunity for negotiated detente rapidly slipping away as the East German experience toughened the Kremlin's manner.[36]

Neither the rejection of Soviet peace feelers nor the passive response to the East German uprising offered much guidance to the positive substance of the policy of liberation. On the diplomatic front, Washington continued to reiterate the objective of liberation while stressing that only peaceful means were contemplated, a qualification that allowed the timorous allies to join in the chorus. His hopes for an independent Eastern Europe, said Dulles before the UN General Assembly in September 1953, lay in "the vast possibilities of peaceful change."[37] The West Europeans were clearly not in a crusading mood, and aggressive formulations of liberation could not be comfortably accommodated either by allied priorities or by the conventions of diplomacy.

Public opinion in the United States displayed rather more active sympathy for the East Europeans. An elite opinion survey conducted in late 1953 found fervid rejection of any acquiescence in Soviet hegemony over the area.[38] Politicians such as Senator Alexander Wiley, the powerful chairman of the Foreign Relations Committee, Senator William Knowland, and Congressman Charles Kersten, chairman of the Committee on Communist Aggression, continued to agitate for active measures to implement liberation. Their motivation stemmed more from doctrinal conviction than from electoral considerations, for liberation was of marginal utility in winning votes. One disenchanted believer was Arthur Bliss Lane, who resigned from the Republican National Committee before the end of 1953, charging that the administration showed no intention of making good the campaign pledge of liberation.[39]

In the political arena, the Kersten Committee remained a thorn in the side of the administration, calling repeatedly for stronger sanctions against the Russians. It complained in August 1954 that the provision of the Kersten amendment (which was retained in the Mutual Security Act of 1954) for creating military units of East European refugees had not been acted upon. Indeed, the Pentagon was most reluctant to comply and suggested that "more good will be accomplished . . . by allowing the Kersten Amendment to lapse or at the most leaving it on the books with no actual implementation."[40] In fact, there already existed in the U.S. zone in Germany a so-called Labor Service Organization. Financed through the army civilian personnel budget, it consisted some 8,000 East European refugees formed in lightly armed, paramilitary units. Anticipating budget cuts, though, the army was planning to reduce if not eliminate these units.

In February 1953, Eisenhower instructed the National Security Council to investigate the feasibility of a "Volunteer Freedom Corps" composed of infantry battalions recruited by the U.S. Army "from stateless, single, anti-Communist young men, coming from the countries behind the Iron Curtain." Qualified recruits, suggested the president, should be "developed into specialists in anti-Communist underground and in political offensive work in their respective countries." He complained that he was "disappointed in the progress made by the United States Army in carrying into effect the Lodge Act, the objective of which was to produce from stateless, anti-Communist young men an elite of officer material," observing that out of more than 6,000 applicants only 395 had been accepted. "It would seem possible," wrote Eisenhower, "in these days of tension, with a zeal equal to need, to recruit up to 250,000 men for the Volunteer Freedom Corps." [41]

Three months later, an ad hoc committee composed of representatives from State, Defense, the CIA, and the Psychological Strategy Board duly delivered NSC 143/2, an elaboration of the president's proposal that had the endorsement of the army chief of staff. Questioning the President's optimistic projection, it estimated that up to 33,000 escapees would be available for recruitment. Although it acknowledged the goal of securing additional combat manpower, the committee stressed the psychological value of the project. It would boost the morale of East European anti-Communists, "eliciting more escapees, and compounding the problems of the authorities in the Soviet-dominated areas," and "possibly provoking the Soviet rulers into self-defeating counter-policies which we can exploit." Recruits to the Volunteer Freedom Corps would be prepared for "fighting to liberate their peoples in case of war." The U.S. ambassador to the United Nations endorsed the notion that "escapees can give the U.S. the initiative in psychological warfare, and can be the biggest, single, constructive, creative element in our foreign policy." [42]

For reasons that are unclear but probably include the lingering reservations of the Pentagon, allied objections, and the changed circumstances of the post-Stalin thaw, the proposal never reached the stage of enabling legislation. Although the ad hoc committee considered that the Kersten amendment was not wholly suitable for the purpose of setting up the VFC, it had prudently appended an interim proposal to expand the Labor Service Organization with Kersten amendment funds. The military raised various legalistic and practical problems, while the French objected to the notion of basing a 5,000–man LSO unit in their country. Eventually, a derivative scheme code-named "Red Sox/Red Cap" was devised, then aborted after the Hungarian debacle of 1956. NSC 143/2 was quietly rescinded in 1960.[43]

The Problem of Emigres. Psychological objectives as well as humanitarian concerns informed the American approach to the problem of the several hundred thousand refugees from Eastern Europe, many of them lingering in camps in Western Europe. Inadequate assistance was considered responsible for deteriorating morale among the emigres and an asset for Communist counterpropaganda.

Various programs therefore were devised to supplement the work of the International Refugee Organization, the Intergovernmental Committee for European Migration, and United Nations as well as voluntary agencies. The U.S. Escapee Program, established in 1952, within three years resettled some 25,000 escapees overseas. Under the Refugee Relief Act enacted in 1953, nearly 100,000 nonquota immigration visas had been issued by April 1956. The Defense Department was responsible for the Labor Service Units and the Alien Enlistment Program, which by 1956 accounted respectively for 10,000 and 976 escapees.[44] Finally, it was officially claimed that some $4,300,000 out of the Mutual Security appropriations had been spent on providing transit facilities for refugees.[45]

Such programs helped to placate the emigres and other Americans of East European extraction, but many of them expected more. The rhetoric of liberation galvanized refugee politicians, and the Free Europe Committee continued to serve as their mentor and channel for covert CIA funding, preserving the semblance of an arm's length relationship between the government and emigre groups that (apart from the Estonians, Latvians, and Lithuanians) did not enjoy diplomatic status. In September 1954 the FEC organized a conference of representative East European notables in New York that ceremonially founded the Assembly of Captive European Nations (ACEN). The ostensible purpose of the new body was to coordinate activity in service of the goal of liberation. ACEN would periodically issue appeals for a consistent and nonviolent pursuit of liberation and took a hard line on East-West trade, diplomatic recognition and UN membership, and peaceful coexistence. For the purposes of domestic politics, ACEN was a useful safety valve and display of public concern for the satellites. It helped to keep the fractious emigre politicians in line and pacify congressional crusaders.

The demonstration effect of ACEN in the satellite target areas was fraught with greater risk. Its messages of encouragement and the inclination of its member groups to regard themselves as virtual governments-in-exile gave the East Europeans a false impression of American activism in pursuit of their liberation. Soviet and Western propaganda both reinforced the impression that East and West were locked in an inexorable and uncompromising struggle for supremacy. For most East Europeans, war seemed the only realistic way to escape Moscow's embrace, and they sought assurances to this end from Western propaganda.[46] The scope for unwitting deception and self-deception was dangerously great.

U.S. Propaganda Efforts.   The principal Western propaganda organs, Radio Free Europe and Radio Liberation (after 1956, Radio Liberty), remained under the control of the Central Intelligence Agency. The responsible official, Cord Meyer, recalls that he was relieved to find broad agreement among the CIA, the State Department, and the two watchdog congressional committees that the electoral rhetoric of roll-back "did not affect the standing injunction that the radios were not to provoke premature and suicidal internal revolt by any implied promise of external assistance." Meyer reported directly to Allen Dulles, who took an active interest in East European developments and emigre politics. He collaborated with the State Department in drafting an annual guidance directive for each target country and then "hammered out an agreement with the radios on its provisions." The directives were supplemented by daily advice in times of crisis. Meyer's staff conducted random sample checks of broadcasts to ensure compliance, and he maintains that "our control function, although publicly not evident, served to keep the broadcasts responsive to official policy" and that he resisted agency pressures for disinformation campaigns against particular East European leaders.[47] The administration and Congress frequently paid tribute to the importance of the radio operations. They kept alive the hope of eventual self-liberation, argued Dulles, and he pointed to the satellite regimes' jamming efforts as confirmation of the effectiveness of psychological warfare.[48]

Paradoxically, the official myth of self-liberation was only reinforced by the disturbances in 1953 in Czechoslovakia and East Germany. The Psychological Strategy Board was requested to prepare "recommendations as to policies and actions to be taken during the next sixty days to exploit the unrest in the satellite states." A week later, the NSC approved with amendments the report of the board.[49] The recommended policy, contained in the still only partially declassified NSC 158, set the following psychological objectives:

a. To nourish resistance to communist oppression throughout satellite Europe, short of mass rebellion in areas under Soviet military control, and without compromising its spontaneous nature.
b. To undermine satellite puppet authority.
c. To exploit satellite unrest as demonstrable proof that the Soviet empire is beginning to crumble.
d. To convince the free world, particularly Western Europe, that love of liberty and hatred of alien oppression are stronger behind the Iron Curtain than it has been dared to believe and that resistance to totalitarianism is less hopeless than has been imagined.

Other recommendations included: encouragement of passive resistance; support for German unity based on free elections followed by a peace treaty; discussions with allied governments to implement the Volunteer Freedom Corps; and consideration of bringing Soviet repression of the East German revolt before the United Nations.[50]

NSC 174: U.S. Policy toward the Satellites. In December 1953, the policy review culminated in the adoption of NSC 174, "United States Policy toward the Soviet Satellites in Eastern Europe," designed to supersede NSC 58/2 and NSC 158. Its ultimate general conclusion was that the "detachment of any major European satellite from the Soviet bloc does not now appear feasible except by Soviet acquiescence or by war." While such a detachment would not decisively impair Soviet strategic military capability, it would be a "considerable blow to Soviet prestige" and impair Soviet conventional military capabilities in Europe. The main policy conclusion was that it is nevertheless "in the national security interests of the United States to pursue a policy of determined resistance to dominant Soviet influence over the satellites in Eastern

Europe and to seek the eventual elimination of that influence. Accordingly, feasible political, economic, propaganda and covert measures are required to create and exploit troublesome problems for the USSR, complicate control in the satellites, and retard the growth of the military and economic potential of the Soviet bloc." NSC 174 urged preparations to "exploit any future disturbances similar to the East German riots," but it also stressed the importance of avoiding "incitement to premature revolt" and "commitments on the nature and timing of any U.S. action to bring about liberation" or the creation of false hopes of U.S. intervention.

This policy, as the staff study argued, represented the feasible middle course between liberation by military force (which would "probably mean war with the Soviet Union and most probably would be unacceptable to the American people and condemned by world opinion") and acceptance of the fact of Soviet control ("inconsistent with the fundamental principle of the right of the satellite peoples to freedom" and contrary to the Western need to reduce Soviet power). A further, and somewhat tortured, rationale for the middle course was that "though it may preclude reaching any general accommodation with the Soviet Union in the foreseeable future, [it] might contribute to the creation of conditions which will induce the Soviet leadership to be more receptive to negotiated settlements in line with U.S. objectives towards the satellites." Soviet domination over Eastern Europe had "created a fundamental disequilibrium on the continent and a continuing pressure on Western Europe" that was unacceptable to the United States.[51] On December 23, 1953, the president approved NSC 174 and designated the Operations Coordinating Board as the responsible implementing agency.

The OCB's first progress report, delivered the following July, noted soberly that implementation of NSC 174 amounted to no more than "holding actions" and that "the hard facts of the situation make it unrealistic to expect that conspicuous progress towards achieving the long-range policy objectives of NSC 174 will be made under present circumstances."[52] Planning for future disturbances similar to the East German riots was confined to "fixing responsibility on the puppet regimes and/or the Kremlin, propaganda exploitation and possible use of the forums of the United Nations." The report reiterated the basic dilemma:

The desire for liberation from Soviet domination is undoubtedly strong among the captive peoples, many of whom would welcome militant Western action to liberate them, even to the extent of resort to a war of liberation by the West. Neither the U.S. nor other free world countries are willing to take such extreme steps, nor is the U.S. prepared to undertake or foster activities which it would not back up with military support in the event of ruthless Soviet suppression and reprisals. Furthermore, our European allies are strongly against taking what they estimate to be provocative action. Consequently, the U.S. must limit its activities to a scope which is considered inadequate by at least the activists among the captive peoples and some of the emigres.

More concretely, improved services for refugee resettlement had been developed, a one-megawatt transmitter was established in West Germany, and NATO members had conferred in January 1954 on the coordination of propaganda. New operational plans, anticipated the OCB, would "primarily involve actions which will permit propaganda exploitation to the peoples of the satellites states and several diplomatic moves."

A policy designed principally to maximize Soviet difficulties among people perceived to be friendly to the West placed impossible demands on the managers of psychological warfare. As the staff study leading to NSC 174 recognized, "continuing and careful attention must be given to the fine line, which is not stationary, between exhortation to keep up morale and to maintain passive resistance, and invitations to suicide." Radio Free Europe's policymakers had no choice but to act on the assumption that the divisions in the Kremlin and the uncertainty these induced in the satellite regimes could be exploited if the latent popular opposition was properly guided. The policy directive issued for Czechoslovakia on June 30, 1953, stressed the need to raise the workers' consciousness of their power to extract concessions and to undermine the loyalty and self-confidence of the regime's servants. Implementation took the form of "Operation Prospero," an intensive propaganda barrage through the airwaves and millions of leaflets dropped from balloons over Czech cities.

The Kremlin's "New Course."   When later in 1953 the Prague regime began on Moscow's instructions to adopt certain reforms in the context of the New Course, RFE strategists concluded that their efforts could bear fruit and a few months later launched a second broadcast and

leaflet campaign, "Operation VETO." The campaign attempted to propagate ten demands for incremental change and to demoralize leading
Communists by publicizing their misdeeds and corruption. The underly-
ing strategy envisaged the growth of an organized opposition, which
with proper external guidance could exploit a "favorable confluence" of
internal and external events to win major concessions and perhaps national autonomy.[53]

At least in retrospect, the notion that with a little Western guidance
the satellite nations could seize the hypothetical opportune moment and
by their own effort liberate themselves from totalitarian rule seems
improbably optimistic. Yet such optimism was liberally professed by the
managers of psychological warfare and their emigre employees as well
as by the president and the secretary of state. Disclaimers of any intent
to drive the East Europeans to suicidal rebellion did not eliminate the
ambiguities of the strategy, if only because the target audiences entertained few doubts regarding the will and capability of their domestic and
Soviet masters to preserve order and assumed that American encouragement implied a commitment to provide material assistance. Whereas
many propagandists found in the East German uprising encouraging
evidence of popular opposition to communism, East Europeans and the
more sober Western observers saw that the self-appointed leaders of the
working class had no compunction about shooting workers to retain
power. The teleological quality of the liberation strategy advocated by
the more enthusiastic cold warriors overrode the prudential axiom that
he who wills the end wills the means.

Of course, psychological warfare had a short-range objective as well:
to destabilize, however marginally, the Soviet bloc and thereby reduce
its offensive potential. The operational policy of liberation therefore also
involved exploitation of the East Europeans' legitimate grievances and
aspirations for the purpose of enhancing Western security. No doubt
most proponents and agents of psychological warfare managed to reconcile the idealistic and pragmatic aspects of their crusade at a small
cost in self-deception. They drew confidence from the short-term results,
for propaganda obviously irritated the target regimes. Jozef Swiatlo, the
CIA's asset in the Polish secret police, finally moved west in December
1953, bringing with him vast evidence of corruption in leading circles.
Drawing on these revelations, RFE mounted a radio and leaflet operation in the fall of 1954 that impelled the Polish authorities to save face

by purging some exposed officials, notably the minister of security, General Stanislaw Radkiewicz.

The Kremlin's New Course had its most dramatic impact on Hungary, where the ultra-Stalinist methods of Matyas Rakosi were now perceived by Soviet leaders to be dangerously counterproductive. The fall in the standard of living and rule by terror had alienated even the working class, the peasantry seethed with resentment at forcible collectivization, much of the former middle class had been reduced to penury and internal exile or imprisonment, thousands of arbitrarily purged Communists languished in jail, and a growing number of the party's intellectual servants and sycophants were becoming disenchanted and restive.

In June 1953, Rakosi was summoned to Moscow and ordered to relinquish the prime ministership (which he held along with the party leadership) to a Malenkov protege, Imre Nagy. The latter, also a Soviet-trained veteran Communist, had been in disgrace for daring to oppose the precipitous collectivization of agriculture. Nagy understood his mandate to be a more consumer-oriented economic policy and in general the creation of a less oppressive political mechanism. His patently popular reforms were opposed by Rakosi, who feared above all a public investigation of the party purges. When Malenkov fell from grace in early 1955, Rakosi's intrigues bore fruit, and he persuaded the Kremlin to dismiss the increasingly liberal Nagy. The political impact of the New Course in Hungary could not, however, be so readily undone. The party's unity and self-confidence had been shattered, dissident intellectuals and rehabilitated victims of the purges were no longer held in check by the cult of the infallible leader, and the population at large began to emerge from its repressed and submissive condition.

Having assessed the promise of Nagy's New Course, Radio Free Europe in October 1954 launched "Operation FOCUS" to incite Hungarians to step up the pressure for reforms. The operation resorted to the tested tools of radio and balloon-carried leaflets and drew on the talents of emigre academics and politicians, notably the former Peasant party leader Imre Kovacs, to tailor the messages to local susceptibilities. Leaflets carrying the letters NEM (for the Hungarian equivalent of National Opposition Movement) or the numeral 12 (standing for the demands of a fictional opposition movement) inaugurated the campaign. Also dropped from Hungarian skies were light-metal medals depicting the Freedom Bell and carrying the comforting message "Hungarians for Freedom—All the Free World for the Hungarians." The radio broadcasts elaborated on these themes and urged Hungarians to demand economic reforms and political rights from the regime.[54] The operation ended following Nagy's demise, and while it probably contributed little to the rise and suspension of the New Course, it left a strong impression of Western sympathy for the aspirations of anti-Communist Hungarians.

The RFE and Voice of America broadcasters in the East European languages were emigres whose understandable feelings of solidarity with their oppressed countrymen disposed them to reinforce hopes of liberation. Policy directives and periodic monitoring could not prevent the nuances and ambiguities of liberation from receiving different interpretation in Washington, Munich, and Eastern Europe. Meanwhile, when Budapest or Prague protested at the propaganda campaigns, the State Department simply professed the fiction that RFE was a private organization drawing attention to obvious popular grievances.

While psychological warfare continued to rage, the other unmentionable tool of foreign policy, covert action, suffered from earlier setbacks, notably the Albanian fiasco. In the fall of 1953, a meeting was held in the White House to consider what counter measures might be taken by the United States in the event of another eruption such as the East Berlin rising. On the request of Allen Dulles, now director of central intelligence, Richard Bissell assembled a small staff to study the question and reached the now-familiar conclusion that clandestine operations had little chance of success against the Soviet bloc.[55]

The discouraging prospects did not prevent the CIA's role in the cold war from expanding steadily. By 1952, Frank Wisner's Office of Policy Coordination had acquired close to 3000 employees, forty-seven overseas field stations, and an annual operating budget of $82 million. Wisner continued to hold the title of deputy director of plans and enjoyed the enthusiastic support of Allen Dulles, who was more interested in covert operations than in research and analysis. National Security Council directive 5412 of March 15, 1954 restated the scope of the secret war, which included all the standard propaganda, subversion, resistance, and economic tactics "and all activities compatible with this directive necessary to accomplish the foregoing." NSC 5412/1 (March 1955) and NSC 5412/2 (November 1955) provided for the review and oversight of clandestine action by a group composed of presidential, State, and Defense nominees known as the "5412 Committee."[56]

CIA activities in Eastern Europe, however, were largely limited to the infiltration of agents for intelligence gathering and, of course, psychological warfare. The satellite regimes periodically protested U.S. covert activities, which the United States officially denied. Allen Dulles did, however, allow in an interview in March 1954 that in the face of Communist subversion, the Americans would be stupid not to respond in kind.[57] Military Special Forces units received some instruction in East European languages and were deployed in West Germany, but the idea of creating paramilitary refugee units acquired immediacy only in the wake of Khrushchev's secret speech in 1956.

Trade Sanctions. Official American policy toward the satellites pursued their diplomatic and economic isolation. Only in December 1955 did the administration decide that the deadlock over United Nations membership was becoming counterproductive and agree to a package deal whereby Albania, Bulgaria, Hungary, and Romania were admitted to the world body. Harold Stassen, the new director for mutual security, appointed General William J. Donovan as special consultant on East-West trade control and developed a program for even tighter restrictions on exports to the Soviet bloc.[58] The volume of America's trade with the East continued to decline, but that of Western Europe with the East surged after 1953. In particular, West Germany began to reassert its historic economic influence. Its trade with the East grew by 175 percent between 1952 and 1954, although even then it scarcely reached one-fifth of the prewar volume. Over half of this trade was with East Germany.

Western controls over the export of capital goods of strategic value were effective and undoubtedly impeded the modernization of East European industry. Washington took a dim view of its allies' greater readiness to trade with the enemy, and free trade and economic warfare were uncomfortable bedfellows. In September 1955 a recommendation was submitted to the Council of Europe for the establishment of a central organization to oversee all East-West trade. This, it was argued, would overcome the East's advantage of having a trading monopoly that forced Western prices down while maintaining high Eastern prices. Common action could raise the volume of trade as well as give the allies greater flexibility in using trade as a bargaining tool and for sanctions. Approved by the Council's Assembly, the proposal was rejected by the Committee of Ministers ostensibly on the ground that it was contrary to Western free trade principles.[59] An enduring pattern emerged in the 1950s wherein the West Europeans gradually revived their historic commercial links with the East while the United States, putting principle before profit, stood aloof and disapproving, and in time becoming envious (see chapter 5).

Economic sanctions did not palpably undermine the stability of Soviet rule in Eastern Europe, although they helped to preserve the West's technological superiority and therefore military security. On the other hand, Washington and its allies showed little readiness to use trade as a positive reinforcement of desirable political trends. There was some disposition on the part of the administration to detect and act on positive developments in the satellites such as Imre Nagy's New Course. An NSC policy directive in early 1955 recommended that the United States encourage "greater emphasis on internal problems" and "exploit differences" within the bloc.[60] The scope for constructive external influence was judged to be negligible, however, and differentiation among the satellite regimes was recognized more in terms of the immediate advantage to Western security than in the context of rollback. The relevant guidelines for covert operations disclosed that March enjoined the CIA to "create and exploit troublesome problems for International Communism, impair relations between the USSR and Communist China and between them and their satellites, complicate control within the USSR, Communist China and their satellites, and retard the growth of the military and economic potential of the Soviet bloc."[61]

Yugoslavia's Case.   The one exception to the tactics of isolation and subversion remained Yugoslavia, which continued to benefit from American economic and military aid. In the seven years following Tito's expulsion from the Soviet bloc, the United States spent close to $1.5 billion, most of it in the form of outright grants, to assist him in maintaining his secessionist regime. The investment paid some dividends. In October 1954 Tito settled his long-standing dispute with Italy over Trieste by retaining the hinterland but abandoning claim to the city. He had earlier signed a treaty of friendship and cooperation with Greece and Turkey that in August 1954 became a mutual defense pact. Western security in the eastern Mediterranean was enhanced, and the example of "national" communism provided by Yugoslavia had an unquestionably unsettling effect on the other regimes of Eastern Europe. An additional benefit for Washington was the working relationship established between the CIA and the Yugoslav intelligence service.

Tito's successful consolidation and expanding links with the developing world tempted the new leadership in the Kremlin to woo him as well. Stalin's unrelenting hostility toward Tito was judged to have been counterproductive, and in May 1955 Khrushchev and Bulganin journeyed to Belgrade to make amends. Blame for the estrangement was laid on Beria (and soon on Stalin himself). The Soviets agreed to coexist peacefully, thus establishing the revolutionary notion that there could be several roads to socialism. The concept was enshrined in the Belgrade Declaration, which formally ended the feud and normalized Soviet-Yugoslav relations. As a result, while Dulles and his advisers were not sanguine about making headway on the status of the satellites at the forthcoming Geneva summit, it was noted that Western pressure might nonetheless have some effect since "what we ask for is less than what the Soviets gave Tito."[62]

The Soviets, of course, had given Tito nothing but grudging recognition that he was beyond their reach. Still, Dulles tried to exploit the Moscow-Belgrade thaw and paid a quick visit to Tito at his Brioni retreat during a lull in the foreign ministers' conference at Geneva that autumn. The resulting communique asserted the right of East Europeans to determine their futures free of external interference, and Dulles waxed optimistic about the coming disintegration of the Soviet empire. "I don't mean to suggest that there will be an early breakaway of the satellites from Moscow," he observed. "But I think there will soon be visible signs of evolution toward governments which command more popular support than those which now exist, and which are markedly less the paid hirelings of Moscow." He reported to the Senate Foreign Relations Committee in January 1956 that Tito "undoubtedly is eager to get the best he can out of both sides, and that is something which I did not think we necessarily want to deny him if, in the process of doing that he creates, as he is doing, a very large measure of unsettlement in the satellite countries."[63] The possibility that the East Europeans might not prudently settle for a version of Titoism was scarcely entertained.

Continuing Quest for Liberation.   On the diplomatic front, Washington's insistence that the status of the satellites was an international issue was rejected by Moscow. Moscow refused to be party to a summit if Eastern Europe were on the agenda of the Geneva meetings, and Washington regretfully conceded. Dulles suggested to the president that he pursue the question in private, but Eisenhower saw little purpose in futile debate. Asked about liberation at a press conference before the summit, he retorted, "You are certainly not going to declare war, are you? So there, instantly, you fix yourself limitations on how far we, as a people, will go in accomplishing this thing." [64] The allies were even more reluctant to spoil the emerging detente with talk of liberation, and they persuaded Eisenhower at the last minute to tone down his proposed references to Soviet tyranny. [65] As noted, the summit produced no progress on Germany or European security and disengagement, let alone on the satellite question. Its real significance lay in the tacit acknowledgment by both sides that the division of Europe could not and would not be altered.

The trouble was that if peaceful coexistence meant the transfer of the East-West contest to areas less explosive than Europe, it undermined the fundamental revisionism of the policy of liberation. Since this was a central element in American foreign policy doctrine, it had to be professed even if shorn of operational significance.

In its second progress report on NSC 174, the OCB acknowledged that keeping alive the hope of liberation was becoming more and more difficult, since "any movement toward a relaxation of tensions between East and West is bound to be widely interpreted in the satellites as a weakening of Western determination to achieve their liberation from Soviet control and a disposition to accept their status as permanent." Encouragement of passive resistance was "somewhat incompatible" with detente and efforts to negotiate and to foster evolutionary change: "It may be that the U.S. will have to undertake to follow simultaneously two policies with inconsistent courses of action, representing divergent approaches to the one objective." The report saw no likelihood of Titoism emerging elsewhere but recommended that "attention should be given to determining what further courses of action might be taken to induce the Soviet and satellite leadership to be more receptive to negotiated settlements and what degree of stress should be placed on encouragement of Titoist tendencies or 'national Communist movements' " as well as to a more differentiated approach to the satellites.[66]

Secretary of State Dulles tried to square the circle by arguing that insofar as the summit had attenuated the danger of war, the Soviets could no longer claim they needed to dominate their western approaches for reasons of security.[67] The Kremlin saw different implications in peaceful coexistence. In September 1955 Adenauer visited Moscow to negotiate the release of ten thousand German prisoners of war and the reopening of diplomatic relations. The Soviet Union thereupon concluded a treaty with East Germany to reinforce the latter's claim to sovereign and equal status. The United States remained adamantly opposed to recognition of the GDR and wedded to the objective of reunification (if only because that hope was considered to be the "main psychological barrier to full acceptance of the GDR regime by a majority of East Germans"), but the OCB warned that "we must be prepared to fight an already discernible tendency on the part of some elements in West European countries to favor concluding security agreements with the USSR based on a divided rather than a unified Germany."[68] To the extent that the integrity and permanence of the Soviet bloc appeared to be the essential component of peaceful coexistence, Washington's revisionism was bound to suffer.

The Promise of De-Stalinization. The spirit of Geneva was short-lived, for 1956 turned out to be a calamitous year for Moscow and Washington with regard to their respective alliances. In the Kremlin, collective leadership proved to be a transitional phase as Khrushchev consolidated his personal power and proceeded to proclaim the end of Stalinism. He stunned the delegates at a closed session of the Communist Party of the Soviet Union's twentieth congress in February with a seven-hour speech criticizing Stalin's despotic rule, economic mismanagement, and intolerance of different routes to socialism. Rumors regarding the thrust of the secret speech soon reached the West, and by April Secretary of State Dulles was commenting liberally on its implications for the spread of Titoism to other East Europeans "who would much rather have their own national brand of communism than be run from Moscow."[69] Khrushchev disbanded the Cominform, renewed his peace offensive by announcing troop reductions, and sealed the reconciliation with Tito by welcoming him to Moscow in June.

What did Khrushchev's formal rejection of Stalinism mean? And what opportunities did it present to the West? Allen Dulles ordered that the secret speech be obtained at any cost. The deputy director for intelligence, Robert Amory, Frank Wisner, and the chief of counterintelligence, James J. Angleton, Jr., all set about the task. Amory made a direct though necessarily secret and ultimately unsuccessful approach to the Yugoslav foreign ministry. Wisner was somewhat more successful and secured, probably from Polish sources, an abridged version. The real coup was pulled off by Angleton, who got the full text by way of Israeli intelligence.[70]

The question of how to handle the coveted prize generated heated debate within the CIA. Angleton and Wisner urged that it be exploited to sow confusion and unrest in the Soviet sphere, that excerpts and doctored versions be leaked selectively and with careful timing while the CIA marshaled its psychological warfare and covert action forces to extract the maximum advantage. Others, notably Ray Cline, argued for the immediate release of the full and authentic text on the grounds that publication of this unprecedented self-indictment by a totalitarian regime would in itself be a tremendous propaganda victory for the United States. Allen Dulles agreed, and with the concurrence of his brother and the president, the State Department forwarded the speech to the *New York Times,* which published it on June 4.[71]

Outside the Soviet bloc the revelations served to dispel any remaining doubts about the horrors of Stalin's tyranny and cast Khrushchev in a favorable light as a courageous reformer. In American political circles, reaction was mixed, particularly in view of Tito's recent visit to Moscow. In June, Senator McCarthy introduced a bill to terminate aid to Yugoslavia, and during hearings on the Mutual Security bill the secretary of state had to argue strenuously that Tito was not the Kremlin's puppet and that American aid reinforced the attractiveness of his national Communist model in the satellites. Support for Tito, Dulles insisted, was an essential part of the American strategy of liberation.[72] Nevertheless, to forestall congressional action and with an eye to the ongoing election campaign, Dulles temporarily suspended the military and economic aid program for Yugoslavia, only to reinstate it in October.

The potential effect of de-Stalinization on the satellites was the subject of much speculation in Washington, but no consensus emerged. The National Intelligence Estimate of May 1955, drafted well before Khrushchev's bombshell, had predicted that "popular resistance of an organized and active kind is unlikely to appear in the Satellites" over the following five years.[73] The frequently revised "Basic National Security Policy" summary of the NSC recommended in its March 15, 1956, version (NSC 5602/1) that the United States continue to promote evolutionary changes, and to "assure the satellite peoples of the continuing interest of the U.S. in the peaceful restoration of their independence and political freedom."

A week later, after hearing a report by Allen Dulles on the significance of Soviet efforts to discredit Stalin, the National Security Council directed its Planning Board to prepare revisions of NSC 174, NSC 5505/1 ("Exploitation of Soviet and European Satellite Vulnerabilities"), and NSC 5602/1.[74] Someone in the CIA even suggested that the time was ripe for a visit by Vice-President Nixon to the satellite countries, but Allen Dulles dismissed the idea as crazy.[75] Reports from Moscow indicated that the Soviet leaders were divided on the merits of de-Stalinization, and Dulles told the Foreign Relations Committee in June that "Khrushchev is on the ropes and, if we can keep the pressure up, [. . .] there is going to occur a very great disintegration within the apparatus of the international Communist organization."[76]

By the early summer of 1956 Cord Meyer was receiving warnings from the satellite watchers at Radio Free Europe that "events were moving toward a confrontation with the Soviets in Poland and Hungary." The experts at the State Department were skeptical, and Meyer records that Allen Dulles later chided him for not bringing these warnings more forcefully to his attention.[77] Other branches of the CIA eagerly seized upon the chance for a major upheaval in Eastern Europe, and Allen Dulles must have approved preparations to exploit these tendencies. Behind Wisner's and Angleton's urgings to hold back the secret speech from immediate publication lay Operation Red Sox/Red Cap. Conceived by Wisner's directorate, the operation involved the training of hundreds of refugees from Czechoslovakia, Hungary, Poland, and Romania at a base near Munich. The plan was to prepare these paramilitary forces for infiltration into the satellites at the opportune moment to foment or aid national uprisings against Soviet rule. The forces, recalls Angleton, were not up to snuff in the spring of 1956, and he and Wisner wanted time to ready them before using elements of the Khrushchev speech to destabilize the satellite regimes.[78]

The scheme was bold, fraught with risk, and carried the American policy of liberation to its logical conclusion by proposing to pursue the covert war beyond the iron curtain via indigenous rebels. Its authors possessed a passionate belief in the justice of America's cause in the battle against communism. But these self-styled Knights Templar were dangerously isolated from the world of high politics, elections, and diplomacy. The distance between the White House and the CIA has seldom been greater than in the case of liberation.

De-Stalinization presented new opportunities and problems for America's propaganda agencies. In May the USIA launched a country-by-country review to better attune Voice of America programming to the diversity among the satellites. Radio Free Europe hammered home the message that the political system had to be changed to prevent the recurrence of tyranny, but it also warned against overestimating the Kremlin's tolerance.[79] CIA balloons were dropping Khrushchev's translated speech all over Eastern Europe. America's message to the East Europeans was riddled with ambiguity: Your regimes are our common enemy; they must be overthrown; press for reform; avoid rash action; you have our moral support; we are seeking to reduce tensions with the Soviet Union. The Kremlin, for its part, acknowledged the existence of internal opposition in the satellites and conveniently blamed America's "lying propaganda."[80]

Although Secretary of State Dulles and the psychological warfare agencies persisted with their exhortative rhetoric, the European allies and many Americans soon came to the conclusion that liberation was a dead letter, at best a peculiarly American profession of faith in the ineluctable forces of history advancing the cause of freedom. The 1956 election campaign confirmed this impression. Eisenhower presented himself as the agent of peace, in Korea and in negotiations with the USSR. The Republican platform made passing reference to liberation of the satellites by peaceful methods, as did Vice President Nixon in campaign speeches. Eisenhower in his acceptance speech at San Francisco promised to end the cold war by bridging "the great chasm that separates us from the peoples under communist rule." These dutiful references differed little from those issuing from the Democratic camp. The latter went so far as to denounce the Republican administration for its "heartless record of broken promises to the unfortunate victims of Communism" and for "standing silent when the peoples rise in East Germany and Poland."[81] Indeed, developments in Poland and Hungary soon thrust the issue of liberation back into the limelight.

Rumbles in Poland. Emboldened by the hints of greater permissiveness emanating from Moscow, Polish dissidents stepped up their pressure. On June 28, workers in the industrial city of Poznan took their economic grievances to the streets and attacked party and security police offices. Americans at the trade fair being held in the city were begged for Western aid. Armored troops took three days to quell the revolt. Scores were killed or wounded, hundreds imprisoned. A semblance of order was restored, but the scent of revolution was unmistakable and the party's leaders began to take steps to win back some public support.

When in the early evening of June 28 Allen Dulles telephoned his brother with news of the riots, Foster exulted, "When they begin to crack, they can crack fast. We have to keep the pressure on."[82] However, Radio Free Europe responded with great caution, warning the Poles against suicidal insurrection. The State Department commented that "all free peoples will be watching the situation closely to see whether or not the Polish people will be allowed a government which will remedy the grievances which have brought them to a breaking point."[83] As in the earlier case of East Germany, American surplus food was offered and rejected.

An embarrassed Kremlin lashed out at the Americans, accusing them of having financed the Poznan rebels. Fortuitously for the Soviets, two amendments to the Mutual Security Act had just been introduced in the Senate offering a $25 million subsidy to private organizations dedicated to Eastern Europe's liberation.[84] The sponsors, Senators Paul Douglas and Everett Dirksen, had evoked the liberation promises as well as the recent Polish events in support of the amendments. Foster Dulles told his brother Allen that he found nothing objectionable in the Dirksen amendment, but neither measure was passed.[85] The Soviets nevertheless seized the occasion to warn the West against attempts to subvert the satellite regimes and warn the East Europeans against nationalistic and opportunistic tendencies. Meanwhile, in Poland and Hungary the momentum of reform accelerated.

The leading figure in the quiet Polish revolution was Wladyslaw Gomulka. In the early postwar years he deplored Soviet removal of German property from the annexed lands, resisted the collectivization of agriculture, and opposed the anti-Tito campaign. At Soviet insistence, he was removed in 1949 from the Polish Workers party leadership. Under the Stalinist Boleslaw Bierut, the Warsaw regime struggled like its neighbors to collectivize and industrialize, to isolate the Catholic church and Russify Polish culture. The expansion of industry proceeded apace, but most Poles resented the party's oppressive rule and especially Soviet domination. In August 1956, Gomulka was readmitted to full party membership and became a symbol and rallying point for nationalists within and outside the party.

The trials of the Poznan rioters were conducted with a degree of openness that only encouraged dissidents, and by early October popular unrest and sporadic demonstrations by workers and students amounted to an incipient revolution. Moscow's displeasure was represented most forcefully by General Konstantin Rokossovsky, a defense minister, member of the Polish Politburo, and Soviet citizen. Apart from Rokossovsky, the Polish party leaders showed steady nerve, independent spirit, and unity of purpose in the face of Soviet pressure, going so far as to reorganize the workers' militia into a force free of Soviet influence. On October 15 the Politburo agreed to nominate Gomulka as first secretary at the forthcoming meeting of the Central Committee.

On the morning of October 19, a few hours after the confirmation of Gomulka's appointment, Khrushchev arrived in Warsaw accompanied by much of the Soviet Politburo. At the same time some of the seven Soviet divisions stationed in Poland began to move upon the capital. Barred from joining the meeting of the Central Committee, a furious Khrushchev demanded the appointment of a more compliant party leadership. In the extraordinary test of wills that followed, he accused the Poles of selling out to the Americans, while Gomulka threatened to broadcast to all Poland the nature of the Soviet blackmail unless the ominous troop movements were halted. "We will not talk while cannons are pointing at Warsaw," said Gomulka.[86] Workers, students, and the militia were alerted to the possibility of violent confrontation. Khrushchev blinked first; the Soviet forces halted their advance, and a bloodbath was narrowly avoided. Rokossovsky was forced to reveal to the Central Committee the next day that the party leadership had asked the

Soviets to stop their saber rattling. He was then stripped of his offices and repatriated to the Soviet Union along with most other military advisers.

Gomulka's victory owed as much to the Soviet leaders' sober reconsideration of his merits as to their reluctance to wage war. His renunciation of Stalinism and assertion of the right to pursue the Polish route to socialism was doctrinally compatible with the new Khrushchevian line, and the united front presented by the Polish party did after all guarantee the preservation of Communist rule. On November 18, with the lessons of the Hungarian revolution already recorded, Gomulka secured in Moscow tangible assurances of support—cancellation of Poland's debt, new Soviet credits, recognition of Poland's right to consultation in the deployment of Soviet forces, and a pledge to let Poles still held in the Soviet Union return to their homeland. He undertook in turn to safeguard Communist supremacy and endorse Soviet foreign policy, notably with regard to the forcible reintegration of Hungary into the Soviet bloc. This was a small price to pay for the free pursuit of domestic reform, which included the decollectivization of much of agriculture, a revival of marginal private enterprise, the establishment of workers' councils in factories, the rehabilitation of victims of Stalinism, and the release of Stefan Cardinal Wyszynski from house arrest. Gomulka appeared to be the agent of national reconciliation, and his regime even expressed a desire for closer relations with the West.[87]

The Polish quiet revolution seemingly vindicated Western policymakers, including Secretary of State Dulles, who had anticipated a peaceful evolution toward Titoism. Back in July 1956, Henry Cabot Lodge, the U.S. ambassador to the United Nations, had suggested to Dulles the introduction in the Security Council of a resolution to set up a Peace Observation Commission for Poland. The Soviets would exercise their veto, of course, but the initiative would have a positive political effect on Polish-Americans. Alternatively, the United States could propose a UN investigation of the Kremlin charges that the Americans had instigated the riots. Observed Dulles, "From a political point of view it is not too bad to let some think we did." The two men agreed that the matter was "not simple and there could be a lot of dividends if it is played right," but Dulles thought that the British and the French would not endorse open allegations of Soviet interference, commenting that "they are weak when things are breaking our way."[88] On October 22, Lodge again proposed action at the United Nations, and Dulles agreed all the more readily since he had heard the representations of leading Polish-Americans. Events in Hungary were about to draw attention away from Poland, but for the moment Dulles could confidently tell a caller that "the continuous sequence of concessions demonstrates the weakness of the Communist regime and will ultimately lead to free elections." [89]

Radio Free Europe played its part admirably, warning the Poles not to demand immediate Soviet military withdrawal or free elections and urging them to support Gomulka's compromise. So calming was this message that Warsaw suspended the jamming of RFE during the crisis. The CIA had, according to Robert Amory, "virtually real-time solid information leaked to the Polish editors by their friends on the Warsaw Politburo and gladly passed on to encourage US assistance in case the Soviets cracked down." He urged the Pentagon's operations chief, General Wheeler, to prepare for World War III, arguing that if the Polish army turned on the Russians "the land war balance in Eastern Europe will be decisively tipped in our favor if material support can only be given them." [90]

Although Wheeler and his staff promptly set to work on a "crash analysis and planning program," the White House displayed only serene confidence. On October 20 the president sent an anodyne message of sympathy to the Poles. The next day, on the CBS program "Face the Nation," Dulles expressed doubt that the Soviets would resort to military measures but stressed that in such an eventuality the United States would definitely not intervene. By then the most critical moment had passed in Warsaw, and the secretary's reassurance to the Soviets was superfluous, although they no doubt drew comfort from it a few days later in the midst of the Hungarian conflagration. The course of action recommended by the NSC's Planning Board included bilateral talks, inducements to reorient Polish trade toward the West, and "economic and technical assistance in moderate amounts sufficient to give the Poles an alternative to complete dependence on Moscow." [91] In the event, Eisenhower decided to quietly extend economic aid to the Poles, though this took a tangible form only in mid-1957 and Gomulka's reformism proved to be short-lived.

The winds of change were blowing through Eastern Europe. Favorable and irreversible forces appeared to be at work, and if all this owed little to Washington's efforts, America's strategic interests were nevertheless well served. A more immediate threat to these interests was emerging in the Middle East, for on October 19 Dulles learned that despite his efforts at conciliation three of America's closest friends were preparing a concerted attack on Egypt. Within a week, the Hungarian and Suez crises would shake both the Eastern and Western alliances to their foundations and dispel the comforting illusions of peaceful coexistence. Another fatal casualty would be the myth of liberation.

Eruption in Hungary. In Hungary, the Party's crisis of confidence, set in motion by the New Course, deepened despite the return to undivided power of the hated dictator Matyas Rakosi. The liberal tendency associated with the dismissed Imre Nagy and officially branded "revisionist" was gaining ground among Communist intellectuals. The party press displayed unprecedented independence in criticizing "dogmatic" leadership. In fact, by the spring of 1956 a discussion forum officially sanctioned as a safety valve and known as the Petofi Circle became the scene of devastating denunciations of economic mismanagement and political oppression. The unrepentant Rakosi plotted to purge his tormentors, but the Kremlin intervened and in July had him replaced by another Comintern veteran, Erno Gero. Rakosi had become expendable not only because of his unpopularity but also because he was a bete noire of Tito, who despised him for his savage attacks of earlier years and charged that his hands were soaked in blood.

Under Gero the Hungarian party tried to recover its balance. Nagy was grudgingly readmitted to party membership, the purged Laszlo Rajk was posthumously rehabilitated, and promises of economic reform and socialist legality were made. In mid-October, at Soviet insistence, Gero traveled to Belgrade to beg Tito's forgiveness for calumnies conveniently attributed to Rakosi (who had retired to the Soviet Union) and to the former secret police chief. Back in Budapest, the classic prerevolutionary situation was in evidence: a divided and demoralized ruling elite, a restive and outspoken intelligentsia, and an alienated population yearning for change. Encouraged by the news from Poland, the Writers' Union, the Trade Union Council, the Petofi Circle, and student groups outbid each other with ever-bolder manifestos. By the morning of October 23, the demands included free multiparty elections and the withdrawal of Soviet troops. Later that day a student demonstration of solidarity with the Poles was first prohibited, then sanctioned by Gero.

The streets of Budapest filled with marching protesters, and that evening the first shots of the revolution were fired into a crowd by secret police guarding the broadcasting center.

In thirteen days the revolution went through stages of armed confrontation, democratic consolidation, and final repression. Gero tried to buy time by appointing Imre Nagy prime minister while calling for Soviet military help. The Warsaw Treaty, evoked in official justification of the appeal, provided for assistance only in the case of external threat and guaranteed noninterference in the members' internal affairs, but neither in 1956 nor in 1968 did the pact inhibit intervention. In fact, Soviet troops had been conducting maneuvers for three days and reached Budapest before dawn on October 24 to crush what Gero called "counterrevolutionary gangs." Most Hungarian soldiers remained inactive or defected to the revolution, and after a few bloody but inconclusive skirmishes it became evident that the regime could count only on the secret police and the Soviets to prop up party rule. Two Soviet Politburo members, Anastas Mikoyan and Mikhail Suslov, hurried to Budapest in order to have Gero replaced as first secretary by the more moderate Janos Kadar and stabilize the situation. Kadar professed his support for Prime Minister Nagy, and the latter appealed to the rapidly proliferating revolutionary groups to lay down their arms, promising sweeping reforms and the withdrawal of Soviet troops.

Responding to popular pressures, Nagy gradually expanded his government to include representatives of the postwar non-Communist parties and promised the formation of a new national army. Deserted by most of its members, the Communist party (renamed the Hungarian Socialist Workers party) was reduced to a hard core of beleaguered veterans holed up in the Central Committee building and district offices. Freedom fighters laid siege to the Budapest party committee's headquarters, and some summary executions ensued. As revolutions go, the Hungarian uprising was an uncommonly civilized affair, and the people's wrath claimed relatively few victims, mostly secret policemen. But eight years of Stalinism dissipated whatever genuine support the Communists once enjoyed, and Kadar anticipated that his party would have to function as a minority opposition. The famous Marxist philosopher Gyorgy Lukacs was more blunt: communism had been "totally disgraced" in Hungary, and in free elections the party could count on no more than 5 to 10 percent of the popular vote.[92] The revolutionary spirit swept the country, political parties old and new emerged, and the liberated Cardinal Mindszenty made a triumphal return to Budapest. The new political consensus favored a pluralistic democracy, some form of mixed economy, and, above all, national autonomy.

The news that Mikoyan and Suslov carried back to the Kremlin after their second visit to Budapest, on October 27, could not have been encouraging. The Soviet leadership was divided on the appropriate response, as were its allies. The Chinese initially recommended against intervention, but the more vulnerable satellites, notably Czechoslovakia and Romania, which had large and now restive Hungarian minorities, were clamoring for swift action.[93] The first military intervention in Budapest had been at best a standoff. It failed to eliminate political challenges to party rule. The bloodshed it caused was denounced around the world as a demonstration of Soviet brutality, and the subsequent tactical withdrawal from the capital implied acquiescence in the democratic revolution engulfing Hungary. No doubt Khrushchev would have preferred a political solution, as he confided to the Yugoslav ambassador on October 24.[94] Between October 29 and 31, the Soviet Politburo decided on the tactics to follow. Hungary was abandoning communism; the Americans had made clear they would not intervene; and the Western allies were divided over the impending military action against Egypt. The imperatives of confirming the integrity of the Soviet bloc were clear, the risks—apart from inevitable propaganda damage—minimal.

Soviet Deception and Intervention.   Preparations for a decisive military strike were set in motion. In the meantime, on October 30 the Kremlin issued a remarkably conciliatory declaration affirming its acceptance of different roads to socialism and respect for the complete equality, territorial integrity, and sovereignty of other socialist states. The declaration was presumably designed to dampen unrest in the other satellites, reassure Tito, and deceive the Hungarians. Mikoyan and Suslov were dispatched once again to Budapest on October 31 to try to still Nagy's apprehensions. Along with Moscow's ambassador, Yuri Andropov, they repeatedly assured the Hungarian leader that Russian troop movements were merely preparations for withdrawal and that negotiations for a full evacuation could commence.

Reports of a massive influx of Soviet reinforcements convinced Nagy that he had been deceived, and on November 1 he secured his cabinet's support (including that of Kadar) for the fateful step of appealing to the United Nations. He proclaimed Hungary's withdrawal from the Warsaw Pact and requested the "four great powers" to recognize and guarantee Hungary's neutrality. Speaking to his countrymen, he observed that "our people are as united in this decision as perhaps never before in their history."[95] Andropov promptly demanded that Nagy retract this measure, then invited the Hungarians the next day to join in negotiations on a Soviet withdrawal. It is worth reiterating that Nagy resorted to the provocative proclamation of neutrality only *after* receiving evidence of the Soviet intent to overthrow his government by force.

Khrushchev and Malenkov paid lightning, secret visits on November 1 to Brest, then to Bucharest, to brief the Polish and other satellite leaders on the impending suppression of the Hungarian revolt. A more difficult job of persuasion awaited them the next day, when they appeared at Tito's Brioni retreat. The other Communist leaders, Khrushchev assured Tito, all agreed on the necessity of military intervention. The Western powers were "mired deep in the mud of Egypt." The counterrevolutionaries in Hungary were killing communists and bringing back capitalism to the very frontiers of the Soviet Union. The Soviets could not afford to let things take their course and appear stupid or weak. Tito argued against resort to force but finally contented himself with urging the appointment of Kadar as Moscow's new lieutenant.[96] Kadar by this time had been persuaded to serve the inevitable. Spirited out of Budapest by the Soviets, he was held in readiness in the Carpatho-Ukrainian city of Uzhgorod for the impending formation of a new "Hungarian Revolutionary Worker-Peasant Government."

In the late hours of November 3, a Hungarian military delegation met with its Soviet counterpart at the Soviet military headquarters outside Budapest to continue discussions on withdrawal. The meeting was interrupted by the appearance of the head of the KGB, General Ivan Serov, who summarily arrested the Hungarians. At dawn the next day, the Soviets launched a massive assault on Budapest. A shattered Imre Nagy broadcast to his people that "Soviet troops attacked our capital with the obvious intention of overthrowing the legal Hungarian democratic government" and claimed that "our troops are in combat." In fact, he did not give the order to fight, for the formation of a new Hungarian national army had hardly begun.

Fighting continued sporadically for a few days, and several weeks passed before the resistance of workers' councils in the factories was crushed. Kadar was brought back to Budapest in a Soviet armored car and set about the thankless task of restoring Communist rule. Cardinal Mindszenty sought sanctuary in the U.S. legation; Nagy and his retinue in the Yugoslav embassy. Some two hundred thousand Hungarians fled abroad. The dead, and burned-out Soviet tanks, littered the streets of a devastated city. Execution, imprisonment, or deportation was the fate of thousands of patriots. Nagy was enticed from his refuge and executed in June 1958 after refusing to recant at a travesty of a secret trial. A spontaneous and movingly courageous attempt by a small nation to discard communism and foreign domination had come to a tragic end.

Washington Faces Two Crises. The outbreak within a few days of both the Hungarian and Suez crises sorely tried the fortitude and nerve of Washington's policymakers. Suez was not as much of a surprise as Hungary. Deputy Under Secretary of State Robert Murphy claimed subsequently that Washington had neither advance warning nor a contingency plan for the Hungarian uprising.[97] The State Department and the CIA had undoubtedly observed the mounting tension in Budapest, but the eruption of a full-scale revolt on October 23 was spontaneous and could hardly have been accurately predicted. As Allen Dulles later observed, "We were not caught by surprise as to the general conditions or the general reactions, except in Hungary it went beyond what we expected." He awakened Cord Meyer with the news that "all hell has broken loose in Budapest." The common belief that Communist rule was immovable, recalls Meyer, impeded the formulation of realistic contingency plans for such a revolt. Momentarily the secretary of state was elated: "We kept alive the yearning for freedom. It worked in Yugoslavia; it will work in Poland and Hungary. The great monolith of Communism is crumbling!"[98]

Eisenhower records that the developing crisis in Hungary was on the agenda of numerous White House meetings, but the disposition of policymakers was to wait and see.[99] The new Hungarian prime minister was a Communist and had apparently sanctioned the call for Soviet assistance. From his vantage point in Moscow, Ambassador Bohlen reported that there did not appear to be any open divergence between the Soviet and Hungarian governments.[100] Perhaps, as Dulles claimed, the aid to Tito was paying dividends in Hungary as well as Poland, and evolution toward national communism would be condoned by Khrushchev. The latter was regarded as a bold reformer who was still consolidating his position, and provocative American action might weaken his grip and even raise the risk of global conflict. The hope in official Washington was that the Polish and Hungarian situations would evolve at a pace tolerable to Moscow and in a direction favorable to the West.

After news of the bloody clashes with Soviet troops reached Washington, on October 25 the president issued his first public comment. The United States, he said, noted the "renewed expression of the intense desire for freedom long held by the people of Hungary" and deplored the intervention of Soviet forces. He told a Republican rally in Madison Square Garden that evening that the United States would do all in its power peacefully to help the Hungarians, and confided to a journalist: "Poor fellows, poor fellows, I think about them all the time. I wish there were some way of helping them." [101]

The options for an American response were the subject of intensive debate within the administration and in the press. Action at the United Nations was one common idea urged by Hungarian-American leaders and recommended by the *New York Times*. Dulles discussed this with Lodge, worrying "from a political standpoint" that "it will be said that here are the great moments and when they came and these fellows were ready to stand up and die, we were caught napping and doing nothing." He thought that there was more of an excuse to take Hungary to the Security Council than there had been with Poland and that the British and French would reluctantly go along. [102] The next day, Lodge suggested an observation commission, while Dulles toyed with the possibility of a circular letter to UN members or a resolution initiated by other states on the Security Council such as Cuba or Peru. Dulles and the president agreed action should be concerted with the allies, who might otherwise suspect an election gambit. [103]

The National Security Council convened on the morning of October 26 to take stock of the situation. Allen Dulles reported that Khrushchev appeared to be in trouble, and the president voiced great concern that the Kremlin might be "tempted to resort to extreme measures, even to start a world war." The tentative consensus was that the United States should extend a guarantee of noninterference to alleviate Soviet apprehensions and induce a more permissive attitude toward Hungary and Poland. [104] The NSC instructed its Planning Board to prepare "a comprehensive analysis of the developments in Hungary and Poland, and possible courses of action in the light thereof which the United States should consider," deferring action on the latest policy guidance, NSC 5616.[105]

Secretary of State Dulles was scheduled to make a major foreign policy address in Dallas on October 27. This opportunity was used to deliver the authoritative American response to the Hungarian revolution. He twice consulted the president the night before, and they agreed the world should be assured that America wanted genuine independence for the East Europeans; if this was granted, the problem of European security would be altered. The president and Dulles also agreed that the issue should be broached with the Soviets only in private, backstage discussions at the United Nations.[106] In his Dallas speech Dulles offered America's economic aid without any condition as to "any particular form of society" that might emerge. In other words, Titoism was an acceptable, indeed desirable, outcome.[107]

The prospects for peaceful evolution dimmed the next day when the State Department learned that fresh Soviet troops were flooding into Hungary.[108] Ominous news also arrived from the American ambassador to Tel Aviv: full-scale mobilization by the Israeli forces.[109] The final plans for the Anglo-French-Israeli operation to topple Nasser had been developed just as the Hungarian revolution broke out, and the conspirators evidently saw no reason to postpone action. Moscow's preoccupation with Hungary might well have been regarded by them as fortuitous, although Dulles promptly warned French and British diplomats that the operation would undermine Western attempts to forestall repression of the Hungarians.[110]

Dulles's reassurance to the Soviets was meanwhile reiterated at the United Nations on October 28 by Lodge and in Moscow the following day by Bohlen, who on Dulles's instructions also reminded Khrushchev, Bulganin, and Zhukov that the United States continued to favor an earlier Western proposal linking a "treaty of assurance" to German unification.[111] Dulles had cleared these instructions with the president, who suggested that "this would be a good time really to talk with the Russians." The secretary warned that they had to be "extremely careful not to do anything which could be misinterpreted in the satellite countries to indicate that we were selling them out and dealing with their hated masters behind their backs," and Eisenhower agreed.[112] This, on available evidence, was the only American attempt to place the Hungarian events in the context of East-West negotiations on European security. There was apparently no response, nor any follow-up.

The State Department was equally cautious in its appraisal of the political orientation of the Nagy government, which by this time had made clear its radical departure from Communist orthodoxy. The new American minister to Hungary, Edward T. Wailes, was scheduled to leave for Budapest on the afternoon of October 30. When the question of having Wailes meet with the president arose in a discussion between Dulles and a White House aide, the secretary observed that "it is not important . . . because the present government is not one we want to do much with." The diplomat complained that he had not been briefed on his assignment.[113] Nor, apparently, had there been contact between Nagy and the remaining American diplomats in Budapest, and Hungary's permanent representative at the United Nations was a Stalinist who enjoyed the confidence of neither the new regime nor the West. The momentary lapse in communication and inadequate intelligence may therefore serve to explain Dulles's cool response to the emergence of an ultra-Titoist regime—the very development he had so confidently anticipated.

Soviet charges that American agents and money had fomented the uprising were publicly dismissed by the secretary of state.[114] CIA operatives in Western Europe were rushed to the border to make contact with their agents in Hungary, and some arms were supplied to the rebels, but there is no corroborated evidence of calculated and covert collusion to precipitate an uprising. To be sure, the CIA's operational departments reacted with enthusiasm. For Frank Wisner and his aides in the Directorate of Plans, the long-awaited opportunity had come. Air resupply facilities, stocks of arms, and communications equipment were ready. The Hungarian uprising, recalls a onetime director of central intelligence, was "exactly the end for which the Agency's paramilitary capability was designed."[115] Wisner, on a European inspection tour, pressed the case for active rollback, for unleashing the Red Sox/Red Cap forces to aid the Hungarians and spread the spark of revolt in the satellites.

If Allen Dulles favored paramilitary intervention, he was soon overruled by the president. This was the moment of truth for the CIA. In William Colby's words, "Whatever doubts may have existed in the Agency about Washington's policy in matters like this vanished."[116] Hungarian specialists like James McCargar were reduced to speculating about the desirable political composition of a new Hungarian government. The agents at the Hungarian border could offer little more than cautious encouragement to contacts who were becoming increasingly anxious about Soviet and American intentions.

Frustrated by the collapse of all his plans and preparations, Frank Wisner was also furious at the coincidental Suez operation and at not having received any warning from his British counterparts. Did Britain not understand what its action would do to Hungary, where Khrushchev was about to make concessions? The revolution turned into a personal tragedy for this cold warrior. When the final Soviet assault got under way, he flew to Vienna to observe the dismal sight of freedom fighters and refugees flooding across the border. At his next stop, the CIA station in Rome, he was visibly on the brink of a nervous breakdown, and he never fully recovered. Recurring fits of depression and other illness eventually drove him to suicide, "a casualty of the realities of the Cold War."[117]

One of the realities of the cold war was propaganda, and Radio Free Europe served as a convenient scapegoat for both East and West. Admittedly, its performance during the revolution was a controversial mix of encouragement and excessive suspicion. Until November 1, RFE's commentators treated the Nagy regime as a Communist Trojan horse, blaming it for the initial call for Soviet help, although some policy advisers would have preferred to withhold judgment. On the other hand, RFE offered some tactical advice to the rebels, served as a transmission belt for their demands, and was generally identified with the goals of the revolution. In retrospect, Cord Meyer agreed that the tone of the broadcasts was "more exuberant and optimistic than the situation warranted." Reports on UN debates and Western expressions of sympathy implied the promise of tangible assistance.

On the morning of November 4, as fighting raged in the streets of Budapest, the station broadcast a review of a newspaper report suggesting that if the Hungarians held out until after the American election, Congress might approve armed intervention. The commentator added that "a practical manifestation of Western sympathy is expected at any hour."[118] The next day's policy guideline was somberly realistic in observing that "none of our audiences will be too receptive to strong propaganda words and strident voices while the victims of Soviet imperialism lie unburied."[119]

Investigations by the CIA and the West German government largely exonerated RFE of any wrongdoing, although a few broadcasts were found to be in violation of standing policies and daily guidances. The real issue, of course, was not so much the occasional transgression by overzealous emigre broadcasters but rather the perceptions induced by American psychological warfare. Surveys among refugees indicated that while few blamed RFE for incitement, a great many construed Washington's liberation rhetoric and the very existence of RFE as an American commitment to come to their assistance at the appropriate moment against the Soviet Union. Not surprisingly, they felt that the Hungarian revolution, by creating a constitutional regime that requested recognition and protection of Hungary's sovereignty and neutrality, had presented the West with the ideal opportunity for constructive action.[120] That these illusions persisted despite Washington's prudent emphasis on peaceful evolution and Titoism owed more to fundamental misperception on both sides than to willful deception or self-deception.

The most damaging misperception, displayed notably by Dulles, involved the transferability of Titoism. Tito, initially the most orthodox of Communist leaders, had secured Yugoslavia's autonomy with only modest assistance from the allies and enjoyed a domestic following that only grew after his refusal to do Stalin's bidding. No other East European Communist leader commanded such popular support and such strong and reliable defense forces. Dulles's hope that the virus of Titoism would spread was understandable and consonant with American interests, and Gomulka's success momentarily lent it some strength. Titoism held out the promise of liberation without additional or more tangible American commitments.

Israel's lightning advance on October 29, followed the next day by the prearranged Anglo-French ultimatum to Nasser, compelled Washington to concentrate its attention on the Middle East. The implications for the outcome of the Hungarian crisis were evident. Allen Dulles shared his brother's concern that "a spark in the Middle East could give the Soviets a shield to do things they can't do now" and that "the clock might be turned back in Central Europe." In a telephone conversation with Eisenhower on the afternoon of October 30, the secretary of state observed "what a great tragedy it is just when the whole Soviet policy is collapsing the British and French are doing the same thing in the Arab world."[121]

The CIA's director hailed Moscow's October 30 declaration as "one of the most significant to come out of the Soviet Union since the end of World War II," although by then U.S. and British military intelligence had learned that some Red Army units had been placed on full battle alert. The president doubted Moscow's sincerity, and in a major public address on the two crises, delivered in the evening of October 31, he toned down Foster Dulles's proposed references to irresistible forces of liberation in Eastern Europe.[122] Instead, Eisenhower noted that the use of force to fulfill the wartime pledges regarding Eastern-Central Europe would not have been in anyone's interest, but that the United States "did help to keep alive the hope of these peoples for freedom." He reaffirmed Dulles's statement that the United States did not look upon new East European governments as potential allies but was ready to offer them economic aid.[123]

Washington's dilemma was aggravated by Nagy's declaration of neutrality and appeal for recognition. The American legation in Budapest reported that the revolution was clearly leading to a democratic form of government and that "the potentiality of U.S. influence in this period is tremendous"; it recommended urgent consideration of "further U.S. statements."[124] The director of central intelligence, for his part, construed the occurrences in Hungary as a "miracle."[125] The less favorable developments were the Suez crisis and the movement of Soviet reinforcements into Hungary. The critical moment had arrived for reassessing Washington's response. There was no shortage of advice: congressmen, emigres, diplomats were all lobbying the State Department for some form of support for the Hungarians in their hour of need.

Policy Options and Decisions. Since October 26, the members of the National Security Council Planning Board had been struggling with the development of policy recommendations in a fluid and complex situation. A revision of NSC 5616 was in preparation, and according to Robert Amory, he and some other members of the Planning Board were urging forceful action. He recalls that intelligence reports of Soviet troop movements led them to conclude that the Suez crisis had helped the Kremlin to decide on swift repression: "Appalled by the combination of a God-given chance to witness a significant roll-back of this iron curtain by the unaided guts and verve of the Magyar people and a sense of helpless foreboding at what would happen to them if the Russians felt certain that the West would not lift a finger," Amory desperately searched for a workable strategy. The option of conventional military intervention would have required the acquiescence of the European allies and direct access. The key allies, Britain and France, were otherwise engaged and in any event would not have agreed to NATO taking an aggressive stance. Austria was certainly not ready to compromise her neutrality and would not even condone the use of her airspace for an airlift. Claiming that his country was "trembling on the thin edge of war," the Yugoslav ambassador urged Robert Murphy that everything be done to confine the conflict to Hungary.[126]

Even if conventional military intervention was unfeasible, there remained, at least in Amory's view, the option of a surgical nuclear strike. The United States possessed a substantial stockpile of thermonuclear weapons, and the strategic balance was still clearly in America's favor. He therefore advanced the idea of a preemptive attack directed at Lvov and mountain passes in the Carpatho-Ukraine and western Romania, designed to obstruct rail and road access to Hungary: "So I drafted a one-page ultimatum for the President and the Secretary of State to consider, calling for a halt to all further Soviet reinforcement of its forces in Hungary on pain of our taking military measures at our disposal [. . .]. I said that if Khrushchev were to ask Marshal Zhukov if he was ready for nuclear war with the United States, the latter would have to answer no; hence, the ultimatum by itself might well work."[127]

It is highly unlikely that any American president would ever have seriously considered taking such risk for the sake of freeing a small, faraway country, or for the marginal strategic benefits that might have accrued from a successful ultimatum. Eisenhower was certainly not an impetuous man, and if Amory's proposal was ever conveyed to him, he must have dismissed it out of hand. In his memoirs the president indulged in some safe speculation: "I still wonder what would have been my recommendation to Congress and the American people had Hungary been accessible by sea or through the territory of allies who might have agreed to react positively to the tragic fate of the Hungarian people."[128] In fact, neither the American people nor the West Europeans were ready to risk war over Hungary, where no vital national interests were at stake. From this perspective, the Suez crisis could be seen as more help than hindrance, for it allowed the United States to display moral consistency in deploring all foreign intervention. Dulles later explained to the

French foreign minister that American acquiescence in the Suez operation would have only encouraged the interested American ethnic groups to press for military action to liberate the satellites.[129]

The National Security Council received its Planning Board's assessment of the Polish and Hungarian situations on November 1.[130] The report viewed the events as "a serious defeat for Soviet policy [which] may cause the Soviet Union to reappraise the value of continuing its control through the presence of its forces in the light of the increasing costs of such a policy." The West should therefore "strive to aid and encourage forces in the satellites moving toward U.S. objectives without provoking counter-action which would result in the suppression of 'liberalizing' influences."

The report reflected the heated debates over possible courses of action, which included public pressure through the United Nations to inhibit further Soviet intervention; immediate covert support of the rebels; open recognition of their belligerent status, and overt military support and recognition of their government; a disarmament proposal involving Hungarian neutrality on the Austrian model and an indication of American willingness to "consult with NATO on the probable withdrawal of some U.S. forces from Western Europe if the Soviet does withdraw all its forces from Hungary" (even at this stage, Defense and the Joint Chiefs of Staff objected to assurances that the United States would not look upon Hungary or other satellites as potential military allies); disaster relief and economic measures similar to those proposed for Poland; and, most pessimistically, assistance to Austria in dealing with refugees. The Planning Board urged the administration as a matter of high priority to "exploit fully throughout the world propaganda opportunities afforded by the recent events in Poland and Hungary" and (in evocation of NSC 174) "to determine U.S. courses of action in the event of future revolutionary actions or uprisings" in other satellites.

The NSC evidently dismissed not only the more warlike options but also those involving recognition and military disengagement. The State Department's disposition was to avoid any official endorsement of the Nagy regime and its claim to neutrality. Only some moderate version of Titoism was considered to have any chance of survival in Hungary, and if Nagy overextended himself, then the United States should not encourage him. The department's circular to major embassies on November 2 still gave credence to the Kremlin's earlier profession of readiness to significantly loosen its control over the satellites and claimed that it was not clear whether the Soviet Union had decided that developments in Hungary necessitated armed repression.[131] Coming after Nagy's renunciation of the Warsaw Pact and reports of massive reinforcements, such an estimate was misinformed or, more likely, disingenuous. That same day, an incoming cable from Ambassador Bohlen in Moscow warned that the Soviet promise of negotiation with the Nagy government was probably a device to gain time for military preparations.[132]

More consistent with Washington's real appraisal of the situation was the advice relayed to Nagy to avoid too great a show of friendship for the West and the reassuring message sent to Moscow—apparently via Tito on the occasion of his secret meeting with Khrushchev on November 2—that the United States did not favor governments unfriendly to the Soviet Union on the latter's borders.[133] But confirmation of the Kremlin's decision to intervene soon reached Washington. In the late afternoon of November 2, Allen Dulles twice called his brother with news of the Soviet military buildup. That same day, a convoy of U.S. diplomatic personnel and dependents trying to leave Hungary was turned back by Soviet troops near the Austrian border. Wailes cabled at 1400 hours GMT on November 3 that Soviet forces had encircled Budapest and other Hungarian cities and that in the "veiled form of negotiations" the Soviets would probably issue an unacceptable ultimatum to the Nagy government: "This could lead to slaughter." Two hours later, Bohlen reported that after "considerable discussion" the Soviet leadership had decided on military intervention.[134]

Only after the Soviet assault was under way, in the early hours of November 4, did the Hungarian government dispatch a direct plea for help to the United States. Addressed to President Eisenhower, it claimed that although the Hungarians were "determined to resist with desperation the attack upon them, there is no doubt that in this unequal struggle [Hungary] will be defeated if it does not receive help. In this moment the most necessary kind of help is political, not military." Hungarian Minister of State Istvan Bibo urged Eisenhower to negotiate a simultaneous withdrawal of foreign forces from Hungary and Egypt.[135]

The president issued a statement on November 4 reporting that he had conferred with Foster Dulles (who had been taken to Walter Reed Army Hospital the previous day), Acting Secretary of State Herbert Hoover, Jr., Allen Dulles, and other advisers to "discuss the ways and means available to the United States which would result in . . . [the] withdrawal of Soviet troops from Hungary" and had sent a message to Premier Bulganin asking that the Soviets desist "in the name of humanity and in the cause of peace." But a more provocative message was already on its way from Bulganin threatening a nuclear attack if the British and French did not withdraw from Egypt. Washington officially dismissed the Soviet threat as a diversionary tactic, but Eisenhower privately worried that the Soviets were "furious and scared," in a "most dangerous state of mind," and he apprehended the risk of war. Bulganin's reply on Hungary was dismissive, "almost the last provocation that my temper could stand," recalls Eisenhower. Despite the reported "emotional urges" of some cabinet members, the prevailing view was that military intervention would incur the risk of world war and that nuclear stalemate had created two impregnable spheres of influence in Europe.[136]

Having ruled out intervention and even overt diplomatic support for the Nagy government, Washington was reduced to showing its sympathy for the revolution with humanitarian gestures and a belated propaganda offensive at the United Nations. On November 1, the president allocated $20 million from his emergency fund for Hungarian relief, and the International Red Cross was mobilized, but only some medical supplies reached the Hungarians. Later, of course, the United States and other Western countries made generous provision for the resettlement of Hungarian refugees. Action at the United Nations materialized only after the signs of impending Soviet intervention were unmistakable, when it could serve to condemn but hardly to prevent the crushing of the revolution.

The United Nations and Hungary. At the October 28 session of the UN Security Council the situation in Hungary did receive some attention. Statements of concern by Western delegates were met by Soviet charges of foreign provocation, and further debate was postponed sine die on the grounds that the Hungarian government had made no approach to the United Nations and that the situation in Hungary was too confused to warrant international action. The British delegate, Sir Pierson Dixon, waxed eloquent on the urgency of a UN response, but when Foster Dulles queried Lodge the next day regarding the feasibility of sending an international observation commission to Hungary, the ambassador reported that the British did not like the idea.[137]

The Suez invasion soon overshadowed Hungary at the United Nations, and Secretary General Dag Hammarskjold pragmatically chose to concentrate his efforts on the more manageable of the two crises. Nagy's request of November 1 for recognition and protection of Hungary's neutrality was handled in an extraordinarily dilatory manner by the Secretariat, and at the first meeting of the General Assembly's special emergency session, convened to address the Suez issue, Hungary received only passing mention. Hammarskjold later reflected that Suez "had a time priority on the thinking and policy-making of the main body in the UN. That was not their choice. It was history itself, so to say, which arranged it that way." [138]

Indeed, any UN response to the Hungarian crisis was dependent on the political will of the Western allies, and their division over Suez undoubtedly weakened this will. When on November 2 Lodge reported that the British and French were pressing for a condemnation of the Soviet Union, Dulles retorted that "it is a mockery for them to come in with bombs falling over Egypt and denounce the Soviet Union for perhaps doing something that is not quite as bad." [139] The fear of war was an even more compelling deterrent to early American initiatives at the United Nations. The president's view at the time was that "if the United Nations, overriding a certain Soviet veto, decided that all the military and other resources of member nations should be used to drive the Soviets from Hungary, we would have a major conflict." [140]

The Security Council indulged in inconclusive debates on Hungary (revolving mostly around the credentials of Nagy's envoy) on November 2 and 3, but in the end Lodge merely observed that "adjournment for a day or two would give a real opportunity to the Hungarian Government to carry out its announced desire to arrange for an orderly and immediate evacuation of Soviet troops." [141] His public optimism stood in sharp contrast to the growing evidence of Soviet preparations for intervention. Only after that intervention was a fait accompli did the United States and its friends mobilize the United Nations for a series of impassioned debates and resounding resolutions condemning the Soviets and asking a helpless Hammarskjold to investigate the situation. Endorsed by the majority of UN members, this exercise in propaganda reflected and reinforced the virtually universal abhorrence of Moscow's brutal action. No one expected that resolutions could alter the reimposition of Soviet rule. The United Nations remained a safe forum for the verbal rituals of East-West discord. The eventual report of the UN "Special Committee on the Problem of Hungary" found and deplored that the constitutionally formed government of a member state had been overthrown by the armed action of another. It recorded that most Hungarians had expected more than sympathy from their Western friends.[142]

Liberation Policy in Retrospect. Following the Hungarian debacle, the administration was subjected to a barrage of criticism for its sins of omission and commission. A special report of the House Committee on Foreign Affairs concluded that the "failure of the United States to have a plan or plans of action concerning the Hungarian events indicates either a serious weakness in our intelligence services or a serious misapplication by the administrators of our foreign policy of the facts reported." For four fatal days, said the report, the United States was "paralyzed by inaction. This inaction in effect weakened the morale of the freedom fighters and emboldened the Soviets to take their ruthless action without fear of countermeasures from the free world."[143] Many would charge that Washington had misrepresented its commitment to rollback.

The inadvertent and calculated ambiguities of the policy of liberation were thrown into sharp focus by the Hungarian revolution. The official formulation of that policy had always stressed peaceful means, although there was consistent discrepancy between the president's vague affirmations of American interest in the welfare of East Europeans and his secretary of state's professions of active support for the spread of Titoism. Dulles's confidence in the inexorable and controlled evolution of national communism was shared to some extent by the intelligence community but reflected an idiosyncratic self-deception with regard to both Soviet tolerance and the disposition of the satellite peoples to limit their expectations. The tactics of psychological warfare had led many Americans and East Europeans to believe that the U.S. commitment to liberation represented more than principled exhortation.

Granting that the Hungarian revolution went beyond the expectations and hopes of the Eisenhower administration, the question remains whether its response to the crisis served the best interests of the United States. Those interests would have been advanced by the emergence of a national Communist regime and even more by a democratic and neutral Hungary. Washington's calculation that an essentially passive attitude would alleviate the Kremlin's fears and forestall Soviet intervention might well have been mistaken. It is more likely that America's assurance of nonintervention strengthened the hand of those advocating a quick reimposition of Soviet control.

Similarly, the prompt recognition and symbolic guarantee of Hungary's independence and neutrality by the United States acting alone or through the United Nations and the dispatch of an international observation commission could have at least delayed the Soviet decision to intervene, and any delay would have increased the chances of consolidating the gains of the revolution. The combination of such diplomatic steps and a less halfhearted attempt to seize the occasion for renegotiating European security would have carried no serious risks. More aggressive measures such as covert operations to provoke unrest in the other satellites and the flexing of America's nuclear muscle in the form of some ultimatum to the Kremlin to desist were technically feasible but politically inconceivable.

The administration's failure to fully explore the opportunities presented by the Hungarian revolution can be explained by certain preconceptions regarding the domestic dynamics of change in the satellites as well as by an excess of prudence, manifested first and foremost by Eisenhower but reinforced notably by the Pentagon's opposition to any serious reconsideration of the military status quo in Europe. These inhibitions and constraints might still have allowed for bolder initiatives had the Suez crisis not intervened. That ill-conceived and cynically timed adventure effectively incapacitated the Western alliance and comforted the Kremlin at the moment of greatest challenge to both East and West in Europe in postwar history. The Hungarians were punished for trying to undo the political legacy of World War II in Eastern Europe. For the United States as well, the revolution served as an unwelcome moment of truth. It finally laid to rest the rhetoric of liberation, but the dilemmas of policy remained.

3

Walls and Bridges

As the mirage of early liberation dissipated, both the United States and the peoples of Eastern Europe settled in for the long haul anticipated in the original concept of containment. There would be no more attempts at destabilization, no more invitations to the East Europeans to seize the Titoist option. The Soviet Union's forceful reminder that it was the sole arbiter over its sphere of dominance compelled the United States to adjust policy to the possibilities of evolutionary change.

The lessons of Hungary also informed Khrushchev's pursuit of de-Stalinization. Poland was allowed to make concessions to the Roman Catholic church and to private farming. Police terror and cultural Russification were gradually relaxed throughout the region, but orthodoxy was reimposed in agriculture when in 1959–60 a new collectivization campaign (sparing only Poland) turned peasants into workers and completed the creation of a classless "socialist society." By the early 1960s, when the extensive approach to industrialization (promoting growth by imputs of capital and labor rather than by technological improvements in productivity) had exhausted the region's resources without generating adequate productivity and competitiveness, economic reform came on the agenda in Czechoslovakia and Hungary. It was arrested in the case of the former by the 1968 invasion, but that same year Hungary inaugurated a "new economic mechanism" that aimed to reconcile central planning with the forces of the market.

Khrushchev had attempted to invigorate the Council for Mutual Economic Assistance (CMEA) by promoting more efficient regional integration. Romania balked at adjusting its industrialization program (to fit the CMEA's vision of Romania as a breadbasket) and adopted a nation-building strategy that encompassed a more autonomous foreign policy. Tito's nonalignment, Romanian voluntarism, and the concurrent Sino-Soviet rift all seemed to indicate that without Stalin's firm hand the Communist world was drifting toward "polycentrism." Though the staunchly Stalinist Albanian regime broke with Moscow in 1961, seven years later the Brezhnev Doctrine set the limits to polycentrism in the rest of Eastern Europe.

In the Brezhnev era the Kremlin continued to tolerate Romania's independent posturing as well as a degree of economic experimentation and recourse to Western trade and credits, but its abhorrence of political liberalization was once again displayed in the suppression of Poland's Solidarity. Only with the advent of Mikhail S. Gorbachev did the profound economic and political malaise of Eastern Europe win recognition. The lifting of the Brezhnev Doctrine's procrustean discipline unleashed a whirlwind of change, first in Hungary and Poland, then in the rest of the region. By early 1990, the question was not whether the Kremlin had really relinquished its grip on Eastern Europe, but whether it could hold the Soviet Union together.

Washington's policies, variously designated as peaceful engagement, bridgebuilding, and differentiation, had aimed to promote liberalization. Their effect on the nature and rate of change was tangible but marginal. Reform in Eastern Europe remained governed by domestic factors and, most critically, by the Kremlin. Doctrinally unwilling to accept the permanence of Soviet rule over Eastern Europe, the United States was compelled to exercise its limited leverage in aid of the disintegrative and ultimately liberating forces that George Kennan had predicted in 1947 would dissolve the Soviet empire. A gradualist strategy was pursued with only minor modifications by presidents Eisenhower through Bush, with greater or lesser emphasis on the foreign policy dimensions of human rights, economic interaction, and military security and geopolitics in America's quest for change in Eastern Europe.

Peaceful Engagement and Bridgebuilding. The Eisenhower administration had to suffer some harsh criticism in the wake of Hungary's
failed revolution. A congressional study characterized that event as "the
lost opportunity of our generation," deploring America's apparent unpreparedness while recognizing that military intervention would have
been inappropriate.[1] The National Security Council concluded that the
United States had no alternative course of action but recommended
policies to prevent its recurrence.[2]

First, the concept of rollback had to be buried. Psychological warfare
to destabilize the Soviet domain had backfired, and the propaganda
organs, especially Radio Free Europe, were now attuned to a more
modest evolutionary approach. Operation Red Sox/Red Cap was deemed
to be inconsistent with American aims and capabilities and raised the
risk of provoking a European war. The CIA, which apparently contemplated renewing the offensive and inciting an uprising in Czechoslovakia,
was ordered to wind down the operation.[3]

The basic U.S. policy continued—to "assure the satellite peoples of
the continuing interest of the United States in the peaceful restoration of
their independence and political freedom."[4] The secretary of state took
pains to indicate the continuity in his approach, telling congressional
leaders that he still favored national communism "as means to [an] end,"
economic aid for "semi-independent" Poland, and diplomatic condemnation of the Soviet Union at the United Nations. But he stressed that
"we do not ourselves incite violent revolt. Rather we encourage an
evolution to freedom."[5] It had all been said before, but the disclaimers
had acquired new force, and there would be no more covert war to
obtain liberation. Khrushchev warned that "if we are confronted with
conditions such as Dulles likes to put forward such as the liberation of
East European countries from 'slavery,' it might take 200 years before
we ever come together. For on these matters we are inflexible."[6]

The intractability of the problem reduced the frequency of official
policy statements in Washington. When the Kremlin in early 1958 proposed a summit meeting, Eisenhower, sensitive to domestic opinion,
requested that the East European question figure on the agenda. As
expected, Khrushchev retorted that there could be no dialogue if the
United States did not accept the status quo.[7] He was even more incensed
when, in July 1959, the president complied with a unanimous resolution

of Congress to proclaim Captive Nations Week in honor of the "enslaved peoples" of Eastern Europe.. Vice President Nixon tried to appease the Soviets by stressing the peaceful and moral nature of the resolution, but even at the height of detente in the 1970s American administrations could not overcome Congress's attachment to this annual ritual. Eastern Europe thus remained a chronic irritant in U.S.-Soviet relations even after the rhetoric of liberation was abandoned.

Nevertheless, a selective approach to the region was pursued long before the term "differentiation" entered the official vocabulary. Poland was the first satellite to benefit from positive action. Aid for Communist countries was controversial in Congress, but a U.S. organization called the Polish-American Congress became an advocate of economic assistance and individual contacts.[8] In 1957, the administration moved cautiously to extend Export-Import Bank credits, sell agricultural commodities for Polish currency, and conclude a cultural agreement. Poland's most-favored-nation tariff status, revoked in 1951, was restored in 1960 after settlement of American claims. Vice President Nixon was greeted by enthusiastic crowds in Warsaw on his way back from Moscow in July 1959. But already in 1958, Eisenhower had observed regretfully that such concessions seemed to have little effect on Polish (and Yugoslav) policies, and indeed Gomulka soon turned more intransigent domestically and more subservient to his Soviet mentors.[9]

If Poland momentarily raised hopes for evolutionary change, the new Kadar regime in Hungary incurred only ostracism and, at the United Nations, annual resolutions demanding the withdrawal of Soviet troops and respect for human rights. Finally, in 1963, the United States made its peace with Kadar, allowing the United Nations to restore Hungary's full membership and selling Hungary some surplus wheat. By then, most political prisoners had been amnestied, and the State Department reported to Congress that "we hope that the actions of the United Nations have had a helpful influence in this regard."[10] Even so, the Assembly of Captive European Nations protested vehemently at the implication that the West had accepted the finality of the East European status quo.[11] Three more years passed before Washington and Budapest agreed to raise their diplomatic representation to the ambassadorial level. Elsewhere, in 1960, the settlement of American claims in Romania was followed by a cultural and scientific exchange agreement, and in 1963, a similar deal was made with Bulgaria (full diplomatic relations having been restored in 1959).

The Policy of Peaceful Engagement. Normalization of relations as a goal was inherent in a gradualist strategy that called for the calibrated application of economic and other benefits. Although, as Allen Dulles reported to Congress in January 1959, the satellites "would revolt tomorrow if they had any chance of getting free," there was no practical alternative to what became known as peaceful engagement.[12] The term was coined by two academics, William E. Griffith (a former policy adviser at Radio Free Europe) and Zbigniew Brzezinski (eventually the most influential voice in American policy toward Eastern Europe), in an article published in *Foreign Affairs* in 1961.[13] They recommended that the United States address both the regimes and the people in stimulating diversity and evolutionary change leading to a neutral belt of states enjoying "genuine popular freedom of popular choice in internal policy while not being hostile to the Soviet Union." The United States should not compromise in its advocacy of full self-determination, but "a general attitude of disapproval does not preclude our attempting to improve our political, economic and cultural relations with the East European states, providing these regimes refrain from hostile acts toward us."

Though this incremental approach hardly represented a radical departure from established practice, its formulation coincided with evidence of polycentric tendencies in the Communist world and with the accession of John F. Kennedy to the presidency. One of his most influential foreign policy advisers, Walt Rostow, reported that the Sino-Soviet split "could give rise to increased factionalism in national Communist parties, weaken the overall thrust of world Communism, and facilitate the emergence of more independent and nationalistic Communist states, especially in Eastern Europe."[14] Eastern Europe did not figure prominently in Kennedy's "Grand Design," but he indicated in his first State of the Union message that he would seek congressional authority to selectively expand economic relations with the satellites.[15]

In October 1962, at a Pulaski Day meeting in Buffalo, Kennedy reiterated the principled and pragmatic dimensions of peaceful engagement: "There are varying shades, even within the Communist world. We must be able to seize the initiative when the opportunity arises, in Poland in particular and in other countries as time goes on," but "we must never—in any statement, declaration, treaty, or other manner—recognize Soviet domination of Eastern Europe as permanent."[16] A year later, Secretary of State Dean Rusk professed confidence in the prospect of peaceful change:

The darkest night of Stalinist terror and oppression is past. Historic forces of nationalism are visibly at work. Gradually the smaller Communist nations of Eastern Europe seem to be finding for themselves a little more autonomy. . . . We would like to do what we can to encourage these trends within the Communist world . . . [and think they] are more likely to be furthered by a somewhat relaxed atmosphere than by an atmosphere of crisis or severe cold war.[17]

Kennedy's disposition to liberalize trade with the East was reinforced by a report from the State Department's Policy Planning Council in July 1963, which argued that the "ability to use trade flexibility in Eastern Europe would add greatly to the present limited capacity of the United States to shape the course" of events in that region.[18] But the mood of Congress, affected by successive Berlin crises, the Cuban missile confrontation, and the deepening conflict in Vietnam, was anything but accommodating, and neither Kennedy nor his successor, Lyndon B. Johnson, could obtain significant discretionary powers to offer economic incentives to communist regimes (see chapter 5).

Apart from Poland, which remained at the top in the rank order of East European countries as much for reasons of domestic politics as for the performance of the Gomulka regime, Romania was singled out as a promising testing ground for economic leverage. The American minister in Bucharest, William Crawford, had been lobbying for measures to exploit the emerging Soviet-Romanian economic discord, and the Romanians were eager to obtain American help. Negotiations resulted in June 1964 in a trade agreement that extended Eximbank credit guarantees, but legislative constraints prevented the administration from offering long-term credits or MFN tariff status. The upgrading in December of the Bucharest legation to an embassy brought small comfort to the disappointed Romanians.[19]

The Johnson administration persevered in trying to persuade Congress and domestic opinion that peaceful engagement could serve American interests in Eastern Europe. The prospects, argued Secretary of State Dean Rusk in February 1964, were favorable in Poland, where "a good deal of the national autonomy and domestic liberalization which the

Poles won in 1956 persists," in Romania, which had "asserted a more independent attitude and has expanded its trade and other contacts with the West," and even in Hungary, which had "turned to a more permissive policy of national conciliation." Yugoslavia's "success in defending its independence made other peoples in Eastern Europe wonder why they could not do likewise."[20] The bridge-building metaphor was employed by Johnson in his Virginia Military Institute address on May 23: "We will continue to build bridges across the gulf which has divided us from Eastern Europe. They will be bridges of increased trade, of ideas, of visitors, and of humanitarian aid."[21]

When Brzezinski joined the State Department's Policy Planning Staff in 1967, he was intent (as related in his memoirs) on developing "a more forward-looking approach toward Eastern Europe."[22] His objectives remained modest: evolution into more socialist and less Communist "semidictatorships" on the Yugoslav model.[23] Upon leaving the department at the end of the year, Brzezinski delivered himself of a more visionary program calling for an "institutionalized multilateral framework" including East-West economic and political "assemblies" and a European Security Commission based on the two alliances, all in the interest of attenuating the division of Europe.[24] The political climate was hostile even to his less radical urgings. Although the president invoked the bridge-building theme again in a speech in October 1966, his ambassador to Poland, John A. Gronouski, observed regretfully that the program "ran into deep trouble under the sustained attack of those to whom peaceful engagement is being 'soft on communism.' "[25] Congress was not disposed to discriminate among Communists at a time when Americans were fighting them in Vietnam.

The Berlin Crisis. Indeed, despite autonomous stirrings in parts of Eastern Europe, the Soviet Union was not about to let evolutionary tendencies weaken its western bulwark. Moscow had become committed to the consolidation of the GDR, which West German Chancellor Adenauer, and therefore his allies, refused to recognize as a sovereign entity. Khrushchev tried to use Berlin for leverage, threatening in November 1958 to hand over his zone to East German administration unless the West agreed within six months to turn Berlin into an independent and demilitarized district; a similar threat was issued in 1961. On both occasions the West called Khrushchev's bluff and stood firm, and the policy developed by the Kennedy administration in mid-July 1961 differentiated between the two halves of the city. The president was prepared to risk war to defend the status of West Berlin but not for Western rights in East Berlin and unimpeded access between the Western and Soviet zones.[26]

The crises only swelled the flood of East Germans fleeing into West Berlin. The West Germans welcomed this mass migration, offering the defectors citizenship and aid in resettling. The CIA's psychological warfare operations had included active inducement of East Germans, especially professionals, to move West. By the summer of 1961, when the monthly rate rose to 10,000, over three million Germans had taken the route. On August 6 alone, there were two thousand defectors. A week later the East German regime began to seal off its zone with what became the infamous Wall, a hundred-mile-long barrier equipped with minefields and 285 watchtowers that confirmed the division of Germany and Europe.

The measure was not wholly unexpected. There had been numerous intimations since early spring that the refugee problem would drive the GDR and the Soviet Union to take some preventive step. Fearing that tighter border controls might precipitate popular unrest in the East, Kennedy and the allies wanted to avoid any provocative gesture, and especially any hint that the West might intervene militarily. Although Washington felt that the GDR should be punished for the border closure with economic sanctions, neither Bonn nor London favored such a step unless the West's presence in Berlin was threatened.[27] At a press conference in East Berlin on June 15, Ulbricht had declared that "nobody has the intention of building a wall," and in the circumstances the denial should have aroused suspicion.[28] This and other signals and rumors caused little alarm in NATO capitals, for the nature of the threat remained uncertain, and what was threatened was not of vital interest. The actual preparations were detected, notably by West German intelligence, but Kennedy had already considered the contingency and decided not to challenge it.[29]

Fearing another East German uprising, the Kennedy administration limited its response to diplomatic protests and demonstrative military movements on the access routes to West Berlin. General Clay, the legendary hero of the airlift, was dispatched to reassure the West Berliners, but he had no mandate to challenge the border closure. When two years later the president proclaimed, "Ich bin ein Berliner," he was emphasizing the West's determination to preserve West Berlin. As for the Wall, his administration was secretly relieved that it alleviated an unstable situation while presenting the West with a lasting symbol of Communist brutality. The hemorrhage debilitating the GDR was stemmed if not entirely stopped. Over the next twenty-five years the Wall would claim the lives of seventy-four East Germans. But the Wall facilitated the consolidation of the GDR, the agreements that normalized intra-German relations, and the status of Berlin, and thus, paradoxically, the pursuit of peaceful engagement. In the era of detente, such achievements outweighed the human costs of an iron curtain.

A nuclear test ban treaty had been concluded with the Soviets in 1963, and five years later the Johnson administration was anticipating agreement on nonproliferation and the beginning of negotiations on the limitation of strategic weapons. It also prepared to reintroduce its politically controversial East-West Trade Relations bill. Bonn's emerging *Ostpolitik* superseded the long-standing Hallstein Doctrine, which had precluded diplomatic relations with any state (other than the Soviet Union) that recognized the GDR, and it registered its first success in breaching the Warsaw Pact's reciprocal ban with the establishment of diplomatic relations with maverick Romania in January 1967. West Germany's new found flexibility facilitated a NATO agreement in December of that year to pursue negotiation with the Soviet bloc on issues of European security. It seemed that, despite the bitter war in Vietnam, progress could be made on East-West detente and reconciliation in Europe.

The Prague Spring and the Brezhnev Doctrine.   These hopes were momentarily reinforced by the wave of liberalization that swept Czechoslovakia in the early months of 1968. Mounting opposition to the Stalinist rule of Antonin Novotny culminated in January in his replacement by Alexander Dubcek. The Kremlin had sanctioned this step but not what followed, for in April the new, reformist party leadership adopted an "action program" that called for sweeping economic and political reforms. Dubcek saw no contradiction between this "socialism with a human face" and loyalty to the Soviet Union and the Warsaw Pact, but the lifting of censorship and other totalitarian controls unleashed popular pressures for quick and radical change.

The exhilarating freedom of speech in this Prague spring thoroughly alarmed the Kremlin, which convened a meeting of the alliance in Warsaw on July 14. Ulbricht and Gomulka were as belligerent as the Soviets. The Czechoslovaks had declined the invitation and received a stern warning that "this is no longer your affair alone. . . . Never will we consent to allow imperialism, by peaceful or non-peaceful means, from within or without, to make a breach in the socialist system and change the balance of power in Europe in its favor." In its reply, Prague invoked the declaration on noninterference that the Soviet Union had issued on October 30, 1956, a dubious reference point in light of what followed in Hungary.[30] A confrontation between the Soviet and Czechoslovak leaders at Cierna on July 29 failed to budge the latter. The Bratislava communique five days later adopted a more conciliatory tone, but this was merely a smoke screen to cover up preparations for invasion.

The Prague leaders deluded themselves that their version of socialism could survive a war of words. Three days before the invasion, Hungary's Kadar tried to caution Dubcek against ignoring the Russian warnings, observing in parting: "Do you *really* not know the kind of people you're dealing with?"[31] The answer came on the night of August 20, when Soviet and Warsaw Pact forces invaded Czechoslovakia without even the pretense of an invitation such as that provided by Kadar in 1956. The Poles and East Germans participated more willingly than the Hungarians, who had hoped that Prague's economic reforms would reinforce their own strivings and had to be persuaded with the threat of Soviet economic sanctions; and the appearance of bloc unity was marred by Romania's absence. Soon there descended the long, dark night of "normalization," of purges and proscription of any talk of reform.

The Kremlin after the event tried to evoke in mitigation "perfidious plans of NATO warmongering circles" and the aggressive intent of West Germany, and indeed the troops participating in "Operation Danube" had been fed tales of bourgeois anarchy and impending NATO intervention.[32] In fact, Washington's response to the Prague spring bordered on paralysis. There developed what one analyst has characterized as a process of tacit bargaining, initiated by the Soviet Union, to link the extension of detente to American noninterference in Czechoslovakia.[33] Although there is no concrete evidence that Washington was a willing party to such a bargain, its signals to the Kremlin were conciliatory to a fault.

The State Department on May 1 issued an expression of benevolent interest in the Czechoslovak developments, and some tentative steps were taken to improve economic relations, but the administration evidently calculated that in the short run anything more than passive sympathy could be of disservice to the Czechoslovak reformers.[34] The Soviets attempted to reinforce the spirit of detente, belatedly implementing a commercial air agreement and ratifying a consular convention with the United States, while sending signals that included denunciations of bridgebuilding and Western interference as well as military exercises in June in Czechoslovakia. President Johnson hoped to regain some popularity by advancing detente, and after the nonproliferation treaty was signed in July, he set his sights on Strategic Arms Limitation Talks (SALT) and a summit.

Washington took pains to assure the Soviets of its limited interest in the mounting confrontation between them and the Czechoslovaks. On May 21, Under Secretary of State Eugene Rostow volunteered the gratuitous reminder that the United States had not intervened in the East German and Hungarian revolts.[35] On July 14, the United States signed a new cultural agreement in Moscow. Five days later, the State Department declared that "we have not involved ourselves in any way" in the Prague crisis, and on July 22 Rusk met Ambassador Anatoly Dobrynin to refute Soviet charges of American interference.[36] On the following day the Soviet Union announced massive ground and air maneuvers on its western reaches (designed, in fact, to cover up preparations for the invasion), whereupon a previously scheduled NATO exercise was relocated away from the Czechoslovak border area.[37]

The Johnson administration hoped that the Soviet Union would not intervene forcefully as long as Dubcek professed adherence to the Warsaw Pact.[38] To be sure, twelve years earlier the decision to intervene had been taken even before Imre Nagy proclaimed Hungary's neutrality, but surely Brezhnev would not act rashly to disrupt detente. This comforting assumption was reinforced by the invitation to a summit conference that Dobrynin handed to Johnson on August 19. Although the overture might have been purely diversionary, it arguably reflected the Kremlin's impression that the United States would not allow a police action by the Soviet Union in its own backyard to derail detente. Ambassador Llewellyn Thompson had reported earlier from Moscow that Soviet military preparations pointed to a high probability of invasion, but the president records in his memoirs that "we could only try to avoid any action that would further inflame the situation."[39] The Czechoslovaks, he notes, had indicated they would offer no resistance nor welcome Western offers of assistance.

Neither policymakers nor the intelligence services distinguished themselves in the Czechoslovak crisis. An early warning from West German intelligence of the Soviet decision to intervene had met with conditioned skepticism in Bonn and at NATO headquarters. American intelligence even managed to lose track of a Soviet combat group in Poland, only to rediscover it two weeks later in the invasion force. And when CIA Director Richard Helms belatedly tried to raise the alarm at a White House meeting shortly before the invasion, his attempts at persuasion were as futile as (in his words) "peeing up a rope."[40]

President Johnson learned of the invasion from Dobrynin, who insisted that this "rendering of direct assistance" should not harm Soviet-American relations.[41] The CIA reported to the president that the Soviet Politburo had been divided up to some three weeks earlier and that "the decision to execute the plan of intervention came at a fairly late stage."[42] Given this ambivalence in Moscow, the United States probably made a mistake (as Brzezinski later argued) in not taking seriously the possibility of invasion and warning the Soviets of the potential damage to detente.[43] There can be no certainty as to the deterrent effect of such a warning, though it apparently worked years later in the 1980 Polish crisis. In the event, Washington was reduced to protesting a fait accompli.

After an emergency session of the National Security Council, Rusk told Dobrynin that the summit meeting was off, and the president went on the air to denounce the invasion and urge the invaders to withdraw. When a few days later the CIA reported that Soviet troops were massing on Romania's borders, with the possibility that the Kremlin was intent on eliminating dictator Nicolae Ceausescu as well, Johnson issued a public warning against "unleashing the dogs of war." But the Romanians were more likely to offer armed resistance than the Czechoslovaks, and the threat dissipated.[44] The Kremlin also made threatening noises about its right to intervene against West German aggressiveness, prompting the United States to declare that such action would meet with immediate allied response.[45] These were probably diversionary tactics to safeguard tangible gains: nipping dangerous reform in the bud and strengthening the Warsaw Pact's northern tier by extracting from Czechoslovakia's cowed leaders agreement on the stationing of Soviet troops in their country for the first time since the end of World War II.

The West registered its displeasure with the Soviet invasion at the United Nations, but condemnation was short-lived and perfunctory. It was also marred by mutual recrimination. Washington's passivity was attributed by some, notably President de Gaulle, to an unholy pact to preserve the division of Europe, impelling Secretary of State Rusk to publicly deny that "there must have been some 'spheres of influence' agreement between us, that perhaps there was 'an arrangement' made at the Yalta Conference, that perhaps the Soviets acted in Czechoslovakia with some 'carte blanche' from the United States, that we concurred or connived in that aggression." But the United States, he said, acknowledged "the reality of the Soviet military position and the existence of the Warsaw Pact," and Johnson, like Eisenhower, "recognized that there was little we could do, through the use of military force, to assist any of those countries without automatically engaging in general war with the Soviet Union." [46] It was all sadly reminiscent of the Hungarian fiasco, leaving the same suspicion that Washington had been ill-prepared and derelict in failing to explore all preventive options.

The administration soon returned to its pursuit of detente and a summit meeting, and even Brzezinski argued that the invasion did not invalidate the bridge-building strategy, claiming rashly that "it was the success of this policy that forced the Soviet Union into this criminal act." [47] It was more a case of illusions shared by Czechoslovak reformers and American policymakers regarding the Brezhnev regime's readiness to accommodate significant liberalization. That the individual East European countries' scope for reform was limited by the socialist community's collective interest as defined in Moscow received redundant confirmation in the so-called Brezhnev Doctrine.

That rationale for qualified sovereignty was first expressed in a Soviet note to Bonn on September 2, which stated that "the entry into Czechoslovakia was founded on the obligation which the countries of the socialist camp had mutually undertaken for the protection of their unity." A few weeks later, *Pravda* explained that "antisocialist degeneration" could not be sheltered by "abstract sovereignty." And at the Polish party's congress in November, Brezhnev himself elaborated that "when external and internal forces to socialism try to turn the development of a given socialist country in the direction of restoration of the capitalist system, when a threat arises to the cause of socialism in that country, this is no longer merely a problem for that country's people, but a common problem, the concern of all socialist countries."[48] The Warsaw Treaty's prohibition of interference in internal affairs, flouted in 1956, was now explicitly subordinated to a commitment to preserve Soviet-style socialism. There was still no alternative to the gradualist rationale of peaceful engagement and bridgebuilding, but it was clearer than ever that American policies and actions could scarcely influence, let alone expedite, the rate of evolutionary change.

Detente and Differentiation.   Although activism and bold initiatives marked the Nixon-Kissinger approach to foreign policy, Eastern Europe was only a residual beneficiary. Washington's priorities were disengagement from Vietnam, detente with the Soviet Union, and rapprochement with China, not to speak of crisis management in the Middle East and elsewhere. Henry Kissinger, first as national security adviser and then as secretary of state, pursued a global balance of power strategy that concentrated on America's major interlocutors and on a traditional diplomacy that depreciated the people-to-people approach and meddling in domestic affairs.

Eastern European policy was subordinated to the higher politics of detente on the assumption that peaceful coexistence (a Soviet term that now entered the American diplomatic vocabulary) would be beneficial to evolutionary change in the region. As Kissinger observed before he joined the White House staff, the invasion of Czechoslovakia had only confirmed that "no Western policy can guarantee a more favorable evolution in Central Europe; all it can do is to take advantage of an opportunity if it arises." Greater Western European unity and autonomy would exert a growing attraction on the East, and "the major initiatives to improve relations between Western and Eastern Europe should originate in Europe with the United States in a reserve position."[49] Disparaged by Brzezinski as "benign neglect" and "moral indifference," this approach nevertheless earned some tangible benefits in bilateral relations and, somewhat inadvertently, in the eventual Conference on Security and Cooperation in Europe.[50]

Policy statements focusing on Eastern Europe became less frequent and essentially reflected continuity. In his first report to Congress in

February 1970, President Richard Nixon noted that "reunion of Europe will come about not from one spectacular negotiation, but from an extended historical process" in which the Soviet Union would overcome its fear of Germany and discover that reconciliation was the best guarantee of its security:

It is not the intention of the United States to undermine the legitimate security interests of the Soviet Union. The time is certainly past, with the development of modern technology, when any power would seek to exploit Eastern Europe to obtain strategic advantage against the Soviet Union. . . . By the same token, the United States views the countries of Eastern Europe as sovereign . . . We are prepared to enter into negotiations with the nations of Eastern Europe, looking to a gradual normalization of relations. . . . Progress in this direction has already been achieved in our relations with Romania. . . . A similar relationship is open to any Communist country that wishes to enter it.[51]

Two years later, the president assured East European nations of "ample opportunities for economic, technical, and cultural cooperation on the basis of reciprocity. The East European countries themselves can determine the pace and scope of their developing relations with the United States."[52]

Leaving the initiative to the West Europeans and to the East European regimes was a far cry from the spirit of the Captive Nations Resolution, which the administration would have preferred Congress to repeal. By the fall of 1974, with Nixon out and domestic qualms about detente on the rise, Kissinger had to argue strenuously in defense of the "imperative of coexistence":

We must know what can and cannot be achieved in changing human conditions in the East. . . . There has always been a fear that by working with a government whose internal policies differ so sharply with our own, we are in some manner condoning these policies or encouraging their continuation. . . . In that view, demands for internal changes must be the precondition for pursuit of a relaxation of tensions with the Soviet Union. Our view is different. We shall insist on responsible behavior by the Soviet Union and use it as the primary index of our relationship.[53]

Although the immediate target of Kissinger's plea was the move in Congress to link trade concessions to Jewish emigration from the Soviet Union, it reflected his general view that the primary concern of American diplomacy was the foreign policy and actions of other states, not their domestic affairs and human rights practices. As he observed to the columnist James Reston a few weeks later, the growing interdependence of the global economy and the inability of socialist dictatorships to adequately foster economic modernization would induce favorable change: "The pressure of this realization on Communist systems is going to bring about a transformation apart from any conscious policy the United States pursues, so long as there is not a constant foreign danger that can be invoked to impose regimentation."[54] Faith in the inexorable forces of history informed Kissinger's view of detente as it had Kennan's logic for containment.

Kissinger's Differentiation.   Kissinger made external behavior the principal criterion for improving relations with Eastern Europe. The purpose of what became known as "differentiation" was, as Kissinger recalls in his memoirs, to "encourage sentiments of national independence."[55] The guidelines set down in the National Security Decision Memorandum (NSDM 212) of May 2, 1973, reportedly specified the condition of "satisfactory" foreign policy conduct by East European regimes as well as the settlement of private American claims. Economic favors, commercial, cultural, and scientific agreements would be calibrated to the merits of each state, the descending rank order being Poland and Romania, Hungary, Czechoslovakia, and Bulgaria.[56] East Germany was not yet recognized by the United States; Albania remained in self-imposed isolation (benefiting, until 1978, from Chinese aid), and Yugoslavia (which Nixon visited in 1970) was already a model of cooperative relations.

This model of differentiation was distilled in the administration's extensive statement on East European policy, delivered by Deputy Secretary of State Kenneth Rush in April 1973. He outlined three basic principles: First, to deal with each country "as an independent sovereign state entitled to be free of all outside interference," without any desire to intervene in its domestic affairs; second, to expand trade and encourage receptivity to foreign investment (Rush indicated that the previous fall American ambassadors had been directed to "place trade promotion at the very top of the list of our policy priorities"); and third, to "promote a deepening of political and economic relations between the countries of eastern and western Europe."[57]

U.S.-Romanian relations benefited most from the priority assigned to external conduct. Romania's refusal to cooperate in CMEA integration, to sever relations with Israel as the other Warsaw Pact members (apart from the GDR, which had no such relations) did in 1967, and to participate in the invasion of Czechoslovakia was favorably appraised in Washington. The Romanian prime minister had secretly visited China in 1967, and the Brezhnev Doctrine only intensified Bucharest's quest for new linkages to counter Soviet pressure. Hardly had Nixon taken office when an invitation arrived from President Ceausescu. Despite the misgivings of the State Department and of Ambassador Thompson, the White House seized the opportunity to signal its activist approach, particularly to China, and to impress on the Soviet Union that peaceful coexistence did not preclude American diplomatic forays into its western approaches. In Bucharest, during the first presidential visit to an East European capital, Nixon declared that "we stand ready to reciprocate the efforts of any country that seeks normal relations with us."[58] The visit infuriated the Russians, who retaliated with a token delay in the start of the SALT talks, but it inaugurated a phase of active diplomatic collaboration between Washington and Bucharest.

Nixon had asked Ceausescu for help in approaching the Chinese, and in December 1969, Romanian Deputy Foreign Minister Gheorghe Macovescu brought him a message from Beijing. The following October, when Ceausescu returned Nixon's visit and received the full red carpet treatment at the White House, he was given another message for the Chinese, to the effect that the United States was eager for rapprochement and even willing to compromise on Taiwan; three months later the Romanians relayed Zhou Enlai's invitation to the president.[59] Romania was not the only channel of communication, but its eagerness to cooperate earned Ceausescu another visit to Washington in December 1973. In July 1972, Secretary of State Rogers signed a consular convention in Bucharest. An agreement on the exchange of scientific and technical information was concluded in September 1973, and U.S.-Romanian trade was growing rapidly. While Ceausescu's domestic rule remained thoroughly repressive, he had performed useful services and ostentatiously breached Warsaw Pact solidarity.

In Poland, the deteriorating domestic situation was marked by the harsh repression of student dissidence and an anti-Semitic campaign in 1968, and it culminated two years later in strikes against food price hikes and Gomulka's replacement by Edvard Gierek. Gierek promptly launched an ambitious program to revitalize Poland's economy with the help of Western credits and technology. When Nixon visited Warsaw in April 1972, on his way back from the Moscow summit, the two countries signed a consular convention and agreed on rescheduling the debt Poland had incurred in its earlier grain purchases. Gierek's visit to Washington in October 1974 led to the expansion of economic relations and a package of agreements on the creation of a joint economic council by the two chambers of commerce, a tax convention, and cooperative research.

Relations with Hungary improved as well, reflecting the remarkable transformation of the Kadar regime from agent of Soviet repression to promoter of economic and political liberalization. Cardinal Mindszenty, who had taken refuge in the American legation when the revolution was crushed, was finally persuaded by Nixon and the pope to accept exile in September 1971. With this diplomatically awkward legacy of the revolution eliminated, Secretary of State Rogers visited Budapest in July 1972 and signed agreements on consular facilities and scientific cooperation. The following March, Hungarian Deputy Premier Peter Valyi came to Washington to seal the settlement of American claims and receive the administration's promise to submit to Congress a recommendation for most-favored-nation (MFN) tariff status.

Some modest progress was made with respect to Czechoslovakia and Bulgaria as well. A consular agreement was signed with the former in July 1973 and the latter in April 1974. Negotiations resumed in September 1973 on American claims in Czechoslovakia valued at $72 million. Congress, however, balked at the proposed settlement ($29.5 million and the return of 18,400 kilograms of Czechoslovak gold held by the United States), adding to the Trade Act of 1974 an amendment requiring the State Department to seek more favorable terms; final settlement came in 1982. In the Jackson-Vanik amendment to the 1974 Trade Act Congress imposed severe constraints on the administration's freedom to dispense economic favors. Romania was granted MFN in 1975, but Hungary had to wait three more years for the same benefit.

German Compromises and the CSCE. Washington's recognition in September 1974 of the German Democratic Republic was the culmination of a series of historic diplomatic compromises, originating for the most part in Europe. In the late 1960s, with America absorbed in Vietnam, France and West Germany took the lead in seeking detente with the East. De Gaulle pursued his vision of a reconciled Europe free from superpower domination with an active Eastern policy, visiting

Poland and Romania in 1967 and 1968, but the invasion of Czechoslovakia served to remind him of the limits of East European autonomy, and France subsequently concentrated on detente with the Soviet Union. Germany and Berlin had long been the key stumbling blocks to European detente, with the Western allies hostage to Adenauer's adamant refusal to formally acknowledge division. Willy Brandt's coalition government, formed in October 1969, adopted an invigorated *Ostpolitik* that accommodated itself to realities and the decisive role of the Soviet Union.

Although the previous two administrations had encouraged Bonn to be more flexible, Kissinger and Nixon were apprehensive that Brandt's unilateral opening to the East might preempt American initiatives toward detente and divide the alliance.[60] Nevertheless, in August 1970, Bonn and Moscow concluded a nonaggression pact that entailed recognition of current frontiers, and in December the West Germans confirmed their acceptance of the Oder-Neisse frontier in a treaty with Poland. A treaty with Czechoslovakia two years later affirmed the inviolability of that common frontier. The Warsaw Pact's long-professed fears of German revanchism and territorial revisionism were presumably laid to rest by these treaties, but there remained the deadlock over recognition of the GDR.

Surrender of the goal of unification was politically even more contentious in West Germany than formal acceptance of the territorial losses. The Federal Republic regarded itself as the legal continuation of a united German state, and in its Basic Law the "entire German people is called on to achieve in free self-determination the unity and freedom of Germany." On the other hand, after 1955 the East Germans adopted with Soviet approval the doctrine of two separate states and pursued a policy of *Abgrenzung* (demarcation). The Warsaw Pact (apart from Romania) demanded full recognition of the GDR as the precondition for normalizing relations.

With his "two states within one German nation" formula, Brandt tried to reconcile the irreconcilable. In East Germany, the replacement of the intransigent Ulbricht by Erich Honecker heralded greater flexibility. Tough negotiation produced in December 1972 a German treaty that fudged the issue of sovereignty. The two countries declared that their relations were of an "interstate" nature and agreed to exchange not embassies but "permanent missions." The treaty also enshrined respect for each other's territorial integrity, although article 9, which registered that the agreement did not supersede other existing treaty commitments, allowed West Germans to argue that residual allied rights left open the frontier question pending a peace treaty. Thus, the normalization of state-to-state relations did not, at least in the West German view, represent a conclusive resolution of the national question.[61] The Christian Democrats nevertheless preferred to withhold public assent, leaving the Bundestag to ratify the treaty by the narrowest of margins.

In the meantime, the four former allied powers had come to grips once again with the Berlin conundrum, and a Quadripartite Agreement was signed in September 1971. It was, inevitably, an imperfect compromise. The Soviet Union tacitly gave up its efforts to force the West out of Berlin and agreed to continued allied presence and access and to political self-rule for the West Berliners. The West accepted that West Berlin would remain a distinct political entity, with special institutional links to the Federal Republic; Bonn would also look after West Berlin's international representation, although the Soviet Union did not formally recognize its right to do so. A more tangible concession by the West was the de facto recognition of East Berlin as the capital of the GDR. The Quadripartite Agreement confirmed the continuing four-power responsibility for the entire city, but in practice the Soviets tended to treat East Berlin as an integral part of the GDR and to depict West Berlin as the only occupied area.

For the Soviet Union, the German and Berlin agreements were steps toward a comprehensive East-West agreement on European security that would legitimate its sphere of influence in Eastern Europe. Having achieved military parity at great cost to other economic sectors, the Brezhnev regime sought symbolic recognition of its equal superpower status and the access to Western trade and technology that detente could bring. Its quest for a European security conference dated back to the mid-1950s, and when the Warsaw Pact conceded that the United States and Canada were valid partners in such an exercise, the pressure within NATO to respond became irresistible.[62]

A negotiated disengagement from Vietnam was Nixon's top priority, and the need to secure Soviet support was a key element in the complex linkage diplomacy pursued by Henry Kissinger. The summit meeting in Moscow in May 1972 marked a high point of detente. The SALT I agreement was signed, as was a statement of "basic principles" governing U.S.-Soviet relations. The principles affirmed peaceful coexistence and noninterference, mutual recognition of security interests "based on the principle of equality and the renunciation of the use of force," and the need to "promote conditions in which all countries will live in peace and security and will not be subject to outside interference in their internal affairs." Lest that injunction be read as invalidating the Brezhnev Doctrine, the final principle registered that the agreement did not affect "any obligations with respect to other countries earlier assumed" by the two signatories.[63] Nixon also agreed "in principle" to proceed with the security conference (the eventual Conference on Security and Cooperation in Europe, or CSCE) so avidly sought by the Soviets, and they reciprocated by agreeing to the mutual and balanced force reduction talks (MBFR) advocated by the United States and NATO.

The CSCE, in fact, had more support in Western Europe than in Washington, where prevailing political opinion feared that it would only produce a gratuitous and undesirable legitimation of Soviet dominance in Eastern Europe. The administration treated it as a bargaining counter, and as one of Kissinger's aides put it later, "we sold it for the German-Soviet treaty, we sold it for the Berlin agreement, and we sold it again for the opening of the MBFR."[64] The exploratory talks on MBFR began in Vienna on January 31 and the formal negotiations on October 30, 1973; sixteen years later, with little achieved, they were superseded by a new offspring of the Helsinki process, the Conventional Forces in Europe (CFE) talks. The CSCE opened with preliminary consultations in Helsinki in July 1973 and produced, in July 1975, a Final Act that launched a continuing series of review conferences.

That the Helsinki process served admirably to focus world attention on human rights violations in the Soviet sphere owed little to Kissinger. His focus was an artful balance of power diplomacy, not vulgar psychological warfare. Detente required that Communist regimes not be offended with reminders of their shortcomings. Responding to domestic criticism, James Keogh, who in 1973 replaced cold warrior Frank Shakespeare as director of the U.S. Information Agency, argued that detente meant "we do not interfere in the internal affairs of other countries. We're not in the business of trying to provoke revolutions and uprisings."[65] The same restraint had to be exercised by Radio Free Europe and Radio Liberty, whose presence was beginning to embarrass Bonn in this heyday of detente and *Ostpolitik*.

For all its tangible achievements, the Nixon-Kissinger strategy of detente gradually lost domestic political support, much like containment had in the early 1950s. It was, charged its detractors in the media and Congress, soft on communism. President Gerald R. Ford was subjected to violent attacks when he traveled to Helsinki to seal the Final Act, and he included Warsaw and Bucharest in his tour to display American support for East European autonomous tendencies. In December 1975, at a supposedly confidential briefing of American ambassadors, State Department counselor Helmut Sonnenfeldt declared that "it must be our policy to strive for an evolution that makes the relationship between the Eastern Europeans and the Soviet Union an organic one. Any excess of zeal on our part is bound to produce results that could reverse the desired process for a period of time. . . . So our policy must be a policy of responding to the clearly visible aspirations in Eastern Europe for a more autonomous existence within the context of a strong Soviet geopolitical influence." Seizing on the ambiguous term "organic," two journalists construed his unexceptionable remarks as a new "doctrine" condoning Soviet domination. In the ensuing political furor, Sonnenfeldt was compelled to reassure Congress that the Ford administration remained devoted to the goal of self-determination for the East Europeans.[66]

Carter and Differentiation.   The "Sonnenfeldt Doctrine" canard was not alone in bringing Eastern Europe to the fore in the 1976 election campaign. In June, Kissinger tried to undo the damage by declaring that the United States recognized "no spheres of influence and no pretensions to hegemony. We are determined to deal with Eastern Europe on the basis of the sovereignty and independence of each of its countries."[67] To presume sovereignty in order to reinforce it was a cardinal rule of Kissinger's differentiation. Gerald Ford's rendering of the same notion in October in his second televised debate with Jimmy Carter was politically disastrous: "There is no Soviet domination of Eastern Europe, and there never will be under a Ford administration." In answer to a followup question, Ford insisted that Romania and Poland (as well as Yugoslavia) were independent and autonomous.[68] His formulation dismayed many, particularly voters of East European origin, who were already susceptible to the view that the Helsinki Final Act was a sellout on the order of Yalta.

Ford subsequently told a delegation of ethnic leaders that he had made a mistake in not expressing himself clearly, but the original blooper probably contributed to his defeat.[69] Jimmy Carter made his own contribution to controversy in the final debate by declaring he didn't believe that "our security would be threatened if the Soviet Union went into Yugoslavia." Now it was Kissinger's turn to remind voters of America's long-standing interest in preserving Yugoslav independence.[70]

Early in that election year, Brzezinski had sent a foreign policy brief to Jimmy Carter arguing that "only a more comprehensive and a more reciprocal detente can enhance peace and promote change within the Communist system" and that "the abandonment of the policy of benign neglect toward Eastern Europe is desirable, for the United States ought to be at least as interested in Eastern Europe as the Soviet Union is in Latin America."[71] In his role as national security adviser, he steered the Carter administration toward a more activist approach to the region that culminated in attempts to manage the Solidarity crisis in Poland.

The interagency debate on Eastern Europe revolved around the merits of differentiating according to foreign policy independence, or domestic liberalization, or both, and of expanding relations without any differentiation. No East European country could satisfy both differentiating criteria, while the last option precluded discriminating leverage. The outcome was a policy that reflected Brzezinski's preference for a more balanced version of differentiation. The guidelines called for developing closer relationships with Eastern Europe for its own sake and not merely as a by-product of detente with the Soviet Union; for rewarding internal reform as well as foreign policy independence; and for developing regular contacts with "representatives of the loyal opposition in Eastern Europe—liberal intellectuals, artists, and church leaders" as well as with the regimes.[72]

This new version of differentiation departed from its predecessor in the greater weight assigned to internal reform. Brzezinski also pressed for a more assertive U.S. posture in the CSCE on human rights and more funding and scope for Radio Free Europe as "an instrument for the deliberate encouragement of political change." The initial NSC policy review had advocated better coordination of Western economic policies toward the Soviet bloc, and the president, sensitive to West European concern about his human rights crusade, assured a NATO summit in May 1977 that "our aim is not to turn [Eastern Europe] against the

Soviet Union but to enlarge the opportunities for all Europeans to work together in meeting the challenges of modern society."[73]

Indeed, despite its addition of human rights to the foreign policy agenda, the Carter administration was intent on pressing forward with detente, SALT II, and rapprochement with China. The special effort to improve relations with Eastern Europe would not, it was hoped, impede detente with the Russians. Deputy Assistant Secretary of State William H. Luers observed at a congressional hearing that the Soviets "are reluctant to use military power, and they are prepared to tolerate a good deal more diversity than they were 10 or 15 years ago." American policy "is to be cooperative with the individual countries of Eastern Europe, to move at a pace which is comfortable to them in their relations with us and the Western world, to provide them the opportunity to promote their own diversity and their own pluralism." The East Europeans no longer expected that an uprising would win significant Western help; rather, opposition elements had adopted more subtle ways of pressing for change, notably by invoking the Helsinki Final Act. Luers's successor, George S. Vest, reaffirmed that "we intend neither to leave our relations with Eastern Europe hostage to relations with the Soviet Union, nor to conduct a policy that is reckless and destabilizing."[74]

Exploiting Diversity within the Soviet Bloc. The unanswerable question was what degree of diversity the Kremlin would tolerate. The satisfaction of material needs could dampen yearnings for democracy; in the 1970s, therefore, the Soviet Union encouraged its client states to invigorate their economies, if necessary by drawing on Western credits and technology. The move would also reduce the burden on the Soviets. Western banks were more than ready to recycle petrodollars to the region. The expectation was that structural reforms to make the East European economies more market and consumer oriented would expose Communist regimes to the necessity of political liberalization as well. What would happen if popular demands went beyond Soviet tolerance, or if the economic reforms failed, were questions that governments East and West preferred not to entertain.

"We wanted to show that the road to Eastern Europe did not necessarily lead through Moscow," observed Brzezinski in 1978.[75] The implication that previous administrations had believed and acted otherwise was no easier to demonstrate than to now completely decouple East

European and Soviet policy. Although the Carter administration did abandon Kissinger's restraint in the pursuit of human rights in the Helsinki process and refine the strategy of differentiation, continuity rather than radical change marked its approach to the region. In the event, trade expanded, bilateral contacts and agreements multiplied, and at the margin Poland and Hungary benefited from the enhanced emphasis on domestic liberalism in the policy of differentiation.

Romania's Ceausescu remained a prized asset for Washington. He was instrumental in facilitating the historic Jerusalem meeting between Egypt's Anwar Sadat and Israel's Menachem Begin in November 1977 that led to the Camp David accords on a peace treaty. Ceausescu was rewarded with another gala reception in Washington the following April, when President Carter declared that they shared a commitment to personal freedom, lavish praise indeed for the dictator of a police state. According to Ceausescu's senior intelligence adviser, who subsequently defected, he had devised a strategic deception operation codenamed "Horizon" to create an impression of independence and gain access to Western credits and technology. He apparently also nurtured cordial relations with the PLO's Yasser Arafat and Muammar Qaddafi, and his intelligence services collaborated with the PLO in a plot against Jordan's King Hussein in 1975.[76]

If all this was known in Washington, it evidently did not detract from Ceausescu's utility. He continued to spurn the Soviets over China, hosting the new party leader, Hua Guofeng, in 1978 (when the Chinese leader also visited Yugoslavia). Romania's deviation from Warsaw Pact orthodoxy in the Helsinki process and on arms control issues pleased Washington, and when in late 1978 Ceausescu rebuffed Soviet pressures for greater military integration and expenditures, the administration hurriedly dispatched Treasury Secretary Michael Blumenthal to Bucharest to show approval. For the time being, Romania's compliance with Jackson-Vanik in respect to Jewish emigration allowed the administration to overlook its other shortcomings in the sphere of human rights.

Kadar's "goulash communism" and his comparative tolerance of cultural freedom also qualified Hungary for special treatment, and in 1977, the State Department proposed that the Crown of St. Stephen and other national treasures, in American safekeeping since the end of the war, be returned. Despite public protests by Hungarian-American organizations, Carter was satisfied by the regime's promise to put the relics on permanent public display.[77] In January 1978, a delegation led by Secretary of State Cyrus Vance made the ceremonial transfer in Budapest. A more tangible accolade came two months later with a bilateral trade agreement that extended MFN to Hungary. In ostensibly accepting the terms set by Jackson-Vanik, Hungary, like Romania, had chosen not to follow the lead of the Soviet Union.

The original Communist heretic, Yugoslavia, continued to benefit from American patronage, although occasional clouds passed over the cordiality. Outspoken criticism by the U.S. ambassador in 1975–76 of Tito's human rights abuses embarrassed both governments and led to the envoy's resignation.[78] In May 1977, Yugoslavia failed to notify Washington that it transferred to Ethiopia a number of obsolescent M-47 tanks that had been provided in the 1950s as part of the U.S. military assistance program, thereby violating the Arms Export Control Act. When the Yugoslavs professed ignorance of the provision, no penalties were imposed. Tito's nonalignment was not to be endangered.[79] After the 1979 Soviet invasion of Afghanistan had soured detente and raised fears of renewed Soviet aggressiveness, Deputy Assistant Secretary of State Robert L. Barry delivered an uncommonly forceful warning that "attempts to undermine Yugoslavia's unity, territorial integrity, and independence would be a matter of grave concern to the United States."[80] Fresh assurances of support were conveyed by Carter when he visited Belgrade in June 1980, a month after Tito's death.

The president and his national security adviser both considered Poland to be the most important East European country. Gierek seemed intent on economic reform. Poles were free to travel and practice their faith, and an oppositional counterculture flourished with only sporadic official interference. Riots in 1976 over a proposed hike in meat prices signaled that the Poles were not satisfied by the improvements in consumption. The regime prudently rescinded the price increases, but only after jailing numerous citizens who were involved in the rioting. Intellectuals formed a Committee to Defend the Workers (known by its Polish initials as KOR) to seek the release of imprisoned protesters. Other opposition groups emerged, some openly anti-Communist and anti-Soviet, and economic grievances combined with nationalism to deepen the cleavage between rulers and ruled. The election of a Polish pope, and his triumphal visit in 1979, brought further inspiration to this profoundly Catholic nation.

Communist rule and the machinery of a police state remained in place, but in July 1977, faced with growing unrest over food and other consumer-goods shortages, Gierek made a conciliatory gesture toward both his domestic and American critics by including ten political dissidents in a general amnesty. Despite some apprehensions in the State Department about the Kremlin's reaction, Carter and Brzezinski decided to make Poland the site of their first presidential state visit, and they arrived in Warsaw on December 29, 1977. The official meetings were marked by great cordiality, with Carter evoking Polish independence and inviting closer relations.[81]

Gierek's efforts to revitalize Poland's economy were running into trouble, for the substantial Western loans and technology transfer had not produced satisfactory results in terms of productivity, exports, and domestic supply. American commodity assistance through direct credits and guarantees rose steadily to $670 million in 1980. Economic assistance intensified when in mid-1979 Brzezinski received "quite explicit signals from some Polish leaders that the situation was deteriorating rapidly and that the pro-Soviet elements in Poland were deliberately interfering with Polish economic programs so as to keep Poland dependent on the Soviet Union." Poland's economic troubles could hardly be attributed to sinister sabotage alone, but by late 1979 Brzezinski was advising the president that the situation was moving toward a critical stage representing "a significant change in the Soviet world and a sign of decreasing Soviet control."[82] Whether American economic assistance had contributed materially to this change and could sustain peaceful evolution was a cause-effect conundrum that defied resolution.

The detente of the 1970s had undoubtedly facilitated closer Western relations with Eastern Europe, and Carter's campaign for human rights was logically linked by Brzezinski to a differentiated approach. Differentiation reinforced positive tendencies in Hungary, Poland, and Romania, but suffered from inherent dilemmas and contradictions. For example, symbolic and material rewards for foreign policy deviance could indirectly help the preservation of repressive domestic rule. Moreover, differentiation rested on the expectation of incremental change, and not of radical challenge to the political order. It was understood, given the asymmetry between Soviet and American interests in Eastern Europe, that Western leverage could not be a decisive factor. Although the possibility of another East European crisis remained, gradualist assumptions did not condition American policymakers to anticipate and plan for any such crises.

Detente, already strained by the Soviet deployment of SS-20 missiles in Eastern Europe and NATO's reluctant disposition to reciprocate, as well as by America's assiduous courting of Mao's successors, did not survive the invasion of Afghanistan in December 1979. That crisis dashed President Carter's hopes of winning Senate approval for the SALT II agreement as he entered an election year during which his administration also had to grapple with the Iranian hostage crisis and a revolution in Nicaragua. Yugoslavia condemned the Afghanistan invasion, and some East European regimes privately expressed reservations, but only Romania broke Warsaw Pact ranks by absenting itself from the UN vote on the issue. The subsequent Polish drama only reinforced growing American skepticism about the prospects for detente and evolutionary change in Eastern Europe.

The Polish Crisis.   On July 1, 1980, the Polish government once again took the economically rational but politically perilous step of raising meat prices. Protest strikes spread from Warsaw to the Baltic, and Radio Free Europe was instrumental in fanning the flames of discontent. By the middle of August, the strike leaders, advised by KOR, were demanding free trade unions. Washington's immediate reaction was to maintain a low profile, though Carter declared as early as August 22 that "we hope, and I might say we expect, that there will be no further Soviet involvement in Polish affairs."[83] Learning from the lesson of 1976, the Gierek regime took the path of appeasement. On August 30, after three days of negotiations, it concluded an agreement with the Interfactory Strike Committee in Gdansk to permit the formation of independent trade unions, on condition that the latter recognize the leading role of the party and not challenge Poland's alliance commitments. Thus Solidarity was born, and it eventually became a mass movement with ten million members. A week later, Stanislaw Kania replaced Gierek as first secretary of the beleaguered Polish United Workers' party (PUWP).

Even before the Gdansk accord, an interagency task force had been considering Washington's options, and on August 29, Carter sent letters to Prime Minister Margaret Thatcher of Britain, President Valery Giscard d'Estaing of France, and West German Chancellor Helmut Schmidt inviting coordination of Western responses. At the same time, however, the United States was having difficulty in coordinating its own response. The AFL-CIO responded enthusiastically to the formation of the first democratic trade union in Eastern Europe and immediately planned to send some $25,000 in financial aid. Brzezinski was "distressed" to learn that Secretary of State Edmund Muskie (with Carter's approval) warned Lane Kirkland (the AFL-CIO president) that the action could be "deliberately misinterpreted" by the Russians and assured the Soviet embassy that the administration had no part in the scheme.[84] Indeed, the Soviet media was already deploring the rise of "anti-socialist elements" in Poland and alleging Western interference; on September 23, *Pravda* accused Brzezinski of conducting psychological warfare through RFE and the VOA.

Washington had better intelligence sources in Poland than it had had twelve years earlier in Czechoslovakia, notably in the person of a senior staff officer, Col. Ryszard Kuklinski. He had been a reluctant participant in the Warsaw Pact invasion and, in disillusionment, became a CIA source. The idea of resorting to martial law, he reports, was conceived as early as August 1980, and by November preliminary plans had been drafted, then shelved.[85] Concurrent Soviet military activity on Poland's borders impelled Carter on September 20 to publicly pledge U.S. noninterference and invite the Russians to do likewise; four days earlier, he had announced that the Commodity Credit Corporation would make another $670 million available for grain.

The American strategy, inspired by Brzezinski and developed by the NSC's Special Coordination Committee, was twofold: first, to avoid the apparent mistake of 1968 by publicizing Soviet military moves and the Western sanctions that an intervention would precipitate, and second, to induce moderation on the part of the Warsaw regime with economic incentives. Meanwhile, Brzezinski urged official and unofficial Polish visitors to strive for compromise but to present a united front if the Soviets tried to intervene. *Pravda* promptly construed this advice as an invitation to armed resistance, leading Brzezinski to issue an elliptical denial, acknowledging the need to resolve the crisis in the context of "certain historical and geographic realities."[86]

Soviet and Western Pressures. After the Polish Supreme Court confirmed Solidarity's legal status on November 10, signs of Soviet military preparations multiplied as the East Germans sealed off their border with

Poland. At Brzezinski's urging, Senator Charles Percy told Foreign Minister Gromyko in Moscow that the "use of troops in Poland would change the face of the globe" and lead to a huge arms buildup. On December 3, the president sent a message to Brezhnev expressing "growing concern" and warning that U.S. policy toward the Soviet Union would be "directly and very adversely affected" by military intervention.[87] Two days later, Soviet bloc leaders meeting in Moscow issued a communique expressing confidence in the ability of the PUWP to "overcome the current difficulties" and assuring Poland of the fraternal support of their Warsaw Pact allies.[88] This thinly veiled evocation of the Brezhnev Doctrine was reinforced the same day by a CIA report that the Soviets were planning to move into Poland (ostensibly as part of the "Soyuz 81" exercises) on December 8 with fifteen divisions (along with one East German and two Czechoslovak divisions) and that the Polish General Staff was debating whether to put up resistance.[89]

The Kremlin suspected that in delaying martial law the Kania leadership was playing a double game and planning to make radical concessions to Solidarity. Military intervention would be followed by the installation of a hard-line regime and mass arrests. Moscow secretly discussed operational coordination with the Polish military, including Defense Minister General Wojciech Jaruzelski, who was reduced to bargaining for the participation of a few Polish units. Amidst the rising tension, discussions in Washington ranged over the options of forewarning the Polish opposition, seeking UN action, and even blockading Cuba in retaliation. On December 7, the CIA confirmed the imminence of invasion, and an enlarged Special Coordination Committee meeting agreed on presidential messages to Brezhnev and other leaders. The first message, to which Brezhnev never replied, was a terse restatement of the previous warning. The others (addressed to Schmidt, Giscard, Thatcher, Canada's Pierre Trudeau, Italy's Arnaldo Forlani, Australia's Malcolm Fraser, Japan's Zenko Suzuki, NATO Secretary General Joseph Luns, UN Secretary General Kurt Waldheim, and India's Indira Gandhi, who was about to host Brezhnev) indicated the probability of Soviet intervention and invited diplomatic support. Brzezinski used Lane Kirkland and other channels to warn Solidarity; he personally telephoned the pope, and instructed RFE and the VOA to broadcast the White House statement without delay.[90]

This feverish activity was aimed at depriving the Soviets of the element of surprise. They might, Brzezinski hoped, be deterred by international diplomatic pressure and the possibility of resistance by the forewarned Poles, who, in turn, might be sobered by news of the threat. But by December 10, the CIA reported that some twenty-seven divisions were ready and likely to move within the next six days.[91] Czechoslovakian and East German troops were prepared to participate in the assault.

Though Giscard sent a strong note to Moscow, other allied support was not as forthright. Bonn was particularly reluctant to stake its detente with the Soviet Union on the latter's nonintervention ("best proof yet of the increasing finlandization of the Germans," recorded Brzezinski in his diary).[92] But a European Community summit in Luxembourg on December 1 promised food aid for Poland and indicated that flouting of the UN Charter and the Helsinki Final Act principles would have "very severe consequences."[93] The following week, NATO foreign ministers met to consider joint steps in case of invasion, including increasing defense expenditures, cutting off credits to Poland and the Soviet Union, canceling technology transfers (notably those involved in the Soviet-West European gas pipeline project), closing Western ports to Soviet ships, and terminating MBFR and CSCE talks. In the event, the allies— including West Germany—agreed on economic sanctions and a minor military buildup, and the communique issuing from the meeting on December 12 warned that detente would be imperiled by intervention.[94]

The U.S. Senate, meanwhile, passed a unanimous resolution to the same effect. The AFL-CIO worked on plans for a comprehensive boycott of Soviet goods by international transport workers. And Brzezinski instructed the Pentagon to prepare a list of weapons that might be offered to the Chinese, anticipating that the initiative would leak and become known to the Soviets. In the midst of these alarums, while *Pravda* mocked Brzezinski for thinking that "he can act tough without getting into any fights," farmers at a meeting in Warsaw founded Rural Solidarity.[95]

By the end of December, the Soviets had suspended their invasion plan. American and allied pressure, doubts about the Polish army's loyalty, preparations for popular resistance, and Jaruzelski's renewed offer to eventually resolve the crisis by internal means had evidently acted as a deterrent. Brzezinski regarded the outcome as one of the Carter administration's signal successes.[96] But as the president noted in his last State of the Union message, "although the situation has shown signs of stabilizing recently, Soviet forces remain in a high state of readiness, and they could move into Poland on short notice."[97]

Invasion had been deterred, but its threat overwhelmed the second part of the administration's strategy, the consolidation of reforms. In November the Polish government had approached Washington with a request for a $3 billion financial aid package (and other Western governments for an additional $5 billion). Tentative allied consultations followed, but such an immense subsidy to a mismanaged and technically bankrupt socialist economy could not be lightly entertained, least of all by a defeated president. Nor is it too likely that a quick and positive response in principle from the West could have strengthened the position of the more reform-minded Communists such as Kania, drawn them together with Solidarity into a common front, and generated the necessary structural reforms, all without provoking Soviet intervention.[98] The request was therefore put off. When, a year later, new CCC credits and a partial rescheduling of debt were offered, Kania was gone and the countdown to martial law reaching its end.

The incoming Reagan administration carried on with established strategy but remained divided on the option of significant economic leverage. Although Secretary of State Alexander Haig would publicly dangle the lure of aid, linking it to internal reform, President Ronald Reagan's tax-cutting priorities and the preference of some of his advisers for a more "red-blooded" policy to declare Poland in default and bring the Soviet Union "to her knees" militated against prompt action. Recalls Haig, "Some of my colleagues in the NSC were prepared to look beyond Poland, as if it were not in itself an issue of war and peace, and regard it as an opportunity to inflict mortal political, economic, and propaganda damage on the USSR."[99] Thus Washington concentrated its efforts on keeping the Soviets out.

Preparing for Martial Law.   Caught between the millstones of the Kremlin and Solidarity, the Polish regime struggled to maintain some order and stave off disaster. When Solidarity leader Lech Walesa threatened a one-day strike in support of free Saturdays and the legalization of Rural Solidarity, suspension of censorship, the release of political prisoners, and a new union law, the leadership made a concession on the first demand; but ten days later, on February 9, 1981, it responded to Soviet pressure by appointing General Jaruzelski prime minister. On the following day, the Supreme Court ruled that Rural Solidarity could register only as an "association," not as a trade union. In a tough speech to the Sejm (the Polish parliament) on February 12, Jaruzelski warned against the creeping process of destabilization and called for a ninety-day moratorium on strikes.

Soviet-Polish consultations in Moscow produced a communique, issued on March 4, that professed faith in the ability of the PUWP to "reverse the course of events and . . . liquidate the dangers that threaten the socialist gains" and evoked again the common responsibility to defend an "indissoluble" socialist commonwealth.[100] Two weeks later, when the police brutally dispersed a sit-in protest by Rural Solidarity members in Bydgoszcz, Walesa declared that unless a full investigation of the incident was conducted he would call a general strike for March 31. An eleventh-hour compromise offered little to Solidarity, but the strike was called off as the threat of Soviet intervention waxed again.

Hopes for a political accommodation were raised by the scheduling of an extraordinary congress of the PUWP for July 20 under rules that strengthened the voice of party reformers. The latter, meeting in Torun on April 15, called for a more democratic party that permitted factions. The Czechoslovak party had been moving in the same heretical direction in 1968; the Russians now responded by denouncing revisionist elements in the PUWP and dispatching on April 23 a delegation led by Politburo member Mikhail Suslov to impress on the Poles the imperative of orthodoxy.[101]

Jaruzelski had submitted a detailed report, "On the Status of the State's Preparations for Imposing Martial Law," at the March Kremlin meeting but pleaded, then and in countless other discussions, for time to prepare the party, army, and security forces. A powerful military and KGB delegation led by Marshal Viktor G. Kulikov arrived in Warsaw in late March to study the situation, and a week later Kania and Jaruzelski were taken to see Brezhnev, who put pressure on them to speed things up. Neither would agree to set a firm timetable for martial law. Meanwhile, the prospect of mass resistance, including parts of the Polish army, and renewed Western warnings once again deterred the Russians from acting on their own.[102]

Washington was aware of the martial law preparations but failed to devise an adequate contingency plan because (according to Haig) the allies could not reach a consensus.[103] Worse still, a State Department spokesman declared on February 10 that Polish action to restore order would be regarded by the United States as an internal matter; his subsequent clarification, that such action would still be "a matter of very great concern to us," did not dispel the impression that Washington's priority was to deter Moscow. When Haig invoked the principles of detente proclaimed at the 1972 summit, Soviet Foreign Minister Andrei Gromyko refused to discuss Poland's internal affairs and charged Western interference.[104] The administration hinted that military sales to China were still under consideration, and on April 3, Reagan told Brezhnev that arms control talks were contingent on nonintervention in Poland.[105] NATO defense ministers issued a similar warning, but a North Atlantic Council statement on Poland a month later refrained from asserting that linkage, reportedly at Bonn's insistence.[106] The Reagan administration was in any case cool to the resumption of arms control talks, and it had refused to press for Senate ratification of the SALT II treaty signed by Carter in June 1979. Nevertheless, mainly to pacify West European public opinion, it agreed in June to new negotiations on intermediate-range nuclear forces (INF) and strategic arms reductions (START), thereby effectively decoupling arms control from the Polish crisis.

Apart from these verbal signals and the publicity given to Soviet military moves, some modest steps were taken to "bridge" Poland's debt crisis. On February 27, the United States deferred for four months the repayment of $88 million in CCC credits; on March 18, Bonn guaranteed an additional $71.4 million in private credits for Poland; on March 24, another EC summit raised the prospect of economic aid; and two days later the White House issued a warning against external or internal repression, adding that peaceful resolution would bring economic benefits.[107] When tensions momentarily seemed to ease in April, the United States agreed to provide $70 million worth of surplus food (payable in zlotys, thus more a gift than a sale) and, together with the other members of the "Paris Club," the group of Western Governments that had advanced credits to Poland, developed the outlines of a partial rescheduling arrangement. At the same time, however, Reagan sent a contradictory signal to the Soviet Union by lifting the Carter grain embargo imposed in response to the Afghanistan invasion. In August, the Poles expressed interest in rejoining the IMF and signed the rescheduling agreement, though neither initiative survived martial law.

Moscow's impatience with the Poles was fully displayed in the formal complaint addressed on June 5 to the Central Committee of the PUWP. It charged that the Polish party had "retreated step by step under the onslaught of internal counter-revolution, which relies on the support of imperialist subversion centres abroad" and promised (quoting Brezhnev) that the Soviet Union "will not abandon socialist Poland, fraternal Poland in its time of need—we will stand by it!"[108] Haig, on his way to Beijing, called a special press conference in Hong Kong to decry this interference in Polish affairs, and a few days later the United States announced that it had decided in principle to sell lethal weapons to China.[109]

Solidarity's Demands and the Coup. The Polish party congress was anticlimactic, for Soviet pressures successfully prevented the reformers from gaining ground. Frustrated, Solidarity turned increasingly toward total political confrontation. Undeterred by another round of Warsaw Pact maneuvers, it proceeded at its September national congress in Gdansk to call for a national referendum on self-management, and invited workers in other socialist states to follow its lead. Moscow demanded that the PUWP and the government "immediately take determined and radical steps in order to cut short the malicious anti-Soviet propaganda and actions hostile to the Soviet Union."[110] The demand was reinforced by the threat of economic sanctions (of some consequence given Poland's dependence on and trade deficit with the Soviet Union). The Polish cabinet met in emergency session and declared that since the obvious goal of Solidarity was to take power, it would brook no compromise and use all means at its disposal.[111]

Washington responded with deliberate caution. "There are interventionist implications in the Soviet note," said Haig, "and we don't welcome that. On the other hand, it is also not a blatant threat of the kind some might be even more fearful of." The president on September 22 sent a note to Brezhnev urging that the Polish people be left alone to deal with their problems.[112] That martial law was becoming the more likely form of suppression was scarcely reflected in the administration's public stance. Moscow's propaganda barrage only intensified as Solidarity reconvened its congress from September 26 to October 7. Its program demanded dismantlement of the party-state's economic dominance, cuts in defense spending, and more pluralistic elections.

On October 18, Jaruzelski added the leadership of the PUWP to his other functions as prime minister, defense minister, and commander-in-chief. Harassment and arrests of Solidarity activists led to wildcat strikes, which in turn gave the government the excuse to deploy military teams —ostensibly to supervise supplies and help maintain law and order, in fact to condition the population to martial law. Haig professed to take comfort from the fact that "this was less than martial law," and on October 27, Washington came forward with an additional $27 million in food aid.[113] By then, the deadline and mechanism for imposing martial law had been worked out in consultation with the Soviets.[114] Solidarity organized a nationwide, one-hour work stoppage on October 28, and over the next few weeks Jaruzelski went through the motions of negotiating with the union the creation of a "Front of National Accord," but these moves were evidently designed to deceive the opposition. Warsaw Pact coordination proceeded at meetings of foreign ministers in Bucharest, defense ministers in Moscow, and news agency heads in Prague, all on December 1, while Jaruzelski presented the Sejm with a request for emergency powers, including a strike ban. When Walesa threatened a general strike, the regime charged that Solidarity was taking "the position of a political opposition embarking on an open struggle against the socialist authority and a struggle for power."[115]

The option of a major economic aid program had meanwhile come under discussion again in Washington, and an offer of $100 million in CCC credits reached Warsaw on December 11.[116] But the opportunity, if it ever existed, to reinforce peaceful compromise was long past, for the offer coincided with another directive from the Soviet party to the Polish leadership and the secret return of Marshal Kulikov to supervise the impending coup. The following evening, security forces surrounded the Solidarity headquarters in Gdansk, and at 6 a.m. on the December 13, 1981, General Jaruzelski went on the air to declare a "state of war" as a patriotic necessity to deal with the pervasive "chaos and demoralization."[117] The operation was meticulously planned and executed. The Solidarity leaders were caught unprepared, and the cutting of all internal telephone communications effectively impeded the organized mass resistance anticipated by the CIA.[118]

"I would say, in general, that all the Washington parties were surprised," recalls Secretary of State Haig.[119] Indeed, the American policy of publicizing preparations for military intervention and for martial law had drawn the net of suspicion around the CIA's prime source, Col.

Kuklinski, and he prudently defected in early November. Thus, Washington apparently had no advance knowledge of the precise time of the coup and could not warn Solidarity.[120] Ignorance, in this case, probably prevented unnecessary bloodshed.

From the start, Brezhnev's Kremlin had regarded Solidarity as anathema, and if it wavered between invasion and the martial law option, it was in all likelihood never prepared to condone the emergence of a free trade union movement that would inevitably weaken the party's monopoly rule and inspire political heresy in other parts of Eastern Europe. A hypothetical united front of party reformers and opposition, supported by the army, obviously would have raised the cost of intervention. Whether the prospect of a bloody war over Poland might have steered the Soviets to attempt less forceful means of suasion lies at the limits of fruitful speculation.[121]

For Washington, the Polish crisis was yet another East European lesson in frustration. The basic approach, in Haig's rendition, had been to warn off the Soviets without "excessive provocation" and to "offer humanitarian aid to the Polish people, but not even hint that the United States would under any circumstances go beyond that."[122] The strategy probably helped to forestall invasion, but neither the Soviets nor the Poles expected more forceful American action. The West conceivably could have come forward with massive economic aid or, alternatively, threatened the Poles with default, but such radical departures were beyond the capacity of the lame-duck Carter administration or his successor in the midst of a divisive policy review. In all likelihood, neither the carrot nor the stick would have altered the Kremlin's perception of deadly threat to its sphere of dominance. In terms of military security, Poland was a key constituent of the Warsaw Pact's northern tier, the gateway to Germany. To be sure, a different Soviet regime might have taken a more sanguine view of the domestic reforms advocated by Solidarity, but in 1981 Soviet interests were defined by the aging Brezhnev.

Martial law, coming on top of the invasion of Afghanistan, reinforced the administration's belligerent stance vis a vis the Soviet Union.[123] Reagan put Vice President George Bush in charge of a task force to study American responses, and ten days after martial law a series of sanctions were imposed on Poland. A bitter dispute erupted between Departments of State and Defense over appropriate sanctions, with the Pentagon favoring a ban on the sale of equipment for the $10 billion Soviet-West European gas pipeline project by European subsidiaries of American corporations. Reagan sided with the Pentagon, and the State Department's representative explained to Congress that "we hope by this action to put further pressure on the Soviets to restore the reform and renewal process in Poland."[124]

The administration was already aggrieved at the allies' comparatively complacent reaction to martial law. Bonn's dogged attachment to detente and stability was reflected in Chancellor Schmidt's concurrent visit to Honecker and his insensitive remark that the two German leaders regretted the necessity of martial law. It matched the initial reaction of French Foreign Minister Claude Cheysson that "of course [France] was not going to react" to an internal Polish affair.[125] The pipeline measure provoked more acrimony among the allies, compelling the president to suspend the licensing ban in November 1982.

The early sanctions against Poland were economically damaging but politically fruitless, and when in October the military regime formally banned Solidarity, Reagan turned the screw by suspending the country's MFN status. The option of forcing Poland into default had its advocates in Congress and among Reagan's advisers, but prudence prevailed. Instead, the administration sought to extract the maximum propaganda advantage from the Polish disaster. In early 1982, the USIA beamed a television spectacular, "Let Poland Be Poland!" to Western and Eastern Europe. The AFL-CIO and the CIA provided covert assistance to the remnants of Solidarity, and after 1983 the new National Endowment for Democracy became the overt source of such sustenance.[126] Poland's ambassador to Washington had defected after martial law, and when in early 1983 the time came to rotate American ambassadors in Warsaw, Jaruzelski imposed unacceptable conditions and the post was left vacant. U.S.-Polish relations had sunk to a postwar nadir. For the moment, Solidarity endorsed the American sanctions in the hope that they would impel Jaruzelski to compromise.

Differentiation Policy Continues.   The decade that began inauspiciously with the consolidation of Soviet rule and orthodoxy in Poland ended with the Soviet empire in incipient disintegration and optimistic plans for reintegrating the East Europeans into the democratic world. The impetus for this dramatic transformation came from Moscow, inviting Washington to reconsider the tactics if not the long-term objectives of differentiation.

Cold war with Poland suited administration officials, notably in the Pentagon, who were pressing for a tougher policy of economic isolation and destabilization of the Soviet bloc.[127] In the absence of allied consensus, what emerged was the old policy of differentiation enhanced by more aggressive rhetoric on Communist human rights violations (along with a more lenient attitude toward the practices of friendly regimes). The administration's policy review once again addressed the option of making American favors conditional on internal liberalization as well as foreign policy independence, but once again the existing strategy of rewarding one or the other was reaffirmed in a National Security Decision Directive (NSDD-54) of· August 1982.[128] As before, stacking the criteria of foreign and domestic deviance would have left the United States with no opportunities for leverage in Eastern Europe, where despite the Polish setback domestic pressures for economic reform and human rights were accumulating.

Differentiation in the conduct of bilateral relations remained the minimal realistic response to these stirrings. With Poland's demotion, Romania became the most promising target for rewarding liberalization. Secretary of State Haig visited Bucharest in February 1982 to praise Romanian independence, as did Vice President Bush the following September. Romania earned much credit in Washington for attending the 1984 summer Olympics in Los Angeles, which was boycotted by the rest of the Warsaw Pact in retaliation for the American boycott of the 1980 Moscow event, but clouds were gathering over the special relationship. The American ambassador, David Funderburk (a political appointee and Romanian expert), recommended against such visits "because of the wrong signals [they] would send regarding what Ceausescu represents," and tried to convince the State Department that Ceausescu's ostensibly independent foreign policy covered extensive collaboration with the Soviet Union, while his domestic rule was the most repressive in the bloc. The State Department, charged Funderburk, downplayed and dismissed his protests because its "overriding concern" was to protect the MFN relationship from congressional challenge.[129] The criticisms that he vented publicly when he resigned in 1985 became, three years later, conventional wisdom.

This continuity in differentiation policy was occasionally overshadowed during the first Reagan administration by denunciation of Soviet rule in language that evoked the darkest days of the cold war. "Star Wars" and "evil empire" supplanted the soothing vocabulary of detente. In an address to the British parliament on June 8, 1982, the president called for a "crusade for freedom" to relegate Marxism-Leninism to the "ash heap of history." [130] Three years later, on the fortieth anniversary of Yalta, he reiterated the American commitment to "undo this boundary" between repression and freedom: "We do not deny any nation's legitimate interest in security. But protecting the security of one nation by robbing another of its national independence and national traditions is not legitimate." [131] It was not all idle rhetoric, for the administration pursued human rights with unprecedented vigor in the Helsinki review process and moved to establish a National Foundation for Democracy to nurture the seedlings of pluralism in Eastern Europe and elsewhere.

Moscow reacted predictably to these challenges to the legitimacy of the East European status quo and to Vice President Bush's reminder on September 21, 1983 that "the Soviet violation of the [Yalta] obligations is the primary root of East-West tensions today." Speaking in Vienna on his way back from a visit to Yugoslavia, Romania, and Hungary, Bush delivered a blunt exposition of American policy to support and encourage "all movement toward the social, humanitarian and democratic ideals" without seeking to "destabilize or undermine any government." Differentiation meant that the United States would "engage in closer political, economic and cultural relations with those countries such as Hungary and Romania which assert greater openness or independence" but not reward "closed societies and belligerent foreign policies" (e.g. Czechoslovakia and Bulgaria) or those, specifically East Germany and Bulgaria, that served as Soviet proxies in aiding terrorists and revolutionaries. [132] Dissidents in Eastern Europe were comforted by such statements, though too much praise made the comparatively liberal Budapest regime nervous about Soviet reaction.

Gorbachev's Revolution. It befell Mikhail Gorbachev, who in March 1985 took over the Kremlin after the brief tenures of Yuri Andropov and Konstantin Chernenko, to take stock of the grim legacy left by his predecessors. The status of military superpower had been achieved at ruinous cost to the civil economy, and Reagan's defense modernization program promised only more costly competition. The Soviet Union remained technologically backward in most spheres; consumer goods were in chronically short supply, and an inefficient agriculture required continuing reliance on grain imports. On top of this, Brezhnev had bequeathed rampant corruption and a military commitment that threatened to turn Afghanistan into a Soviet version of Vietnam. The peoples of the Soviet Union were not in a revolutionary mood, but neither they nor the system displayed the productivity needed to catch up to the West.

The East European empire was dubious asset. It had turned into an economic burden and a political embarrassment. The activity of isolated dissidents could be overlooked, but the Solidarity experience left no ambiguity as to the predominant popular mood in the region. The majority of East Europeans seethed with nationalistic resentment at Soviet suzerainty and, far from regarding the Soviet Union as their model, looked westward for economic and political formulas for salvation.

Impelled by this sobering reality, Gorbachev launched a revolution to revitalize the Soviet economy. The restructuring, or *perestroika,* aimed at political and administrative institutions as well as the economic mechanism. The stagnation and conservatism of the Brezhnev apparatus was to be challenged with *glasnost* (literally, "openness"), the unleashing of the intelligentsia's critical and creative forces, and with a degree of democratization that would invigorate popular participation in the process of government. In the West, the initial skepticism soon gave way to ebullient optimism that Marxism-Leninism was on its last legs, though Gorbachev's revolution generated more problems—in the economy and with the national minorities—than solutions.

Gorbachev's "new political thinking" in foreign policy reflected the urgency of concentrating on these domestic problems. The ideological rationale for securing a respite in the East-West military competition was that, after all, capitalism and imperialism did not necessarily spawn a threatening militarism. In the new detente, armaments could be reduced to a level of "reasonable sufficiency" (allowing for a transfer of Soviet resources from the military to the civil economy) while cooperative relations could ease access to Western technology, trade, and investment. All this inspired Gorbachev's soothing evocation of "our common

European home" to woo the Germans, in particular, but others as well (witness his seduction of Reagan at the summits), and justified his withdrawal from Afghanistan.

Gorbachev infused Soviet East European policy with unprecedented permissiveness. The "entire framework of political relations between the socialist countries must be strictly based on absolute independence. . . . The independence of each Party, its sovereign right to decide the issues facing its country and its responsibility to its nation are the unquestionable principles," wrote the new leader in his handbook for *perestroika*.[133] Although he also stressed collaboration and common interests, his spokesmen and advisers insisted that the time was past when the Soviet Union would intervene militarily in Eastern Europe in the name of the socialist commonwealth.[134]

The signs of a new Soviet approach to Eastern Europe multiplied. On his visit to Yugoslavia in March 1988, Gorbachev formally reaffirmed the principle of noninterference. At an extraordinary Soviet-American symposium on East-West relations and Eastern Europe, held in July 1988 in Alexandria, Virginia, Soviet spokesmen acknowledged Stalin's role in the "revolutionary transformations" after the war. They noted that his successors' "hegemonic aspirations" as well as major mistakes by the satellite parties had been responsible for the subsequent crises. A return to the Brezhnev Doctrine, said the delegation's head, academician Oleg T. Bogomolov, was "completely unacceptable and unthinkable." To be sure, Gorbachev in his book had blamed not "socialism" but the local parties and Western subversion for the crises, yet his permissiveness gradually extended to the abandonment of Leninism in Eastern Europe.[135]

Were the East Europeans, as the perceptive scholar Charles Gati speculated in an article in *Foreign Affairs,* on their own? And what were the limits of the Kremlin's newfound tolerance? Poland's Mieczyslaw Rakowski, later premier and then party leader, secretly warned his colleagues in late 1987 not to expect Soviet help if they lost control. And in 1988, when the new Hungarian party leader Karoly Grosz followed established practice in seeking the Kremlin's ruling on a policy matter, he was told by Gorbachev to be "guided by his conscience."[136] In his travels in Eastern Europe Gorbachev proved a most diplomatic advocate of *perestroika,* stressing the need for economic revitalization without urging (publicly, that is) the adoption of a particular model. But his cautious criticism of Ceausescu and the Russian reformers' acknowledgment of the similarity between Dubcek's "socialism with a human face" and *perestroika* bode ill for the region's more conservative regimes.

The Hungarians and the Poles were the first to take Gorbachev's cue by treading gingerly on the slippery slope of political concessions in mid-1988. With Soviet permissiveness confirmed, the liquidation of the Leninist party-state came with dramatic suddenness. At the beginning of 1989, all of the East European parties still clung to their doctrinal leading role. A year later, all except the Albanians had effectively surrendered it in response to popular pressure. The transition was relatively peaceful except in Romania. In July 1989, the Hungarians presented President Bush with a piece of the barbed wire from the dismantled fence on their Austrian border. By December, the Berlin Wall had been breached and the East Germans were busily selling pieces of it to Western souvenir hunters.

Reagan's Responses to Perestroika. As the Gorbachev revolution began to unfold, the possibility of hastening the peaceful emancipation of Eastern Europe acquired new salience. "The West typically heeds Eastern Europe only in crisis," editorialized the *New York Times* in November 1987. "This is a good time to break that pattern with a thoughtful and unified approach to nudge inevitable changes in desirable directions." [137] Brzezinski observed that Eastern Europe was entering a phase of systemic crisis, the "organic rejection by the social system of an alien transplant." Though these countries were in his view "potentially ripe for revolutionary explosion," gradual change was preferable and had to be deliberately promoted, among other things, "by the development of more expansive East-West economic contacts." [138]

The Reagan administration overcame its initial mistrust of Gorbachev to move ahead on arms control but kept up its pressure on human rights. Visiting West Berlin in June 1987, the President issued a rhetorical challenge: "General Secretary Gorbachev, if you seek peace—if you seek prosperity for the Soviet Union and Eastern Europe—if you seek liberalization: Tear down this wall." In his proclamations of Captive Nations Week and Helsinki Human Rights Day and other statements, Reagan repeatedly called on the Soviet Union to fulfill the Yalta pledges, to allow free elections, and to repudiate force as a means of preventing liberalization in Eastern Europe. [139] The linkage of human rights concessions to new conventional force reduction talks was sustained at the CSCE review conference in Vienna, which had been underway since November 1986 (see chapter 4). As the president's National Security Strategy Report affirmed in January 1988, "We have never recognized Soviet hegemony in the region as legitimate or healthy because it is based on military power and dictatorship, not democratic consent. We wish to develop our relations with each country of the region on an individual basis."[140]

In the summer of 1987, Secretary of State George Shultz gave a special mandate to his deputy, John C. Whitehead, to invigorate American engagement in Eastern Europe. That region, said Whitehead in an address to the Washington Institute of Foreign Affairs the following January, was ripe for change:

[The] long run Soviet interest in maintaining a hegemonic relationship with Eastern Europe has not changed, although the Soviet definition of what this means in practice may have evolved. . . . there is no question that a confluence of easing East-West tensions, the reform process in the U.S.S.R. and enlightened self-interest present the United States and the West our most important opportunity in Eastern Europe in the four decades since Winston Churchill's [Fulton] speech.

We in the U.S. now have a unique and perhaps short-lived chance to influence change in Eastern Europe in the direction of political and economic liberalization. These countries are looking for new solutions to their stubbornly familiar problems. Our challenge is to make sure they look to the West for some of these solutions, and that meaningful political as well as economic change occurs in a peaceful and permanent manner.[141]

At the time, the permissiveness of *perestroika* was inducing more diversity than ever in Eastern Europe. Hungary and Poland were caught up with reform, and Bulgaria was tentatively toying with it, but the Romanian, Czechoslovak, and East German leaderships were obviously discomfited by the new winds from Moscow. Washington's active engagement therefore had to be calibrated to the circumstances of each country as the pace of diplomatic contacts increased. Within less than two years, Whitehead visited each East European country at least twice. After a trip in January and February 1988 to Czechoslovakia, Poland, Romania, and Bulgaria, he reported that "I have the feeling they have a lot of latitude. . . . I see practically no chance, no evidence of the Russians intervening in any way."[142]

Whitehead briefed the East European regimes on American approaches to arms control and, in the spirit of differentiation, reminded them that American trade and other economic benefits were contingent on liberalization.[143] He made an effort to meet with religious leaders and opposition figures, such as Charter 77 activists in Czechoslovakia. This kind of symbolic legitimation of political opposition in Eastern Europe soon became common practice for visiting Western statesmen and diplomats. *Perestroika* reduced the relevance of foreign policy deviation as a criterion for differentiation, and the main thrust of U.S. strategy became encouragement of domestic reform. The sole casualty of this shift was Romania, now out of favor in both Moscow and Washington; by 1988 Whitehead was reflecting that "it was illogical that Romania should have had MFN status, given their human rights performance."[144]

Washington was under no illusions that American leverage alone could have a decisive influence on change in Eastern Europe, and it sought to coordinate policy with its allies. While France and Britain tempered their enthusiasm for Gorbachev with sustained pressure on human rights, the "Gorbymania" sweeping West Germany did not dispose Bonn to adopt a politically more differentiated *Ostpolitik*. Moreover, the Germans had the biggest potential economic leverage in the region. On the eve of a NATO ministerial meeting in Madrid in June 1988, an American official indicated that there were differences among the allies on the linkage of aid for economic reform to political liberalization and that Secretary of State Shultz would "insist on political reform up front."[145] In the event, no formal decision was taken, but the foreign ministers agreed to treat East European countries individually and not as a bloc, and the allies' responses to developments in Hungary and Poland followed roughly parallel paths.

Bilateral Relations. The pattern of the Reagan administration's bilateral relations altered more with respect to Poland and Romania than with the others. The conservative regimes of Gustav Husak and his successor Milos Jakes in Prague remained largely impervious to *perestroika* and Western lures and continued to repress the burgeoning opposition groups and religious protesters. The consular convention ratified in 1973 remained a dead letter for fourteen years as human rights abuses put U.S.-Czechoslovak relations into a deep freeze. It was finally implemented in 1987, when on his visit to Prague Whitehead professed to find signs of improvement; a civil aviation pact as well as a cultural and scientific exchange agreement were also signed that year. A measure of "improvement" was permission for two American physicians to conduct a postmortem on the activist Pavel Wonka, who had died in prison. They found no evidence of torture, but the State Department called upon the government to release all political prisoners and abide by its human rights obligations under the Helsinki Final Act.

Relations with Bulgaria improved marginally when the Zhivkov regime appeared to jump on the *perestroika* bandwagon. The Bulgarians had acquired a bad reputation for harboring international drug traffickers and terrorists, but in 1988 they agreed in bilateral talks to be more vigilant. Their interest in improving economic relations was signaled by the visit to Washington in April that year of trade minister Andrei Lukanov, the highest-ranking Bulgarian visitor since the war. But the concurrent campaign to assimilate ethnic Turks worsened and led, a year later, to massive emigration, prompting Washington to recall Ambassador Sol Polansky in August 1989.

East Germany remained at the bottom of Washington's list for priorities and favors, partly because it was regarded as Bonn's special preserve and partly because it continued to symbolize Stalinist orthodoxy. The regime had suspended its "shoot to kill" policy at the Wall prior to Honecker's visit to West Germany in September 1987, and Washington took some comfort from this and from travel concessions for East Germans. Talks on trade expansion began in April 1988, but the regime's resistance to reform, the Jackson-Vanik requirement, and outstanding U.S. claims (including those of Jewish victims of the Nazi era and their survivors) in the amount of some $70 million made the prospect of American concessions remote.

In contrast, U.S. relations with Hungary flourished. The dynamic new ambassador, Mark Palmer, worked tirelessly to foster cordial relations with both official and opposition reformers, encourage commercial contacts, and facilitate private funding and initiatives (notably by the American-Hungarian financier George Soros) involving cultural exchanges and the creation of the first Western-style business school in Eastern Europe, the International Management Center in Budapest. Impelled by mounting foreign debt and the failure of partial economic reforms, the Hungarians assiduously nurtured their relations with Western countries and were the first Warsaw Pact country to establish relations with the European Community.

Whitehead's successful visits to Budapest paved the way for a trip to Washington in July 1988 by the new party leader, Karoly Grosz. The United States, Reagan told him, was "encouraged by your recognition that economic reforms cannot succeed unless they are accompanied by political reforms as well." [146] Within a year, Grosz had been eclipsed by more radical reformers and a new American president had come to Budapest bringing fulsome praise and modest material rewards.

While the erstwhile favorite of differentiation, Ceausescu's Romania, withdrew into isolation in reaction to international criticism, Jaruzelski's Poland slowly emerged from the isolation it incurred with martial law. Poland was unique among East European countries in having a significant constituency in the United States, including influential politicians on Capitol Hill. The Polish-American Congress supported the conditional normalization of relations, and American economic sanctions were progressively suspended, culminating in the restoration of MFN in 1987 (see chapter 5).[147]

Jaruzelski's self-confidence was displayed in the release of all remaining political prisoners in September 1986, and although the bulk of the population remained profoundly alienated from his regime, Solidarity appeared to be a waning force. The following August, after two fact-finding missions to Poland by Congressman Stephen Solarz (D.-N.Y.), a senior member of the House Foreign Affairs Committee, Congress gave final approval to a $1 million grant to Solidarity through its Brussels office. Solidarity intended to apply the funds to health care, principally diagnostic clinics, but a year later the government refused to authorize the autonomous foundation formed to administer the project. The idea of a church-sponsored fund to channel Western aid to private farmers had been abandoned earlier for the same reason.

Secretary of State Shultz and PUWP Secretary Josef Czyrek had agreed in March 1987 to upgrade diplomatic relations, leading in September to the nomination of John Davis, a veteran diplomat who was serving in Warsaw as charge d'affaires. The administration considered more substantial American aid to ease Poland's economic crisis, an option that had some backing among State Department specialists but little support at Defense and the Treasury.[148] The conditional offer that Vice President Bush took to Warsaw in September linked aid to fundamental economic reforms and political liberalization. "The more you proceed toward greater freedom and pluralism the more we will endeavor to find new

ways to help you," he declared on Polish television.[149] Bush found
Jaruzelski willing to relax the rules on free associations and to allow for
a semblance of electoral competition but adamantly opposed to accommodating Solidarity, a prospect he described as "suicidal."[150] The vice
president could consequently promise support for consolidation and
rescheduling of Poland's debt by the Paris Club but no additional financial assistance.

The thaw in official relations was thus superficial, and Bush underscored America's distaste for the regime by laying a wreath on the grave
of Father Jerzy Popieluszko, a pro-Solidarity priest murdered by security
police in 1984, and by meeting with Lech Walesa. He urged Walesa to
press for political pluralism, and indeed that general demand came to
overshadow the opposition's call for reinstatement of Solidarity's legal
status. On his return, Bush reported to the Polish-American Congress
that "Jaruzelski resists any linkage with economic aid that might make
it appear as if the United States is dictating the internal policies of
Poland. I told him that genuine economic progress would be impossible
without meaningful movement toward pluralism and national reconciliation."[151] Jaruzelski did submit an ambitious economic reform plan as
well as a proposal for limited electoral pluralism to a national referendum in late 1987, only to receive what he construed as a rebuff. He
could only offer economic austerity, and most Poles had no confidence
in his regime.

The Polish domestic political deadlock allowed for only marginal
progress in what the State Department called the "process of U.S.-Polish
re-engagement" during last year of the Reagan administration. The Poles
stopped jamming Radio Free Europe and complied with American requests to shut down the Warsaw office of the terrorist Abu Nidal organization. In February 1988, the Polish-U.S. joint trade committee met
for the first time since martial law began. The Warsaw regime finally
agreed to register a church-linked farm foundation, and Whitehead indicated that up to $10 million in American funds might be provided for
this purpose. Concurrently, the Rockefeller Brothers Fund developed
another program to aid Polish private agriculture. But when in May a
new wave of strikes led to the forceful intervention of the militia at the
Nowa Huta steel works, Washington put further consideration of economic aid "on hold." The United States, said a White House spokesman,
strongly urged the government to "begin a productive dialogue with all

segments of Polish society, including Solidarity," and the Senate proceeded to pass a resolution condemning the Jaruzelski regime.[152] Western insistence on the need for national reconciliation as a precondition to economic aid remained firm.

That message was impressed on Polish Foreign Minister Tadeusz Olechowski on the occasion of his visit to Washington in July 1988. Secretary of State Shultz told him that "the potential exists in your country for bold steps, maybe great and historic steps, that would capture the imagination of Europe and the world. The people and government of the United States are ready to respond."[153] Another wave of strikes in August finally persuaded Jaruzelski that vital domestic and foreign support required such bold steps. It fell to the Bush administration to respond to the resulting radical transformation of the Polish political climate.

Bush Moves beyond Containment. The foreign policy review of the new administration showed unprecedented challenges and opportunities in East-West relations. Reform in Eastern Europe and the Soviet Union and Gorbachev's diplomatic offensive in Western Europe, including arms control proposals that threatened to divide NATO, demanded American leadership and initiative. In his first major address on these issues, delivered at Texas A & M University on May 12, 1989, President Bush declared that containment had worked but the time had come to move beyond it. The United States, he said, "now has as its goal much more than simply containing Soviet expansionism—we seek the integration of the Soviet Union into the community of nations." He called upon the Soviets to reduce their military forces, cooperate in solving regional disputes and other global problems, "achieve a lasting political pluralism and respect for human rights" at home, and adhere to the obligation incurred at Yalta by abandoning the Brezhnev Doctrine.[154]

Two weeks later, speaking in Mainz, West Germany, the president elaborated four proposals to "heal Europe's tragic division." The first was to

strengthen and broaden the Helsinki process to promote free elections and political pluralism in Eastern Europe. As the forces of freedom and democracy rise in the East, so should our expectations. And weaving together the slender threads of freedom will require much from the Western democracies. In particular, the great political parties of the West must assume an historic responsibility

—to lend counsel and support to those brave men and women who are trying to form the first truly representative political parties in the East, to advance freedom and democracy, to part the Iron Curtain.

His second proposal was to "bring *glasnost* to Berlin," to turn the city into a center of East-West commerce. The third, to work together on environmental problems. And the fourth, to bring about a less militarized Europe through "solid, verifiable agreements" between the two alliances (see chapter 6).[155]

In the meantime, roundtable talks between the Warsaw regime and Solidarity had produced an accord on more democratic elections. This development accelerated the administration's policy review concerning Eastern Europe. Hailing the accords as "a watershed in the postwar history of Eastern Europe," Bush outlined a modest and conditional economic aid package:

If Poland's experiment succeeds, other countries may follow. And while we must still differentiate among the nations of astern Europe, Poland offers two lessons for all. First, there can be no progress without significant political and economic liberalization. And second, help from the West will come in concert with liberalization. Our friends and European allies share this philosophy. . . . The Soviet Union should understand . . . that a free democratic Eastern Europe as we envision it would threaten no one and no country.[156]

In its reformulation of the policy of differentiation, the Bush administration displayed a judicious blend of optimism and prudence. With regard to aid, it stressed conditionality and collective Western responsibility. And it continued to insist that overcoming the division of Europe did not entail a threat to Soviet security. All this had been said before; what had changed was the political climate in the Soviet Union and some of its dependencies and in Western Europe.

The West Europeans rose to the challenge by adopting a "global, consistent and dynamic approach" toward Eastern Europe. The EC Commission's president, Jacques Delors, and the Belgian foreign minister, Leo Tindemans, had argued the case for a coordinated policy within the European Community, and on April 24, the EC foreign ministers agreed to this experiment in political cooperation.[157] Emulating the American strategy of differentiation, they decided to put a trade accord with Poland on the fast track and to formally suspend the already faltering trade negotiations with Romania because of the latter's human rights violations.

Gorbachev offered increasingly explicit reassurances about the scope for autonomous change in Eastern Europe. "How the Polish people and the Hungarian people will decide to structure their societies and lives will be their affair," he said at a news conference with President Mitterrand on July 5, as the triumphant Solidarity was about to take its place in the Polish parliament; the "right to free election is . . . of vital importance." To be sure, he anticipated that reform would give socialism a second wind and, speaking earlier at the Sorbonne, cautioned the West against expecting Eastern Europe to "return to the capitalist fold" and "cultivating the illusion that only bourgeois society represents eternal values." But there was no hint of the Brezhnev Doctrine in his address to the Council of Europe in Strasbourg the next day:

> Social and political orders in one country or another changed in the past and may change in the future. But this change is the exclusive affair of the people of that country and is their choice. Any interference in domestic affairs and any attempts to restrict the sovereignty of states—friends, allies or any others—are inadmissible.[158]

Indeed, a remarkable harmony seemed to prevail between Washington and Moscow over the developments in Eastern Europe. After his visits to Poland and Hungary, President Bush took pains to give Gorbachev credit, indicating that he had told his interlocutors, "We are not here to poke a stick in the eye of Mr. Gorbachev—just the opposite, to encourage the very kind of reforms that he is championing, and more reforms." And Gorbachev, for his part, reportedly conveyed to the administration his appreciation for its relative restraint in responding to the changes and clamor for aid in the East.[159]

Washington's message to the East Europeans had to be finely tuned to reinforce the reform process without offending Moscow and arousing unrealistic expectations of Western assistance. "I don't want to overpromise, do too little or too much," said the president on his way to Warsaw on July 9.[160] Accordingly, the president found a friendly but sober welcome in Warsaw and Budapest in July. He evenhandedly praised Jaruzelski and Walesa and stressed that there could be no substitute for Poland's own efforts at recovery, though the United States "stands ready to help, as you help yourselves."[161] The proffered aid was modest indeed, although Congress would eventually increase it (see chapter 5).

The Temptation of Disengagement. It became evident that Washington was passing the torch to the West Europeans at the economic summit in Paris immediately following the President's East European tour. Poland and Hungary dominated the Group of Seven's agenda, and it was decided to charge the European Commission with coordinating aid. For long the Americans had been the strongest political advocates of Eastern Europe's emancipation, and the West Germans economically the most engaged in the region. Since the West Europeans were destined to bear most of the burden of direct aid and debt rescheduling, and in order to spare the Kremlin's sensibilities, it made diplomatic sense to superficially depoliticize the West's response by enhancing the role of the European Community.

In fact, George Kennan, the father of containment and the Marshall Plan, responded to the East European revolution by counseling U.S. disengagement. He told the Senate Foreign Relations Committee on January 19, 1990:

The problems of the designing of a new political and economic relationship of the Eastern European countries to the remainder of Europe is primarily one for the Europeans themselves to confront, and I see no reason why we should take any prominent part in it. Let the other Europeans draw up their own plan, and implement it with such of their own resources as they can spare for it. If we can help in minor subsidiary ways, so much the better; but the initiative, the responsibility, and the main burden of implementation must be theirs.[162]

To be sure, Kennan advocates continuing American involvement in the creation of a new security structure for Europe, but he generally supports a much less active concern for this troublesome region.

America's interest in Eastern Europe appears on the decline at the same time as that of the Soviet Union, a coincidence that confirms transcendence of the policy and reality of containment by a new process of regional reintegration. If in the short run differentiation brought some disappointments, notably in Poland and Romania, it was because distant America's leverage was but a minor factor in the calculations of determined Soviet and other dictators. The bridges that had been built reached nations more than they reached individual governments. Until Soviet power turned more benign, Washington's peaceful engagement served mainly to sustain the promise of eventual reintegration.

How far American policy had moved beyond containment was vividly revealed in the midst of the Romanian revolution, when on Christmas Eve, 1989, Secretary of State James A. Baker declared that the United States would welcome a Warsaw Pact military intervention in aid of the reformist forces.[163] (French Foreign Minister Roland Dumas had similarly urged Soviet or Western intervention.) In the event, the Soviet Union remained aloof, and the Ceausescu dictatorship fell without external aid. Baker's invitation might have seemed disingenuous in light of the concurrent U.S. "police action" to seize Panama's General Manuel Noriega, but it reflected the administration's judgment that Gorbachev's Soviet Union had become a force for democratization and self-determination in Eastern Europe.

American official and popular interest in Eastern Europe has tended to wax at moments of crisis and wane in times of detente. Yet the potential and need for engagement as well as the leverage is far greater in the latter than in the former circumstance. As the Soviet empire disintegrates, the East Europeans' need grows for help in developing stable democracy, productive economies, and closer association with the West. Their success will depend in part on the will and ability of the Bush administration as the stimulus of the Soviet threat disappears. Conditionality will become more difficult to calibrate, and the resurgent nationalisms will test diplomatic impartiality.

The speed of democratization in Eastern Europe outpaced Western expectations, and the Bush administration suffered some criticism for the alleged timidity of its response. "We don't need to be out there trying to micromanage the desire for change in these countries," retorted the president; "we want to be ready and available . . . to help financially, if we don't go broke in the process."[164] The consolidation of change would require more than money, for, as Ronald Reagan observed on the fortieth anniversary of Yalta, the freedom of Europe was unfinished business. As America and its allies began to devise the architecture of post-cold-war Europe, the East's initial euphoria over its escape from socialist authoritarianism was rapidly dissipating in the face of grim economic realities. After the sacrifice of generations on the altar of Communist utopia, the new democracies faced the prospect of demanding more sacrifice for the distant rewards of the free market.

The East Europeans' recognition that their newfound freedom owed much to America's unflagging crusade was vividly displayed in the official expressions of gratitude that greeted former President Reagan on his visits to East Berlin and Warsaw in September 1990. But freedom offered no guarantee against political turbulence as conflicting economic demands and interethnic rivalries began to reappear. In the spheres of human rights, economic rehabilitation, and regional as well as continental security, explored in the remaining chapters, many tasks awaited America and its allies. Recognition of these necessities and opportunities prompted in mid-1990 the naming of Deputy Secretary of State Lawrence S. Eagleburger as coordinator of U.S. assistance to Eastern Europe and plans to shift nearly eighty State Department positions to the region. Containment had paid off; the potentially most constructive phase of peaceful engagement was only beginning.

4

Human Rights

The principle of inalienable individual freedoms is deeply rooted in the American political culture, as is the belief that these freedoms have universal validity. Ideological universalism has been a constant factor in the U.S. world outlook, confirmed by force of example as well as by active engagement of the Wilsonian variety. In modern times, the powerful popular appeal of human rights has induced regimes of all colors to seek legitimacy by professing to respect them or to seek their realization. But much as the notion of democracy, or rule by the will and consent of the majority, has been debased in its appropriation by countless authoritarian regimes, so have human rights been used and misused to fit other ideological preconceptions and formulas for political power.

Contending philosophical approaches and tactical accommodations continue to confuse and devalue human rights, yet never before has the concept enjoyed such prominence and power in international and national political life. For this, the United States deserves a large share of the credit. To be sure, many compromises have been made and many abuses condoned or ignored; as the United States acquired increasingly global interests, human rights considerations were often subordinated to calculations of security and political advantage. But in the ideological contest of the cold war, the clear and consistent advocacy of human

157

rights was targeted on the Communist world, and for Washington, Eastern Europe became the prime battleground.

That human beings possess natural rights not bestowed by temporal authority or dependent on time and circumstance was a belief affirmed and elaborated by political philosophers of the Enlightenment, notably Locke, Montesquieu, and Rousseau.[1] The rights to life, liberty, and property require recognition of certain civil and political rights. No regime can claim to rule by consent if it fails to guarantee the right of emigration. No rights are secure without the rule of law, which demands an independent and neutral judiciary. The right to the rule of law implies a constitutional order in which the citizen is free to express and propagate his views, to choose and recall his legislative representatives, and to have recourse to safeguards against the abuse of political power.

The moral universalism of this liberal doctrine came under challenge from both Marxism and a relativist tendency to treat the hierarchy of rights as contingent on material and cultural circumstance. In keeping with their economic determinism and class dogma, Marxists have dismissed the rights of man as a self-serving invention of the bourgeoisie designed to protect its privileged status, property, and freedom to exploit the majority. Human rights, in the Marxian view, are inseparable from class, and the only legitimate rights are those of the proletariat as it realizes its historically preordained mission. Individual rights derive from, and are subordinated to, the collective rights and obligations vested in class membership and articulated by the political vanguard of that class, the Communist party.

The Marxian and relativist approaches to the problem of rights come together in their dogmatic or expedient focus on the satisfaction of material desires. To be sure, man has certain irreducible needs for physical survival, for security, health, and subsistence, and it would be absurd to insist that political and civil rights take precedence over these essential claims. But the elevation of open-ended economic, social, and cultural desires to the status of entitlements or "rights" makes a mockery of the principle that universal rights are natural, inalienable, concrete, and enforceable. That principle can, however, be sustained in the case of political and civil rights. Freedom of speech, for example, can be unambiguously codified and enforced in all societies regardless of their material circumstances. The "right" to sanitation, on the other hand, is simply one of a multiplicity of social needs among which, given the scarcity of resources, hard choices have to be made.

The so-called social, economic, and cultural rights are therefore not analogous to fundamental freedoms. By invoking economic and social rights, however, the state legitimizes a theoretically unlimited degree of intervention in the private sphere to marshal human resources for the benefit of others. The individual's right to liberty thus becomes a contingent rather than a primary claim. The primacy of political and civil rights, on the other hand, allows for a participatory process in which the individual can articulate his personal desires and social values, thereby influencing the choice of priorities in the allocation of communal resources. A direct threat to national security or some other crisis may require the temporary suspension of political and civil rights without denial of their immanent validity and supremacy. Their permanent, doctrinal subordination, however, demeans the dignity of the individual by turning him into a politically impotent subject.

By vesting freedoms in the individual rather than in society, the liberal doctrine of natural rights affirms the essentially pluralistic nature of human communities. It follows that the political organization of these communities must aggregate and serve multiple interests without violating individual basic rights. From this perspective, democratic process is less a right than an instrument for the preservation of the rights to life, liberty, and property, and for this purpose the optimal political system is based on pluralistic representation and government limited by law as well as by institutional checks and balances.[2]

The diffusion of human rights by force of moral example and through international institutions was advocated by Kant and many others as the road to "perpetual peace." As long as the rights of man were not universally recognized and respected, the anarchic nature of international relations threatened the liberties and security of those who had secured them within their own society. Moral conviction aside, therefore, enlightened self-interest militates in favor of active diffusion of human rights and their instrumental corollaries. Ironically, the first attempt to realize the Kantian vision, the League of Nations, coincided with the greatest historical challenge to the liberal doctrine of human rights, that of the institutionalization of Marxism, transformed by Lenin into a doctrine of state power and world revolution. America's timorous abandonment of Wilsonian internationalism further weakened the impact of the fragile and partial moral consensus that had emerged. The global confrontation inaugurated by Lenin's triumph pitted a distorted Marxian version of human rights against the liberal belief, and totalitarian government against limited government.

Other totalitarian and authoritarian regimes have come and gone, but only in the late 1980s did the Marxist-Leninist construct begin to crumble. The philosophical distinctions between the Marxist and liberal doctrines were accommodated without being directly addressed in the 1948 Universal Declaration of Human Rights, a nonbinding enshrinement of political and civil rights that also made reference to economic and social rights. Disagreement over the primacy of rights between the West on one side and Marxist as well as the growing number of third world regimes on the other persisted, and the outcome in 1966 was two United Nations International Covenants, one on civil and political rights and another on economic, social, and cultural rights. By mixing rights, needs, and welfare-state objectives, the declaration and the covenants lend themselves to selective application and dilute the principle of fundamental liberties.[3]

This dilution impelled Congress to take a position that some construed as inconsistent with America's human rights advocacy. The U.S. Constitution includes treaties among the supreme laws of the land, and the Senate therefore refused to ratify the covenants (and the enforcement provisions in the Optional Protocol and Optional Article) on the grounds that they intrude into the sphere of domestic legislation. The Carter administration, sensitive to the apparent contradiction between these reservations and its human rights campaign, tried without success to accommodate the legalistic objections to ratification. Since the covenants were not backed by an authentic international moral consensus and were practically unenforceable, the Senate's refusal to ratify them was understandable if also embarrassing to the administration. In the final analysis, as Assistant Secretary of State Richard Schifter observed in March 1988, "our total effort in the human rights field is not seriously impeded at the present time by our failure to have ratified the human rights covenants."[4]

Self-Determination and Eastern Europe. Although a democracy's foreign policy should aspire to at least a degree of idealism, traditional diplomacy shied away from addressing human rights in other sovereign states. The United States and, more briefly, revolutionary France, broke with this tradition. America's anti-imperial ethos prevailed in policy toward Europe's overseas dependencies and produced spontaneous sympathy for the republican and nationalist revolutions that shook the imperial order of Central Europe in the mid-nineteenth century. Hungary's Lajos Kossuth, leader of the failed revolution against Habsburg rule, received an enthusiastic welcome in the United States. The Democrats' Young America movement of that time called for the abandonment of neutralism and the active propagation of republicanism throughout the world.

America's own imperial drive in the late nineteenth century was rationalized in terms of ideological universalism, a belief the rest of the world would benefit from the adoption of American values. At the end of World War I, Woodrow Wilson's Fourteen Points invoked the universality of "the principle of justice to all peoples and nationalities, and their right to live on equal terms of liberty and safety with one another, whether they be strong or weak." The application of Wilson's prescription of national self-determination for the Poles and other East Europeans was flawed by many a political compromise, and America's hasty return to isolation undermined the capability of the League of Nations to preserve the new, imperfect order.

Advocacy of the right to national self-determination remained the principal manifestation of the human rights element in U.S. foreign policy, notably in the Atlantic Charter and the Yalta Declaration on Liberated Europe. In his Four Freedoms appeal, President Roosevelt evoked the classical liberal principles of human rights by specifying freedom of speech and expression, and freedom of worship, and appended the more problematical freedoms from want and from fear. He later added that neither in America nor in the rest of the world could true individual freedom exist without economic security and independence. This stretching of the liberal rights doctrine reflected Roosevelt's ideological preferences as well as the mood of the times, but it did not alter the precedence of political and civil rights, which Washington affirmed implicitly as well as explicitly in its advocacy of self-determination for the East European nations.

The political clauses of the peace treaties with Hitler's former allies enjoined them to guarantee human rights and fundamental freedoms, "including freedom of expression, of press and publication, of religious worship, of political opinion and of public meeting." These clauses, observed George Kennan, a foe of idealism in foreign policy, "we know full well will never be implemented" in the countries occupied by the Soviet Union.[5] They nevertheless reflected America's disposition to legitimate foreign intrusion into the domestic sphere of human rights. To be sure, the United States also actively pursued economic objectives that were in its immediate commercial interest—free trade, multilateralism, security of foreign investment, and freedom of navigation on the Danube. Still, America's tangible economic stake in Eastern Europe was minimal and could hardly be regarded as a hidden materialistic motive for advocacy of political and civil rights.

Moralism in the Cold War.   The new "people's democracies" copied the Soviet approach by enumerating in their own constitutions a commendably comprehensive list of rights, subordinated to the pursuit of social revolution. The judiciary was enjoined to apply laws in defense of socialism. General political rights were qualified by the leading role of the Communist party. While the class struggle officially had been brought to a successful conclusion in the Soviet Union, East Europeans were still in the midst of it, and therefore "class enemies" were legally deprived of political and civil rights. Rights were contingent on corresponding obligations; citizens had the duty as well as the right to work, and to espouse socialism in return for its benefits. Since law was regarded as an instrument of revolution, socialist legality in the Stalinist period was the will of the party, in practice of the ruling oligarchy. Arbitrary arrests, torture and imprisonment, massive deportations and compulsory resettlement, the seizure of private property, prohibition of emigration, discrimination in employment, education, and housing on grounds of class and political or religious belief, the practical elimination of freedom of speech and association all flouted elemental notions of human rights. In theory, the party was the servant of the working masses and "substituted" for the latter in managing revolutionary change. In reality, the Stalinist political system totally subordinated the individual to the capricious will of the "workers' vanguard."

As the Soviet-imposed experiment in totalitarian social engineering began to unfold behind the iron curtain, the United States found itself reduced to ineffective professions of moral outrage. American and UN protests at violations of the human rights and demilitarization clauses of the Bulgarian, Hungarian, and Romanian peace treaties were countered by satellite ruling party claims (endorsed by the Soviet Union) of domestic jurisdiction; the State Department observed fruitlessly that "persecution of all political leaders and parties not amenable to the dictates of the minority ruling group and denial of freedom of expression cannot properly be justified under any Article of the Treaty."[6] Finally, the United States and its allies at the United Nations resorted to blocking the admission of these three countries (as well as Albania), and the Soviet Union reciprocated by blocking Western applicants. The logjam of twenty-one states awaiting admission was finally broken in a package deal at the end of 1955, American acquiescence in the case of the satellites taking the form of abstention.

Violations of human rights in Eastern Europe were grist to the mills of the Voice of America and Radio Free Europe. The Truman Doctrine's offer to "assist free peoples to work out their destinies in their own way" did not directly apply to the already-captive East Europeans, but Dean Acheson observed in 1950 that the United States would "maintain undiminished its concern for their rights and their welfare," and the affirmation of human rights was a central task of psychological warfare.[7] Behind the iron curtain, recalled Truman in his 1952 State of the Union address, "minorities are being oppressed, human rights violated, religions persecuted. We should continue and expand the activities of the Voice of America, which brings our message of hope and truth to those peoples."[8] Later in that presidential election year, John Foster Dulles developed the GOP's liberation policy plank, calling for a "great new Declaration of Independence" on behalf of the East Europeans and invoking natural law: "We should be dynamic, we should use ideas as weapons; and these ideas should conform to moral principles."[9]

America's moral high ground with respect to Eastern Europe was shored up by legalistic reminders of the allies' wartime pledge of self-determination. The Soviet Union and its allies routinely protested at such verbal interference in their internal affairs. Washington maintained diplomatic relations with the satellite regimes but at the same time denied their claim to autonomy and popular legitimacy, thereby reserving the right to champion the political and civil rights of their subjects. From the founding of the Comintern forward, the Soviet Union had

scarcely respected the conventions of sovereignty and political impermeability, and the United States, having assumed ideological leadership of
the "free world," felt free to reciprocate.

To champion the entitlement of East Europeans to self-determination
and other liberties was good politics, particularly in the domestic arena,
but it was no substitute for an operational policy. As Vice President
Nixon explained lamely after the Hungarian revolution, "Our only weapon
here was moral condemnation, since the alternative was action on our
part which might initiate the third and ultimate world war." [10] America's
advocacy of human rights in Eastern Europe was fundamentally sound
and honest but constrained by considerations of national security. To
reconcile idealism and realism is the unhappy but necessary task of
democratic statesmen, and the inevitable compromises that are made
almost invariably incur the wrath of idealists, or realists, or both.

A chastened Eisenhower administration rode out the storm of criticism by concentrating its fire at the United Nations on the Soviet Union
and its new client regime in Hungary. The latter was deprived of full
membership rights at the United Nations, and for years the "question of
Hungary" regularly reappeared on the General Assembly's agenda. Finally, in 1963, after the Kadar regime had begun to show more liberal
tendencies and had amnestied most political prisoners, the General Assembly approved one last time an American-sponsored resolution calling
for the withdrawal of Soviet troops and the restoration of basic human
rights, and the matter was laid to rest.

Succeeding administrations had little choice but to profess faith in
evolutionary change in Eastern Europe and to selectively offer inducements and rewards. The Hungarian tragedy confirmed the division of
Europe, but de-Stalinization promised to allow the East European regimes greater latitude in courting domestic popularity. For Washington,
there remained the chronic problem of how to normalize relations and
gain leverage over regimes that were regarded as fundamentally illegiti-
mate and less than autonomous. Moral absolutism did not facilitate
diplomatic flexibility. In July 1959, Congress unanimously approved the
Captive Nations Resolution, which denounced the "enslavement" of
millions by Communist imperialism and requested that the president
designate a "Captive Nations Week" of prayers for the enslaved peoples,
to be repeated annually "until such time as freedom and independence
shall have been achieved for all the captive nations of the world."

Khrushchev commented: "This resolution stinks." [11] Nevertheless, Captive Nations Week (the third week in July) became a perennial fixture on the American political calendar.

Detente Diplomacy and Human Rights. The logic of the strategy of peaceful engagement was compelling, and its intellectual guardians tried to reconcile idealism and realism by arguing that disapproval of the status quo did not preclude pragmatic efforts to improve bilateral relations. [12] To be sure, the language of congressional politics was blunter than the language of diplomacy, and the satellite regimes bridled at reminders that they enslaved their subjects. Faced with the Proxmire-Lausche initiative in June 1962 aiming to restrict United States economic aid to Yugoslavia and Poland, Secretary of State Dean Rusk felt compelled to reaffirm that the United States was not "permanently writing off to Soviet domination" the East Europeans. [13] And when the Polish ambassador complained about a speech by Arthur Goldberg criticizing his government's repression of religious freedom, Rusk's soothing response was, "Mr. Ambassador, could you perhaps allow us some fifteen percent of our speech-making for domestic purposes? We allow a much larger percentage for yours." [14]

Although the principle of self-determination remained common coin in American domestic political discourse, the gradualist approach required that it be toned down in the conduct of foreign relations. In the era of detente and arms control negotiation, it became counterproductive to belabor the obvious. For the West, detente diplomacy subsumed the expectation, or rather the hope, that liberalization in Eastern Europe would progress peacefully. The Warsaw Pact invasion of Czechoslovakia momentarily dispelled these illusions. "Socialism with a human face" unleashed nationalistic and libertarian impulses that the Kremlin would not condone. The Brezhnev Doctrine affirmed that the interests of the socialist camp and of the world revolutionary movement took precedence over the sovereignty of individual socialist states. Dean Rusk protested that "what they are asking us to accept is that in this 'Socialist commonwealth' the Soviet Union has the right to use its armed forces to determine what happens inside independent countries, and that is very difficult for the rest of us to accept." [15] But the brutal suppression of the Czechoslovaks' right to self-determination and the reimposition of a despotic regime proved to be a passing disturbance as far as the flow of detente diplomacy was concerned.

Human rights advocacy was out of tune with the realpolitik style of the Nixon administration. At his confirmation hearing in 1973, Henry Kissinger warned that "it is dangerous for us to make the domestic policy of countries around the world a direct objective of American foreign policy." [16] It is all the more ironic, then, that the entrenchment of human rights on the world agenda would become the shining legacy of a conference that the administration joined with great diffidence. In Kissinger's linkage approach to East-West relations, the European security conference persistently advocated by the Soviets since 1953 was a price to pay for progress on higher United States priorities, notably talks on mutual and balanced force reductions. [17] The Kremlin's campaign reinforced suspicion that such a conference could only serve its interest in legitimating its political predominance in Eastern Europe and in weakening the cohesion of the Western alliance. On the other hand, Washington's relative neglect of Europe in the Vietnam years and its preference for bilateral negotiation with the Soviets had created (in Kissinger's words) "enormous eagerness" on the part of the West European allies for such a conference.

The "Declaration on Basic Principles of United States-Soviet Relations," signed by Nixon and Brezhnev at the Moscow summit in May 1972, made repeated reference to non-interference in internal affairs but did not mention human rights. Kissinger considered public confrontation with the Soviets over human rights to be counterproductive, and indeed Jewish emigration rose in this period of traditional diplomacy. Paradoxically, it was America's NATO allies who now championed human rights and humanitarian diplomacy and deplored Washington's low-profile approach to these issues.

The European Security Conference. Notwithstanding Washington's reservations, the European allies and nonaligned participants were eager to engage in this unprecedented diplomatic review of the political state of the continent. The Conference on Security and Cooperation in Europe (CSCE) has been described as a "minimal Concert of Europe and North America," a "surrogate World War II peace treaty," and the "high water mark of the detente era." [18] It was, in fact, an extraordinarily laborious exercise in the superficial accommodation of conflicting interests. Its novelty lay in its inclusiveness with regard to both participation and terms of reference. The thirty-five participants included all the states of Europe except Albania as well as the United States and Canada; the agenda ranged from security to economic relations and human contacts.

The Soviet Union wanted a symbolic, multilateral confirmation of the political and territorial status quo as well as easier access to Western markets and technology. The Kremlin hoped for a quick conference leading to a concise endorsement of the inviolability of frontiers (meaning the permanent division of Germany) and the political impermeability of Eastern Europe. The West, on the other hand, wanted to preserve the possibility of peaceful change and political evolution in the Soviet sphere, the West Europeans being particularly keen to consolidate detente by the normalization of relations in all spheres. Arguably, the fundamental conflict was over the legitimacy and immutability of the Brezhnev Doctrine.

The great achievement of the CSCE was to firmly entrench human rights on the international diplomatic agenda, thereby subverting traditional notions of sovereignty. This achievement did not come easily. The Soviet Union, though ready to raise human rights issues when it suited its interests, notably in South Africa, fought vigorously against this tendency, extending the principle of nonintervention (which denotes aggression) to noninterference in the domestic affairs of sovereign states. In the initial debates on principles, the Soviet delegate argued that human rights were not relevant to interstate relations and that self-determination was not an issue in Europe.[19] The Warsaw Pact position was that social justice formed the basis of individual freedom, that these matters were wholly within domestic jurisdiction, and that communication and contact across borders were dependent on the foreign policy interests of states.

It was not the United States, with the oldest tradition of idealism in foreign policy, that introduced the case for linking individual rights and the freer movement of people and ideas to international security in the CSCE, but France and Italy. In Washington, a damage-limiting strategy overshadowed the potentiality of human rights advocacy. Kissinger questioned the utility of making progress in detente contingent on domestic reform in the Soviet sphere.[20] By default, then, it was mainly the

European Community members who developed and promoted the proposals on easier human contacts and freer flow of information (known in CSCE lingo as "Basket Three" proposals; the issues under negotiation at the CSCE were grouped into three "baskets," with the first two encompassing security and economic matters respectively), while the Americans urged caution and "greater realism."[21]

Apart from the question of inviolability of frontiers, with its implications for the German problem, human rights proved the most troublesome.[22] The requirement of unanimity made for protracted semantic debate; it took a subcommittee fifty-six sittings over three months to reach a lowest common denominator formulation of human rights. The Soviets countered Western pressure on human rights by stressing the principle of nonintervention in internal affairs. They also tried, unsuccessfully, to render Basket Three commitments virtually meaningless by subordinating them to the "laws and customs of the participating states."[23] The Warsaw Pact strategy was to go for broad rather than detailed directives, for institutional cooperation rather than individual contacts, and for facilitating only communication that "strengthens peace and security."[24] But external developments reinforced the new salience of human rights. On September 17, 1973 the United States Senate unanimously passed a resolution invoking the Universal Declaration of Human Rights and calling on Moscow to allow free circulation of ideas and emigration. In the Soviet Union, leading dissidents Alexander Solzhenitsyn and Andrei Sakharov issued public pleas for intellectual freedom. The relative mildness of the sanction (arrest and expulsion) against Solzhenitsyn in February 1974 was perhaps attributable to the CSCE.

Initially, Kissinger remained aloof from the CSCE, and the American delegation tried to avoid a confrontation with the Soviets that might draw the secretary of state into that diplomatic arena. But as United States-Soviet relations took a turn for the worse and domestic hostility to the CSCE grew, Kissinger took the lead in pressing the West's case. His interventions with Soviet foreign minister Andrei Gromyko in February 1975 in Geneva and in May in Vienna helped to break impasses over the inviolability of frontiers and provision for peaceful change, as well as the human contacts and information sections of Basket Three. The Soviets were in a hurry to end the conference, and a trade-off in compromises over Baskets One and Three allowed the CSCE to conclude with the ceremonial signing of the Final Act on August 1, 1975.

The Helsinki Final Act. The Final Act, characterized by Poland's Edward Gierek as the "Magna Carta of inter-European relations," did not have the binding force of a treaty.[25] It represented, rather, a minimal diplomatic compromise on the desirable parameters of relations among the participants. The need for consensus had produced artfully vague and often ambiguous formulations that invited selective emphasis and interpretation. The Declaration on Principles enjoined the signatories to "respect each other's right freely to choose and develop its political, social, economic and cultural systems." Principle VII invited respect for "human rights and fundamental freedoms, including the freedom of thought, conscience, religion or belief"; the signatories, it went on, "will promote and encourage the effective exercise of civil, political, economic, social, cultural and other rights and freedoms all of which derive from the inherent dignity of the human person and are essential for his free and full development," and "confirm the right of the individual to know and act upon his rights and duties in this field."

The issue of minority rights had divided both East and West, resulting in anodyne statements of the right of national minorities to equality before the law and the recommendation (in Basket Three) that their cultural contribution to international cooperation be facilitated. Basket Three also provided for "cooperation in humanitarian and other fields." The recommended practices—facilitation of travel, family reunification, freedom of information, better working conditions for journalists, dissemination of foreign cultural products—laid the greatest burden of adaptation on the socialist states.

The reiteration of conventional human rights principles was less significant than the provision that the signatories "endeavor jointly and separately . . . to promote universal and effective respect for them." The message was clear: the rights of individual citizens were no longer a purely domestic political matter but also a valid issue of international relations linked to security. Thus, the Final Act went well beyond the exhortation of the UN Declaration in legitimating external scrutiny of national human rights practices.

The conversion of the CSCE into an ongoing "process" offered a framework for such scrutiny. Originally the Warsaw Pact had envisaged the creation of a permanent advisory body to institutionalize pan-European consultation on security matters, an idea that aroused no enthusiasm in the West. But as human rights and free movement of people became issues central to the CSCE, the positions were reversed, with the Soviet Union hostile to and the West more supportive of a permanent forum to follow up on implementation of the Final Act. Significantly, some of the smaller Warsaw Pact countries—especially Romania—welcomed the presumption of autonomy bestowed upon them by the CSCE and were less hostile than the Soviet Union to a follow-up process that would enhance their image as independent states. They would not have welcomed the prospect of international scrutiny of their domestic human rights conduct. Yet the continuing multilateral review finally agreed to was destined to greatly enhance the prominence of human rights in East-West relations.

President Ford observed at the signing of the Final Act that history would judge the CSCE not by the promises made but by the promises kept. Few anticipated the enormous impact that it would have on the process and substance of East-West relations. The low-level style of negotiation that characterized most of the CSCE had perhaps facilitated Soviet verbal concessions on human rights, but it also failed to draw the attention of the mass media and the public. Much to Moscow's delight, the prevalent judgment in the West, reminiscent of the Yalta myth, was that the Soviet Union had won on points by securing solemn confirmation of the political status quo in Europe. "No journey I made during my Presidency was so widely misunderstood," recalls Ford in his memoirs.[26]

In fact, the West had conceded nothing in the affirmation of the inviolability of frontiers, regardless of the cosmetic clause on peaceful change. The few who took the trouble to read the Final Act realized that the diplomatic wall behind which socialist regimes freely violated political and civil rights had been breached, and that the liberal principle of individual liberties had gained at the expense of the socialist premise of collective rights.

The perception that the CSCE reflected tacit American acquiescence in Soviet hegemony over Eastern Europe and a passive approach to human rights in the region was unwittingly reinforced in the last year of the Ford administration, notably in the flap over the mythical "Sonnenfeldt Doctrine" (see chapter 3). To be sure, the Kissinger version of differentiation stressed foreign policy deviation and not human rights. This perception was inadvertently reinforced by Ford in his election debate in October 1976, when he affirmed that there was no Soviet domination of Eastern Europe. Retorted Jimmy Carter: "I would like to see Mr. Ford convince the Polish-Americans and the Czech-Americans and the Hungarian-Americans in this country that those countries don't live under the domination and the supervision of the Soviet Union behind the Iron Curtain."[27] What Ford meant was that the United States treated the East European regimes as sovereign in order to encourage them to become more independent, but he managed to sound legalistic and politically naive. In the event, the genie of human rights had been let out of its diplomatic bottle, and as detente waned the United States was drawn into a moral crusade whose time had come.

Domestic Battle over the Radio Services. Ironically, the most tangible and sustained manifestation of America's commitment to human rights in Eastern Europe almost failed to survive into the Helsinki era. After the trauma of 1956, Radio Free Europe was recast into a less propagandistic medium, with emphasis on professionalism in news and research. What a former director called the "romantic-heroic period" was over, but RFE, styling itself a surrogate home service for the East Europeans, continued to serve as a conduit for accurate information and varied opinion that were lacking in the official and exclusive media.[28] Although article 19 of the UN Declaration of Human Rights enshrined the right "to receive and impart information and ideas through any media regardless of frontier," the Soviet and East European governments ceaselessly denounced Radio Liberty and Radio Free Europe as threats to peace. They broke international conventions by systematic (though not officially acknowledged) jamming, both ground wave and sky wave, at a cost that surpassed that of the radios. Jamming of other Western radios such as the VOA and the BBC was relaxed, then reimposed after the invasion of Czechoslovakia. Hungary and Romania suspended jamming in the 1960s, although at least in the case of the latter listening to foreign broadcasts remained a punishable offense. The electronic curtain was less effective in rural areas and in the period of atmospheric "twilight immunity," and Radio Free Europe continued to reach an audience of some thirty million.

In February 1967, *Ramparts* magazine disclosed that from its inception, RFE had been financed by the CIA, the money being channeled through dummy and legitimate foundations to the National Security Agency. Although President Johnson had some doubts about the radios' effectiveness, the administration was not prepared to liquidate them. A special committee chaired by Under Secretary of State Nicholas Katzenbach concluded that the radios continued to serve United States foreign policy interests. General Lucius Clay was brought back to head the Free Europe Committee while CIA Director Richard Helms struggled to convince the responsible congressional committees that if the radios' private status was a deception, they were nevertheless "government proprietaries" eligible for covert CIA funding.[29]

The cover-up was initially successful, but in January 1971, Senator Clifford Case made the revelation official and denounced the deception of Congress, of American taxpayers, and of the donors to the erstwhile Crusade for Freedom. The real leader of the attack was Senator William J. Fulbright, who characterized the radios as "outworn relics of the cold war" and seemed obsessively intent on shutting them down. A protracted battle ensued involving supporters and detractors in Congress as well as the administration. A reluctant State Department assumed temporary guardianship, and emergency funding kept the radios alive while alternative administrative and financing scenarios were debated and President Nixon appointed a study commission, chaired by Milton S. Eisenhower, to report by February 28, 1973. Fulbright's next spoiling tactic was to demand West European contributions. While the radios had some tacit support among the allies, they were not about to help finance them.

The Eisenhower Commission concluded that "the broadcasts of Radio Free Europe and Radio Liberty had not deterred but rather contributed to the search for long-term detente." Nonetheless, there remained the question of ensuring that the radios would operate "in a manner not inconsistent with broad United States foreign policy."[30] The hypothetical option of allied cosponsorship, with the consequent multiple accountability, entailed risks for the radios' professional independence and was rejected. The commission recommended federal financing by annual congressional appropriations channelled through a new, quasi-governmental agency—the Board for International Broadcasting, appointed by the president—that would exercise oversight but free the radios from direct government control. This was duly enacted in Public Law 93–129 on October 19, 1973. President Carter's human rights crusade encompassed free flow of information, and his report on international broadcasting, submitted to Congress March 22, 1977, confirmed the value of RFE and RL (as well as the VOA) and recommended new transmitters.[31] The radios were compelled to trim budgets and consolidate their Munich operations, but their broadcasting and research remained invaluable and far out of proportion to their modest cost.

Radio Free Europe and Radio Liberty remained a prime target of Warsaw Pact invective, and the best that the West could secure at the CSCE was an ambiguous provision in Basket III that had the signatories "note the expansion in the dissemination of information broadcast by radio, and express the hope for the continuation of this process, so as to meet the interest of mutual understanding among peoples and the aims set forth by this Conference." At the Madrid follow-up meeting, the Warsaw Pact interpreted the "so as to meet" clause to allow jamming, while the West argued that it expressed the purpose of expanding broadcasts.[32]

Congress and Human Rights.   The RFE financing crisis had more to do with political vendettas and congressional prerogatives than with Eastern Europe. Congress had maintained a watching brief over the satellite countries reaching back to the Kersten amendment of the early 1950s and the obstruction of trade liberalization in the following decade. Congressional initiatives and the Carter administration's efforts in the mid-1970s gave human rights unprecedented prominence in United States foreign policy and provoked domestic and diplomatic controversy regarding philosophy as well as practice. The principal motive force of American involvement in Europe for over a century was given a new lease on life. The mass media, public opinion, and nongovernmental organizations came to be possessed by a moral fervor rare in peacetime.

Thanks to the activism of conservative Republicans and Democrats of the conservative, Henry M. "Scoop" Jackson wing, human rights considerations were repeatedly imposed on foreign policy in the Helsinki era. Congressional amendments prohibited security and economic assistance to human rights violators. The essential human right of emigration was the inspiration, and the Soviet bloc the target, for the Jackson-Vanik amendment (section 402 of the 1974 Trade Act), which prohibited most-favored-nation tariff status and credits for "nonmarket economy" countries that unreasonably restricted this right.[33] (The implementation and impact of these restrictive measures will be considered below and in chapter 5). Administrations generally regarded congressional human rights initiatives as an unwelcome intrusion into areas of executive responsibility.

Of more profound and enduring consequence for the substance and conduct of policy toward Eastern Europe was the innocuous initiative of a Republican congresswoman from New Jersey, Millicent Fenwick. She had toured the Soviet Union with a congressional delegation shortly after the Helsinki accord and had been moved by the pleas of dissidents for sustained Western pressure on human rights. In May 1976, she introduced a bill for the creation of a commission to monitor compliance with the Final Act that would "embody those principles which have distinguished this Nation above all others: our respect for human dignity, the importance of the individual and the freedom to pursue one's own thoughts and beliefs and religion." [34] The commission was to be an independent advisory agency consisting of an equal number of members from each legislative chamber as well as executive nominees representing the Departments of State, Defense, and Commerce. With the support of Senators Claiborne Pell and Clifford P. Case, the bill passed and was signed into law (Public Law 94–304) without publicity by President Ford on June 3, 1976.

There was strong resistance in the Ford administration to this extension of Congress's constitutional right of oversight into what promised to be ongoing involvement in the conduct of foreign policy. The State Department reported that its procedures for reports on implementation and compliance with the Final Act were sufficient, as was the monitoring provided by existing congressional committees and subcommittees. The Commission's first chairman, Congressman Dante Fascell (D-Fla.) was soon complaining about the secretary of state's uncooperative attitude. He charged in November 1976 that Kissinger and the Soviets were colluding to try to prevent a visit by commission members to the Soviet bloc. [35]

Despite these unpropitious beginnings, the Commission on Security and Cooperation in Europe, commonly known as the Helsinki Commission, soon became a leading force in the institutionalization of the CSCE process and the public diplomacy of human rights. The popularity of its mandate attracted energetic politicians as well as an expert staff. Through its frequent hearings with officials, scholars, interest groups, and East European dissidents, and through its direct participation in the CSCE review conferences, the Helsinki Commission acquired a credibility and authority that perhaps justified the fears of traditional diplomatists but at the same time represented a quintessentially American manifestation of idealism in foreign policy.

Carter and Human Rights. The Helsinki Commission did benefit indirectly from the Carter administration's stormy romance with human rights. This was a cause that appealed to the conservative Scoop Jackson wing as well as the liberal George McGovern wing of the Democratic party, and that suited Jimmy Carter's moral impulse. In the campaign, human rights served as the central theme of a foreign policy approach distinct from that of Nixon and Kissinger. Unlike Ford, declared Carter, he would invite Alexander Solzhenitsyn to the White House. Encouraged by the American public's positive response, Carter stressed human rights in his inaugural address. The more pragmatic expectation, recalls his national security adviser, Zbigniew Brzezinski, was that human rights policy would "sustain domestic support for our policies by rooting them clearly in our moral values." [36] But, as had been the case with liberation twenty-four years earlier, it was easier to proclaim a principle that to turn it into an operational policy.

It soon became apparent that Communist regimes would not be the primary target. Joshua Muravchik, a Scoop Jackson Democrat and author of the most thorough analysis of the issue, records that "the foreign policy team of the Carter administration included a network of individuals in key positions affecting human rights policy who shared a 'McGovernite' or 'left-liberal' worldview and whose human rights passions were focused on the depredations of rightist regimes. It included no one, at least among its political appointees, who shared the 'Jacksonite' worldview and whose human rights passions were directed to the acts of Communist governments." [37] To be sure, Brzezinski himself saw in human rights "an opportunity to put the Soviet Union ideologically on the defensive," but to his disappointment this priority was not shared by either the administration's human rights activists or by Secretary of State Cyrus Vance. [38]

There was no dearth of criticism of Communist human rights practices in the early days of the Carter administration. The State Department denounced the reprisals against Czech dissidents who in January 1977 had issued the "Charter 77" appeal for implementation of the

Helsinki human rights provisions. Similar reprisals in the Soviet Union drove Andrei Sakharov to invite Carter's support. The president's measured response, drafted by Vance and Brzezinski, may have brought spiritual comfort to Soviet dissidents, but their harassment continued.[39] After much hesitation, Carter on February 29 received the exiled Soviet dissident Vladimir Bukovsky but kept photographers at bay. The ambivalence had to do with domestic as well as international politics. In order to make progress on SALT II, the administration had to satisfy both Brezhnev, who was furious at the human rights campaign, and the Senate, where human rights concerns and hostility to arms deals with the Soviets ran strong.

By mid-1977, after an acrimonious meeting between Vance and Brezhnev, the Carter administration had toned down its pursuit of human rights in the East: agreement on SALT was not to be jeopardized. Criticism of violations continued, but the administration preferred to avoid direct attribution of the abuses to totalitarian ideology. "Old ideological labels have lost their meaning," declared Carter expansively when he met Gierek in Warsaw in December 1977.[40] Though eager for more American aid, his hosts disabused him of this hopeful assumption.

The Carter administration's priorities in human rights were soon adapted to a calculation of interest and leverage that focused on the non-communist world. In an address at the University of Georgia on April 30, 1977, Secretary Vance offered the new and authoritative definition of human rights. First came the right to be "free from governmental violation of the integrity of the person," from arbitrary arrest and torture; second, the satisfaction of economic and social needs; and last, the right to enjoy civil and political liberties. The ordering was deliberate and consistently reiterated.[41] It was designed to appeal to the third world and to address principally the brutal practices of right-wing dictatorships. As Muravchik observes, "integrity of the person" is more a category of violations than of rights; implicitly this priority paid tribute to the capacity of established totalitarian regimes to deny fundamental rights with only a modicum of overt violence against the individual.[42] In an Eastern Europe cowed by the experience of Stalinist terror, only a few were willing to risk arbitrary arrest and imprisonment in pursuit of political and civil rights. The administration's bias was deplored by Brzezinski, who blamed the State Department. He complained to Carter that "our human-rights policy was in danger of becoming one-sidedly anti-rightist," but in pursuing SALT and courting the Chinese and the Romanian regimes, he followed a realpolitik worthy of Kissinger.[43]

There was, therefore, some force in Jeane Kirkpatrick's charge that the effect of Carter's priorities was to favor the Communist enemy over the authoritarian friend.[44] The fact that the denial of civil and political rights was inherent in Leninism was glossed over in the Carter crusade. This ideological relativism and the gradual muting of criticism of Soviet and East European violations did not fail to disappoint East Europeans who had expected much from the coincidence of Carter and Helsinki.

To be sure, America's leverage upon human rights in Eastern Europe remained minimal, and advocates of quiet diplomacy could always point to Kissinger's success in inducing Moscow to facilitate Jewish emigration. The Jackson-Vanik amendment arguably had been temporarily counterproductive in this respect, although it did induce some improvement in Romanian emigration practices. Moreover, other considerations tended to override human rights where potential leverage existed. The United States invariably supported multilateral aid for Romania and Yugoslavia. Neither had a shining human rights record or more pressing "basic human needs" (the escape clause in section 701 of the International Financial Assistance Act) than non-Communist countries that earned a negative vote, but both had contributed to a more or less tangible fragmentation of the Soviet empire. Political pragmatism offered less justification for the fulsome praise heaped upon Tito and Ceausescu on the occasion of their visits to the United States in the spring of 1978, when President Carter lauded both leaders for their dedication to human rights.[45]

Human Rights Monitoring and the Belgrade Review. By the middle of the 1970s an extensive network for the scrutiny of human rights had emerged. The Harkin amendment to the Foreign Assistance Act had mandated the State Department to produce annual reports on human rights practices. In 1976, Congress extended this requirement to cover all UN members, not just United States aid recipients, and legislated the establishment of a coordinator for human rights and humanitarian affairs at the State Department. The following year, at the urging of the Helsinki Commission's chairman, the office was expanded into a bureau headed by an assistant secretary.

The law establishing the commission required the president to submit semiannual reports (Implementation of Helsinki Final Act) on CSCE compliance by the Warsaw Pact signatories. The State Department, not without complaining about the burden, assigned an officer in each embassy to report on human rights. One result, observed the assistant secretary for human rights and humanitarian affairs, Richard Schifter, was the sensitization of the entire bureaucracy to human rights issues.[46] The situation in Eastern Europe was also addressed in the Helsinki Commission's published hearings and its *CSCE Digest,* in the North Atlantic Assembly's quarterly Bulletin, as well as in the publications and lobbying of numerous nongovernmental organizations such as the New York-based Helsinki Watch and the London-based Amnesty International.[47]

This proliferating monitoring industry constituted a international lobby that undoubtedly promoted public awareness of human rights violations and exerted some salutary pressure on the violators as well as Western policymakers. East European dissidents valued the moral support, and in some cases the publicity reinforced quiet diplomacy to deter or alleviate reprisals against them. Admittedly, positive results were mostly achieved in countries with relatively tolerant regimes or where the United States had some economic leverage, notably Poland, Hungary, and Romania. But even if the immediate and tangible benefits were few, the advocacy efforts put Communist regimes on the defensive and raised both the domestic and international cost of violation and denial.

After a preparatory meeting from June 15 to August 5, 1977, the first CSCE review conference was convened at Belgrade on October 4, only to disband five months later with little accomplished but the airing of acrimony and agreement on further meetings. Brzezinski records that he "pushed hard and I believe effectively for a more assertive United States posture in CSCE" and "horrified" the State Department by considering a "confrontationist approach."[48] The State Department's preference for low-keyed and balanced negotiation was also opposed by the Helsinki Commission, which demanded the addition to the United States delegation of commission members and other public figures.

The West Europeans, already skeptical about the thrust and conduct of Carter's human rights crusade, did not welcome the prospect of a confrontational approach. The West Germans were particularly apprehensive that their improved relations with the East might be jeopardized. The East Germans warned that Basket Three was not "a license to undermine the socialist countries ideologically" while insisting that the objective ideological class struggle was inevitable. They stressed the primary role of the state in implementing the objectives of Basket Three and asserted that "the dissemination of ideas endangering peace as part of the exchange of cultural and spiritual values and information was expressly prohibited," a reference to what were identified further on as "subversive radio stations." The general Warsaw Pact position was reflected in the claims that the East had the superior record in implementing economic and social rights and that "citizens of the socialist countries are much better informed on political and cultural life in the West than vice versa."[49]

At the preparatory talks, the United States delegation maintained a low profile while the West Europeans pressed for procedures that would allow more public sessions and a full review of implementation. But a more aggressive American stance was foreshadowed by the appointment of a former Supreme Court justice and UN ambassador, Arthur Goldberg, to lead to the review conference a delegation that included public members as well as professional diplomats. Nor was there any sign of mellowing in the East. Undeterred by the impending review, the Soviet authorities arrested eleven members of the Moscow Helsinki Watch Group; in Czechoslovakia, several Charter 77 founders were arrested and put on trial. After heated debate in the NATO caucus, the European and American positions were reconciled, and in a series of speeches Goldberg castigated the Communists for their human rights record. The Soviet Union tried to argue that each country was responsible for monitoring its own compliance, and to invoke the principle of noninterference, which Goldberg argued referred to compulsion and not persuasion. By retaliating in criticism of Western human rights practices, the Soviet Union in effect conceded the legitimacy of the exercise.

The verbal violence of the Soviet-American confrontation made the front pages and caused some unease in Western Europe. It also strained the solidarity of the Warsaw Pact, for Hungary and Poland reportedly argued for moderation while Romania simply skipped many bloc caucuses.[50] The Belgrade conference rewarded human rights advocates with a public condemnation of the Soviet bloc, but it failed to advance the CSCE process. The brief final communique made no reference to human rights but simply called for three experts' meetings followed by another review at Madrid. Albert W. Sherer, Jr., a career diplomat who had led the United States delegation to the preparatory talks only to be eclipsed at the formal meeting by Goldberg, reflected with some bitterness on the latter's outspoken self-righteousness, which he construed as being designed to "protect Carter's credibility on human rights."[51]

The choice of confrontation over low-profile diplomacy owed much to the president's sensitivity to domestic political concerns, championed most forcefully by the Helsinki Commission. But the American hard line at Belgrade had no direct negative or, for that matter, positive consequences. Detente was fast dissipating, and the coup de grace was soon to be administered by the Soviet invasion of Afghanistan. By the time the next review meeting convened in Madrid, another administration was preparing to take office.

Reagan's Crusade for Democracy. The Carter record, and human rights, were grist for the 1980 presidential campaign. Adopting Jeane Kirkpatrick's critique of a moralism that damaged America's friends more than her enemies and downgraded the centrality of the East-West conflict, Ronald Reagan initially seemed intent on attenuating and recasting official human rights advocacy. The objective was not to condone violations in what Reagan branded the "evil empire," but rather to spare friendly regimes, however authoritarian and repressive. Carter's apparent double standard had been rationalized at least partly on grounds of available leverage. Higher national security considerations were invoked in justification of the new double standard. In the event, the shift in emphasis scarcely altered America's approach to human rights in Eastern Europe.

That human rights had won a solid political constituency was made clear to Reagan when the Senate Foreign Relations Committee refused to confirm Ernest Lefever for the post of assistant secretary of state for human rights and humanitarian affairs. The reason for the rejection was that he had expressed reservations about making humanitarian concerns the focus of foreign policy. While many—in the Congress and elsewhere—believed that Carter's practice had been flawed, few were prepared to surrender the principle. By the end of 1981 the principle was reaffirmed, notably in an internal State Department memorandum that stated, "Human rights is at the core of our foreign policy." Echoing Brzezinski, the memo observed that "we will never maintain wide public support for our foreign policy unless we can relate it to American ideals and to the defense of freedom." Human rights would "give us the best opportunity to convey what is ultimately at issue in our contest with the Soviet bloc." A positive effort to promote democratic values would be accompanied by a negative policy toward violators, differentiated in favor of America's friends.[52] Elliott Abrams, who reportedly drafted the memo, was duly appointed to the post left vacant by Lefever's rejection.

The general principle was preserved, but the operational definition of human rights underwent significant alteration. Whereas the Carter administration had emphasized the ideologically neutral notion of the "integrity of the person," Reagan reverted to the philosophically firmer ground of political and civil rights (whose observance would safeguard the integrity of the person) and linked them to the American tradition of democracy through limited government. The Reagan administration's intent, stated Abrams, was to "treat not only the symptoms but the disease." The president, in his address to the British House of Commons in June 1982, denounced Soviet human rights practices and promised to actively foster the "infrastructure of democracy."[53]

The most tangible manifestation of Reagan's ideological crusade was the National Endowment for Democracy, established in December 1983. The bipartisan board of this federally funded private corporation included Kissinger, former Vice President Mondale, AFL-CIO President Lane Kirkland, and Helsinki Commission chairman Dante Fascell; its first chairman was a onetime RFE president, John Richardson, and its president a former Kirkpatrick aide, Carl Gershman. The NED receives its federal funding from the United States Information Agency and disburses it mainly through four "core grantees": the AFL-CIO's Free Trade Union Institute, the Center for Private Enterprise of the Chamber of Commerce, and the National Republican and National Democratic Institutes for International Affairs.

The NED has implemented its mandate to foster democracy and political pluralism by subsidizing independent labor, business, and civic groups, education and training in the practical organization of democratic politics, and publishing by political exiles and dissidents. Clearly, in many respects the NED attempted to pursue openly what the CIA had done secretly for many years with mixed success. Observed Gershman, "We should not have to do this kind of work covertly. It would be terrible for democratic groups around the world to be seen as subsidized by the CIA. We saw that in the 60's, and that's why it has been discontinued. We have not had the capability of doing this, and that's why the endowment was created."[54]

The Endowment checks with the CIA via the State Department to ensure that potential recipients are not already benefiting from other United States aid, and recipients know the source of the largesse. Still, given the conditions of semilegality or even illegality in which some NED beneficiaries, such as Solidarity, operated until 1989, the principle of full openness had to be qualified to protect them from reprisals. The difficulty of identifying viable projects left Eastern Europe with only a modest share of NED funding. Solidarity's underground publishing network was one major recipient; exile publications were also subsidized, and independent groups in Hungary received copying and printing equipment.

Romania and Reagan. No such opportunities arose in retrograde Romania, ruled with an iron hand by the neo-Stalinist Ceausescu regime. That regime's diplomatic departures from Warsaw Pact orthodoxy, however, had earned it MFN tariff status as well as the enduring favor of the State Department. United States-Romanian trade surged, though with an imbalance heavily in favor of the latter; in 1983, the Commerce Department estimated that loss of MFN would cost the Romanians $200 million in exports (out of a total of $340 million) and American exporters a similar amount. For the first six years of Jackson-Vanik, the Carter and Reagan administrations managed to convince Congress that the leverage of MFN had produced improvement at least in one area of human rights, that of emigration—specifically the emigration of Jewish Romanians. American Jewish organizations exerted sustained political pressure to extract this concession, and as long as the flow of emigrants did not ebb, they lobbied in effect for the extension of MFN. Fearing that once suspended, MFN would never be granted again to Ceausescu's Romania, the State Department was also a staunch advocate of renewal.

By 1982, economic as well as human rights problems threatened to upset this ostensibly cordial relationship. Early in the year, against the background of Poland's debt disaster, Romania reached its own liquidity crisis and technically defaulted on loans by United States financial institutions, forcing the Export-Import Bank to make good on $8 million of unpaid loans. The administration also accused Romania of dumping steel on the United States market. The persecution of Christian activists, a decline in Jewish emigration levels, and continuing cultural discrimination against the two-million-strong Hungarian minority drew growing attention from the human rights constituency in Washington; in April and May, several members of Congress jointly sent messages of concern to Reagan and Ceausescu. The Romanians hastily responded by sending Foreign Minister Stefan Andrei as well as Chief Rabbi Moses Rosen and a parliamentary delegation to lobby on Capitol Hill.

President Reagan on June 2 formally recommended renewal of the waiver, acknowledging that the maximum number of emigrants admissible to the United States had been permitted to leave over the previous twelve months (overall, Romanian emigration had grown fourfold since 1973), but indicated that unless Romanian emigration procedures improved he might recommend otherwise in 1983. Concurrently, the State Department attempted to counter criticism by revealing that it had been communicating to Bucharest American concern over religious and ethnic persecution.[55] The Romanians, in response, quickly granted more emigration permits, resolved some individual humanitarian cases, amnestied twenty-seven prisoners (including some whose crime had been to distribute Bibles), and promised to discuss emigration procedures with American Jewish organizations. A partially mollified Congress voted down the resolutions of disapproval, but a "Sense of the Senate" resolution passed on September 24 instructed the administration to pursue the issue of human rights.

Six weeks later, the Romanian government decreed that would-be emigrants had to reimburse the state in hard currency (which citizens were forbidden to hold) for the cost of most of their education, a prohibitive tax that was explicitly ruled out by Section 402 of the 1974 Trade Act. The main recipients of Romanian immigrants, West Germany and Israel, lodged diplomatic protests, and the measure was roundly condemned at the Madrid CSCE follow-up meeting, but Washington played for time. In January 1983, the president dispatched Under Secretary of State Lawrence Eagleburger to Bucharest to warn that implementation of the decree, scheduled for the following month, would mean suspension of MFN, and to try to work out a face-saving compromise. Two months later, the president made the threat public, and congressional officials visiting Romania confirmed that Congress would sustain a negative recommendation.[56] At the end of May, West German Foreign Minister Hans-Dietrich Genscher struck an apparent deal with Ceausescu, securing withdrawal of the offensive decree and promising to have Romania's bilateral debt rescheduled. Emigration levels rose, and Reagan recommended another extension of MFN.

Despite Jackson-Vanik's narrow focus on emigration, the annual hearings conducted by the Subcommittee on Trade of the House Ways and Means Committee and the Subcommittee on International Trade of the Senate Finance Committee gradually became occasions for general human rights reviews. The Helsinki Commission concerned itself with the emigration issue in the broad context of human rights. Its reports on CSCE implementation painted an increasingly bleak picture of violations in Romania, as did the president's semiannual report for the period ending May 31, 1983, which noted the "extensive harassment" of religious, political, and cultural dissidents. The regime's totalitarian reach was displayed in a decree requiring the licensing of all typewriters and registration of the typeface. The promise of suspension of the emigrant education tax was overshadowed by growing awareness on Capitol Hill of Romania's dismal rights record, generating support for the new disapproval motions. But a coincidental Supreme Court ruling in the *Immigration and Naturalization Service v. Chadha* case rendered unconstitutional a one-house veto of executive action, the procedure allowed for in Jackson-Vanik. Now, only by a bill or joint resolution could Congress reject a presidential request for waiver. The ruling took the wind out of the sails of the disapproval motions, and MFN was extended for another year.[57]

For four years more, the administration clung to the belief that, on balance, extension of MFN to Romania served American interests, although each year it came closer to losing the case in Congress. The Ceausescu regime's human rights abuses received increasing international exposure. In particular, the issue of minority rights, which had been studiously downplayed by the State Department, rose in prominence, thanks in part to the Hungarian government's now open concern and to the lobbying activity of Hungarian-Americans. Ceausescu's primary tactic for winning popular legitimacy had been to wave the standard of Romanian nationalism. As a consequence, the large Hungarian minority suffered from overt and covert measures of dispersal, discrimination, and cultural assimilation. Transylvania historically had been linked to Hungary until it was awarded to Romania at the Versailles Peace Conference; Hungarian irredentism was partially satisfied by the

Vienna Award of 1940, but in the postwar settlement all of Transylvania once again reverted to Romania. Bucharest was therefore ever ready to allege that foreign interest in the minority threatened Romania's territorial integrity.

The State Department's view remained that the very limited influence afforded by MFN ought not to be jeopardized by unrealistic demands, and it opposed a congressional initiative to recognize the Transylvanian Hungarians' right to self-determination.[58] Deputy Assistant Secretary of State Thomas W. Simons, Jr., told the Helsinki Commission on the occasion of its hearing on East European minorities in May 1987 that "we do not intend to be drawn into debates about deeply rooted historical questions which still provoke deep emotions on all sides. . . ." He conceded that even if "assimilation into the majority culture is a natural byproduct of development, as it is in the United States as well, there is nevertheless serious evidence that Romanian Government authorities today seek actively to push the natural process of assimilation forward, in practice, if not as a matter of policy."[59] Other witnesses were not so diplomatically disingenuous in comparing American and Romanian practices.

The State Department used human rights leverage as the main rationale for extending MFN, but it became increasingly difficult to sustain. There was much embarrassment at State in 1985 over the scathing public denunciation by the retiring ambassador, David Funderburk, of Ceausescu's despotism and the administration's relative complacency. He had fought a running battle with his superiors over what he perceived to be an unhealthy "convergence of interests" between the State Department and the Romanian regime. A regime that turns bibles into toilet paper, observed Funderburk in reference to the reported fate of thousands of books donated from the West to the Transylvanian Reformed Church, does not deserve MFN status. The leading Romanian dissident, Mihai Botez, also criticized America's extraordinary forbearance.[60] And even one of Funderburk's targets, Deputy Assistant Secretary Mark Palmer, testified before the Helsinki Commission in June 1985 that "Romania is, in human rights terms, certainly one of the biggest challenges and one of the biggest offenders in Eastern Europe."[61]

Indeed, far from ameliorating his domestic policies, Ceausescu turned more repressive and became a pariah to both East and West. By 1986, the margin of approval in the House on the president's waiver recommendation had narrowed to 216–190. The following summer, both chambers passed resolutions condemning Romania and voted for a six-month suspension of MFN pending presidential certification of progress on human rights. The Helsinki Commission's Steny Hoyer reported after a visit to Bucharest at the end of August that "we received no assurances from Ceausescu that the human rights situation would improve." [62] The administration was ready to throw in the towel. Seeing the writing on the wall, in February 1988 the Romanian government announced that rather than submit to further calumny it would voluntarily surrender MFN.

The Romanian experience offered little satisfaction to advocates of human rights. Higher emigration had been induced by Jackson-Vanik, though the bargain of emigrants for commercial favors and, in the case of West Germany and Israel, for outright ransom, was hardly in the spirit of the Final Act. [63] On rare occasions, publicity and diplomatic pressure had some effect, such as the release of the long-imprisoned priest Gheorghe Calciu, but on the whole the regime remained impervious to American and Western blandishments. The State Department displayed remarkable bureaucratic rigidity in clinging against all evidence to a positive image of Ceausescu as a Warsaw Pact maverick. To be sure, he had performed some useful diplomatic services in the past. There was, perhaps, another reason for Washington's lenient attitude. The *Washington Post* reported in May 1990 that over the ten years preceding Ceausescu's downfall, the CIA had paid over $40 million to obtain advanced Soviet military technology, including air defense systems, from Romania. Two of Ceausescu's brothers were involved in the transactions, presumably with the dictator's tacit approval. [64]

The Madrid Conference. Despite its initial reservations, the Reagan administration took full advantage of the opportunities presented by the CSCE process to probe the human rights record of Communist regimes. During his election campaign Reagan had questioned its value, but on the tenth anniversary of the Final Act he ignored the advice of some hard-line conservatives that in light of continuing Soviet violations he should simply repudiate it. As his relationship with Gorbachev warmed, he tactically and temporarily relaxed the pressure for Soviet compliance. [65] Nevertheless, the linkage of human rights to progress on security-related issues was sustained to the end of the Vienna follow-up conference.

The Belgrade experience had made the Soviet Union and its allies wary of the Helsinki process, and during the preparatory phase of the Madrid follow-up conference, in the autumn of 1980, they tried to block procedural provision for a thorough review of implementation. These tactics, added to the invasion of Afghanistan and recurring human rights violations, reinforced the resolve of the Western participants. A wind of liberty as a universal right had finally swept away the West's Soviet apologists, and Thatcher's Britain as well as Mitterrand's France shared the human rights perceptions of Reagan's America. At Madrid, NATO's united front and its practice of regular consultation with the neutral and nonaligned participants (NNa) resulted in procedures that allowed for not only an initial lengthy review of compliance but also subsequent exposure of new violations.

The Carter White House had appointed as chairman of the Madrid delegation former Attorney General Griffin Bell, and as cochairman Max M. Kampelman, a Scoop Jackson Democrat; the latter became chairman when the Reagan administration took office. The delegation now included some thirty public members. Congressional hearings and Helsinki Commission staff reports had generated voluminous information and advice that emphasized human rights and informed the American approach at Madrid.[66] More than one hundred pressure groups conveyed their views to the conference, including thirty-seven associations of East European emigres and fourteen Helsinki Watch committees. In the opening days of the meeting, emigre dissidents and representatives of human rights organizations conducted in Madrid a veritable "counterconference" to lobby for their cause.[67] This public involvement and the Western practices of naming dozens of victims of repression, holding press conferences, and releasing speeches delivered in closed session turned the Madrid meeting into a media event that focused on human rights.

That focus was foreshadowed in the opening address of Griffin Bell, who warned delegates they would "hear often over the next several weeks that the words of the Final Act on human rights and human contacts must be interpreted in different ways when applied in different social systems. This argument is untrue—and profoundly harmful to the spirit of our enterprise."[68] The United States concentrated on reviewing fulfillment and submitted only a few new proposals, for meetings of experts on human rights and family reunification. France, with NATO support, proposed a conference on confidence-building measures and a cultural forum. The Eastern priority, announced at the Warsaw Pact meeting in Warsaw on May 15, 1980, was a conference on military detente and disarmament in Europe, part of Brezhnev's "peace program." Some initiatives canceled each other out: an Eastern proposal on the right to work was countered by a Western one on the right to strike. A European Community proposal to ban jamming was met by Soviet-Czechoslovak proposal to terminate RFE and Radio Liberty. The bargaining, mediated by the NNa, would be over a mutually acceptable set of security and human rights recommendations.

The NNa's draft of a concluding document was almost completed when martial law was imposed in Poland on December 13, 1981. The CSCE process had offered some encouragement to Polish dissidents, and as Solidarity rose many hoped that the Madrid meeting might serve as a deterrent to repression. But for Brezhnev and Jaruzelski, blatant violation of several Helsinki principles was a price worth paying for reaffirming undivided Communist rule. The Madrid review phase came to an end a few days later amid discord. Differences arose between Washington and Bonn: the former was disposed to have the meeting adjourn as long as repression continued in Poland, while the latter preferred to keep the dialogue going at all costs. When the meeting reconvened on February 9, 1982, the chairman, by alphabetical rotation, was the Polish delegate, and he resorted to procedural chicanery in an attempt to prevent several foreign ministers, including France's Claude Cheysson, from delivering their speeches.

Despite long procedural wrangles, the human rights violations of martial law were fully exposed and denounced, with Kampelman aptly quoting from Bertolt Brecht that "the people have lost confidence in their government. The government has, therefore, decided to elect a new people." [69] Determined to prevent "business as usual" and to secure a long recess, the West resorted to procedural delaying tactics. On March 5, 1982, in the drafting committee charged with finalizing the concluding document, Western delegations remained silent in what one historian called a triumph of allied solidarity. [70] When after eight months the meeting reconvened on November 9, the focus shifted from implementation (though Romania's new education tax on emigrants was deplored) to recommendations; the West introduced a flurry of new amendments on such issues as security of individual Helsinki monitors, free trade unions, and jamming.

After much difficult negotiation and mediation, consensus was finally reached in July 1983 on a concluding document, and the Madrid meeting came to an end on September 9, 1983.[71] The Soviet downing of a South Korean airliner figured prominently in the closing speeches of Secretary of State George Shultz and other Western foreign ministers. The Madrid results, though modest, represented an improvement over Belgrade. The Soviet desire for a military security conference was satisfied, and the West's persistence paid off with some minor embellishments of the Final Act's human rights provisions. The participants formally agreed to "take the necessary action in their respective countries to effectively ensure" the rights enumerated in Principle VII. On trade unions, it was agreed that the "participating states will ensure the right of workers freely to establish and join trade unions, the right of trade unions freely to exercise their activities," but these rights had to be exercised "in compliance with the law of the state." This was the escape clause for the East, which had no intention of allowing free trade unions in the wake of Solidarity, but even so, the compromise was a victory for the West. On this as on other issues where agreement was reached, the CSCE process was a battle over form as much as substance, but the results were more than symbolic.

The Helsinki Commission's stocktaking of the first ten years of the CSCE review process recorded some progress.[72] The Final Act had liberated Western governments from the inhibitions of traditional diplomacy by providing a reference point and continuing framework for addressing the human rights deficiencies of state socialism. Although tangible improvements were slow in coming, and owed much to the reformist tendencies of a few East European regimes in quest of domestic legitimacy, international standards and Western pressure were instrumental in raising the awareness of human rights among both rulers and subjects. Observed the Polish Helsinki Committee, "Above all, the CSCE process strengthens resistance to anti-Western propaganda or at least weakens its effectiveness. . . . The societies' awareness that one normative standard exists helps give social demands a rational form and increases the chances of a peaceful resolution of the conflict."[73] These pressures helped to induce a progressive reinterpretation of "socialist legality" by the more liberal regimes in favor of the legal rights of the individual and of impartial justice. The slow erosion of the ruling parties' arbitrary authority over political and civil liberties had begun.

From 1975 onwards, Western governments and Eastern dissidents invoked the Final Act in seeking implementation of the human contacts provisions of Basket III. The State Department regularly submitted "representation lists" of pending family reunification cases, and the compliance and general emigration record of the East European countries (notably Hungary) improved.[74] Though their motives were not humanitarian, Czechoslovakia and some others began to allow, and indeed to urge, political dissidents to emigrate. Contacts among Eastern and Western religious organizations multiplied. Billy Graham paid pastoral visits to Hungary in 1977 and Poland in 1981. Rigid state control over the dissemination of information allowed little improvement in the Eastern public's access to Western media, but domestic censorship was eased in Poland and Hungary, and Hungarian television began to broadcast unprecedentedly open discussions between Eastern and Western experts on aspects of detente. The oral exchange of information was fostered by easier travel as well as by such established United States government facilities as the USIA's American Participant Program, which sponsored lecture tours by American experts; the USIA's International Visitor Program, which brought East Europeans to the United States; and the Fulbright and International Research and Exchanges Board (IREX) programs for academic exchanges. Cultural exchanges also benefitted from the spirit of Helsinki.

In sum, the pressure legitimized by the CSCE process was not wholly without effect. "And yet," said Secretary Shultz at the commemorative meeting in Helsinki, "10 years after the signing of the Final Act, no one can deny the gap between hope and performance. Despite the real value of the Final Act as a standard of conduct, the most important promises of a decade ago have not been kept."[75] The Helsinki agenda nevertheless had usefully served to marshal the West's diplomatic resources and public attention against reprehensible practices in the East, and to nurture a powerful constituency for human rights. Nowhere was this more evident than on Capitol Hill, where (in what had become an annual ritual) a joint resolution was passed on August 2, 1985 calling on the president to "use every opportunity to stress the inherent link—explicitly stated in the Helsinki Final Act and the Madrid Concluding Document—between respect for human rights and the achievement of lasting peace." [76] In 1988, Reagan responded by proclaiming a Helsinki Human Rights Day.

Ottawa/Budapest/Bern. The measure of the distance to be traveled was vividly revealed in the Ottawa meeting of experts on human rights in May-June 1985. At the outset, the Soviet delegate deliberately misinterpreted the Madrid mandate for the meeting (to address "questions concerning respect, in their States, for human rights and fundamental freedoms, in all their aspects") by arguing that each country was simply required to report on its domestic human rights situation; unfortunately for him, the official Russian text did not support his contention. Despite the Warsaw Pact's initial refusal to discuss specific violations, the United States launched a lengthy debate with details of numerous individual cases, and the East retaliated by condemning social abuses such as unemployment in the West.

The head of the United States delegation, Richard Schifter, pointed out the illogic in the Soviet contention that human rights were contingent on detente: "Does it stand to reason that if foreign countries establish friendly relations with a particular government that government, in turn, will—so to speak—reward the foreign countries by dealing kindly with its own citizens?" The Western participants and most of the NNa's stood by Principle VII's linkage, which made respect for human rights a condition of friendly relations. Schifter also reiterated the Western distinction between individual rights and social objectives: "The rights guaranteed in the United States Constitution . . . are rights which every citizen can call upon the courts to protect. We view what are here referred to as economic and social rights as . . . the goals of government policy in domestic affairs." After expounding on the shortcomings of the Soviet social and economic system, Schifter ended by citing the conclusion of former Communist intellectuals such as Arthur Koestler to the effect that "the price in terms of personal freedom was not worth paying to attain the promised goal of a future paradise." [77]

Another Soviet diversionary tactic was to introduce a "human right of the third generation," the "right to live in peace." The Soviets argued that in the nuclear age this "right" was the fundamental prerequisite for the fulfillment of other rights and demanded that it be included in the meeting's recommendations. The West would not condone the implicit downgrading of political and civil liberties, while the East rejected even an NNa compromise report that called for a further meeting of human rights experts. The Ottawa meeting disbanded without tangible results.

Some of the smaller Warsaw Pact members had shown only grudging solidarity with Soviet initiatives at Ottawa. Another notable development was the beginning of a debate on minority rights. Turkey's complaint regarding new Bulgarian measures to assimilate Muslim ethnic Turks led to an examination of minority issues that exposed Warsaw Pact differences. The Bulgarian representative, observed Richard Schifter, claimed that "these ethnic Turks of Bulgaria never existed, that if they did exist, they are giving up their Turkish ethnic identity voluntarily, and that, at any rate, their ancestors were ethnic Bulgarians who hundreds of years ago were forcibly Islamicized." The facts were that the close to one-million-strong minority had been "subjected to harsh oppression, forced to change their names and to end their cultural and ethnic ties." Schifter praised the Hungarian representative's "thoughtful and informative presentation" on minority rights, criticized the persecution of Hungarian minority spokesmen in Czechoslovakia, and managed to avoid naming Romania in relating that "governmental restrictions on the free flow of information about the past and present of minorities have intensified; churches, cultural monuments, and other artifacts of minority cultures have been destroyed; limitations on the use of native languages and cultural facilities have increased; histories have been rewritten, persons who decry these developments have been harshly persecuted."[78] The multilateral Helsinki process thus allowed the United States to overcome its diplomatic reluctance to address the thorny issue of East European minorities.

The airing of that issue at the Budapest Cultural Forum in October 1985 annoyed the Romanians so much that they blocked any concluding statement. At Western insistence, the delegations included prominent artists and writers as well as government officials, and Solidarity, Charter 77, and Hungarian dissidents addressed briefs to the forum, but the meeting only confirmed the conflicting views of the West and the official East regarding intellectual freedom. "Nothing else is worth writing about except peace," declared a Soviet delegate. In the event, the forum was overshadowed by a concurrent independent cultural symposium organized by the International Helsinki Federation for Human Rights. This counterconference, held in private apartments after the Hungarian government denied it the use of public facilities, allowed for open discussion of such problems as censorship and the cultural privations of the Hungarian minority in Romania. For dissident intellectuals in the East, the Helsinki process was indeed a "framework for hope."[79]

Human contacts were the focus of the Bern meeting in April-May 1986, which also ended without consensus. The issues were of particular concern to the United States, for as the delegation's head, Michael Novak, observed at the outset, a tenth of America's population was of East European origin. The Soviet position was that since employment, housing, medical care, and social security were guaranteed, no one had any reason to leave, and that human contacts such as family reunification depended on progress in detente. Again, the United States rejected this linkage. Novak argued that "the rights to family reunification are prior to questions of foreign policy" and that "there is a crucial difference between fundamental human rights, such as the right to emigrate, and the normal commercial or cultural activities of normal times. The first may never be abridged. The second do follow the rhythms of international life."[80]

After suffering through a painstaking review of violations that left only Hungary unscathed, the Soviet bloc was ready to accept a Swiss formula that included some new provisions, such as prohibition of state interference with international telephone and postal communication. But Washington found the document "too thin, containing loopholes damaging to compliance," exemplified by the qualification "when personal and professional circumstances permit" appended to the right to travel.[81] Despite a last-ditch appeal from West German Foreign Minister Genscher to Secretary Shultz, the United States refused to endorse the compromise.

The Vienna Meeting. By the time the third CSCE review conference convened in Vienna in November 1986, Soviet orthodoxy was being shaken to its roots by a new leader, Mikhail Gorbachev. A meeting that began with lengthy criticism of Soviet and East European human rights violations ended twenty-six months later with agreement to hold the last of a series of conferences on the "human dimension" of the CSCE in, of all places, Moscow. In the interval, Gorbachev's notions of restructuring, openness, and democratization had materialized in a process of change that affected both the domestic and foreign policies of the Soviet Union and the climate for reform in Eastern Europe. Political and civil liberties in particular acquired new meaning, and in May 1988 the CPSU

Central Committee would pass a resolution inviting "the exercise of constitutional freedoms (freedom of speech, the press, conscience, assembly, meetings, street processions and demonstrations, etc.) and firmer guarantees of personal rights, such as the inviolability of the person and the home, and privacy of correspondence and telephone conversations."[82] Though the Gorbachevian squaring of the Leninist circle fell short of Western liberal democracy, it alleviated domestic repression and narrowed the gap between East and West on many issues of human rights.

Gorbachev's reformist zeal initially met with widespread skepticism in the West, and particularly in the United States, but there were also glimmerings of hope for rapprochement. The cordiality of the Reykjavik summit contrasted with the continuing brutal intervention in Afghanistan. A few prominent prisoners of conscience were released, notably the Moscow Helsinki Group leader Yuri Orlov, and, in December 1986, Andrei Sakharov and his wife were allowed to return from internal exile to Moscow. But the death in prison of the dissident writer Anatoly Marchenko cast a pall on these auspicious changes. Still, the new Soviet regime displayed unprecedented openness in a public relations campaign designed to earn it some credibility on human rights.

The American approach to Vienna was, as usual, to emphasize human rights. The delegation, headed by Ambassador Warren Zimmerman, included as vice-chairmen Helsinki Commission chairman Alfonse D'Amato and cochairman Steny Hoyer as well as fifteen public members representing a variety of civic, human rights, and ethnic organizations. Groups from North America and Europe mounted demonstrations, symposia, and exhibits in Vienna to take advantage of the momentary attention of world media. The United States and its allies focused on violations of human rights principles in the Soviet Union and Czechoslovakia. Recognizing that their earlier retrenchment behind the principle of noninterference had been ineffective, the Soviet Union and its most like-minded allies, Bulgaria, the GDR, and Czechoslovakia, complained that such criticism was unproductive and responded both by claiming positive achievements and by accusing the United States, Britain, and Canada of racism and neglecting the poor.

Reviewing Basket III compliance, the United States addressed a plethora of specific concerns that included mistreatment of minorities; penalties for unauthorized contact with foreigners; restrictions on travel and emigration; censorship; and more.[83] There was a certain division of labor among the allies; Canada took the lead in promoting minority rights and Britain in calling for the end of broadcast jamming. The key Western proposal at Vienna was for more systematic monitoring and discussion of problems in the sphere of human rights and humanitarian contacts. For the first time in the Helsinki process, a Warsaw Pact member cosponsored a Western proposal when Hungary endorsed a Canadian initiative on behalf of the fundamental human rights and cultural identities of national minorities. But the most surprising proposal came from the Soviet Union, which invited a follow-up meeting on humanitarian cooperation to be held in Moscow. Taken aback, the NATO allies initially dismissed the idea on the grounds that the USSR could not guarantee unrestricted access to such a meeting. The Soviets showed their ambivalence on human rights during the fifth session (January-March 1988) by attacking Western proposals for follow-up and tabling amendments to the Concluding Document. They insisted that domestic law, rather than international norms, governed the freedom of individuals to promote human rights.

In the final phase, the major issues were the format and mandate of new security meetings, on which the West was divided (see chapter 6), and the Moscow venue for a review of the "human dimension." As happened at Madrid, it fell to the NNa group to mediate between East and West in drafting a concluding document. The biggest potential spoiler turned out to be Romania, which in June 1988 declared that it would accept no additional commitments on human rights, while at the same time introducing new amendments on economic and social rights. But Warsaw Pact solidarity was fraying, and in November and December 1988, the United States and Britain conducted bilateral discussions with the Soviet Union on conditions for the Moscow meeting. By this time, Gorbachev had earned some credits in human rights. The number of emigrants had risen to 80,000 in 1988; some 600 political prisoners had been released over the preceding two years; and *glasnost* had unleashed an extraordinarily open political debate in the Soviet Union, including a new assertiveness among the non-Russian nationalities. The jamming of Western broadcasts was also gradually suspended, so that by the end of 1988 even Radio Liberty and Radio Free Europe enjoyed unhindered access to their vast audiences.

These auspicious developments and concessions led the United States and Britain to announce on January 4, 1989, their consent (conditional on sustained improvements in human rights) to an eventual session in Moscow. President Reagan, said his spokesman, had agreed to the schedule of follow-up meetings "as a means of encouraging continuation of the significant progress that has taken place in the Soviet Union over the past three years."[84] But the Vienna meeting did not end in perfect harmony. Evidently irked by the spreading criticism of his repressive practices, particularly in regard to minorities, Ceausescu had ordered the Romanian delegation to secure last-minute revision of seventeen human rights provisions. This gambit failed to win the support of even Romania's allies, and Ceausescu's envoy, fearing his master's wrath, reportedly broke down in tears at a Warsaw Pact caucus.[85] As the conference was drawing to a close two weeks later, the Romanian delegate declared in the closed plenary that while he joined the consensus "we feel no commitment to implement those provisions to which Romania does not agree or considers inadequate." Canada (speaking for NATO) and Austria (on behalf of the NNa) rejected this qualification as contrary to the CSCE rules of procedure, and U.S. Ambassador Warren Zimmerman categorized it as "absurd and illegal."[86] Romanian Foreign Minister Ion Totu nevertheless reiterated the reservation during the concluding ceremonies. Such open rejection of accountability and the binding quality of consensus was unprecedented in the history of the CSCE and threatened to subvert the entire process.

Secretary Shultz was guardedly optimistic in his address, praising Gorbachev while criticizing some of his allies. Crackdowns on dissidents in East Germany and in Prague, where police had brutally dispersed a peaceful demonstration the previous day, were, he said, "in glaring contradiction to the solemn international commitments" that had just been made. "In Romania, the economic and social conditions, as well as the political and civil rights of all citizens, are being eroded at a discouraging rate, and in both Romania and Bulgaria, minorities have been particularly hard hit by government policies of recent years."[87] Still, as Richard Schifter observed, the Vienna agreement provided the most significant new guarantees of human rights since the Final Act of 1975 and, more importantly, reflected at least on the part of some Communist signatories a more serious intention of living up to their commitments.[88]

Much of the progress embodied in the Vienna agreement lay in terminological nuance and emphasis. The signatories undertook to bring their laws and regulations into conformity with their CSCE commitments and to respect the right of individual citizens to exercise their freedoms, including that of emigration. New commitments to respect freedom of religious practice and education were denounced by Ceausescu as taking "mankind back by 500 years to the age of the Inquisition." [89] Several provisions addressed the cultural rights of ethnic minorities; Bulgaria and Romania attempted, unsuccessfully, to append to each mention of minorities the ominous phrase "where they exist." As before, the reiterations and elaborations on human rights lay the greatest burden of adaptation on the socialist states.

Human Rights after Vienna. The West's desire to further institutionalize the monitoring of human rights compliance was met by new provisions for the exchange of relevant information and bilateral meetings. The Vienna agreement also set the schedule for an Information Forum (London, April-May 1989) and for three meetings (in Paris, June 1989; Copenhagen, June 1990; and Moscow, September 1991) of a Conference on the Human Dimension to "achieve further progress concerning respect for all human rights and fundamental freedoms, human contacts and other issues of a related humanitarian character." The fourth major follow-up meeting of the CSCE was scheduled to convene in Helsinki in March 1992.

The London Information Forum marked the further erosion of Warsaw Pact solidarity. The Soviet Union trumpeted the achievements of *glasnost* and criticized Western visa practices while distancing itself from its more conservative allies. The West concentrated its attacks on Romania and Czechoslovakia; in Prague, police had just beaten up a BBC correspondent who was covering an unofficial demonstration. The East Europeans, particularly Bulgaria and Czechoslovakia, continued to denounce Radio Free Europe, and Western requests that all jamming be deemed illegal went unheeded.[90]

At the Paris meeting of the Conference on the Human Dimension, the split in Communist ranks was confirmed. Romania stood alone in its insistence that the entire mechanism for reviewing human rights compliance constituted interference in internal affairs. Hungary, meanwhile, denounced Romania's treatment of ethnic minorities, announced the opening of its borders, and cosponsored with the United States and Austria a proposal to abolish exit visas as well as offering other proposals on freedom of association and minorities. Even the Soviet Union joined in the criticism of Romania's erection of a barbed-wire barrier on its border with Hungary.

Bulgaria bore the brunt of criticism in the later stages of the Paris meeting when its discriminatory policies took the form of encouraging a massive exodus of ethnic Turks to Turkey. The American delegation, which included several Helsinki Commission staff members, took the lead in denouncing the retrograde East European regimes; on June 15, 1989, concurrent resolutions were submitted in the Senate and the House condemning Bulgaria's treatment of its Turkish minority. At Paris, the United States tabled a proposal calling for free elections and the establishment of multiple political parties. But Romania's obduracy ensured that no communique would be issued by the conference.

When the CSCE signatories met in Sofia from October 16 to November 3, 1989, for a conference on environmental protection, their presence emboldened local ecological and human rights groups to mount public demonstrations. This conference, too, ended without issuing a concluding document, for Romania refused to accept the draft's approval of independent environmental activism. On the last day, in a remarkable show of solidarity, all the other delegations added their names as cosponsors to the document. A week later, the Bulgarian dictator Todor Zhivkov was ousted.

When the last remaining East European dictator, Romania's Ceausescu, perpetrated a massacre of demonstrators at Timisoara in December 1989, the CSCE provided the venue for one more condemnation of tyranny. At the plenary session of the Confidence and Security-Building Measures negotiations in Vienna on December 20, United States Ambassador John Maresca delivered an impassioned statement of the West's outrage.[91] And then Ceausescu, too, was gone.

By the time the second Conference on the Human Dimension ended in Copenhagen on June 29, 1990, free elections had been held in all of the former Soviet satellites except Poland, which was still saddled with a legislature chosen on the basis of a restrictive formula. The Warsaw Pact members no longer met as a group, and even Albania had joined the CSCE process, as an observer. The quality of democracy in Eastern Europe remained uneven, but the new regimes all professed respect for political and civil rights, and in contrast to earlier meetings the conference devoted little time to review of implementation. The main exception was the concern expressed by the American delegation and twenty-one others on June 14–15 at the violent repression of anti-Communist demonstrations in Bucharest.

The U.S. delegation, headed once again by Max Kampelman, concentrated on securing entrenchment of free elections and political pluralism. The work of the conference was divided among four drafting groups focusing on the rule of law and democracy; minorities and tolerance; improvements to the Conference on the Human Dimension mechanism (coordinated by Hungary); and human rights, human contacts, and related issues of a humanitarian character. The resulting concluding document reflected remarkable consensus on all issues except minorities. It listed as essential elements of democratic societies representative, constitutional government, separation of state and political parties, subordination of the military to civil authority, and an independent and impartial judiciary. It declared that political legitimacy is based on the will of the people expressed through periodic and genuine elections, that individuals and groups had the right to establish political parties, and that foreign and domestic observers could enhance electoral propriety.

The concurrent ethnic tensions in Romania, Bulgaria, Yugoslavia, and the Soviet Union and the recurring incidence of anti-Semitism enhanced the urgency of addressing minority rights and racism. These controversial issues cut across country groupings, dividing West and East alike, as debate raged over the definition of individual vs. group rights and administrative autonomy. Austria, Czechoslovakia, Hungary, Italy, and Yugoslavia jointly proposed that the CSCE guarantee the protection of minority rights. The outcome was a compromise affirming that the rights of national minorities were essential to peace, justice, stability, and democracy. The rights enumerated included preservation of ethnic culture and free association, contacts across frontiers, and participation in public affairs to promote minority interests; racial and national intolerance were roundly condemned. The conference invited further consideration of the thorny issue, at an experts' meeting and at other venues such as the Council of Europe.

At Copenhagen the CSCE reached a high point of consensus on the principles of human rights. The Helsinki process had served the cause well from the phase of bitter confrontation to the comparative cordiality that came to prevail at the end of the decade. With the further institutionalization of the CSCE promised at the November 1990 summit, there were grounds for optimism that international scrutiny and mediation could promote application of the principles professed.

From Leninism to Liberalism.   America's pursuit of human rights in Eastern Europe has consumed immense time and energy, in the CSCE process as well as in the routine diplomatic and public spheres. Yet it is scarcely possible to draw up a precise balance sheet, if only because of the complexity of cause and effect in the political evolution of the Soviet sphere. To be sure, publicity and quiet diplomacy had won Eastern concessions on numerous individual cases of emigration, family reunification, and harassment of dissidents. After Vienna, even the repressive regimes in Prague and Sofia had set to the task of adjusting their practices to the new criteria regarding, for instance, the issuing of passports.

The laborious CSCE process had a salutary impact on specific issues of individual rights, and it continued to serve as a useful forum for denouncing the most egregious violators. The real test of the West's human rights crusade nevertheless lay less in the result of such humanitarian pressure than in the comprehensive restoration of political and civil liberties in Eastern Europe. The Western liberal example, America's psychological warfare and human rights crusade, and the CSCE process all served to undermine the popular legitimacy of Leninism. These pressures contributed materially to the wave of liberalism that swept through Eastern Europe in 1989 as Gorbachev relaxed the Soviet Union's imperial grip and set the ruling parties adrift.

The classical concept of rights inherent in the individual, advocated by the West, clashed with official East European political cultures in which rights are granted by society, that is by its self-appointed leaders. The illegitimacy of that notion may not have been always self-evident to all East Europeans. Historically, the authoritarian and paternalistic aspects of their political inheritance conditioned them to a certain extent for Communist bureaucratic rule, though for all its pretense at egalitarian social justice and scientific management, communism soon proved more oppressive than earlier forms of social control. Nevertheless, by the end of the Second World War, most East Europeans leaned more toward the liberal version of rights and limited government than to the collectivism and dubious, "socialist" legality of the Soviet-sponsored alternative. Even the uncertain appeal of Communist utopia was dispelled by the bitter experience that followed. Thus, the West's contemporary crusade for political and civil liberties and for unqualified self-determination found a receptive audience in Eastern Europe.

At the beginning, in their revolutionary-Stalinist phase, the Communist parties relied on agitprop tactics of mass mobilization to generate ritualistic displays of popular support. By the late 1950s, as the parties settled into a more bureaucratic-managerial style of rule, some of them allowed and indeed encouraged a certain depoliticization of social life. The implicit bargain was that the parties would rule and provide material welfare for a politically passive society. This strategy did induce widespread political apathy as well as the "internal emigration" of frustrated intellectuals. Dissent did not die out, but it took economic failure and growing evidence of the rulers' incompetence and moral weakness to stimulate more active challenges to Communist authority.

By the mid-1980s, the popular and intellectual appeal of Marxism had dissipated not only in the West but also in the East, where previously much dissent (from ideological conviction or for tactical reasons) took the form of Marxist revisionism. Only a few Communists continued to profess faith in the reformability of socialism. The Polish dissident (and onetime Marxist) Adam Michnik observed, "The debate about how to improve socialism has become irrelevant because nobody in Poland knows any longer what socialism means. Our discussions concentrate instead upon how to achieve freedom."[92]

The most stinging rebuke to the Communists came from the younger generation, from those nurtured by the state to become the models of socialist man. A 1987 survey of architecture students in Budapest revealed that the majority did not regard Hungary as a democratic country, denied that most Hungarians supported the party's policies, felt that Hungary would have been better off without socialism, did not believe that socialism could only be built in a one-party system, and considered the "bourgeois democratic system" appropriate for Hungary.[93] A national debate organized by the Hungarian Communist Youth League on the theme "What Kind of Socialism Should We Build?" generated many impatient demands for pluralism and democracy but no interest in Marxism-Leninism.[94] Barely 4 percent of young Poles, according to a 1986 survey, desired progress toward "some form of socialism."[95] As Mieczyslaw Wilcek, the Polish industry minister, noted after his defeat in the June 1989 elections, "Nobody wants to hear about Marxism and Leninism any more, even in the party."[96] Both Marx's laws of history and Lenin's political system seemed hopelessly discredited in Eastern Europe.

It was of course not the lure of political liberalism but rather economic crisis that drove the Communist elites in the 1980s to desperately seek viable alternatives that could expand the base of political consent while preserving the party's supremacy. The more perceptive reformers recognized that the rational remedy of decentralized, market economics is inherently pluralistic and cannot succeed without institutional and behavioral change in the political realm. Having little choice but to accept blame for the mismanagement that contributed to this crisis, the Communists were eager to share the onus for painful economic austerity, to diffuse and deflect popular resentment by distancing the party from the daily task of government and by sanctioning more participatory processes.

The option of retaining undivided ultimate power while surrendering responsibility for the routine management of economic affairs was tempting but politically unworkable, for the regulation of even a market economy is intimately linked to social and trade policy, to fiscal and monetary variables, all of which demand choices that are the bread and butter of politics. The need for choice is driven by the plurality of interests, which even Communists conceded to be inherent in modern society. The execrable record of Leninist rule robbed of all popular legitimacy the Communists' original claim to possessing the sole scientific formula for human progress. But retreat from utopianism to the more pragmatic outlook, which characterizes Western liberalism, that the function of government is to represent and serve the ever-changing pattern of competing social interests threatened the foundations of Leninism.

The ruling parties' claim to aggregate all valid interests was in practice as untenable as their earlier pretense at representing the consensus of a seamless, proletarianized society. Without the Marxist dogma of scientific socialism, the parties could not justify monopolistic rule, and without the discipline of Leninist democratic centralism, they could not effectively impose such rule. The reality of diverse social interests leads logically to institutionalized pluralistic politics and to codified liberties that nurture and protect a civil society of autonomous and free individuals. How a Communist party worthy of its ideology could accommodate such a fundamentally liberal outlook without surrendering its doctrinal leading role is a question that invites squaring the circle.

The Gorbachevian answer of "pluralism in one party" proved to be a short-lived palliative. The superficial democratization of one-party rule initially envisaged in Hungary and Poland (and in the Soviet Union as well) only intensified the multiple political demands of an emerging civil society. The minuscule non-Communist parties preserved in a permanent state of subordination in all East European states except Hungary had been a politically meaningless remnant of the Communists' postwar "popular front" strategy. Cautious reformers toyed with variations on the theme of qualified pluralism that would entrench a Communist majority or a Communist-dominated coalition, or reserve certain powers to the party in evocation of constitutional monarchy.

The common denominator of all these alternatives was denial of the individual's full political liberty. The most self-serving rationale advanced by Communists for limiting democracy was that the people of Eastern Europe (after forty-odd years of socialist enlightenment) lacked the experience and political wisdom to freely choose their governors. In the case of other reformers, including non-Communists, such approximative approaches were inspired not by attachment to socialism but by estimates of irreducible Soviet imperial interests. When by 1989 Gorbachev had confirmed that these interests no longer required local Communist supremacy, the tentative steps away from Leninism in Eastern Europe turned into a rout.

Hungarian Reforms. The first country to benefit from this retreat was Hungary, where Janos Kadar's comparative liberalism failed to arrest economic decline and undermined the party's self-confidence and credibility. Communist reformers and frustrated middle cadres dumped Kadar and most of the old guard at the May 1988 national conference, and the floodgates of pluralism were opened wide. Already at the beginning of that year a new press law had come into force lifting virtually all state controls on publishing and the media. A stream of new newspapers, opposition periodicals, and books on hitherto taboo topics appeared; in a few days two hundred thousand copies of Arthur Koestler's *Darkness at Noon* were sold.

Hungary's new general secretary, Karoly Grosz, failed to deliver a concrete program and unite the party behind him, and under the impetus of reformers in party and government and opposition forces, the process of political decompression gathered speed. A multiplicity of new political parties, unions, and other associations surged into the breach. The Hungarian Democratic Forum emerged as a nationwide movement for reform. By the spring of 1989 Hungary was in the midst of uncontrolled pluralistic ferment. Nationalistic sentiments were openly displayed at mass demonstrations in 1988 over the Transylvanian minority issue and in 1989 on the reinstated national holiday (March 15) commemorating the 1848 revolution.

The government also responded to popular concerns by active diplomacy on behalf of minority rights in Romania. In an editorial on March 15, 1989, the party daily *Nepszabadsag* accused Ceausescu of operating a dictatorship that had "practically abolished the constitution" and called the six Communist veterans who had addressed a letter of protest to Ceausescu the real representatives of the Romanian people. In another concession, the government suspended work on the ecologically controversial joint Czechoslovak-Hungarian dam project on the Danube.

The Communist reformers' wish to divorce the party from its past culminated in the reevaluation of 1956. Originally defined as a counterrevolution, it had been subsequently described by Kadar as a national tragedy. By May 1989 the event was openly referred to as a popular uprising and revolution and its leading figure, Imre Nagy, as a good Communist and martyr; the following month, Nagy and his associates, who had been executed in 1958 and placed in unmarked graves, were ceremoniously reburied amidst a mass demonstration. Freedom of speech and association put in question not only the party's exclusive leading role but its internal, Leninist discipline. At a meeting in mid-May of the party's proliferating "reform circles," the Stalinist, "Asiatic" model of despotism was denounced along with Kadar's neo-Stalinism, and civil rights, political pluralism, and marketization of the economy were endorsed.

The party's leading reformer, Imre Pozsgay, asserted (ironically, in an interview with Radio Free Europe) that "it is impossible to reform the communist system now existing in the Soviet Union and Eastern Europe" and that a new party would arise based on the European socialist and social democratic pattern; he openly accepted the possibility that the party might one day find itself in opposition.[97] The "bureaucratic, overcentralized model of socialism and the building of state socialism and a party-state" had run their course, declared Prime Minister Miklos Nemeth; a multiparty system was the best guarantee of democracy, and the

Western experience was a "treasure house" for those who wished to avoid mistakes and wrong paths.[98] At a congress in October, the official Hungarian Socialist Workers' party reconstituted itself as the "Hungarian Socialist party," formally surrendering the Leninist leading role and identifying itself with the Western social democratic mainstream. Only a small fraction of the HSWP membership took the trouble to join the new party, while a few true believers denied the legality of the transformation and tried to keep the old party alive. But to all appearances, Marxism-Leninism in Hungary had peacefully passed away.

Meanwhile, an invigorated parliament enacted a constitutional amendment declaring Hungary a republic pure and simple instead of a "people's republic" dedicated to socialism. New laws provided for free, multiparty elections and guaranteed civil rights, affirming that freedom of conscience and religion was a fundamental liberty not granted by the state or any other authority. Pluralism returned with numerous new political parties, and in the two-round election in March/April 1990 Hungarians delivered their verdict on socialism. The old Communist party was excluded from parliament, and the new socialist version won less than 9 percent of the vote. Democratic Forum, the conservative-nationalist party led by Jozsef Antall, secured a comfortable plurality with over 40 percent, followed by the urban-liberal Free Democrats and the reconstituted Independent Smallholders. The first act of the new parliament was to declare October 23 a national holiday in commemoration of the "glorious freedom struggle" of 1956.

Polish Reforms. Hungary's gradual and peaceful abandonment of Leninism coincided with a more dramatic shift to semidemocracy in Poland. Solidarity's challenge had been repulsed by the Brezhnev Doctrine, but the Polish party found itself wholly discredited in the aftermath of martial law, leaving the task of government to General Jaruzelski and his small band of Communist and nonparty collaborators. His attempts at economic reform met with recurrent labor unrest as well as a profound skepticism that manifested itself in the disappointing result of the 1987 referendum on reform measures. The regime's attempts to simulate democracy with an advisory council of selected non-Communists and to win worker support with more responsive official trade unions failed to generate even the minimal political consensus necessary to extract Poland from its economic quagmire.

The church remained the only institution enjoying popular legitimacy while the rump of the proscribed Solidarity soldiered on with calls for pluralism. Meanwhile, in the burgeoning alternative civil society, independent associations proliferated, some, like Fighting Solidarity and the Confederation for an Independent Poland (KPN), openly calling for national sovereignty and an end to communist rule. The regime applied relatively few restrictions on religious and intellectual freedom, allowing a few of the more innocuous independent clubs to be legally registered, tolerating a vast counterculture of underground publications, and sanctioning the reestablishment of the moderate independent journal *Res Publica*. Such concessions did not extend to outright political opposition. The police continued to harass radical dissidents, and an open attempt to revive the old Polish Socialist party in November 1987 was quickly suppressed. Jaruzelski's appeals for national reconciliation were belied by his adamant refusal to open a dialogue with Solidarity.

Two waves of strikes, in April and August 1988, impelled the regime to relent. After the first, censorship was relaxed to allow wider discussion of issues and an "anticrisis pact." In August, after the striking workers in Silesia and on the Baltic coast had reiterated the demand for relegalization of Solidarity, the regime for the first time since martial law opened talks with Lech Walesa. This historic surrender, presumably sanctioned by Gorbachev, reflected not only economic urgency but also a hope that compromise with the politically seasoned Walesa might stem the rampant radicalism of a younger generation of Polish workers. Faced with empty coffers and the threat of anarchy, Jaruzelski opened the door to meaningful political reform.

The subsequent roundtable talks between the regime, Solidarity, and the official trade union progressed through months of tough bargaining to reach a historic agreement in April 1989. The accords anticipated the relegalization of Solidarity, the farmers' Rural Solidarity, the Independent Students' Association, and other pro-Solidarity associations. The institutional structure of government was reformed, with a new state presidency enjoying limited powers; a new, freely elected Senate; and a lower house, the Sejm, that would need a two-thirds majority vote to override Senate veto of its bills, and in which, at least in the first election, the Communist coalition (the Polish United Workers' party and its allied parties) would be guaranteed 65 percent of the seats. The opposition was allowed to publish its own newspapers and given limited access to state radio and television. The accords also sanctioned reforms aiming at a market economy as well as wage indexation to a maximum of 80 percent (ironically, a limitation rejected by the official trade union). Soon after this compromise, the regime moved to legislate normalized relations between state and church, restoring the latter's independence and property and opening the way for full diplomatic relations with the Vatican. .

Walesa hailed the accords as the beginning of the road to a democratic and free Poland, and took pains during the campaign to convince skeptical Poles that partial democracy was but a prelude to full self-determination: "Our representatives in the Sejm and Senate can create a platform from which we will jump into freedom and independence."[99] The June 1989 elections confirmed the worst fears of Poland's Communists. Radio Free Europe broadcasts and financial donations from the West aided Solidarity's vigorous campaign, and one Solidarity election program on television featured Zbigniew Brzezinski, Yves Montand, and Stevie Wonder. The regime protested such "intervention," but the outcome of the election could hardly be attributed to foreign assistance. Poland's voters overwhelmingly endorsed Solidarity's candidates in the open contests and denied even unopposed Communist candidates victory in the first round. Jaruzelski commented stoically, "It was the first time that voters could choose freely. That freedom was used for the crossing-off of those who were in power till now."[100] His own election to the presidency only came about by grace of Solidarity's support.

Hungary was alone among Poland's Warsaw Pact associates to publicly express the obvious: "Whatever may happen in the future, after four decades the people of an East European country have for the first time expressed their real opinion on a system that was imposed on them."[101] When political deadlock finally gave way to the appointment of a Solidarity-led government, Romania's Ceausescu issued a futile call for Warsaw Pact intervention to salvage socialism. "Everything is fine and there's nothing to worry about," said KGB chairman Vladimir Kryuchkov after meeting with the new prime minister, the once-imprisoned Catholic intellectual Tadeusz Mazowiecki.[102]

The Kremlin's professed equanimity was an ominous signal for the other ruling parties, for it confirmed the death of the Brezhnev Doctrine. Earlier in the year, Hungary's party leader had reported after meeting his counterpart in Moscow: "Analyzing the historical lessons of 1956 and 1968, Mikhail Gorbachev said that there must be maximum guarantees today that outside force should not be used to resolve the internal affairs of socialist countries." Gorbachev also opined that the Hungarian reforms were "historically ripe."[103] And Poland's Mieczyslaw Rakowski warned his fellow Communists not to expect help from the Soviet Union; admitting that in the past the Soviet Union had "to some extent violated [Poland's] sovereignty," he declared that Poland is "now absolutely independent in shaping its policies."[104]

Poland's new government included some Communists, among them the interior minister, but its political orientation reflected the massive popular rejection of Marxism-Leninism. Mazowiecki invoked the support of all "patriotic sociopolitical forces" while anticipating that the application of necessarily painful economic remedies would make the honeymoon a short one. Rakowski, for his part, called upon former communists to build a "mighty party of the Polish left," evidently hoping that Solidarity would exhaust its popularity in the thankless task of economic reform.[105]

At its January 1990 congress, the Polish Communist party followed the Hungarian Party's lead in renaming itself "Social Democracy of the Republic of Poland," while a more reformist faction split off to form a "Union of Social Democracy." The former passed a resolution acknowledging the crimes committed by the party in Stalinist times as well as its responsibility for the economic crisis; it also apologized for having punished Poles for their political views but rejected any notion of tangible redress for these wrongs. A concurrent public opinion survey revealed that scarcely 1 percent of Poles still supported the Communists.[106]

The radical economic reforms and austerity measures promulgated by the new coalition in December 1989 were no prescription for popularity, and the Polish political compromise soon began to fray as the other East Europeans moved to unqualified democracy. Popular impatience with growing material hardship and the continuing predominance of former Communists in state administration led to a split in Solidarity ranks between supporters of Prime Minister Tadeusz Mazowiecki and Lech Walesa, the latter advocating more rapid change and promoting his candidacy for president. By late 1990 Poland was catching up to its neighbors with the transformation of Solidarity into competing political parties, and Lech Walesa was elected president.

East Germany and Bulgaria. "We intend to continue in the previous proven way," declared the East German party leader Erich Honecker in June 1988, dismissing *perestroika* as a Soviet remedy for Soviet problems.[107] As the Politburo's chief ideologist, Robert Hager, put it, there was no need to repaper one's walls just because a neighbor was doing so.[108] One source of this arrogance was the East German economy's comparatively high productivity, but the official coolness toward *glasnost* and political reform derived mainly from the proximity of another Germany, stronger, democratic, and economically prosperous. Despite the efforts of the regime to promote a distinct, East German nationalism, the constant exposure of its subjects (through West German television) to images of freedom and plenty continued to undermine its claim to success and legitimacy. The Socialist Unity Party, SED by its German initials, based that legitimacy on a spurious identification of the GDR with German antifascism. In December 1988, the authorities banned circulation of an issue of the Soviet digest *Sputnik* that carried an article arguing that Stalin and the old German Communist party had contributed to Hitler's rise.

Soviet Foreign Minister Eduard Shevardnadze affirmed lamely at a press conference in Vienna that "each state has the right to build its frontiers as it wishes," but what his British counterpart described as a "monstrosity," the Berlin Wall, remained a vivid symbol of the GDR's political insecurity.[109] West German leverage secured periodic concessions to ease cross-border traffic and family reunification, yet the majority of cases recorded by the West German human rights Central Documentation Bureau at Salzgitter involved prison sentences for the offense of "preparing to escape from the republic."[110]

Numerous groups of dissenters formed in the mid-1980s, most of them sheltering under the protective umbrella of the Evangelical church, which became an active proponent of social and political renewal. In 1988, some church leaders issued a call for democratization, declaring that the party "must renounce its monopoly on truth and its fundamental claim to superiority" over all other institutions.[111] The regime's response was to crack down on dissidents and impose tight censorship on church publications. Local elections in May 1989 were manipulated to produce the requisite sweeping Communist victory, a fraud that spurred dissidents to new activism. The rigidity of the Honecker regime was motivated in large measure by the logical outcome of respect for political and civil rights: democratic self-determination, which in turn could revive the prospect of German unification.

Hungary's decisions in early 1989 to dismantle the iron curtain and adhere to the international convention on refugees (the latter in order to obtain financial aid for refugees from Romania) had an unexpected effect on East Germany. Beginning in August, thousands of East Germans took the Hungarian route to escape to West Germany, and when East Berlin protested that this violated a bilateral accord dating back to 1969, Hungary unilaterally suspended that agreement on the grounds that the CSCE Vienna norms on freedom of travel took precedence. By November, some 120,000 East Germans had fled through Hungary, Czechoslovakia, and Poland.

This new exodus presented the Honecker regime with an economic as well as political dilemma, for the GDR could hardly afford the loss of masses of young, skilled workers and professionals. It also emboldened domestic dissidents already inspired by the wave of reform in Poland, Hungary, and the Soviet Union to form pressure groups, notably the New Forum, and mount public protests. Honecker gave orders for the police to use all means to disperse a demonstration in Leipzig on October 9, which drew 70,000 people, but these were countermanded by some of his Politburo colleagues, averting what might have become a replay of the Tiananmen massacre in China a few months earlier. Gorbachev, in East Berlin for the GDR's 40th anniversary celebrations, had also counseled compromise, reportedly telling Honecker that "those who resist history will be punished by life." [112]

Within a week, Honecker was deposed, and the new party leader, Egon Krenz, moved to open the Wall, initiate talks with opposition groups, and promise political reform. At a special party congress on December 8–9, Krenz was replaced by the reformist lawyer Gregor Gysi amid condemnation of the Honecker regime's mismanagement and corruption. Honecker and then Krenz were expelled from the redesigned "Party of Democratic Socialism," and in January, Honecker and three other former Politburo members were charged with treason; according to the indictment, they had systematically trampled fundamental human rights, warped the media with censorship, squandered and embezzled public funds, and sanctioned electoral fraud. [113]

The East Berlin parliament meanwhile unanimously repealed the constitutional entrenchment of the party's leading role, then legislated freedom of the press from government control. The collapse of Leninism in the GDR had come with astonishing rapidity, bringing not only the turmoil of unfettered pluralism but also an issue of self-determination unique to East Germany: whether its people were disposed, and free, to seek unification with their Western conationals. The opening of the Wall unleashed a flood of economic refugees that forced both Germanys to seek a quick and stable political solution. Bonn's promise of economic largess sealed the fate of an independent East Germany. The leading West German parties poured their resources into an election campaign that led in March to the triumph of the Eastern Christian Democrats; they and the Social Democrats swamped the alliance of grass-roots opposition groups, including New Forum, that had momentarily prevailed in the revolution. The reformed Communists managed to win 16 percent of the vote. The resulting coalition government of Christian Democrats, Free Democrats, and Social Democrats committed itself to seek speedy unification. The restoration of human rights in East Germany reopened a "German Question" that was troublesome for both East and West (see chapter 6).

By 1988, a few human rights and environmentalist groups had emerged in Bulgaria, including the Club for the Support of Perestroika and Glasnost, the Independent Association for the Defense of Human Rights, and Eco-Glasnost, but they made little headway against the regime's determination to suppress dissent. The fall of Todor Zhivkov, who had ruled with an iron hand for thirty-five years, came abruptly on November 10, 1989. The palace coup was engineered by his successor, former Foreign Minister Petar Mladenov, and evidently had Gorbachev's approval. The new leadership subsequently charged Zhivkov with corruption and condemned him for his policies of discrimination against the Turkish minority (a measure that provoked nationalist counterdemonstrations). Legal proscription of independent political activity was abolished, as was the party's constitutional leading role. Although Mladenov insisted that reform would take place within the context of socialism, he promised early multiparty elections, the separation of party and state, and a shift to a more market-oriented economy. The "allied" Agrarian party promptly reasserted its independence, and an opposition alliance, the Union of Democratic Forces, emerged to test the promise of democratization.

The June 1990 elections, essentially free according to foreign observers, brought a result at variance with the other East Europeans' first response to pluralistic democracy: the renamed, ex-Communist Bulgarian Socialist party secured a parliamentary majority. The visceral rejection of all remnants of Soviet influence that distinguished the rest of the region was absent from the historically Russophilic Bulgarian political culture. Socialism, if not its authoritarian variant, had struck deeper roots, and the new governing party promised economic reform. The Muslim "Movement for Rights and Freedoms" also secured representation in parliament, and the new government undertook to suspend official discrimination against ethnic Turks. But this apparent continuity and gradualism did not rest on widespread consensus; the first months of Bulgarian democracy were marked by anti-Communist demonstrations, administrative paralysis, and attempts at creating a more broadly representative coalition government.

Czechoslovakia's "Velvet" Revolution.   A few days after the Bulgarian coup, an equally abrupt but more fundamental revolution engulfed Czechoslovakia. After the suppression of the dream of "socialism with a human face," Czechoslovakia under Gustav Husak and his successor Milos Jakes had suffered the protracted nightmare of "normalization." Abjuring political liberalization, the regime concentrated on satisfying the basic material needs of an apathetic populace. The party was purged of all reformist elements, and formal endorsement of the Soviet invasion and normalization became a prerequisite for meaningful employment. Those dissenters who did not choose exile but adhered to the loose Charter 77 organization, the Committee for the Defense of the Unjustly Persecuted (VONS), and Polish-Czechoslovak Solidarity (which links Charter 77 and KOR) were subjected to constant harassment. Ever vigilant for signs of political deviation, the regime readily resorted to repressive measures against the ostensibly innocuous Jazz Section of the Czechoslovak Union of Musicians (for its "counterrevolutionary activity"), rock groups, religious activists, and spokesmen for the cultural rights of the Hungarian minority.

The obvious similarity between Soviet *perestroika* and Dubcek's 1968 Action Program caused acute discomfort to the regime, all the more so since the Gorbachevite critique of the Brezhnev era threatened to negatively reevaluate the Soviet intervention. Dubcek's congratulatory message to Gorbachev and the airing of his views at an Italian Communist conference and on Hungarian television in April 1989 added to the embarrassment. Gorbachev's encouragement produced tentative steps toward economic restructuring, but *glasnost* and political reform remained anathema to the conservative leadership. The new slogan of socialist pluralism held no appeal for General Secretary Jakes, who declared in 1988 that "the broadening of democratization in no case means the creation of space for the legalization of political opposition which, as all experiences to date show, cannot be other than antisocialist."[114]

Despite the regime's efforts at suppression, a ground swell of protest arose in Czechoslovakia as the revolutionary wave swept through its neighbors. The issues had become more diverse since Charter 77's original concern with violations of human rights, and encompassed environmental decay, cultural freedom, military service, and fundamental change in the political system. In early 1988, some 600,000 signatures were collected on a petition calling for religious freedom, and a related demonstration in Bratislava in March was quelled by force. Underground publications proliferated, and numerous new independent groups emerged. In early 1989, on the eve of the anniversary of Jan Palach's self-immolation in protest against the Soviet crushing of the "Prague spring," Radio Free Europe broadcast a cautionary message from the playwright Vaclav Havel. The regime imprisoned him on grounds of incitement, prompting protests from hundreds of prominent intellectuals as well from Western governments and human rights advocates.

When a student demonstration in Prague on November 17, 1989 was brutally dispersed by the police, Czechoslovaks responded with a wave of mass protests and strikes. Faced with a wholly alienated population and lacking Moscow's support, the party leadership resigned a week later. A general strike on November 27 impelled the government to accept the demands of the new opposition group, Civic Forum, and in the new coalition government named on December 3, Communists were reduced to a minority. By the end of December Vaclav Havel had replaced Husak as president, while Dubcek was elected chairman of the federal assembly. In the meantime, censorship was lifted, political prisoners were amnestied, and new laws were drafted guaranteeing civil rights. The beleaguered party, under its new leader, Ladislav Adamec, announced the rehabilitation of those purged after 1968 and its espousal of pluralistic democracy, but its membership and influence were rapidly eroding. Although free elections were scheduled for the spring, in January 1990 the Communists agreed to surrender their majority in parliament.

In his eloquent New Year's address, the new President Havel drew up a dismal balance sheet of the socialist record. After reflecting on economic decline, pollution, exploitation of workers, and falling life expectancy, he stated:

The worst thing is that we live in a contaminated moral environment. We fell morally ill because we became used to saying something different from what we think. . . . The previous regime, armed with its arrogant and intolerant ideology, degraded people into a productive force and nature into a tool of production. . . . It reduced gifted and autonomous people, skillfully working in their own country, to nuts and bolts of some monstrously huge, noisy and stinking machine, whose real meaning is not clear to anyone. . . . We had all become used to the totalitarian system and accepted it as an unchangeable fact and thus helped to perpetuate it. . . . I dream of a republic independent, free and democratic, of a republic economically prosperous and yet socially just_ short, of a humane republic that serves the individual and therefore holds the hope that the individual will serve it in turn.[115]

The rapidity and peaceful character of the revolution testified to the popularity of these sentiments in Czechoslovakia, whose earlier democratic experience prepared it better than some of its neighbors for the tasks ahead. In the elections of June 8–9, Civic Forum and its Slovakian branch, Public Against Violence, won 168 out of the 300 seats in the Federal Assembly, against 47 for the Communist party. A former liberal Communist, Marian Calfa, was named prime minister, and Dubcek was confirmed as chairman of the Federal Assembly. A democratic future seemed assured, although the open assertion of the several national interests soon put in question the viability of the federal union. Slovakian nationalism and separatism was on the rise, provoking long debate over the naming of the state, ending with the compromise formula "Czech and Slovak Federal Republic." The Hungarian minority also secured parliamentary representation but found little sympathy in the increasingly nationalistic Slovakian republican government.

Coup in Romania. The fall of Romania's Ceausescu was not free of violence. That tyrannical dictator, ruling over the poorest country's in the Soviet sphere, remained fanatically opposed to liberalization, arguing (plausibly) that the party "cannot share, and even less relinquish its role, without disappearing sooner or later."[116] The party, in fact, was merely the servant of his corrupt and nepotistic rule. Ceausescu's neo-Stalinist convictions were displayed in the ruthless suppression of dissent by the dreaded Securitate; in monumental construction projects, notably a new palace, larger than Versailles, for which a good part of historic Bucharest had to be razed; and in a massive experiment in social engineering aiming to eliminate over half of the country villages (and what remained of private farming) and the resettlement of farmers in "agroindustrial centers."

Designed ostensibly to increase the stock of arable land and industrialize food production, that "systematization" program also threatened to destroy the historical and cultural inheritance of the Hungarian and German minorities. It exacerbated the already strained official relations between Budapest and Bucharest and drew worldwide protest. Beginning in 1987, thousands of Romanians, mostly ethnic Hungarians, sought refuge in Hungary, where the party newspaper accused Ceausescu of operating a dictatorship that "practically abolished" the constitution and disregarded human rights.[117] In early 1989, Hungary joined Sweden in having the UN Human Rights Commission launch an international investigation of the situation in Romania, while the European Community, France, and other Western countries suspended trade negotiations or resorted to diplomatic sanctions.

Within Romania, the Securitate operated with a vast network of informers to nip protest in the bud. A workers' demonstration in Brasov in November 1987 was swiftly crushed. Ethnic Hungarian dissenters, including the former party official Karoly Kiraly, and others who in the early 1980s managed to disseminate some samizdat material, were silenced. The few Romanians who dared to criticize the regime openly, such as Doina Cornea in Cluj, suffered severe reprisals. An anonymous group styling itself "Romanian Democratic Action" issued a program in 1987 calling for a return to parliamentary democracy, as did the organization "Free Romania" founded by ethnic Romanian refugees in Hungary. In March 1989, six party veterans, including former foreign minister Corneliu Manescu, addressed an open letter to Ceausescu denouncing the village systematization and construction programs, the forced assimilation of minorities, and an economic policy that produced penury. They called on Ceausescu to "restore the constitutional guarantees regarding the rights of citizens. This will enable you to observe the decisions of the Vienna Conference on Human Rights [sic]."[118] Police harassment was their reward.

With the opposition tiny and fragmented, and with Ceausescu impervious to external pressure, there seemed to be no promise of an end to Romania's agony. The unexpected revolution began in the city of Timisoara on December 16, 1989. Ethnic Hungarians were joined by Romanians in defense of the Protestant pastor Laszlo Tokes, who was about to be deported for his criticism of the regime. On Ceausescu's orders, the Securitate turned the ensuing demonstration into a bloodbath, prompting similar demonstrations elsewhere. Upon his return from a visit to Iran, the dictator called for a public rally of support in Bucharest on December 21, but the stratagem backfired. The Timisoara massacre had finally galvanized the opposition. Ordered to marshal troops against the demonstrators, the minister of defense, Vasile Milea, committed suicide, and the army joined the revolution. For a few days, battle raged between rebels and the loyal security forces as a National Salvation Front emerged to fill the vacuum of power. The execution of Ceausescu and his wife on Christmas Day marked the end of a tragic era in Romanian history.

The National Salvation Front was dominated by dissident and opportunistic Communists, including the interim president, the party's former chief ideologist, Ion Iliescu. (Some of them eventually claimed that they had been long plotting to overthrow Ceausescu.) Its early rule was chaotic. The Front first declared the Communist party outlawed ("considering that it is against the national spirit and our ancestors' law"), then opted to put the question to a national referendum, then postponed the referendum.[119] It promised free elections, then decided to contest them as a new party. Prewar parties, notably the Liberals and National Peasants were revived, and in February 1990, the Front agreed to share power with a provisional, multiparty Council of National Unity.

The revolution was applauded by Gorbachev and the West, and the first foreign minister to visit Bucharest after the dictator's fall, Hungary's Gyula Horn, voiced some confidence that ethnic discrimination would be suspended. Yet nationalistic intolerance soon resurfaced, in interethnic clashes and in the pronouncements of the National Peasant party. The close identification of communism with Ceausescu's despotism had left the ideology bereft of popular legitimacy, but the old *nomenklatura* expediently professed democratic principles under the guise of the National Salvation Front. It improved the food supply, suspended Ceausescu's oppressive practices, and thereby managed to win the support of a majority accustomed to paternalistic government.

The election campaign was marked by intimidation and violence against other parties, prompting the State Department to temporarily recall its ambassador, and by a protracted demonstration of students and intellectuals in Bucharest against the rule of former Communists. Iliescu and the Front nevertheless triumphed in the May 20 election, obtaining 263 out of 396 seats in the Deputies' Assembly and 92 out of 119 in the Senate. The reconstituted Liberal and Peasant parties, led by returning emigres, were far behind. Intimidation and even fraud played a part, though not decisive, in the lopsided victory of the Front. And it bode ill for national reconciliation that the electorally strongest party possessed of a credible democratic platform was the Hungarian Democratic Union, which earned the votes of most ethnic Hungarians.

The early record of the Iliescu government indicated that the transition to a fully democratic order in Romania would not come easily. Although the Communist party had ceased to exist, its personnel and appointees (apart from Ceausescu's relatives and most exposed acolytes) remained in place. The Securitate was renamed, but the fear it generated did not dissipate. Antigovernment protests flared up, and in June the government called in miners to brutally disperse a prolonged, student-led demonstration in Bucharest. Freedom of the press and association unleashed not only liberal but also chauvinistic opinion. The initial promises of cultural and educational facilities for the ethnic minorities were soon qualified if not reneged on. For all the official professions of reformist intentions and respect for human rights, it appeared that a cabal of former Communists had hijacked Romania's democratic revolution and was expediently fanning nationalism to bolster its popular legitimacy, much as Ceausescu had done earlier.

Yugoslavia and Albania.   As the last Warsaw Pact domino fell, the winds of change reached beyond the Soviet sphere. The political affairs of Yugoslavia had drawn little attention from the United States and its allies after Tito's declaration of independence. The party's rule remained unchallenged, and human rights were circumscribed, but Yugoslavs were free to travel and seek work abroad and the country's relations with the

West became comparatively cordial. The Titoist experiment with workers' self-management provided a semblance of decentralization without generating real economic efficiency.

After Tito's death, central party and state authority was progressively undermined by ethnic tensions and economic decline. In the more developed republics of Slovenia and Croatia, nationalistic tendencies resurfaced and combined with pressures for political democratization and even full autonomy. In the backward Kosovo province of the Serbian republic, ethnic Albanian nationalism provoked a Serbian backlash and, by early 1990, a state of near civil war. The economic disparities between regions exacerbated ethnic rivalries, and while the Belgrade government toyed with plans for market-oriented reforms, inflation reached a rate of 2,000 percent. Both the federal party and the government seemed powerless to cope of these disintegrative forces, and the Serbian-dominated military talked darkly of the need to restore order and unity.

At its January 1990 congress, the League of Yugoslav Communists decided to give up its political monopoly and recommend legislation instituting a multiparty system. Reformist delegates failed to win support for a social democratic redefinition of the League, more liberal human rights, and greater independence for republican parties, so a few days later the radical Slovenian party seceded from the League. Within a few months, as the republican parties concentrated on their local constituencies, the League effectively ceased to exist. Non-Communist nationalists triumphed in multiparty elections in Slovenia and Croatia, and the two republics declared their "sovereignty" within a yet-to-be-negotiated Yugoslav confederation. Serbia tried to secure at least its own republican rule by curtailing the constitutional autonomy of its provinces of Vojvodina and Kosovo. And when Kosovo's ethnic-Albanian-dominated parliament challenged central authority, Belgrade dissolved it and sent in the troops. Tensions rose in Bosnia-Herzegovina as well, between the Muslim majority and the Serbs.

Thus, democratic pluralism had a peculiarly disintegrative effect on multinational Yugoslavia. There, as in many other parts of the region, the delegitimation of state socialism unleashed historical forces that were not necessarily conducive to unity and political stability. Similar forces had led in the interwar period to the imposition of centralized Serbian rule. There was no guarantee that the federation would withstand the wave of national self-determination as the country drifted toward civil war.

There remained Albania, once a target of covert Anglo-American efforts at rollback, then largely ignored by the West as it withdrew in the early 1960s into Stalinist isolation. It is the only European country not party to the Helsinki Final Act, and the only country where it is against the law to speak to a foreigner without official permission. Enver Hoxha's successor, Ramiz Alia, thundered that "in the countries of the East, the bourgeois and opportunists are working with united forces, with unified tactics and strategies to liquidate socialism." [120] But even this last true believer made a token concession to political pluralism when in January 1990 he announced that henceforth Albanians could choose between two Communist candidates in elections. A few months later, the government suspended its proscription of "religious propaganda" and declared that it was ready to join the CSCE. Its concurrent promise to facilitate foreign travel did not stop the storming of Western embassies in July by thousands of Albanians impatient to escape from the last bastion of state socialism in Europe. In early 1991, faced with mounting protests, Alia finally took the historic step of sanctioning a more pluralistic democracy.

Problems and Needs of Democratization. The year of unexpected revolutions was followed by the year of free elections, and a new Eastern Europe began to take shape. The legacies of national history, both pre-Communist and Communist, marked the variegated pattern of transformation. From Hungary northward, a comparatively stable democratic order was emerging; political turbulence and ethnic cleavages once again turned the Balkans into an unstable region. For all, there remained many obstacles and pitfalls on the path of converting Leninist dictatorship into pluralistic democracy. The pressing and universally popular demand for the dismantling of the totalitarian state's most fearsome agency of enforcement, the secret police, could be satisfied with relative ease. Freedom of the press and other political and civil rights could also be readily reinstated, although as Havel observed, the behavioral transformation into a democratic civil society will have to overcome decades of negative conditioning. And the vested interests of the old "new class" of officeholders and managers, the job security of workers, the universality and adequacy of social benefits are all threatened by the linked process of democratization and marketization. No government or political party could offer a credible, painless panacea to these concerns.

East European reformers resort readily to the Thatcherite "there is no alternative" rationale, but the emerging democratic order bears the heavy burdens of penury and scarcity, of deep mistrust, grudges, and corruption bequeathed by forty years of socialism. Betrayed by the illusion of Communist utopia, the hapless East Europeans are now prey to the new illusion that democracy and the market can work a magic cure. The restoration of political and civil rights allows for government by renewable consent, and the market and private property foster productive competition, but the satisfaction of all needs and desires remains a dangerous hope ready to be exploited by demagogues and ideologues. The only certainties are that the Marxist-Leninist formula has failed the test of history and that the East Europeans' faith in democracy will be sorely tested by the economic and social transformation that lies ahead.

As the East Europeans begin to exploit the intoxicating opportunity for self-determination offered by Gorbachev, the need for the West to watch over human rights alters but does not disappear. Self-determination brings with it domestic political turbulence and the reassertion of national interests that are not necessarily conducive to regional stability and orderly relations in the region and between the two alliances. A military and ideological monolith was far simpler to deal with than the increasingly diverse and unstable Eastern Europe of the 1980s and 1990s. The West's interest in reinforcing reform in the Soviet Union and renegotiating the conditions of European security may strain its principled advocacy of full self-determination for the East Europeans, particularly in the case of the several multinational states, including the Soviet Union.

The notion that the East Europeans need instruction in democracy may appear patronizing and evoke the hoary Communist rationale that the masses are not politically mature enough for more democracy (an updating of the even hoarier assertion that the party must rule in the name of a proletariat that has not reached a sufficient level of class consciousness). To be sure, neither the pre-Communist tradition of paternalistic statism nor the subsequent socialist authoritarianism nurtured the tolerance for opposite views and willingness to compromise that are essential to the successful practice of pluralistic politics. The creative intellectuals who played a prominent role in the dissident movements are sincere champions of human rights, but they are traditionally ambivalent about the merits of market democracy. And new regimes intent on marketization lack the stable constituency of a large propertied and entrepreneurial class. History has bequeathed to these societies sharp class and ethnic antagonisms, and economic reconstruction will create new social cleavages as compromises are made among the competing claims of market-driven growth and redistributive justice and with respect to foreign ownership of industries and the media. As the euphoria over regained national autonomy dissipates, the hard choices demanded by reconstruction may imperil the fragile consensus for market democracy. Effective political pluralism depends on agreement on the rules of the game. It is a game in which the East Europeans have little experience and which in the short run promises psychological relief but few material rewards.

Political and civil rights can be constitutionally guaranteed, and the principles of democracy can be taught in schools, but democratic political behavior is developed mainly through practice and experience. Nevertheless, the West can offer invaluable help to the East Europeans in their return to democracy. The various constitutions, forms of checks and balances, and presidential and parliamentary systems are indeed a treasure house of democratic practice. Western governments and parties should actively support the efforts of East Europeans to devise democratic institutions optimal for their circumstances and should draw their counterparts into cooperative relationships.

At the moment of structural transformation, the emerging, independent political associations, trade unions, and publications labored under severe handicaps. In an environment where the state long controlled most resources and where private assets are minimal, the simplest material needs of organization, not to speak of organizational experience, were in short supply. There are precedents for private as well as public assistance. A foundation established by the Hungarian-born American financier George Soros has expended millions of dollars aiding democratic groups and exchanges in Hungary. Solidarity's role as the predominant and encompassing Polish opposition force and its ostensible trade union status facilitated material support from Western unions, including NED funds through the Free Trade Union Institute of the AFL-CIO.

Indeed, the United States has made a tangible if modest contribution to the process of democratization. Within the global mandate of the National Endowment for Democracy, Eastern Europe figured as a minor target, accounting in 1987–88 for no more than $2,325,000, or 16 percent of total expenditure on projects. Polish projects took the lion's share, $1,707,500, of which $1 million came as a special congressional appropriation for Solidarity. Projects for Czechoslovakia received $194,000, for Hungary $71,500, and for Romania $50,000, with regional projects absorbing an additional $302,500.[121] As the pluralization of the Hungarian political system gathered speed in 1989, the Democratic, Republican, and AFL-CIO institutes jointly developed a substantial funding program to assist free trade unions and parties to become established, including support for publications and training seminars. In this fashion, the NED has usefully fed the "flame of freedom" and complemented diplomatic advocacy of human rights.

As the opportunities and needs grow, in Poland, Hungary, and elsewhere, additional congressional funding for the NED and more active development of East European projects by its "retailers" can reap rich rewards for democracy. Congress in November 1989 allocated $12 million to support democratic institutions in Poland. In the first Peace Corps project in a European country, volunteers were dispatched to teach English in Hungary; the next recipient was Czechoslovakia. Hungarian legal experts working on a new constitution were invited to the United States to study the American political system, and the USIA has sponsored the visit of budding Hungarian politicians to study American electoral practice. Countries with more tenuous democratic traditions, such as Romania and Bulgaria, are prime candidates for similar programs. President Bush's disposition to encourage voluntary action—his "thousand points of light"—was reflected in his announcement in May 1990 of a "Citizens Democracy Corps" to serve as an information clearinghouse for American volunteer programs in aid of market democracy.

In the battle for human rights and self-determination in Eastern Europe and the Soviet Union, Radio Free Europe and Radio Liberty have played a unparalleled and critical role. RFE took advantage of the spread of liberalization to broadcast interviews with reformers and dissidents, and its reporting of political ferment helped to undermine the more retrograde regimes. Even in Hungary, where by 1988 the media had become extraordinarily free and diverse, RFE retained its audience with superior programming in news and commentary. Acknowledging the legitimacy of free communication, the Hungarian government in 1989 permitted the posting of a permanent correspondent in Budapest with full press accreditation. By the following year RFE correspondents were roaming freely in Eastern Europe, and Czechoslovakia had even provided for medium-wave broadcasting of its programs.

The region's new democratic regimes not only lavished praise on RFE for its past service in the cause of freedom but asserted that it had not outlived its usefulness. Indeed, in its cross-reporting, which draws on a unique research capability, it fills an important gap in the political consciousness of East Europeans. The region is a hotbed of nationalistic passions, grievances, and prejudices. There is a shortage of mutual sympathy and, indeed, of mutual interest between the several nations, and RFE remains the most impartial and best-informed agent for nurturing familiarity, concern, and solidarity, even if at times (notably in its treatment of ethnic minority issues) it reflects Washington's diplomatic reluctance to address divisive conflicts.

The rapid spread of democratization and *glasnost* inevitably puts into question the future of the two Munich-based radio services. Their original mandate had an implicit sunset clause: operations would terminate with the restoration of freedom. At a conference sponsored by RFE/RL in November 1989, Deputy Secretary of State Eagleburger argued that "the new openness currently prevailing in the region does not mean that the radios have worked themselves out of a job." They serve as an "insurance policy against the efforts of those who remain the enemies of glasnost" and can "contribute to the success of perestroika as well by creative programming which introduces the listeners to the techniques and building blocks of the free enterprise system and of democratic institutions."[122]

The construction of stable democracy in Eastern Europe will not occur overnight, and for a few years yet Radio Free Europe and Radio Liberty can serve the region, not least as a benchmark for the emerging pluralistic domestic media. But temptation will soon mount in an economy-minded Congress to write their epitaph. When the original policy rationale for these U.S.-sponsored voices disappears, they can silenced or, if audiences and economics warrant, privatized. The European Community, or the Council of Europe, in its efforts toward integrating the East into a united and democratic Europe, might well consider adoption of such a unique asset. And the Voice of America will continue to do its part. Until then, the $200 million annual operating cost of the two radio services will remain a modest but invaluable contribution by the American taxpayer to the peaceful pursuit of human rights.

The Council of Europe, based in Strasbourg, is also well suited to assist the democratization of Eastern Europe. Founded in 1949 as an association of countries possessed of pluralistic institutions and a commitment to liberal human rights, it serves an essentially consultative and advisory function. In 1990 it had twenty-three members. Within the context of democracy, it is explicitly nonpartisan: the members' delegations must include representatives of all major political parties. The Council drafted the 1950 European Convention on Human Rights and has also promoted the socioeconomic rights (notably the right to strike) enumerated in the European Social Charter as well as various forms of cultural cooperation addressed in the 1954 European Cultural Convention.

The Council was active in denouncing human rights violations in the East, and as early as June 1989 it responded to improvements in this sphere by admitting Hungary, Poland, Yugoslavia, and the Soviet Union to special "guest status" that allowed nonvoting participation in the parliamentary assembly. Similar status was granted to Czechoslovakia in March, to East Germany in May, and to Bulgaria in July 1990. Hungary had the longest record of contacts with the Council and, after joining the European Cultural Convention, it was the first Warsaw Pact state to formally apply for membership, in November 1989. His country, said Foreign Minister Gyula Horn, "cannot manage to catch up with European civilization if it is not integrated into Western European organizations." Poland, Yugoslavia, and Czechoslovakia soon followed suit. Council representatives observed the elections in several East European countries, and, as pluralistic democracy is consolidated, full membership is bound to follow. In October the Council's Assembly unanimously approved Hungary's admission, to take effect on November 6, while denying even guest status to retrograde Romania.

East Europeans tend to regard membership in the Council as a badge of eligibility for admission to the European Community. To see the Council as the institutional embryo of a European confederation is premature. It is well suited, however, to play an increasingly active role in inducing and verifying implementation of the CSCE's human rights provisions and in promoting the parliamentary and other contacts that are needed to deepen democratic practice in Eastern Europe.

The inclusion of East European countries in a continental community is an appealing prospect for both East and West, one that should lead to a shared interest in the development of compatible democratic institutions. The European Parliament, which over the years repeatedly passed resolutions condemning human rights violations in the East, as early as 1987 addressed the possibility of parliamentary contacts and in 1988 received visits from groups of Polish, Czechoslovakian, and Hungarian deputies. The Parliament also sponsored the establishment of a Foundation for East European Studies. It was, in early 1990, the scene of a lively debate over the merits of direct aid to East European democratic parties (advocated by center-right groups) versus party-to-party assistance, the option supported by the social democratic group.

Material support from the West for democratic political parties is more problematical. Apart from legal obstacles, there are obvious dilemmas and uncertainties in the choice of recipients; pluralism and partisanship go hand in hand, but the West's responsibility is more to nurture the necessary institutions than selectively to reinforce parties. The East German case of massive political penetration was an exception owing to unique circumstances. The Federal Republic's parties promptly moved in to help their sister parties in the election campaign, an involvement subsequently legitimated by a new East German party law. They swamped the coalition of New Forum and other indigenous opposition groups as well as the revamped Communist party, paving the way for the absorption of East Germany into a common political structure.

Elsewhere, the West's aid to parties was prompted by fear that the ex-Communists would derive unfair advantage from their financial and organizational assets in the initial democratic contest. The fear was perhaps warranted in the case of Romania and Bulgaria, but in the countries that received the most foreign assistance, the Communists' unpopularity was sufficient to seal their fate. Even the region's most resolutely reformist party, the Hungarian Socialist party, performed miserably at the polls, though it had spared no expense in buying the services of a British advertising agency for its campaign.

In the case of Hungary, the bulk of American aid had gone to the Free Democrats. That opposition-group-turned-party seemed to be the most uncompromisingly Western-oriented; some of its leading figures spoke

English and had well-established contacts in the United States. The other major opposition group, the Hungarian Democratic Forum, was more nationalist and populist in character, and had been more disposed to seek compromise with the reform Communists in the early stages of the transformation. The NED's retailers gave modest support to both parties; the Democratic Forum received more substantial aid from Bavaria's CSU party. The revived Social Democrats got some help from the Socialist International, but they expended their energies in internal quarrels and failed to win representation in parliament, allowing the ex-Communists to prevail as the party of social democracy. In the event, the Democratic Forum proved to be far better attuned to the mood of the electorate. The party leader and new prime minister, Jozsef Antall, subsequently hosted a congress of the Christian Democratic International in Budapest.

In Czechoslovakia, the Civic Forum and Public Against Violence had led the revolution and were identified as the principal democratic force by the NED, which granted them $400,000 for technical equipment. The Christian Democrats received some supplies and advice from their British, West German, and Belgian counterparts. They won only forty seats in the federal assembly, fewer even than the second-place Communists, and protested at the selectiveness of American aid.

In these cases, and in the case of Poland's Solidarity, Western aid and advice were helpful, but probably not crucial to the success on the non-Communists. The reinforcement of democratic political groups at the moment of pluralism's rebirth was a logical extension of the West's human rights campaign. With democratically elected governments in place, partisan aid from official sources such as the NED becomes potentially counterproductive. In any case, as the newly victorious non-Communist governments begin the complex process of divesting the old ruling parties of their vast assets, the need for external aid vanishes. Individual parties may forge links with their Western (and Eastern counterparts), but it would be unhealthy for East European democracy and national autonomy if their parties became identified as clients of one or another foreign government.

These experiences reveal the pitfalls but offer little concrete guidance on dealing with unstable situation in the Balkans. On balance, prudence would dictate NED assistance on a nonpartisan basis to all significant groups that credibly profess adherence to the Helsinki principles. The deepening of democracy throughout the region will be aided by education, familiarization with successful political models, and intensive communication. The NED and other Western institutions can facilitate this process with money and programs. So can private initiatives such as the Prague Branch of the New York–based Institute for East-West Security Studies. As the initial impetus of a consensual rejection of state socialism loses strength, the fragile fabric of the new democracy will be tested by old, undemocratic reflexes and new social conflicts. The United States and other Western countries must help strengthen that fabric by bilateral as well as multilateral initiatives.

The CSCE put human rights on the international agenda. In establishing the legitimacy of collective scrutiny and a common standard of fundamental freedoms, it breached the wall of sovereignty that hitherto afforded legal if not moral immunity to deviant regimes. If this radical departure from traditional diplomatic practice occasionally causes discomfort even to democratic governments caught in the act of compromising on civil liberties, all the more reason for the CSCE process to be further institutionalized. The formal self-determination of Eastern European countries is no cause to abandon a worthy collective enterprise. In fact, the ongoing CSCE could help to restrain nationalistic excesses that have so often in the past embittered regional relations, and to forge, in the words of President Bush, "a new consensus on the cornerstones of freedom, rights, and democracy." [123]

The fledgling democracies need moral and material encouragement to avoid the pitfalls of demagoguery, of expedient compromises at the cost of individual liberties, and of chauvinistic neglect of minority rights. "If 1989 was the year of sweeping away," said Secretary Baker in an address at Prague's Charles University on February 7, "1990 must become the year of building anew." Voicing concern particularly about Romania, he warned that "any backsliding in the movement to create legitimate governments will isolate a nation from the support we can provide." [124]

To deplore the denial by totalitarian regimes of human rights may have been simpler and easier than to nurture the seedlings of democracy, but in willing the end the United States and its allies also accepted some responsibility for providing aid and counsel to East Europeans once they began to emerge from the long night of oppression.

5

Economic Levers

The Western alliance, observed a prominent expert, has a capacity for chaotic mismanagement of East-West trade policy that is hard to underestimate.[1] Indeed, the need to reconcile America's security, political, and commercial interests in Eastern Europe has sorely tested the wit and will of successive administrations. Recalcitrant allies, conflicting domestic pressures, and marginal economic leverage have hampered the development of a consistent strategy that could effectively advance all of those interests. The relative decline in America's economic predominance further weakened that leverage even as detente in the early 1970s and in the Gorbachev era invited a redefinition of the costs and benefits of trading with the East. Yet history's devastating verdict on Marxist economics is opening up new opportunities for political advantage and economic profit.

Lenin's revolution presaged a global competition between socialism and capitalism, between planned and market economies. The United States, rapidly emerging as the foremost capitalist power, reacted with abhorrence. The negligible commercial contacts with the Soviet Union were easily sacrificed in order to isolate the Bolshevik virus. The Europeans proved readier to sell the rope that could hang them, and during the Second World War Washington too overcame its ideological inhibitions to supply massive aid to Stalin's USSR. That conflict also impelled the United States to develop the tools of economic warfare, then directed against the Axis. They would later be used in the quite different circumstances of the cold war.

At war's end, the creation of a new global economic order ranked high among Washington's priorities. Following its liberal economic precepts and applying the lessons of the Great Depression, the United States pressed for unrestricted exchanges of goods and capital (through the General Agreement on Trade and Tariffs, or GATT) as well as for international institutions designed to stabilize and promote the process of economic development (specifically, the International Monetary Fund and the International Bank for Reconstruction and Development, or World Bank). From the Kremlin's perspective, these measures and the abrupt termination of Lend-Lease signified American resolve to impose capitalism's dominion.

For Eastern Europe, postwar liberation meant the replacement of German by Soviet domination, and the economic implications were not long in manifesting themselves. Not satisfied with the expropriation of German assets, the Soviets exacted crippling reparations from former Axis camp followers, such as Hungary. Bilateral commercial agreements with Moscow began the eastward reorientation of the region's trade. The United States offered some military surplus in emergency relief, pressed for nondiscriminatory trade, and sought to protect private American assets.

Although their need for reconstruction aid was desperate, by the time of the Marshall Plan, the East Europeans were no longer masters in their own house. The plan ostensibly did not discriminate between Western and Eastern Europe, but its preconditions, notably the requirement for full disclosure of economic data, predictably proved unacceptable to the Soviet Union and its new client states. Czechoslovakia's rejection of the offer, after initial enthusiasm, marked the extent of Soviet rule. Had such tempting bait been dangled at war's end, some of the early East European regimes, such as Czechoslovakia and Hungary, might have been freer to accept it and the attendant links to the West. But Moscow's political influence soon encompassed irresistible economic demands, and by 1947 the Marshall Plan could only confirm the reality of an exclusive Soviet sphere.

Stalin's perception of capitalist hostility became a self-fulfilling prophecy, for as the iron curtain descended, Washington dusted off its arsenal of economic warfare measures, this time against the Soviet Union and its unwilling satellites. In the East, the nationalization of American and other foreign assets, the imposition of the Stalinist command model, complete with irrational, autarkic tendencies, and the shift to a war economy with the onset of the Korean conflict reflected the subordination of the region's peoples to Soviet interests. For Washington, Eastern Europe had become part of an ideologically hostile, militarily aggressive empire at war with the United States and the free world. In the context of the policy of containment, economic statecraft would be applied to the pursuit of a foreseeably protracted conflict. The threat to Western security would be countered by positive steps to consolidate a militarily and economically strong alliance and negative measures to weaken the enemy's capability. The Soviet bloc could hardly be regarded as an economic threat to the West, but the modern notion of total war, justified by ideology, dictated the pursuit of full economic and psychological warfare against the East.

Strategic Embargo.   Planning in Washington for an embargo against the Soviet bloc was under way by late 1947, and on March 1, 1948, in the wake of the Prague coup, licenses were made mandatory for all exports to Europe. The real target was the East. The postwar embargo strategy was first codified in the Export Control Act of February 1949, which provided authority for the denial of militarily relevant exports without specific reference to the Soviet bloc. Consultation with NATO allies led in late 1949 to the creation of a secret agency, the Coordinating Committee for Multilateral Export Controls (Cocom). The founding members were the United States, Britain, France, Italy, and the Benelux countries, soon joined by Canada, Denmark, the Federal Republic of Germany, and Norway, then in 1953 by Greece, Japan, and Turkey.

For the sake of political expediency, and to avoid awkward debates in West European legislatures, Cocom was established without any treaty or other legal status and therefore without formal enforcement authority. The West Europeans were ambivalent about losing what they perceived to be the mutual benefits of East-West trade, notably access to Soviet raw materials. But at a time when Marshall Plan aid exceeded their entire turnover in East-West trade, their self-interest dictated acquiescence to the American insistence on a comprehensive embargo. By

1951, trade between Western Europe and the Soviet bloc had sunk below prewar levels. One measure of the impact of autarkic Eastern economic policies and Western controls was that, overall, the bloc imported only 37 percent as much as it had in 1938.[2]

The embargo lists quickly rose to nearly three hundred items in the early 1950s, effectively reducing East-West trade to a trickle. The net impact on West Germany and Italy was greater than on the other Europeans, whose trade with the East had barely started to recover from the disruption caused by war. The embargo's impact on Eastern Europe cannot be calculated precisely but was undoubtedly far greater. The reconstruction and expansion of the region's industries and infrastructure now had to be pursued without access to the most logical, Western suppliers. But even without an embargo, Stalinist notions of economic self-sufficiency meant binding the East European economies to the Soviet Union. The forced industrialization programs of the East European countries became an exercise in technological obsolescence and inefficiency, shaping a legacy from which they suffer to this day. Meanwhile, Soviet efforts to obtain controlled items met with some success thanks to the readiness of a few Western businessmen to make a quick profit and the occasionally lenient attitude of their governments.

The expectation of some cold war strategists that economic strains induced by the embargo might impel the East Europeans to break away proved politically unrealistic. The U.S. Minister in Bulgaria, for instance, opined in late 1949 that Western sanctions could provide a "fertile field for the development of malcontents who, it may be hoped, will, in their disillusionment over the glories of communism, turn to the West in their search for a way out."[3] Such hopes were dashed by regimes wholly beholden to Moscow and dedicated to the same revolutionary exercise in social engineering. The embargo simply reinforced Communist propaganda regarding the irreconcilability of the two systems. By itself, it neither caused nor significantly accentuated the forced integration of Eastern Europe into a Soviet empire, but that empire justified Washington's decision not to differentiate between the satellites and their master in its conduct of economic warfare.

The State Department concluded in 1950 that "neither restrictive measures nor the offer of Western economic assistance would in themselves cause the satellite countries to break away from the Soviet Union. The economic weapons available to the West are chiefly important as auxiliaries in a coordinated program designed to cause defection by other means." [4] Western trade was not crucial to the satellite economies, and they were not free to accept loans or credits on terms that would have entailed a reduction in Soviet influence. Washington regretfully acknowledged that the embargo could not seriously jeopardize political stability but calculated that it would considerably impair the Soviet bloc's capacity for prolonged war. [5] At most, it may have marginally contributed to the decline in the standard of living in the satellites, and therefore the unrest that led to eruptions in 1953 in East Germany and Czechoslovakia and in 1956 in Hungary and Poland. To this uncertain extent it succeeded in weakening and destabilizing the enemy at a time when the conventional military balance in Europe favored the Soviet Union.

The Korean War only hardened American attitudes to trading with the enemy. Foreign compliance with the embargo had to be secured. An NSC report in November 1950 specified that "shipments of strategic commodities to any Western European country should be denied where there is evidence that such shipments may be transshipped, directly or indirectly, to the Soviet Bloc." [6] The Battle Act of 1951 prohibited U.S. aid to countries that shipped items on the American embargo list to controlled areas, although to pacify the West Europeans it also allowed the president discretionary power to grant exemptions. The Battle Act's goal was of course to safeguard the West's military and economic advantages, and the notion that the measures would ultimately "assist the people of the nations under domination of foreign aggressors to reestablish their freedom" was more a gratuitous expression of American hopes than a calculated linkage of embargo and rollback.

The administration's seriousness of purpose was signaled by the appointment of Averell Harriman as the Battle Act's first administrator, to be succeeded by Harold Stassen. Since in the early 1950s most non-Communist countries received American aid, the Battle Act proved a potent lever, and some fifty-five out of sixty-six countries agreed to cooperate. [7]

American exports to Eastern Europe, which had reached a postwar high of nearly $120 million in the second quarter of 1947, had been virtually eliminated by mid-1951. The one exception was Yugoslavia, which benefited from a relaxation of the strategic embargo as early as 1949 and became a recipient of American aid. Among America's European allies, on the other hand, pressure for reviving trade with the East mounted as the perception of Soviet threat receded following Stalin's death and the armistice in Korea. Rapid economic recovery, the end of Marshall Plan aid, and skepticism regarding the strategic necessity of a comprehensive embargo exposed the divergence in the commercial interests of the United States and Western Europe.

Our allies argued that the USSR's progress in military technology had not been significantly impeded by the embargo, notably in the nuclear field, and the East European economies were growing, albeit at the price of low personal consumption. American business was enjoying global predominance and had little incentive to question the merits of the embargo, but West European industrial concerns were eager to regain their historic Eastern markets. The Federal Republic of Germany had a particular interest in developing its special open exchange relationship with East Germany. The restless West Europeans were accommodated by waivers of Battle Act sanctions, then in 1954 by a trimming of the Cocom lists. Four years later the lists were reduced further, to 118 items. At the same time the United States made its second tactical breach in the embargo by granting Poland a $55 million credit for American exports, in an attempt to reinforce the apparently reformist regime of Gomulka.

Controversy over the Embargo. By the early 1960s the domestic consensus on the merits of the strategic embargo was beginning to fray as private businesses in the United States began to cast covetous glances at Eastern markets where the West Europeans were busily establishing beachheads. The functionalist hypothesis, that freer trade would build mutual confidence and security and induce desirable reforms, struck some political observers as the next logical phase in East-West relations. For the Americans, at least, freer trade had to be justified in terms of political benefits. While the growing eagerness of American business to compete in East European markets could be accommodated by this more pragmatic approach, the requisites of military security ensured that some form of strategic embargo would remain in place.

Debates over the appropriate dimensions of the embargo continued within the administration and Congress and in Cocom and other allied councils. Beginning with the Kennedy administration, U.S. policy moved along two tracks: adaptation of the embargo to changing military, technological, and political perceptions and expansion of credits and non-strategic trade. The functionalist notion of bridge building led President Kennedy to establish an Export Control Review Board in 1961 to facilitate consideration of waivers. President Johnson responded to business pressures by appointing a Committee on U.S. Trade Relations with East European Countries. In 1964, the Export-Import Bank was directed to advance credits to Hungary and Romania, and American exports to the East momentarily surged, to nearly $160 million. But the political climate was not propitious to trade expansion.

The Berlin and Cuban missile crises and the Vietnam War revived domestic political opposition to trade with the enemy. Congress in 1962 passed an amendment to the Export Control Act specifying that not only militarily relevant exports but also goods that could make a "significant contribution" to the target countries' military or economic potential had to be controlled. In 1965, the Cocom lists were expanded to cover 10 percent of generally traded items.[8] American unilateral controls were even more restrictive, and the gap between the two lists, the so-called "embargo differential," caused bitter disputes among the allies. When the foreign subsidiaries of American corporations were required to abide by the longer, unilateral list, the Europeans protested at this extraterritorial extension of U.S. jurisdiction. De Gaulle's France, having withdrawn from the NATO military structure, was momentarily disposed to ignore Cocom, making the other European participants even more restive. Toward the end of the 1960s Bonn launched its new *Ostpolitik* in pursuit of normalized political and economic relations. Traumatized by Vietnam, Washington took a dim view of its allies' grudging participation in the strategic embargo but proceeded to adapt to the changing economic and political realities.

The rising trade deficit and business pressures had their impact on Congress when in 1969 it debated extension of the Export Control Act. The new Export Administration Act acknowledged that the controls, and in particular the embargo differential, had a deleterious impact on American's balance of trade and payments and laid stress on the need for export promotion. The act reaffirmed the strategic embargo, but in more limited form, for goods of military (and not merely economic) significance the export of which would prove "detrimental to the national security of the United States."[9] In the Equal Export Opportunity Act of 1972, Congress called for lifting unilateral controls where comparable items were available from foreign producers, prompting the

Commerce Department to appoint six Technical Advisory Committees to oversee export licensing in areas such as computing and telecommunications. As a result, many goods were decontrolled, exports to Eastern Europe doubled between 1972 and 1973, and in Cocom the United States came to account for over half of the requests for waivers.

The basic approach in the detente period of the 1970s was to expand general trade while refining the controls on strategic trade. The Bucy report, commissioned by the Pentagon and issued in 1976, laid emphasis on the preservation of America's lead in "critical technologies" of actual or potential military application and recommended that controls be concentrated on design and manufacturing knowhow rather than on end products.[10] This view informed the Export Administration Act of 1979, which superseded both the EAA of 1969 and the Battle Act. The new act reiterated the desirability of trade expansion, rationalized licensing procedures, instructed the president to review with the allies the Cocom lists, and stressed the importance of controlling the export of critical technologies.[11]

The Soviet invasion of Afghanistan in 1979 and the Solidarity crisis in Poland shifted the balance once again toward economic warfare. The modernization of the Soviet bloc's military machine, critics charged, owed much to the transfer (overt as well as covert) of Western technology. The evidence was necessarily incomplete. According to intelligence estimates, some $150 million worth of embargoed goods found their way to the Soviet bloc between 1973 and 1977; an East German defector claimed in 1980 that industrial espionage saved his country an annual $70 million in research and development costs.[12] The Carter administration responded by expanding unilateral technological controls and ordering the U.S. Customs Service to crack down on illegal shipments.

The Reagan administration's initial review of East-West trade policy reflected a hard-line approach that issued principally from the Pentagon. As Assistant Secretary of Defense Richard Perle said of the Soviet Union, "at no previous time in history has one nation been able to prey so deeply and systematically on the fruits of its adversary's genius and labor."[13] The Customs Service's Operation Exodus, launched in late 1981, involved cooperation with allied customs agencies to stem the flow, and within two years some 1400 illegal shipments valued at almost $200 million had been seized.[14]

The administration's intent to invigorate economic warfare was manifest in the bill introduced in April 1983 to supplant the EAA of 1979. It aimed to expand both the national and Cocom lists of "militarily critical technology and keystone equipment," to strengthen enforcement mechanisms, including the Cocom secretariat, and to secure foreign compliance by threat of retaliatory penalties. The bill went beyond the established rationale for the strategic embargo, that is, the preservation of national security, in seeking discretionary power for the president to impose economic sanctions in pursuit of foreign policy objectives. The objectives, explained the Commerce Department's spokesman, included deterrence and punishment as well as the simple expression of political disapproval.[15] The bill provoked much debate in Congress, notably over the merits of "foreign policy controls" of symbolic purpose. The allies, having already acceded to numerous American requests for stiffer control procedures, were resistant to further expansion of the multilateral control lists and a congressional proposal for converting the informal Cocom arrangement into a full-fledged international organization. Only in June 1985 was a new EAA enacted by Congress, to remain in force until September 30, 1989. The compromise bill provided for both trade expansion, by eliminating the need for licenses to export low-technology goods to the allies and generally easing licensing procedures, and tighter controls on militarily sensitive technology.

The Pentagon had led the drive for stricter controls, but American industry and research institutions voiced growing alarm at the harmful effect on the international competitive position of the United States. In 1982, a panel of the National Academy complex persuaded the administration to relax restrictions on the communication of basic research findings. In 1984, another National Academy panel, chaired by Lew Allen, Jr., was charged with studying the complex problem of controlling dual-use technology. The title of its report, issued three years later, reflected the basic dilemma: "Balancing the National Interest: U.S. National Security Controls and Global Economic Competition." It found that the executive branch had mismanaged the embargo, which cost the American economy an estimated $9.3 billion in 1985.[16]

The Allen panel's most original recommendation, that the United States control only Cocom-proscribed items, was inspired both by the prospect of more opportunities for American business and the difficulty of enforcing unilateral controls. The panel urged that the coverage of the U.S. and international lists be limited to "items whose acquisition would significantly enhance Soviet bloc military capabilities and that are feasible to control." Since the allies disagree with some American foreign-policy-driven export controls, the United States ought to clearly separate these from controls required by national security.[17]

Changing Objectives and Problems of Enforcement. Initially the main purpose of the strategic embargo had been what might be termed "structural," to retard the Soviet bloc's economic and military development, and for a time the United States managed to maintain broad, multilateral controls. The erosion of this capability and the limited impact of the embargo led to the reconsiderations that culminated in the Allen report. The remaining rationale for the embargo was preservation of the West's technological lead in the military sphere, a fundamental security consideration in view of the imbalance in conventional forces. As detente, and then the growing trade deficit, put a premium on trade expansion, the Department of Defense became an increasingly influential advocate of effective controls, with authority to review all exports to controlled countries as well as some exports to fifteen other countries. Military exports, for which primary responsibility rests with the State Department, are totally excluded from East-West trade and therefore cause no problems, but the licensing of commercial exports remains fraught with controversy. The coverage of the Pentagon's 800–page-long "Militarily Critical Technologies List" far exceeds the Control List of the Commerce Department, which has the formal licensing authority for commercial exports. The 1985 EAA called for integration of the two lists, but the divergent priorities of Commerce and Defense continue to bedevil the process. There is scarcely a technological innovation that does not have potential military application and therefore could not be classified as "dual-use."

What is militarily "critical" and susceptible to effective controls is a question over which conflict frequently arises between the Pentagon—intent on delaying diffusion—and the Commerce Department (and private business) eager to promote profitable trade. The chairman of United Technologies, Harry J. Gray, observed in 1985: "Clearly, our national interests must come first at all times. We must be alert to government policies, however, that place unnecessary and excessive restrictions on technology. Unrealistic barriers to technology exports handcuff America economically and degrade us in the eyes of our friends and allies."[18]

Two years later, an association of leading U.S. computer and electronics trade groups, the Industry Coalition on Technology Transfer, called for a liberalization of export controls that went well beyond the Cocom revisions. At the same time, the Pentagon accused the Commerce Department of an "egregious lapse of responsibility" in allowing powerful computers to be sold to a Soviet-controlled company in Hamburg and reasserted its authority (pursuant to an earlier presidential directive) to review all export license applications.[19] In 1988 the administration earmarked $39 million for operating the control system (compared to $7.3 million in 1980) and set up a separate agency at the Department of Commerce headed by Paul Freedenberg, under secretary for export administration, with a staff of 510 (versus 207 in 1980) to license exports.

The problems of reconciling these interests are multiplied at the level of multilateral controls. The allied nations' military establishments generally share the Pentagon's restrictive disposition, whereas trade ministries and manufacturers tend to regard controls as an impediment. The latter suspect the Americans of occasionally exploiting the controls for economic advantage and resent the extraterritorial application of American laws where U.S. components or subsidiaries are involved. Cocom, which has a small secretariat located in an annex of the U.S. embassy in Paris and an annual budget of some $1 million, has the daunting task of updating lists covering thousands of items, monitoring enforcement, and adjudicating requests for waivers. Cocom is involved in the actual granting of export licenses only for the most sensitive products. The deliberations of Cocom are secret, and unanimity is required for its decisions. The munitions and nuclear energy equipment lists present few problems, for almost all of the items are totally embargoed. Most headaches are caused by the industrial list, which covers dual-use technologies that might enhance the military capability of the target countries. The secretariat spends much of its time controlling the shipments of these technologies between the member countries to guard against illegal diversions to the Soviet bloc.

Enforceability is the key to a meaningful embargo. At a Cocom meeting in January 1982, the allies agreed to stiffen their control mechanisms, but the emerging consensus suffered a severe setback from the subsequent Urengoi pipeline dispute, a case of tactical "foreign policy" controls. To punish the Soviet Union for its misdeeds in Afghanistan and Poland, Washington banned the sale by American multinationals of machinery essential for building a gas pipeline from Siberia to Western Europe, but it soon had to back down in the face of allied protests. The allies painstakingly forged new agreements in NATO on East-West trade, in the OECD on subsidized credits, in the International Energy Agency on energy security, and in Cocom on strategic technology. But particularly in high-tech trade, the weighing of economic gains against strategic losses remains an immensely complex and politically contentious calculation, one in which government agencies, private interests, and allied countries often find themselves at loggerheads.

A political storm was unleashed in 1987 by the Toshiba-Kongsberg case, in which a Japanese and a Norwegian company had shipped controlled machinery for making ultraquiet submarine propellers to the Soviet Union. Congress issued threats of economic reprisals, and the administration began a new campaign to secure compliance in the multilateral control system. The Pentagon called for an international blacklist whereby businessmen indicted for export offenses in one Cocom country would be automatically denied export licenses by the others. Deputy Secretary of State John Whitehead led the delegation to a showdown meeting of Cocom in January 1988. The bargain he offered was to lower U.S. licensing requirements for countries that tightened their own enforcement system. European pressure for a shorter and more enforceable list was spearheaded by West German Foreign Minister Hans-Dietrich Genscher, who told the European Pariliament in Strasbourg that "no responsible Western politician wants to endanger Western security interests, but present trade limitations within Cocom go beyond what is necessary." [20] Cocom agreed, logically enough, to (in the words of a European diplomat) "erect higher fences around fewer items." [21] Evidence of tougher sanctions against embargo breakers, notably on the part of France, was accompanied later that year by Cocom permission to Boeing and Airbus to market their aircraft in the East, with the proviso that the engines and some of the avionics had to be serviced in the West. In August 1988, the U.S. relaxed the curbs on the sale of lower-level computer equipment to Communist countries.

The rapid global diffusion of technology and the emergence of new economic powerhouses in the Far East has turned the American-inspired multilateral control system into a leaky ship. Western participants at a computer trade fair in Warsaw in February 1988 were surprised to find Polish firms displaying more powerful computers than the Westerners were allowed to export, obtained largely in Taiwan and other Far Eastern markets. The problem of diversion of controlled goods through third countries such as Austria and Switzerland is as old as the embargo. "End-use" clauses in contracts offer little real protection as long as there are unscrupulous middlemen willing to disregard the controls. An Austrian firm, Datapoint International, was fined $275,000 in 1987 for shipping controlled U.S. equipment to Bulgaria, Czechoslovakia, Hungary, and Poland. In another instance, the Commerce Department licensed the sale of an American computer capable of simulating nuclear explosions to an engineering college in Zagreb, Yugoslavia, only to discover later that it had reached Moscow via Belgrade and East Berlin.[22] To block as many gateways for diversion as possible, the Commerce Department offered to ease licensing controls for non-Cocom countries that tightened up their own export licensing and customs inspection procedures. A growing number of countries, including Austria, Finland, Singapore, Sweden, and Switzerland, have complied.

That the Soviet bloc became a willing and eager consumer of Western technology is both evident and natural. The Soviet foreign minister, Eduard Shevardnadze, has referred to the embargo as "this cursed list" and complained that it had held up twenty large industrial projects in recent years.[23] Although Soviet leaders, including Gorbachev, have warned against excessive dependence on the West, there is plenty of evidence that the systematic acquisition of Western technology is an integral part of Soviet weapons development. The Soviet government's Military Industrial Commission (VPK) coordinates the collection of "spetsinformatsiya," or special information, by the KGB's "T Directorate," the GRU military intelligence agency, the State Committee for Science and Technology, the Academy of Sciences, and the State Committee for Foreign Economic Relations. An improved wing design for the Sukhoi-25 fighter, a cruise missile guidance system, and armour-piercing shell technology were among the alleged payoffs of special information.[24]

The intelligence resources of the East European countries have served the same ends. According to the Romanian defector Ion Pacepa, in the 1960s, his agents stole the secrets for making an alloy used in space vehicles, and in 1978, Brezhnev and Andropov asked Ceausescu for help in obtaining the design of Texas Instruments microchips. (Then again, as noted in chapter 4, Ceausescu apparently was also selling Soviet military secrets to the CIA in the 1980s.) Polish agents were instrumental in the covert acquisition of American missile and radar technology in the late 1970s. In 1982–83, Hungarian diplomats conspired with Japanese businessmen to smuggle high-tech laser equipment from the United States to Hungary via Japan. Hungarians were also involved in a foiled attempt in 1987 to smuggle computer and microelectronic equipment of "incredible military applications," according to a Pentagon source. The equipment was Japanese-made, with some American components, and had been ordered in Australia by a dummy corporation set up by the Hungarians in Singapore.[25] And when, after unification, the Bonn government began to round up former East German spies, it discovered that numerous miltary secrets, including the Tornado fighter project, had been compromised.

Such instances of high-tech skulduggery were grist to the mill of the Pentagon in its effort to stiffen controls, but opinions were divided on the net benefits accruing to the East from overt and covert technology transfer. According to secret Soviet documents smuggled to the West, the budget in 1979 for acquiring special information was roughly equivalent to the resulting economies in research. The same source reveals that only half of the hardware and one-fifth of the documentation was put to practical use, and that more than 80 percent of the material obtained by the KGB was unclassified.[26] Still, some Western experts have estimated that, thanks to illegal purchases and industrial espionage, the East had managed to reduce the technology gap in computers and microelectronic systems from between ten and twelve years in the 1960s to between three and five years in 1988.[27]

From Eastern Europe's perspective, the situation looked much bleaker. Erno Kemenes, deputy director of Hungary's National Planning Office, observed, "The technology gap between the two parts of Europe is getting wider. This is a problem because technology is playing a larger and larger role in the economy."[28] As the East Europeans tried to modernize the equipment and infrastructure of their faltering economies, they found that the producers in the CMEA (Council for Mutual Economic Assistance, also known as Comecon) were unable to provide the necessary goods in adequate quantity or quality. The CMEA's program for scientific and technological development, launched by Gorbachev in 1985, failed miserably. The East Europeans are therefore increasingly compelled to look westward for high-tech goods ranging from telecommunications equipment to airliners and suffer from the constraints of the strategic embargo. Needing a powerful computer to manage their new income tax system, the Hungarians rejected the available Soviet mainframe as unreliable and settled for a West German Siemens machine that, because of controls, had only half the desired memory.

The Embargo after the East European Revolution. Consensus on the need for a strategic embargo and its scope became even more elusive as the wind of revolutionary change swept through Eastern Europe in 1989. Negotiation on arms reductions, planning for Western aid, and the lure of new markets overshadowed the perception of threat that had inspired the embargo. Pressure mounted, from the Cocom partners and from American industry, for fewer controls. The restrictions (including the deterrent effect on trade of reexport controls) continued to cost the United States an annual $9 billion in lost exports. Facing a trade deficit of over $100 billion, the administration saw the wisdom of compromise.

In May 1989, the administration agreed to relax Cocom's "no exceptions" rule affecting high-tech exports to the Soviet bloc. A bitter interdepartmental dispute erupted in July when the Commerce Department sanctioned export of more sophisticated desktop and laptop personal computers. The ban, it was argued, unnecessarily penalized American companies since comparable equipment was readily available from Asian suppliers such as Taiwan and Singapore. President Bush supported Commerce Secretary Robert Mosbacher's decision, but Defense Secretary Dick Cheney publicly dissented, claiming that the some of the decontrolled technology was not freely available on the world market and would give the Soviet bloc "significant capabilities that they do not now possess" (including, intimated the Pentagon, detection of the Stealth bomber).[29] Another Cocom controversy arose in October over the Italian Olivetti company's sale of machine tools and computer software for the new Soviet YAK-41 jet fighter.

Relaxation of Cocom restrictions was high on the agenda of the East European regimes as they moved toward market economics in 1990. Czechoslovakia, Hungary, and Poland made overtures to Cocom promising not to divert sensitive Western technology to the Soviet Union. Whether in a more pluralistic Warsaw Pact such self-discipline becomes feasible and verifiable remains an open question, but the West acknowledged that the East Europeans no longer represented a serious strategic threat and deserved preferential treatment. At its June 1990 meeting,

Cocom defined the criteria for removing all restrictions on exports to these three countries, slashed the list of controlled items by a third, and loosened the controls in the computer, telecommunications, and machine tool sectors. It was estimated that these measures would eliminate licensing requirements for $45 billion worth of U.S. exports. A new core list, to be developed by the end of the year, was expected to reduce the number of annual applications for export licenses submitted to Cocom from 1,500 to between 150 and 200.[30]

Risk-benefit calculations in a strategic embargo are only broadly indicative, but some basic conclusions can be drawn. First, socialist, centrally planned economies are singularly inefficient in the application of imported technologies. Technology transfer generates demand for more intermediate goods but does not greatly enhance the capacity of the socialist countries to innovate and to compete on world markets. As an American scholar noted, "The most effective barriers to technology transfer are those erected by the Soviets themselves."[31] Second, the Soviet military-industrial sector does have a capability, exceptional by Eastern standards, to absorb and apply Western technology, and it will resort to all means to acquire it. Third, the West's key comparative advantage in the global economy lies in the sphere of research and development, of high tech knowhow and products, but this sphere is marked by rapid diffusion and obsolescence.

The implications of these propositions for the strategic embargo are obvious. Even in a period of detente, the imperative of military security justifies Western efforts to delay the acquisition by the Soviet Union of the latest scientific-technological innovations of direct military applicability. The Pentagon's 1988 report on Soviet military power found that the United States was superior to the Soviet Union in the technology level of fifteen out of thirty-one deployed military systems, and equal in ten.[32] No nation or alliance can afford to surrender such a security asset. The denial of technology that would be of immediate military advantage to the enemy is eminently prudent and rational, but the same cannot be said with any assurance about knowhow and technologies of only potential, indirect, and long-term military applicability.

In the final analysis, as an English economist has noted, "all goods are strategic, since in the long run all are substitutes."[33] Total economic warfare would have justified the denial of virtually all trade with the East. The experience of the 1950s indicates that such warfare is politically unproductive and impossible to sustain effectively in peacetime. Moreover, any notion that the socialist economies represented a threat to the West was dispelled by their dismal performance and prospects. The strategic embargo, despite flaws and transgressions, has served Western security. Its continued utility and viability depend on a realistic and dynamic reassessment of the irreducible core of military-technological secrets, a calculation that should be informed by political and economic considerations as well as by military expertise. Restricted to these essentials, unilateral and multilateral controls can serve the immediate security interests of the democracies without hampering harmony among the allies. Economic competition and freer trade will serve the long-term interests of nations on both sides of the great divide. And as the East Europeans join the democratic community and sever their military links with the Soviet Union, their need for Western technology should be satisfied with only a minimal application of strategic controls.

Economic Leverage: Yugoslavia, Poland, and Hungary. Economic relations between nations are seldom left untouched by politics, and the East-West nexus has been the most politicized of all ever since the Bolshevik revolution. The challenge, it must be remembered, was delivered unequivocally by the practitioners of Marxism-Leninism, who preached an unrelenting struggle to achieve the historically preordained triumph of their socioeconomic system.

The response of the liberal democracies to this challenge was fraught with controversy. Consensus was ruled out in West European countries where Communist parties flourished on memories of anti-Nazi comradeship and the economic distress of the early postwar years. The appeal of communism was gradually diminished by American leadership as well as covert and overt aid, which played no small part in restoring Western Europe's economic and political self-confidence. But beyond a certain elite consensus on the necessity for a strategic embargo, the allies' ostensibly pragmatic attitude toward economic relations with the East stood in sharp contrast to the fundamentally political strategy adopted by Washington.

The Truman and Eisenhower administrations argued that "trade with the enemy" would at best foster the entrenchment of Communist regimes and at worst enhance, directly or by substitution, their capability for military aggression. Denial of trade and credits, on the other hand, would aggravate the structural and productive deficiencies of the Stalinist command economies and, in the logic of containment, hasten the internal disintegration of the Soviet empire. American economic statecraft in the early years showed little faith in the functionalist strategy of commercial engagement and resorted to the tools of denial, sanctions, and rewards. These symbolized what some West Europeans deprecated as naive moral disapproval, as well as the more concrete goal of weakening and dividing the enemy camp.

An early and indirect exception to the policy of economic containment was acquiescence in the maintenance of commercial contact between West and East Germany. Determined to integrate the Federal Republic into Western military defense, Washington endorsed to Bonn's attachment to the principle of one German nation. East Germany's favored economic status survived the failure of half-hearted attempts in the mid-1950s to negotiate reunification and became a permanent, if anomalous, feature of East-West commercial relations.

A more logical application of containment was the favorable treatment extended to Yugoslavia from 1949 onwards. In breaking away from Stalin's embrace, Tito had taken security and economic risks. Alarmed that his model of national communism might find appeal in the rest of Eastern Europe, the Kremlin launched a vicious, regionwide campaign against all real and imagined evidence of Titoism. From Washington's perspective, Titoism and its disintegrative potential deserved encouragement.Accordingly, following adoption of the basic policy regarding economic relations with Yugoslavia (NSC 18/2), a special ad hoc committee was established on February 21, 1949, to examine export license applications. Within five months it had approved exports of more than double the value of all licenses in 1948. In September, the Export-Import Bank approved a $20 million loan and the International Monetary Fund a $3 million drawing. The NSC also exempted Yugoslavia from the ban on exports of aviation fuel and equipment. In April 1950, the Eximbank granted a further $20 million credit to alleviate Yugoslavia's critical balance of payments problem. Later that year, Washington responded to a request for emergency assistance to alleviate the critical food shortage caused by drought.[34] A military assistance program was launched in 1951. By 1955 the United States had spent close to $1.5 billion to "keep Tito afloat."

American military aid helped ward off the Soviet threat to Yugoslavia, and credits assisted the country's industrial development, but this provided little political leverage. Washington had undertaken not to tie the aid to political demands, and when it nevertheless asked Tito not to recognize the rebel regime of Ho Chi Minh, it was sternly rebuffed. The military agreement of November 1951 culminated ten months of tough negotiation; the Yugoslavs agreed to the presence of a U.S. military mission, but they refused to consider any linkage with NATO. One exception was made in 1954, when Yugoslavia entered into a mutual aid agreement, the Balkan Pact, with NATO members Greece and Turkey; shortly thereafter it settled the Trieste dispute with Italy. American wheat and credits probably helped secure Tito's cooperation even though the Yugoslavs strenuously denied that they could be bought with aid.[35]

When the Kremlin in 1955–56 engineered an apparent reconciliation with Tito, many in Congress misinterpreted the significance of the event and called for an end to all aid. The flow of aid waxed and waned with the progression of Soviet-Yugoslav rapprochement and Tito's reassurances that he was not about to surrender his independence and rejoin the Soviet bloc. In July 1956, Congress amended the Mutual Security Act to require the president to halt aid to Yugoslavia unless he could provide assurance that Tito was "not participating in any policy or program for the communist conquest of the world" and that the aid was in the interest of America's national security. In the midst of the election campaign the Eisenhower administration prudently suspended aid until October, when it provided the necessary assurances and reinstated the economic program.[36] An offended Tito rejected the military assistance program, and outright aid stopped after 1957.

Despite Washington's sensitivity to Tito's nonaligned posturing, the logic of sustaining Yugoslavia's independence survived the forceful Soviet reminder in 1956 that Titoism was not an acceptable alternative for the rest of Eastern Europe. The United States and its allies continued to treat Yugoslavia as a favored economic partner. The Kennedy administration provided a technical assistance program of some $500,000–750,000, development loan assistance that amounted to about $10 million in fiscal 1962, agricultural surplus and military sales, the same export licensing status enjoyed by other non-Soviet-bloc countries, and the early restoration of most-favored-nation tariff status.[37] The Yugoslav model of national communism left much to be desired, notably in economic performance, but the example of independence from Moscow it set remained an asset for the West. American economic leverage had played no part in the Stalin-Tito split, but it helped to safeguard the consequences.

Economic leverage was much less successful in its application to Gomulka's Poland. In February 1957, the Poles came to Washington with a request for credits of $300 million. They won a $30 million Eximbank loan and agreement (under the Agricultural Trade Development and Assistance Act) for the sale, payable in Polish currency, of some $65 million worth of agricultural commodities. An additional $98 million in American aid was promised the following February. But the Gomulka regime soon showed that it had little stomach for political or economic reform at home, or for distancing itself from Moscow. Smaller credits and sales of agricultural surplus were sanctioned by Washington for a few more years, and Poland's most-favored-nation tariff status, revoked in 1951, was reinstated in 1960, but the United States received no political reward for its modest economic favors. The lesson seemed to be that where ruling parties were beholden to Moscow, there was little if any scope for promoting tangible evolutionary change through economic leverage.

Hungary in 1956 presented the challenge of revolutionary, not evolutionary, change. Four days after the revolution's outbreak, Secretary of State Dulles declared optimistically that the East European regimes "must know that they can draw upon our abundance to tide themselves over the period of economic adjustment which is inevitable as they rededicate their productive efforts to the service of their own people, rather than of exploiting masters." "Nor do we condition economic ties between us upon the adoption by these countries of any particular form of society," he added, presumably still anticipating the spread of Titoism.[38] The promise of American largess went unrealized as the Hungarians reached for democracy and sovereignty and were crushed. The Kadar regime, imposed by Soviet arms, contemptuously rejected President Eisenhower's offer of $20 million for emergency relief.

East-West Trade under Johnson. Succeeding administrations remained wedded to the strategy of promoting evolutionary change, couched in terms of peaceful engagement, bridge building, and differentiation. At a time when the Soviet Union was attempting to reinvigorate the CMEA with a dose of supranational planning and integration, it was thought that American economic carrots and sticks might serve to encourage a loosening of ties between the satellites and Moscow and induce domestic reform. A less restrictive and more differentiated trade policy, concluded the State Department's Policy Planning Council in July 1963, could secure political advantages.[39] But if in the 1960s West European governments and firms gradually adopted a "business as usual" approach to East-West trade (subject, of course, to the strategic embargo), Washington's more tentative and politically calculated moves in the same direction were repeatedly frustrated by the vagaries of domestic politics. The predominant mood in Congress was one of bipartisan hostility to trade and aid for Communists, and this mood was only reinforced by the Berlin and Cuban crises and, above all, the Vietnam War.

Even nonalignment of the Titoist variety was perceived by many legislators as pernicious and anti-American. In 1962, the Senate passed the Proxmire-Lausche amendment to the Foreign Assistance Act denying the president discretionary power to allocate farm surpluses for aid; the administration managed to secure a compromise amendment that still required the president to give assurances that the recipient was not controlled by the international Communist conspiracy. Another congressional initiative qualified the new Trade Expansion Act to deny the president power to grant most-favored-nation tariff status to Communist countries. Again Kennedy had to fight hard to win back MFN for Poland and Yugoslavia.[40] The farm lobby helped him to prevail in October 1963 in sanctioning wheat sales to the Soviet Union and Eastern Europe, and American exports to the region momentarily surged.

Western Europe's commercial offensive in the East and a perception of polycentric tendencies in world communism encouraged the Johnson administration to call for building economic bridges. In his 1965 state of the union message, the president indicated that the government, "assisted by leaders in labor and business, is now exploring ways to increase peaceful trade" with the East.[41] To loosen the multitude of legislated constraints, Johnson proceeded prudently by first setting up a special presidential committee on East-West trade headed by the chairman of the Cummins Engine Company, J. Irwin Miller. The committee reported at the end of April 1965 that, although the commercial prospects were limited, the United States did have potential exports that could give it bargaining leverage. It stressed the primacy of political considerations, concluding that the "case for expanding peaceful trade comes down to the proposition that we can use trade to influence the internal evolution and external behavior of Communist countries." The report recommended that the president be given greater latitude in granting and withdrawing MFN and that export licensing be made more flexible; it warned, however, against long-term credits that could amount to a subsidy of the socialist economies.[42]

Only in May 1966 did Congress finally receive the draft East-West Trade Relations bill, proposing to give the president power to enter into three-year, renewable commercial agreements and to grant MFN. In his letter of transmittal, Secretary of State Dean Rusk warned that without such authority the United States would miss "significant opportunities" to affect change in Eastern Europe.[43] Nonetheless, the bill was killed by the chairman of the House Ways and Means Committee, Wilbur Mills.

The Chamber of Commerce, the National Association of Manufacturers, and bankers were all keen on boosting exports to the East, but in congress, in the AFL-CIO, and at the grass roots the notion that America ought not to feed and fight communism at the same time outweighed the hypothetical benefits of economic leverage. Impromptu "committees to warn of the arrival of communist merchandise on the local scene" organized boycotts of Polish hams and Czech crystal. Administration officials sharply criticized such initiatives, and the State Department in 1966 issued a pamphlet entitled "Private Boycotts versus the National Interest," but a pervasive anticommunism accentuated by the Vietnam War poisoned the climate for liberalization of trade. East European aid to North Vietnam was grist to the mill of right-wing groups such as the John Birch Society, which collected more than one and a half million signatures to a petition opposing aid and trade with the Communists.

Romania in the early 1960s showed a disposition to distance itself from the CMEA and the Warsaw Pact and to improve relations with the United States and its allies. The administration responded in 1964 by easing licensing procedures and furnishing Eximbank guarantees for credits to fund major industrial projects. Encouraged by the State Department, the Firestone Rubber Company entered into a $50 million contract to build a synthetic rubber plant in Romania. But when the conservative Young Americans for Freedom picketed the company's Akron headquarters and put pressure on its dealers, Firestone beat a hasty retreat and abandoned the project. A company less exposed to consumer pressure, Universal Oil Products of Des Plaines, Illinois, did complete a contract to build a petroleum cracking plant near the Ploesti oil fields. But the total turnover in U.S.-Romanian trade amounted to under $23 million in 1967, the balance being heavily in favor of the United States. The Ceausescu regime resisted Moscow's pressures for a division of labor in the CMEA that Romania regarded as unfavorable to its development, broke ranks with the Warsaw Pact over relations with West Germany and Israel and the invasion of Czechoslovakia, and performed some diplomatic services for Washington, all of which earned it the reward of MFN in 1975. The Romanians repaid the tangible benefits of MFN by allowing more emigration, but violations of basic freedoms attracted ever more attention in the West. Bucharest's ultimate response to American pressure on human rights was to give up MFN in 1988 (see below and chapter 4). On balance, the Romanian experience, like the Polish one earlier, disappointed the advocates of economic leverage.

Nor could the economic tools of foreign policy be applied effectively in the short span of the Prague spring. The prospects for bridge building did appear more promising in early 1968, and President Johnson once again asked Congress for authority to expand trade. Trade in peaceful goods, testified Deputy Under Secretary of State Charles Bohlen before the House Subcommittee on Europe, could help to bring diversity to Eastern Europe.[44] There was an attempt made to resolve the contentious issue of $20 million worth of Czech gold, held by the United States pending agreement on compensation for nationalized American property, but Congress was not about to approve a generous settlement. Mindful of congressional resistance, the administration politely rebuffed the Czechs' request for a $500 million loan while instructing the Commerce Department to ease licensing procedures. Yet there were some positive initiatives in Congress. Democratic Senator Walter Mondale of Minnesota introduced a Czechoslovak trade bill, and Congressman Paul Findley, (an Illinois Republican) proposed an amendment to the Foreign Assistance Act making Czechoslovakia eligible for MFN, but the Warsaw Pact intervention put an end to these probably foredoomed measures. Dean Rusk commented the day after the invasion, "We would not expect that the East-West trade suggestions put forward by the President would be acted upon promptly by this Congress."[45]

Venturing into the uncharted waters of Eastern trade was risky enough, and for firms sensitive about their domestic public image the threat of consumer displeasure served as a potent deterrent. Other companies developed their Eastern contacts through foreign subsidiaries and middlemen, but in the absence of long-term credits and government investment insurance, not to mention marketable East European exports, there was no prospect of rapid expansion of trade. American exports to Eastern Europe (excluding the Soviet Union and Yugoslavia) grew from $87,751,000 in 1961 to $134,953,000 in 1967. This represented 0.3 percent of global exports to Eastern Europe at a time when the American share of world exports stood at 16 percent. The presence of American industry was particularly weak: since the 1960s, Eastern Europe has accounted for scarcely 3 percent of American exports of finished products. The obstacles, apart from restrictive legislation, included distance from the market and lack of experience in dealing with centralized trade organizations. The United States had, of course, the capacity to be a major supplier of Eastern Europe's industrial needs, but, as a leading private exponent of East-West trade noted at the time, it had largely "ceased to count as a source of unique and irreplaceable supplies."[46] Nor was the United States an essential source of credits and investment capital for the East Europeans. In these circumstances, the scope for influence through economic leverage remained minimal.

Trade and Detente from Nixon to Carter. The Nixon administration made only modest progress in liberalizing trade. In Henry Kissinger's linkage approach to the management of detente, commercial relations were made contingent on Soviet cooperation in other spheres. If the Soviets wanted a European security conference to legitimize their zone of influence and gain easier access to Western technology, then they would have to cooperate over Vietnam and West Berlin. Argued the president at a National Security Council meeting, "Better political relations lead to improved trade," and not the reverse.[47] Kissinger believed that technological and economic imperatives would inexorably drive the Communists to detente and acknowledgment of an interdependent world economy.[48] The broad U.S. approach to the East Europeans, (as formulated by Deputy Secretary of State Kenneth Rush in 1973) was to "create a continuing economic relationship . . . by expanding our trade and by encouraging their growing receptivity to foreign investment." He added that it was equally important for the United States to promote closer economic relations between the two halves of Europe.[49] The administration's guarded disposition to expand trade coincided with a growing perception in Eastern Europe that economic growth needed the boost of Western technology and credits and with greater permissiveness on the part of the Soviet mentor.

America's ambivalence regarding East-West trade was fully displayed in the Trade Reform Act finally passed by Congress at the end of 1974. In addition to the agriculture lobby, a growing number of American multinational corporations and banks were pressing—notably through the East-West Trade Council, established in 1972—for more liberal legislation. The AFL-CIO remained opposed, inspired by a mixture of bedrock anticommunism and suspicion that the multinationals' trade with low-wage countries would cost American jobs. Conservative opposition had both purely ideological and security-related sources: why should America trade with an enemy that was exploiting Western technology to enhance its military capability? America's East European ethnic groups were divided on the merits of trade and tended to favor economic leverage for political reform. It was the Jewish lobby that ultimately had the greatest impact on American trade policy because of growing public concern over human rights in the Soviet Union, and particularly over the issue of Jewish emigration.

The high point of detente with the Soviet Union had been reached at Nixon's meeting with Brezhnev in Moscow in May 1972, and one result was a trade agreement that included the promise of MFN. The proposed Trade Reform Act of 1973 was to deliver on this promise. Instead, the Jackson-Vanik amendment linked all trade and financial concessions to the emigration policies of Communist countries; the president's requests for waivers would have to be scrutinized by Congress and could be turned down by a simple majority. (Concurrently, the Stevenson amendment to the 1974 Export-Import Bank Act limited the granting of U.S. credits to the Soviet Union, specifically in energy-sector goods.)

Henry Kissinger warned that the amendment could jeopardize detente and negotiated with Congress the terms of an initial, eighteen-month waiver, but in January 1975, the Soviets flatly rejected the conditions and abrogated the trade agreement. Three months later, President Ford chided Congress that trade and economic sanctions, however well intentioned, could be self-defeating, and observed that Western Europe and Japan had already stepped into the breach. The majority of his audience remained wedded to a more ideological definition of the national interest.[50]

The cool realism of the Nixon-Kissinger strategy in East-West relations did not easily accommodate this moralistic linkage of trade to Communist domestic policy and human rights. The Carter administration won more sympathy in Congress by espousing the cause of human rights, but at the same time it tried unsuccessfully to decouple this issue from trade. The amended version of the EAA in 1977 not only eased licensing procedures but also made the strategy of differentiation explicit in requiring that U.S. trade policy be based not simply on a country's Communist status but "take into account such factors as the country's present and potential relationship to the United States, its present and potential relationship to countries friendly or hostile to the United States, its ability and willingness to control retransfers of United States exports in accordance with United States policy, and such other factors as the President may deem appropriate."[51] But even before Afghanistan and Poland, Congress was not prepared to surrender the restrictive power of Jackson-Vanik, and the administration vacillated in its attitude on economic diplomacy vis-a-vis the primary target, the Soviet Union.[52]

Recent administrations have used MFN as a reward that, despite Jackson-Vanik, was only nominally linked to human rights. As early as 1975, President Ford persuaded Congress that Romania's diplomatic performance on the world stage deserved recognition and that its emigration policy was sufficiently permissive to warrant MFN. The domestic neo-Stalinism of the Ceausescu regime was conveniently overlooked. (Realpolitik also prevailed over moralism in the case of the Carter-Brzezinski decision to grant the People's Republic of China MFN in 1979.) For years thereafter, the Romanians would grant a batch of exit permits just before the annual congressional review to help the administration recommend renewal of MFN (see chapter 4).

Ceausescu cleverly exploited nationalism to win both domestic popularity and Western favors and technology. At the same time, pursuant to a Warsaw Pact agreement covering any newly acquired technology requested by the Soviet Union, he served as an agent of covert technology transfer. When Deputy Defense Secretary Frank Carlucci visited Bucharest in October 1982 to protest this practice, Ceausescu refused to meet with him.[53] The State Department's efforts to protect the special relationship with Romania started to wear thin in the early 1980s. The world's press increasingly depicted Ceausescu as the tyrannical master of a tightly run police state and focused on his systematic policy of

254 *Of Walls and Bridges*

discrimination and forced assimilation of ethnic minorities, notably the Hungarians.

Civil rights in Romania became grist for the annual congressional hearings on MFN, and by 1985 the Ceausescu regime was warning that the benefits of MFN did not warrant all this criticism. Anticipating the inevitable, the Romanian government in February 1988 chose to voluntarily surrender MFN, thereby demonstrating the limitations of U.S. economic leverage. The cost to the Romanians was substantial: their exports to the United States fell from $680 million in 1988 to $354 million the following year.

Hungary was equally keen to expand economic relations with the United States, and the Kadar regime was far more tolerant and reform-minded than the Romanian. It won the accolade of MFN in 1978 and had no difficulty in retaining it through successive reviews. Hungary's and Romania's acquisition of MFN brought a modest surge in their trade with the United States. Overall, the turnover in U.S.-East European trade rose in the 1970s from $400 million to $3 billion, with the balance at the end of the decade heavily in America's favor.

Poland's Financial Crisis. The 1970s were a decade of relative optimism in both East and West toward both detente and the benefits of increased trade. Poland remained a prime target for differentiation, for the positive application of economic leverage. The economic growth produced by the strategy of extensive development began to falter in the 1960s. The Polish economy, like its counterparts in Eastern Europe, was in a state of structural disequilibrium, characterized by production processes wasteful in inputs and replete with outputs that did not meet the standards of the world market. Neither the arbitrary pricing system nor the subsidies for producers and for consumer goods could long conceal the fundamental imbalance and inefficiency of the economy. The outcome was what has been called "the deepest economic crisis in postwar Europe."[54]

Personal real incomes had already been stagnating for some time when in December 1970 the government announced substantial price increases. Faced with an eruption of labor unrest, the new party leader, Edvard Gierek, opted for an economic strategy that aimed to improve the standard of living by increasing the rate of growth. The West was to be the principal source for this revitalization of the Polish economy. The formula was deceptively simple: Western credits would finance imports of Western technology, and the credits would be repaid with the exported products of the modernized Polish industry.

In its implementation, Gierek's strategy revealed a plethora of political and economic weaknesses characteristic of centrally planned economies. The massive new investments in plant and technology far outstripped the abilities of inefficient central and enterprise bureaucracies and the capacities of the construction industry and the creaky infrastructure. Poland became one of the world's top ten owners of industrial robots. Yet hopes of repaying foreign debt with exports faded as the volume of unfinished investment projects mounted. Gierek's half-hearted attempt in 1973 to decentralize economic management was doomed not only by unfavorable external circumstances but also, in the words of a Polish economist, by the "lack of political will and the resistance of the party bureaucracy."[55]

Without the discipline of the market, and with a central planning mechanism that gradually lost effective control, Poland's economy headed for disaster. The rapid growth in nominal personal incomes and domestic consumption created pressure for fewer exports and more imports. Agriculture, formerly a source of hard currency, became a drain on the trade balance. In 1975, Poland's net trade deficit with the industrial West hit a peak of over $2.6 billion. A basic premise of the original development strategy, the boosting of exports, was superseded in practice by a concentration on investments in import-substitution projects. Some 20 percent of the expensive foreign licenses were never used, and another 10 percent duplicated domestic alternatives.[56] Enterprises had little experience or interest in promoting exports. Recession in the market economies in the late 1970s aggravated Poland's trade imbalance. In 1976, Gierek, like Gomulka before him, retreated before the threat of social unrest and rescinded increases in the price of essential consumer goods. The pattern of import-led growth and unrestrained domestic consumption financed by foreign loans was a prescription for bankruptcy.

Clearly, the West was a partner in Poland's financial crisis. The atmosphere of detente predisposed Western governments and private institutions to respond favorably to the economic development strategies of such East European countries as Poland and Hungary. Political as well as economic profit could be drawn from credits and trade that reinforced moves away from the embrace of the Soviet Union. Western producers eager to supply the East's needs and commercial financial institutions awash with petrodollars had a common interest in loans to Eastern Europe. A Bank of America specialist in Eastern lending recalls that in the early 1970s these countries appeared to be excellent risks: they had a good repayment record, their debt level was low, and their conservative central authorities apparently kept tight rein over trade and finance. The bankers also drew comfort from the "umbrella theory," which held that the Soviet Union was the ultimate guarantor of the East Europeans' creditworthiness.[57] By the end of the decade, the total debt of the Soviet Union and Eastern Europe to the nonsocialist world approached $70 billion.[58]

Western governments, including the United States, looked favorably on private lending to Poland, and until 1977 the banks liberally provided loans with no strings attached. The net trade deficit with the industrial West had been reduced to $1.5 billion, but the aggregate debt reached $15 billion, yielding a debt-service ratio of fifty-nine. (Debt-service ratios express interest and principal repayment on foreign debt as a ratio of exports, and international bankers tend to regard a ratio of twenty-five as the upper limit of safety.) Alarmed at the chronic mismanagement of the economy, the banks began to insist on full disclosure of balance of payments and debt information and concrete plans for improving the current account and the balance of trade. The performance of other East European borrowers offered some reassurance. The Hungarians were managing their debt well, and the Bulgarians responded to Western concerns by quickly halving their debt. Some American banks prudently reduced their Polish exposure, while others, fearing that a sudden withdrawal of credit might cause economic collapse, continued to meet part of Poland's credit needs with shorter-term loans.

When President Carter visited Warsaw at the end of 1977, he promised to provide credits to compensate for a growing shortfall in Poland's grain production. Social unrest provoked by food shortages threatened to destabilize Gierek, and the White House wanted to prop up what still appeared to be a reformist regime. The following year, Poland received $400 million in Commodity Credit Corporation credits. In 1979, CCC aid rose to $200 million in direct credits and $300 million in credit guarantees, and in 1980 to $670 million in credit guarantees. By then,

Poland accounted for 37 percent of the CCC's outstanding credits (and Hungary and Romania for another 7 percent).[59]

Brzezinski observes that "in retrospect, it is clear that the sum total of private and government credits extended to Poland was excessive."[60] But the alarm bells had been rung as early as 1977, when a contributor to *Foreign Affairs* forecast presciently that Poland would probably be forced to reschedule its debt in 1980.[61] A study issued by the CIA in 1978 concluded that Poland was a poor credit risk. The report coincided with the president's decision to extend commodity credits and with the administration's advice to U.S. banks to keep on lending to Poland. CIA Director Stansfield Turner records that Brzezinski was "livid" at the publication of an unclassified report that threatened to undermine the president's policy.[62] The administration had humanitarian as well as political motives in alleviating Poland's grain shortage, and it feared adding to Poland's financial troubles by signaling restraint to the bankers.

By the end of 1979, Poland was running a $2.8 billion deficit in its current account balance, and it was faced the following year with the need to repay $5.2 billion in debt principal and $1.9 billion in interest, amounting to some 68 percent of its anticipated hard currency earnings.[63] The crunch came in 1981, when Poland's debt reached $25 billion (with a debt-service ratio of 175) and the only alternative to rescheduling was default. The major proportion of the new credits since 1977 had come from governments. In the United States, Poland's favored status included MFN (restored in 1960) as well as eligibility (granted in 1972) for Commodity Credit Corporation credits for grain and Eximbank credits for imports of U.S. machinery. The latter facilitated several industrial cooperation agreements, notably a joint venture with International Harvester to manufacture crawler tractors. The turnover in bilateral trade rose from $250 million in 1972 to $1.3 billion in 1980, when the United States accounted for 10 percent of Poland's trade with the market economies.

As the Solidarity crisis unfolded, the NATO allies devised contingency plans that included economic sanctions in the event of a Soviet intervention. Yet in April 1981, Reagan made good his campaign promise to the farm lobby and decided to lift the grain embargo on the Soviet Union over the opposition of Secretary of State Alexander Haig, Defense Secretary Caspar Weinberger, and other advisers, giving, recalls Haig, a "sign of weakness" on a "significant bargaining chip."[64]

Both the Carter and Reagan administrations tried to exert positive leverage on the Polish regime by granting new CCC credits and "Food for Peace" aid, and by a multilateral agreement for partial rescheduling of Poland's debt (see chapter 3). The grants obviously did not suffice to dissuade General Wojciech Jaruzelski from doing the Kremlin's bidding, and the rescheduling agreement was aborted by martial law. Washington did not resort to the ultimate economic lever, the threat of forcing Poland into default. That prospect might have deterred Jaruzelski from cracking down, but only if the Soviet Union itself were unwilling to bear the burden of a bankrupt Poland.[65]

When the Polish crisis materialized, Washington was already engaged in economic warfare with the Soviet Union. Responding to the December 1979 invasion of Afghanistan, President Carter had imposed a package of sanctions that included a partial grain embargo. After Reagan lifted the embargo, Haig tried to salvage some leverage by declaring that a Soviet intervention would incur a total trade embargo. The administration took steps to punish the Soviets after the Polish coup.[66] It extended national sanctions to block the sale by U.S. subsidiaries of compressor equipment for the Urengoi-Western Europe gas pipeline project, which it claimed would make the allies dangerously dependent on Soviet energy supplies.[67] The European allies were furious at this American initiative in punitive economic policy. They needed the gas, contracts had been signed, and there was no reason, they argued, to go beyond Cocom in defense of Western security. The early resumption of grain sales to the Soviet Union displayed America's own inconsistency, and Washington did not even wait for the suspension of martial law to conclude a new five-year agreement with the Soviets for agricultural sales. In the end, the United States gave up its attempt to stop the gas pipeline project, and its other post-Afghanistan sanctions against the Soviet Union had little effect other than the demonstration of displeasure.

Sanctions against martial law in Poland were scarcely more effective, reflecting only the outrage of the American public. Incensed at the suppression of Solidarity, AFL-CIO president Lane Kirkland urged Reagan to impose radical sanctions.[68] Within a week of the declaration of martial law, Washington banned grain shipments, Eximbank and other credits, preferential licensing of high-tech exports, and Polish fishing in

U.S. waters; it also suspended the Polish airline's landing privileges and made it known that the United States would not support Poland's admission to the IMF. In May, the United States suspended a scientific exchange program.

When the Polish parliament formally outlawed Solidarity, the United States on October 9 cancelled Poland's MFN status. Washington made it clear that the sanctions were meant to elicit compliance with three conditions: the lifting of martial law, release of all political prisoners, and meaningful negotiation between the regime on the one hand and Solidarity and the Roman Catholic church on the other. After American pressure and prolonged debate, the NATO allies joined the United States in banning new commercial credits.

Economic sanctions offered a quick and expedient way for the West to retaliate, and they were initially supported by the opposition in Poland. The problem of Poland's debt demanded greater circumspection. The Warsaw government had announced in March 1981 that it was unable to meet its repayment obligations, leaving it up to its creditors to reschedule or declare Poland in default. American and European bankers dreaded the losses and international repercussions of default.[69] For Poland, formal default would have meant the potential loss of foreign assets as well as the accelerated maturity of its long-term debt. In the end, the Reagan administration took the prudent course of simply delaying discussion of rescheduling until Jaruzelski made some political concessions. The Commodity Credit Corporation had guaranteed $71 million worth of loans by American banks, and its rules required a formal declaration of default before the guarantee was activated. The administration resorted to an emergency device waiving the requirement, prompting Senator Daniel Patrick Moynihan and other irate legislators to pass a measure requiring the president to periodically justify the waiver on grounds of national security.

Concessions by the Polish and American governments were slow in coming. The lifting of martial law and a partial amnesty for political prisoners in July 1983 led the "Paris Club" of Western creditor governments to begin discussions on rescheduling; commercial banks had taken this step a year earlier and had resumed providing short-term credits. Since projections showed that full debt service would exceed by a huge and growing margin all of Poland's hard currency export earnings, rescheduling was bound to be a protracted and painful process for both borrower and lenders, and indeed by 1989 the outstanding gross debt was nearing $40 billion. After Solidarity leader Lech Walesa called for a removal of sanctions on trade, Washington in January 1984 restored fishing rights and, a few months later, lifted the ban on the Polish airline and on scientific and cultural exchanges. Following a second amnesty in 1984, the administration indicated that it would no longer actively oppose Poland's readmission to the International Monetary Fund, which was duly confirmed in June 1986. The Warsaw regime had previously taken a few austerity measures, but it was clear to all concerned that any IMF rescue program would require comprehensive and unpopular reforms.

By 1985, Western ostracism of the Jaruzelski regime was eroding. He had consolidated his grip on the country, marginalized Solidarity, and drafted plans for economic reform. Yet the conditions for the lifting of U.S. sanctions had been only partially satisfied in the suspension of martial law and the release of most political prisoners; there remained the condition of some positive steps toward pluralism and national reconciliation. In December 1986, Jaruzelski did appoint a Social Consultative Council that included some nonparty notables, but he steadfastly refused to open a dialogue with the illegal Solidarity movement. The Reagan administration found escape from its dilemma in the changing attitude of the Poles themselves, for Walesa and other opposition figures as well as the church, including Pope John Paul II, had come to the conclusion that the remaining sanctions merely caused economic hardship without budging the regime. After consulting with opposition spokesmen in Poland and Polish diplomats at the Vienna CSCE review conference, the administration threw in the towel and announced on February 19, 1987, the lifting of all sanctions.

The balance sheet of economic sanctions against Poland is a mixed one. In October 1986, the *New York Times* editorialized that the Reagan administration had "deftly shown how to express American abhorrence for repression and how to use economic power as a lever for modest change."[70] To be sure, the measures reflected America's outrage at the Soviet-inspired suppression of democratic renewal as well as disappointment with the results of its earlier preferential policies. To pursue business as usual with Poland under martial law would have undermined the credibility of diplomatic protests and made a mockery of the policy of differentiation. Beyond these symbolic benefits, the sanctions probably served as an added inducement to the Jaruzelski regime to lift martial law and release political detainees. It was bound to take these steps sooner or later; Western pressure and ostracism made it sooner. However, Jaruzelski would not expose his monopoly of power to pluralism even in the restricted sphere of trade unions.

Sanctions certainly aggravated Poland's economic troubles. Trade with the West slumped sharply (U.S.-Polish turnover fell to $412 million in 1986), adding to the difficulty of rescheduling debt. But their lifting scarcely altered the pattern of rising debt, inflation, and stagnation. Neither the Western carrots of the 1970s nor the sticks of the 1980s could induce a fundamental and necessary economic reform that required both steadfast political will and a capacity for prolonged sacrifice on the part of the Polish people. Unable to secure even a modicum of popular support for the reforms recommended by the IMF, and faced with a new wave of strikes, Jaruzelski in late 1988 swallowed his pride and set to negotiating a political pact with Solidarity. The outcome was a semidemocratic election that allowed Poles to display their animosity toward the ruling party. The triumphant Walesa pleaded for economic aid, and the West responded with positive measures that will be examined below. Western sanctions contributed marginally to the collapse of communism in Poland, but the country's continuing economic crisis demands a costly commitment to its rehabilitation.

The Record and Legacy of Socialist Economics. Is Eastern Europe becoming the new third world? There is ample evidence that socialist economics has been an immeasurably costly experiment for all the countries of the region. The forced industrialization of the 1950s created the appearance of rapid economic growth. The annual rate of increase in the net material product in the first half of that decade ranged from 13.9 percent for Romania to 5.7 percent for Hungary. Yet the immensely wasteful investment of human and capital resources, managed by bloated and inefficient bureaucracies, failed to generate the productivity and innovation that might have narrowed or even maintained the gap between the socialist and the market economies. Instead, in the observation of the Hungarian economist Janos Kornai, the centrally planned systems only achieved the "constant recreation of scarcity."[71] Economic reforms, where introduced, replaced direct bureaucratic controls by indirect ones, without alleviating significantly the burdens of inefficiency and corruption.

The result was a steady decline in the socialist economies' competitiveness in world trade and in their ability to satisfy domestic demand. As a young Polish worker in Gdansk reflected bitterly, "Forty years of socialism and still no toilet paper." East European consumers are accustomed to comparing their standard of living to that of the industrialized West and not to the third world. That standard varies greatly, from the relative affluence of East Germany, Czechoslovakia, and Hungary to the dismal conditions in Romania and Albania. Most of the regimes were eventually driven to acknowledge the existence of inflation and the fall in real incomes in the 1980s. Queues, shortages, and shoddy goods fed the despair of frustrated expectations. Even life expectancy began to fall in the Soviet sphere.

Both governments and consumers enjoyed a brief surge of hope in the 1970s, when the vogue was to tinker with the planning system and to draw on foreign loans and technology. The average annual growth rate (net material product) in 1971–75 was a probably fictitious 11.2 percent in Romania, 9.8 percent in Poland, 7.8 percent in Bulgaria, 6.3 percent in Hungary, 5.7 percent in Czechoslovakia, and 5.4 percent in the GDR. By the end of the 1980s, the aggregate East European growth rate had fallen below 3 percent, turning these hopes into a profound pessimism scarcely relieved by Gorbachev's reformism. A prominent Soviet proponent of *perestroika,* Abel Aganbegyan, reflected soberly on the unexpected obstacles to reform by noting that "to estimate the depth of the hole you're in is only possible when you start climbing out of it."[72] Some of the East Europeans had started to climb out of their hole earlier and were now slipping back.

After the failure of the strategy of technological import-led growth in the 1970s, most East European regimes turned to export drives and austerity measures to restore economic stability. Unfavorable terms of trade, trade deficits, debt, and domestic inflation characterized the new economic reality. The region's industries remained comparatively inefficient in their use of labor, energy, and raw materials and in the application of technological innovation. They were also dreadful polluters of the environment; some 75 percent of East German industry may have to be shut down when West German pollution standards are applied. Their hopes of becoming suppliers of secondary manufactured products to

Western markets have been dimmed by the rapid rise of Asia's newly industrializing countries. The prospects are no better in the agricultural sector, which lacks the productivity even to satisfy domestic demand. Hungary is an exception, having successfully modernized and in effect privatized much of its agriculture, but Western overproduction and protectionism limit the scope of food exports. As *The Economist* gloomily observed, the East Europeans are in danger of becoming "newly underdeveloped countries."[73]

To be sure, the East European economies suffer from historical handicaps. With the exception of Bohemia, they served as breadbaskets of empire and lagged far behind Western Europe's industrial revolution. Dependence on foreign investment and manufactures retarded the modernization of these backward economies.[74] After 1945, war damage, reparations, and Soviet exploitation set back development. Yet when all is said and done, their greatest handicap in overcoming scarcity and producing wealth has been the Soviet-type centrally planned system, which continued through the 1980s to inhibit their economic potential. This system is succinctly characterized by the Polish economist Jan Winiecki as "illogical".[75] By its fundamental rejection of market-based rationality, it has perversely generated inefficiency, waste, and scarcity. By its egalitarianism and distorted incentives it has nurtured mediocrity, irresponsibility, fear of innovation, and cheating.

Worse still, the hybrid forms of market socialism, attempted in Hungary and currently envisaged in the Soviet Union, suffer from such stresses and new disharmonies that the economy's overall performance may be no better than in the undiluted, centrally planned model. The growth rate of Hungary's GNP since the introduction of its "new economic mechanism" in 1968 has not exceeded the average growth rate of the CMEA six. The record of semimarket socialism in nonaligned Yugoslavia presents an even grimmer picture; the standard of living fell by over one-third in the 1980s, and by the end of the decade hyperinflation had set in. The bitter lesson of these partial reforms was that balanced and sustained growth can only be assured by fundamental, and not merely cosmetic, alteration of the economic structure. That, at least in the short term, is bound to create dislocation and hardship as the security found in an equality of poverty is eroded by wider income disparities, unemployment, and unsubsidized staples.

The Hungarian Lesson.   The problems of socialist economics and partial reforms are well illustrated by Hungary. The new economic mechanism (NEM) launched in 1968 promised to lighten the heavy hand of state control over prices and production plans. Hopes that the NEM would be reinforced by a similar reform in Czechoslovakia were dashed by the Soviet invasion. In the early 1970s, conservative domestic opposition, encouraged by an apprehensive Kremlin, succeeded in halting the reform, mainly on the grounds that it was neglecting the immediate economic interests of industrial labor. Its chief success lay in the agricultural sector, where heavy investment, price reform, and privatization (primarily in the form of autonomous cooperatives, which were allowed to engage in ancillary industrial activity) boosted productivity to the point that the country managed not only to feed itself but also produced a surplus for export.

Even after the reform was relaunched in the late 1970s, and despite heavy use of foreign credits, the productivity and competitiveness on international markets of the state industrial sector showed only modest improvement. The NEM had ostensibly increased the autonomy of enterprises, but it left them wholly dependent on the state for credits as well as subsidies and subject to centrally determined investment priorities. The socialized sector accounted for some 90 percent of all investment, and the record shows that much of this was not planned or applied efficiently. Centrally planned investment grew rapidly until 1979, then was cut back as the debt-service burden mounted.

A flurry of uncoordinated measures allowed for expansion of the second, private economy (distinguished from the third, underground economy). The private sector's contribution to the national income (net material product) grew from 2.6 percent to 7 percent between 1970 and 1986. Workers were permitted to form "working collectives" and use their plant's machinery to produce goods on contract. Small private enterprises were sanctioned. Some of the retail and service sector was privatized. Since basic wages did not keep up with inflation, the regime was expediently encouraging Hungarians to moonlight in order to maintain their standard of living, in effect, to exploit themselves. The young, the pensioners, and others unable to do so were left behind.

These partial remedies managed to create a semblance of consumerism and affluence (earning Western praise for "goulash communism") but could not sufficiently invigorate the industrial sector. Restructuring and technological innovation were also impeded by long-term trade commitments to Hungary's CMEA partners. When an enterprise is geared to export a certain obsolescent product to one of these partners at notional prices, it has little scope or incentive to restructure, innovate, compete for new customers, or even to declare bankruptcy. A standard complaint of Hungarian economists is that in the socialist system it is impossible to determine the real price of anything, including labor; yet without real prices, no manager can rationally plan production and investment.

Faced with a debt-service ratio that is projected to rise to eighty by 1990, the Hungarian regime bravely opted for more liberalization combined with austerity. The decision was impelled by the rapid political democratization of the country, which generated a broad consensus (encompassing former Communist reformers in the reorganized, social democratic Hungarian Socialist party) on the failure of the socialist model and the need for restoring a market economy. It was officially conceded that social, that is, state property was not the most productive form of ownership, and that full employment could not be guaranteed by the state.

Preliminary reforms included lower state subsidies and new income and value-added taxes to reduce the budget deficit and the institution of a competitive banking system and embryonic bond and stock markets to generate domestic capital. "It has become quite obvious," said Justice Minister Kalman Kulcsar when a new reform law was passed in October 1988, "that without a capital market, the commodity and labor markets cannot function adequately either."[76] The measure allowed for full foreign ownership of Hungarian companies and for larger private firms. A "conversion law" provided for the privatization of state firms. Since enterprises presently transfer most of their gross profits to the state in the form of taxes and other mandatory contributions, profitable capitalism may be a distant prospect, although the government anticipates the lowering of both producers' subsidies and tax on profit.

Finally, in December 1989, the lame-duck government of Prime Minister Miklos Nemeth adopted the bitter remedy recommended by the IMF with a budget-balancing program to slash subsidies by 20 percent and shut down fifty unprofitable enterprises, foreshadowing massive consumer price increases and unemployment. In the realm of trade, Hungary planned to cut its exports to the CMEA by 20 percent, reducing its unspendable ruble surplus, and to put its exchanges with the Soviet Union on a hard currency basis by 1991. Such market-driven shock therapy would, it was hoped, spur productivity and generate the exports and hard currency needed to obtain Western technology.

Foreign trade contributes some 40 percent of Hungary's national income. Just over half of this trade is conducted with the socialist countries, some of it settled in convertible currency. The Soviet Union accounts for 28.5 percent of the country's imports and 32.7 percent of its exports (1987). The biggest Western partner is the Federal Republic of Germany, with 13.9 percent of imports and 9.8 percent of exports; the corresponding figures for the United States are 2.5 and 3 percent. Whether the pattern of Hungary's trade is best designed to exploit the country's comparative advantage is questionable, but it reflects the country's earlier political alignment. It has also offered assured sources of energy and raw materials as well as markets for agricultural and industrial exports, though the Soviet Union has of late become disenchanted with trading raw materials for low-quality industrial products. The Hungarians are thus left to choose between a rock and a hard place, for the limited competitiveness of their exports and other impediments, notably West European protectionism, inhibit a major reorientation of export trade, while alternative sources of energy and raw materials would require payment in scarce convertible currency.

"Secure dependence" on the CMEA has not equipped Hungary to compete in other markets. Plants using obsolete East European machinery and Soviet raw materials were designed mainly to serve Soviet import needs. Meanwhile, imports from the West were largely restricted to goods that do not compete with domestic and CMEA products and remain severely limited by the shortage of hard currency. Until recently, joint ventures with Western firms were small-scale and generated little profit for either party. The CMEA pattern of bilateral, long-term trade deals, cleared at notional prices, and the absence of a convertible currency have impeded the adaptation of Hungary's production to world market conditions and discouraged Western firms from using Hungary (or any other East European country) as a base for penetrating the entire regional market.

Hungary's economic performance is a test not only of the ongoing experiment with marketization but also of Western confidence in the viability of East European reform. The latest austerity program was expected to win IMF approval and bring substantial Western economic favors as well as new foreign investment (see below). The immediate consequence was the first drop in personal consumption in over thirty years, and a government commission calculated that Hungary would need an additional $1.5 billion just to keep the standard of living from falling further. The burden of escaping from the accumulated failures of socialist economics will be borne by the hapless consumers of Eastern Europe. In the short term, Western countries and international financial institutions will share responsibility for the imposition of painful austerity.

The East German Alternative. While Hungary opted initially for a hybrid market socialism, the German Democratic Republic concentrated on refining the centrally planned model to achieve economies of scale and more efficient management. The industrial sector was dominated by huge conglomerates, but in retail trade and food services the regime tolerated what was proportionately the largest private sector in the East; private farms also contributed a greater share of agricultural output than elsewhere, except for Poland. A per capita GNP 40 percent higher than that of the Soviet Union made the GDR Eastern Europe's economic powerhouse. It was the Soviet Union's largest trading partner and supplier of manufactured goods, but its superiority in the production of machine tools and opticals, for example, was more a reflection of the backwardness of the rest of the CMEA than of competitiveness on the world market. Although the GDR had more internationally competitive enterprises than any of its socialist neighbors, in technological innovation its industry remained years behind the developed West, and only 15 percent of its exports to its chief Western market, the Federal Republic of Germany, consisted of capital goods.

The relative success of the East German economy was commonly attributed to the ability of diligent, well-trained, and disciplined Germans to make any system work. The GDR possessed another unique advantage: free access to the markets of West Germany (and therefore indirectly to the European Community) as well as to special West German credits and sundry payments, all of which contributed an extra 3–4 percent to its GNP. This significant subsidy was a long-standing paradox of East-West relations, for in terms of positive leverage it secured only minor concessions (on travel and emigration, for instance) but no political or economic liberalization (see chapter 6).

The major East German reform, devised by Gunter Mittag and implemented in 1978–81, was the reorganization of industry into large, vertically integrated *Kombinate* linking firms in related product fields. These combines shared research and development and enjoyed some marginal autonomy in the reinvestment of profits. A respectable growth rate was maintained through the 1970s and early 1980s, but structural and other weaknesses increasingly cast a pall over this eastern version of the German economic miracle: a lack of domestic and regional competition, administrative price setting, huge state subsidies, stagnation in the production of soft coal (the principal domestic source of energy), falling prices for key exports such as bulk chemicals and refined oil products, and a shrinking labor force. Consumers, meanwhile, had to wait over ten years for delivery of a new car.

The revolution in November 1989 brought the promise of pluralism and virtually unrestricted travel, but it also precipitated a political and economic crisis in the East German state. The flood of emigrants aggravated an already acute labor shortage in the GDR, while countless others seized the opportunity to observe at first hand West German affluence and take stock of the fact that at the realistic rate of exchange a West German skilled worker earned several times as much as his Eastern counterpart. The beleaguered East German leaders promised to liberalize trade and private enterprise, to allow joint ventures, to trim taxes and the bureaucracy, and, out of dire necessity, to devalue the Ostmark, conceding that in the past official statistics on the GDR's economic prowess had been "beautified and falsified." [77] Even the East German economic powerhouse, then, had been something of a Potemkin village.

The prospect of self-determination unleashed talk of unification with the Federal Republic on both sides of the crumbling Wall, while neighbors East and West pondered apprehensively the potential economic preponderance of a combined population of 77.8 million with a GNP of $1.1 trillion. Bonn linked its prompt offer of massive aid and investment to democratization and marketization. To salvage a rationale for the retention of a separate GDR, the new prime minister, Hans Modrow, initially insisted that "life points us toward a socialist system in which planning and the market are closely linked." [78] But it soon became clear that even hybrid socialism could not survive open borders. Lured by

West German Chancellor Helmut Kohl's ambiguous promise of a one-to-one exchange rate, East German voters chose full integration into the West German economy. The terms were speedily worked out for the economic union to take place on July 2, 1990. Thus, the East's economic powerhouse was summarily absorbed by that of Western Europe.

Poland's "Big Bang."   Ever since 1957, Poland has flirted periodically with innovative economic measures, but each time the attempt was aborted by political considerations or undermined by social and structural factors. In the post-martial-law period, overdue price hikes were effectively nullified by wage inflation, and the creation in 1986 of conglomerates similar to the East German combines scarcely improved productivity. The predominance of small private farms (accounting for nearly 80 percent of gross agricultural output) remained the main distinguishing feature of the Polish socialist economy and was granted recognition in the 1983 constitution. But agricultural productivity remained low, hampered by shortages of chemicals and machinery, the disincentive of low prices, and diseconomies of scale.

In 1986, the Jaruzelski regime launched the "second stage" of economic reform, designed to encourage small-scale local enterprise, create a capital market, increase labor mobility, and decontrol most prices. The public's response in a 1987 referendum reflected both a mistrust of the government and an understandable distaste for the inevitable belt-tightening that accompanies any stabilization program. Meanwhile, administrative controls over half of consumer prices and one-third of producer prices continued to distort supply and demand, inducing shortages and a thriving "gray market"; interest rates far below the level of inflation discouraged saving and the efficient use of enterprise assets; state subsidies in 1989 still amounted to one-sixth of Poland's gross domestic product and one-third of government spending; and the closing down of unprofitable enterprises, sanctioned by the 1983 bankruptcy law, had hardly begun.

A foreign debt nearing $40 billion was of course a formidable obstacle to economic recovery. Though export earnings rose steadily, they hardly sufficed to service the rescheduled debt and pay for essential imports. Lack of confidence by Western trading partners meant that in 1988 Poland still had to pay cash for 90 percent of its imports. Under the circumstances, there was little prospect of substantial new foreign investment. (There were in Poland some seven hundred companies based on foreign capital, mostly small businesses established since 1977 by foreigners of Polish descent.) With the economy bankrupt and reform stalled by social unrest, Jaruzelski had little choice but to seek an alternative political formula more palatable to Poles and the West.

That the new Polish government would find little inspiration in the cautious incrementalism of *perestroika* was foreshadowed by Lech Walesa's observation in April 1989:

I wish Gorbachev and his reforms all the best. But we still don't know what communism in its final form will look like. In contrast, we know very well which political and economic models in Europe and in the world have passed the test of time, and it is to these models that we must turn as opposed to attempting to "reform" failed ideologies and concepts.[79]

A few months later Walesa told ABC's Barbara Walters that "we will build a system based on democracy and freedom. It won't be capitalism. It will be a system that will be better than capitalism."[80] But the Mazowiecki government soon came to the conclusion that a "big bang" conversion to capitalism (recommended notably by the Harvard economist Jeffrey Sachs, whose similar advice to Bolivia was cited as a positive precedent) was the only realistic remedy and the only one likely to satisfy the IMF and Western creditors.

The economic program unveiled in Warsaw in October called for the creation "in the swiftest possible way" of a market economy based on private property and enterprise. State monopolies would be dismantled; a competitive banking system and other institutions would be established to serve a capital market; prices would be freed and subsidies gradually eliminated; wages would be temporarily frozen and the currency made fully convertible. Unemployment would be alleviated by retraining and social insurance. It was anticipated that the immediate consequences of this shock therapy—industrial recession and a sharp drop in the standard of living—would sorely test the morale of the population; in fact, two months after the deregulation of food prices, inflation reached an annual rate of 450 percent. In the first quarter of 1990, real incomes and output fell by a third, but the inflationary spiral was reversed and the number of private businesses showed a net increase of close to 100,000. The first major protest strike, by rail workers, erupted in May. Unemployment rose rapidly, reaching nearly one million by the end of September. There was little doubt that prolonged recession would soon erode the permissive consensus and that only Western aid could stave off a new political crisis.

By the end of 1989, the remaining East European dominoes had fallen, and the interim regimes in Prague, Sofia, and Bucharest all professed commitment to some degree of marketization. Pursuit of that goal will be no easy task in impoverished societies shorn for forty years of the institutions, managerial class, and work habits that give life to a market. Legislative sanction for a private sector and competitive financial institutions will not generate entrepreneurship, domestic private investment, and a motivated labor force overnight. Price reform is no panacea in economies dominated by monopolistic producers; de-monopolization by the breaking up of state-run conglomerates is no solution unless producers' subsidies are also eliminated; and without subsidies, countless inefficient East European enterprises will go bankrupt, precipitating massive unemployment.

The effectiveness of economic structural reform depends on the availability of skills fundamentally different from those nurtured by the bureaucratic leviathan of state socialism. Eastern Europe may not be short of clever economists, not to speak of bureaucrats, but it lacks a market-oriented managerial class. In the long run, of course, professional education and the market itself will alleviate this weakness. In the short run, the existing managerial nomenklatura and black-marketeers are in a good position to exploit the new opportunities.

The nomenklatura system of political patronage (in Poland, for example, some 900,000 appointments were subject to direct party control) encompassed a diversity of talents and motivations. Contrary to the suspicion, in the words of a Polish journalist, that "all nomenklatura people steal national property," many are not incompetent or corrupt.[81] Others fear the disruptive consequences of a replay of the housecleaning conducted by the Communists in the postwar period and anticipate that self-interest and the profit motive will convert bureaucrats into efficient managers. Some of the East European countries—Czechoslovakia, East Germany, Hungary—have better entrepreneurial traditions than others, but economic transformation will create social tensions in all of them, affecting workers as well as managers.

Moreover, the social turmoil and short-term costs of marketization will only feed the fire of ideologues and opportunistic politicians ready to suppress "capitalist chaos" with the tried and true remedies of command socialism or some other populist chimera. A greater degree of institutionalized political pluralism might absorb some of the social stresses of the escape from socialist economic stagnation, but the economic crisis of Eastern Europe will not be resolved without mutual adaptation in its economic relations with the rest of the world.

Intra-CMEA Trade.   As if foreign debt, falling growth rates, a chronic inability to upgrade the quality of goods produced, and a widening technology gap were not enough, the East Europeans' economic woes are compounded by the structural weaknesses of the CMEA and by a more demanding Soviet Union. The CMEA largely failed to generate the cooperation and division of labor that could facilitate economies of scale, and it offers little in the way of multilateral clearing and free movement of labor and capital. It has provided the security of a protected market for the bilateral exchange of substandard goods, and it has assured supplies of energy and raw materials. This security, however, is now threatened by the Soviet Union's reconsiderations of its economic interests and by the absorption of the GDR into a unified German economy.

The traditional pattern of intra-CMEA trade was the exchange of low-cost Soviet energy and raw materials for East European manufactures and food products, typically of low quality and variety and high production cost (better goods were reserved for hard currency markets). After the early postwar phase of Soviet exploitation, the terms of trade arguably favored the East Europeans until Soviet prices came to reflect the 1970s energy crisis and the higher cost of oil extraction in the more remote parts of the Soviet Union. Moscow began to demand East European investment in its energy development projects, which the countries were not eager to do, and payment in hard currency for increased supplies. Most recently, the dislocations induced by *perestroika* have impaired the Soviet Union's reliability as a supplier of energy; both Hungary and Czechoslovakia experienced serious shortfalls in deliveries of Soviet oil to Eastern Europe were cut by some 30 percent in the course of 1990.

Mikhail Gorbachev is taking a cold, hard look at the costs of empire. While the Soviet Union will remain a prime market and supplier for the East Europeans, the implicit subsidies are bound to be cut in the age of *perestroika.*[82] The East Europeans are also reassessing the hidden costs of the CMEA. Intra-CMEA trade is stagnating (it rose by only 1.5 percent in 1987), yet in the late 1980s it represented a growing share (to some 60 percent) of East European trade as the region's competitiveness in the world market declined. The CMEA economies' inability to adjust to consumer demand created unpredictable scarcities, and the fixed currency exchange rates produced disparities in purchasing power that drove consumers across borders in search of products unavailable at home. This, in turn, caused new supply problems, and most East European governments have in recent years resorted to banning the personal import of certain consumer goods by visitors from other CMEA countries.

The Hungarians accumulated an 800 million-ruble surplus in their trade with the Soviet Union in 1989, and after months of hard bargaining the two sides agreed on a hard currency settlement. Meanwhile, in January 1990, Budapest imposed a temporary and partial moratorium on ruble exports to try to steer its trade westward; "The IMF said they don't want to give loans to Hungary to give loans to the Soviet Union," explained Deputy Trade Minister Piroska Apro.[83] The CMEA obviously can lay no claim to being a dynamic economic community until all its constituent economies are reformed to a common denominator of market responsiveness and allow the free movement of goods in a realistic exchange rate regime.

Symptomatic of the fundamental weakness of central planning is the CMEA's failure to overcome technological stagnation. The much-heralded shift to a new, "intensive" phase of development laid stress on the modernization of industrial processes and products. One of Gorbachev's earliest initiatives was the adoption in December 1985 of a regional "Program of Scientific Cooperation until the Year 2000" that called for major advances in such fields as computers, biotechnology, and nuclear power. But after two years, only 20 percent of the planned contracts between research institutes and enterprises had even been drawn up, let alone produced anything.

Part of the problem, in the view of a Hungarian expert, was that "the Soviets wanted to play the dominating role in each and every one of the projects, but they did not have any experience at all in how to manage such a venture."[84] The program was revised in 1987 and 1988 to make research organizations more accountable for the generation and productive application of scientific-technological innovation and to open up the possibility of East-West cooperation.[85] For now, the East Europeans are left to choose between Soviet computers and commercial aircraft, for example, which are obsolescent and often in short supply, or Western alternatives, which are contingent on the availability of hard currency and the liberalization of Cocom rules.

As presently structured, the CMEA offers neither the advantages of a regional free market nor the largely hypothetical benefits of rational planning by a strong supranational organization. Hungarian foreign minister Gyula Horn complained that it is "not only unsuitable to meet its tasks, but also costs too much in its present form."[86] By the time the CMEA council met in Sofia in January 1990, every East European member was in the midst of revolutionary transformation, and Soviet prime minister Nikolai Ryzhkov had declared that within a year trade should be conducted in hard currency on the basis of world market prices.

Consensus on a new CMEA will be elusive until the economic systems of its members obtain a modicum of symmetry. The conversion of intra-regional trade to world market prices will have a severe impact on the terms of trade of most East European countries, whose manufactured exports to the Soviet Union have been tacitly overvalued. In the case of East Germany alone, the terms of trade between 1970 and 1984 implied a subsidy to the GDR's industry amounting to $4,000 for each Soviet citizen; according to Soviet estimates that still included the GDR, the USSR would gain $10 billion from the conversion of CMEA trade to hard currency.[87] And a much higher proportion of the Soviet exports could be redirected to other markets than East European exports to the Soviet Union. But the Hungarians, Poles, and Czechs appear willing to pay the price of short-term pain for the stimulus to energy conservation, innovation, and productivity that such a reform would bring.

In the final analysis, the interdependence of the CMEA's European members derives not from the institution itself but from their shared economic backwardness. Their obsolescent technology will not be soon replaced by expensive Western alternatives, and convertibility of their currencies will require a devaluation that in the short run at least will favor intraregional trade at the expense of imports from the rest of the world.[88] If the temptation to beggar thy neighbor is resisted, a mar-ketized CMEA could serve as a free-trade holding pattern for the East Europeans even as they seek association with the more advanced economic groupings of Western Europe, EFTA and the European Community.

The CMEA and the World Market. "We want to return to the international market," declared Czechoslovakia's new finance minister, Vaclav Klaus, at the Sofia meeting; "What we want to do is business, not cooperation."[89] That will not be easily achieved, for half of the region's export products that were competitive at the beginning of the 1980s are no longer attractive. Singapore alone exports 20 percent more manufactured products to the OECD countries than all of Eastern Europe, including the Soviet Union.[90] By 1987 the share of East-West trade in world trade had slipped to 3.6 percent, down from a high of 5.5 percent in 1975.[91] The growth rate in East bloc exports to the West fell to 3 percent in 1987. Smaller than expected gains in efficiency, weak export demand, and deteriorating terms of trade were blamed in the annual report of the UN Economic Commission for Europe for an outlook that was "not favorable."[92]

To counteract these negative tendencies, the East Europeans cut their imports from OECD countries by 11.5 percent in 1986 and by another 5.5 percent the following year.[93] Sales to the West picked up somewhat in 1988, yet their balance of trade with the OECD countries continued to deteriorate. The combined trade surplus of the East European six was halved between 1986 and 1987, while their current account surplus fell from over $1.7 billion in 1985 to an estimated $135 million in 1988 (when in fact only the GDR and Romania registered a surplus).[94] And the current account may be in worse shape than it appears, for it includes trade with developing countries financed by risky long-term credits. Meanwhile, debt burden continues to inhibit imports, leaving little prospect of significant expansion in East-West trade.

The commodity profile of East-West trade offers yet another indication of poor performance and prospects.[95] The East Europeans' chief imports are grain, agricultural nonfood items such as wool and hides, steel pipe, and chemicals; their low hard currency export earnings compel them to concentrate on such essentials at the expense of machinery and manufactured consumer goods. Their largest export items include refined oil products (Romania), hard coal (Poland), and agricultural products (Hungary). There are, to be sure, some traditional as well as novel products of attractive cost and quality that do find Western buyers. Hungary, where Rubik's Cube was invented, has of late exported computer software to OECD markets. But even relatively underdeveloped Yugoslavia has a more balanced mix of exports to the West than the members of the CMEA.

The stagnation in East-West economic relations was visible even in the most active of these trading partnerships, with West Germany. The Federal Republic leads other OECD countries in East-West trade mainly because it is a big consumer of the East's low-value-added exports, such as oil, chemicals, wood products, foods, and semimanufactures. These have accounted for over a third of East German and nearly half of Czechoslovak exports to West Germany.[96] West German firms are also involved in subcontracting work, notably for clothing, to East European producers. But to put the Federal Republic's predominance in East-West trade in perspective, the total turnover is no greater than its trade with Switzerland.

Since the advent of Willy Brandt's *Ostpolitik* at the end of the 1960s, West Germany has actively sought to recapture its traditional markets in the East. Apart from the profit motive, the main incentive was the entrenchment of detente. This positive linkage between politics and economics was inspired by Bonn's special interest in security and stability, more particularly in normalizing intra-German relations and facilitating the emigration of German minorities in the Soviet sphere. Having adopted a long-term, functionalist strategy of economic engagement, Bonn resisted the mainly American initiatives to apply negative linkage, such as the gas pipeline sanctions. This policy was buttressed by a solid domestic consensus in favor of trade with the East. Unlike its major European Community partners, Bonn did not directly subsidize credits to facilitate this trade, although the guarantees to exporters provided by the Hermes insurance agency earned Washington's muted criticism.

Bonn did not classify its economic relations with East Germany as foreign trade. Instead, these relations were monitored by the Economics Ministry's "Trust Office for Industry and Trade," which as a matter of political strategy tried to ensure that the level of intra-German trade stayed above 10 percent of the GDR's foreign trade. (Trade with East Germany accounted for less than two percent of total West German trade.) The government instituted a generous clearing arrangement (the so-called "swing") and guaranteed substantial credits over the years to facilitate intra-German trade. One example of the predominance of politics over economics was a deal whereby West Germany sold crude oil to the East and bought back refined oil products, mostly for West Berlin consumption, at more than three times the price of the crude. Since there was plenty of excess refining capacity in West Germany, the transaction was clearly designed to artificially boost trade as much as to serve West Berlin's needs.[97] But even intra-German trade faltered, declining by 9 percent in 1986 and 5 percent in 1987.

The Eastern Debt. The East Europeans' burden of debt adds to the urgency of overcoming economic stagnation but at the same time limits their options. They need imports to modernize and spur economic growth and exports, but boosting imports will at least in the short run only increase their indebtedness. According to OECD estimates, the region's gross hard currency debt had risen to over $100 billion by the end of 1989: $41 billion for Poland, $21 billion for East Germany, $21 billion for Hungary (the highest debt per capita), $10 billion for Bulgaria, $7 billion for Czechoslovakia, and $1 billion for Romania.[98] Only Romania managed, by draconian measures that slashed domestic consumption and debilitated its productive capacity, to virtually eliminate its debt; it passed a law prohibiting new foreign loans, which the post-Ceausescu regime promptly rescinded.

The scale of the debt appears less formidable when compared to what is owed by Argentina, Brazil, and Mexico, but that is small comfort to countries like Hungary or Bulgaria, which are caught in the vise of rising debt-service payments and current account deficits. One cause of this problem is the falling dollar, for many East European countries (like Hungary, and with the notable exception of East Germany) made the mistake of keeping their reserves in dollars while incurring debt in West German marks and Japanese yen.

The debt burden increased Eastern Europe's vulnerability to a crisis of foreign confidence and financial liquidity. In 1989, Poland had the region's highest debt-service ratio at eighty-eight (down from nearly two hundred in 1981); the debt-service ratios of the GDR, Hungary, and Bulgaria were also in the perilous range of forty and above. Unable even to maintain full interest payments, let alone amortize its debt, Poland was reduced to seeking rescheduling agreements with both the Paris Club and commercial lenders. It was the first East European country to explore the possibility of reducing its debt by means of debt-equity swaps (a device that has been used in Latin America), but the virtual absence of capital markets in the East limits the scope of such novel palliatives.

Government credits to Eastern Europe virtually ceased after 1981, and (largely because of American pressure) the OECD countries agreed to forgo competition and set standardized, "consensual" lending rates for commercial credits that they are willing to guarantee. However, commercial banks soon resumed fixed-rate lending (at levels below the consensual rate) to some of the CMEA countries, notably creditworthy Czechoslovakia, and as a result Western nonguaranteed bank debt to Eastern Europe has risen faster than its total debt.[99] West German banks hold the largest share of East European debt; American banks, one of the smallest at some $3 billion. The Germans remain the biggest lender to the East. In early 1988, they granted a DM 1 billion credit to Hungary, a gesture that in light of that country's perilous debt-service ratio could only be construed as a politically calculated show of support for the reform program. In recent years Japanese banks have also become major lenders to Eastern Europe, specifically to Hungary (as well as to the Soviet Union), in the context of a long-term export strategy to develop this market for Japan's capital goods.

Reformers in the East are naturally eager to secure hard currency credits as they struggle to revitalize their economies, but from the Western perspective a positive assessment of the commercial and political risks requires a leap of faith. None of the past, partial economic reforms produced the expected results, and Western loans have not generated the innovation and productivity necessary to repay them. Commenting on an IMF standby loan to Hungary in early 1988, the *Wall Street Journal* noted that "defenders of the IMF would argue that a key tenet of its programs is conditionality. But we've been watching this story unfold for years now, and we've yet to see the most important condition put forward—namely, end Communist rule or you don't get your money."[100]

The record of the IMF's East European members (Yugoslavia, Poland, Romania, and Hungary) suggests that they have done comparatively well in obtaining IMF and IBRD (World Bank) facilities. (Czechoslovakia was admitted in September 1990, and Bulgaria's application was pending.) Far from being handicapped by their socialist character, they seem to have benefited from the application of positive political criteria.[101] Hungary drew on Western approval of its economic reforms when in the midst of a liquidity crisis it applied for IMF membership and was admitted in 1982. Its subsequent admission to the World Bank reflected further favoritism, for some stretching of the Bank's threshold was required to classify Hungary as a developing country eligible for loans. Since then, Hungary has taken advantage of over $1 billion worth of World Bank credits (as well as $1.2 billion in World Bank-organized cofinancing loans), including a $500 million, five-year program for industrial restructuring. In the case of Yugoslavia and Romania, it is plain that the Fund and the World Bank were at least partly motivated by the wish of the United States and its allies to reinforce these countries' independent foreign policies.[102]

The charters of the IMF and the IBRD specify technical and economic, not political, criteria, but they embody a free-market philosophy that is clearly antithetical to the dogma of a Soviet-type centrally planned economy. Yugoslavia's and Hungary's experimentation with market socialism arguably fitted this free-market bias and deserved reinforcement. The same could not be said of Romania, where lip service to reform did not alter the rigidly centralized system, and dealing with this country proved to be a "learning experience" for the Fund. Between 1980 and 1984, Romania benefited from $1.2 billion in IMF facilities and $1 billion in development loans from the World Bank. Nevertheless, in 1983, the Ceausescu regime rejected the Fund's recommendation (induced in part by Western reconsiderations of Romania's political value) that it introduce market-oriented reforms, prompting the suspension of IMF credits. After the facility was renegotiated, Romania chose not to draw from the new standby credit as it pursued its harsh austerity measures to reduce debt.[103]

The intention at the Bretton Woods conference that set up the international leading agencies was to have voluntary and universal membership in the World Bank and the IMF, but both were designed to foster open economies receptive to foreign investment. Romania's admission despite its resistance to economic reform set a bad precedent. Although there is little hard evidence of direct linkage between "conditionality" and structural reform of the economic systems of the other three East European members, the Fund's influence probably played a part in their attempts to liberalize investment, trim unprofitable sectors, establish a realistic price system and exchange rates, and balance budgets by cutting subsidies and other expenditures and raising taxes.

It is plausible to argue that the "emergence of a group of government officials committed to and dependent upon the maintenance of cordial relations with the lending agency . . . enhances the political as well as economic influence of that agency on the policy process of the borrower." [104] Active membership compels the East Europeans to assume the normal obligations of borrowers, such as providing reliable economic information, while easing their access to hard currency credits and markets. IMF approval of a standby facility is generally regarded by commercial lenders as signifying a certain confidence in the economic management of the recipient. The Fund's leverage over economic reform is limited, but it remains in the interest of the United States and its allies to apply and reinforce the principle of market-oriented conditionality in vetting new candidates and in deciding whether to help alleviate the balance of payments problems of the East European members. The World Bank, for its part, has indicated readiness to loan over $5 billion to Eastern Europe over the next three years. In August 1990, it granted a $300 million loan to Poland in support of privatization, bank reform, and social welfare programs.

GATT Membership. East European participation in the General Agreement on Tariffs and Trade (GATT) has offered little specific leverage to the West. Established in 1947 as a device for expanding free trade by reciprocal tariff reductions, GATT could not easily accommodate centrally planned economies that defied standard methods of calculating prices, tariffs, subsidies, and evidence of dumping. Membership normally included the mutual granting of MFN, and the East European economic systems lacked the tariff mechanism necessary for nondiscriminatory trade.

Czechoslovakia was a founding member of GATT and retained its membership, although in practice the mutual nondiscrimination clause could not be enforced. For political reasons, Yugoslavia was granted observer status as early as 1950, and as it moved toward a hybrid model of market socialism it became a full member in 1964. When Poland was admitted to full membership in 1967, structural incompatibility was papered over with a quantitative formula requiring it to increase its aggregate imports from GATT members at an annual rate of no less than 7 percent. Poland's failure to meet this commitment in the early 1980s allowed the United States to suspend MFN. Political considerations also predominated in Romania's admission in 1971, on terms even less enforceable that those granted to Poland. When Hungary was finally admitted to full membership in 1973, the more conventional terms again reflected the West's political desire to encourage its progression to a market economy.[105]

GATT membership, therefore, was used by the West less as a reward than as an inducement to structural reform, and the results were meager. Since the East European members accounted for only a tiny share of world trade, the integrity of GATT was not seriously subverted by accommodation of their centrally planned economies. The Soviet Union's application in 1987 (partially satisfied in 1990 with observer status) and China's interest in reactivating its membership raised more thorny questions about the compatibility of even partially marketized socialist economies with an institution dedicated to free and fair trade. As the East Europeans began to implement more radical structural reforms in 1990, they naturally anticipated unqualified access to the benefits and attendant responsibilities of GATT membership, and Poland was the first to renegotiate the terms of its membership.

Trade with the European Community and the United States. Western Europe is the most natural and proximate trading partner of the CMEA countries, which observed the region's economic integration with a mixture of ideological hostility, envy, and fear. Regarding the European Community as simply the economic dimension of an American-dominated military alliance, the Soviet Union sought to promote the self-sufficiency of the socialist bloc and discouraged CMEA members from seeking bilateral trade agreements with the EC. In the early 1970s, against the backdrop of *Ostpolitik,* detente, and the Helsinki Final Act, the East Europeans nevertheless began to court the Community, and in an essentially defensive reaction Moscow initiated talks to establish a framework agreement between the two trading blocs.

There were numerous obstacles to such an accord. The West Europeans observed that the CMEA lacked the international legal status and supranational authority of the EC and was therefore juridically not competent to negotiate a trade agreement on behalf of its members. The Community's general policy was to expand trade (subject to Cocom restrictions) with the CMEA members by selective bilateral agreements. The EC did not wish to jeopardize this expanding network of bilateral economic cooperation nor to encourage even indirectly the integrated regulation of the trade of the smaller CMEA countries.[106] A formal accord between the two blocs promised little commercial gain and some political costs for the West.

Aborted by the invasion of Afghanistan, talks between the EC and the CMEA were resumed in 1985. Gorbachev's "new thinking" and disposition to normalize relations in "our common European home" produced a Soviet compromise proposal for mutual recognition in an agreement that would facilitate bilateral relations between Brussels and the East Europeans. Bonn was particularly keen to respond positively, but it took three years for the Soviet Union to accept the Community's standard requirement that its treaties be applicable to the entire EC territory, including West Berlin. The declaration signed in June 1988 provided for official EC-CMEA relations and the expansion of economic cooperation without compromising the Community's preference for conducting trade negotiations with the individual East European countries. "We didn't want any agreement that would strengthen Moscow's hold over its allies," observed an Community official, and the declaration ostensibly satisfied this condition.[107]

The signing of the joint declaration was followed in short order by the conclusion of the first comprehensive bilateral trade pact, between the Community and Hungary. The agreement reflected the EC's approval of Hungary's economic reforms and provided for most-favored-nation status as well as the removal of all quotas on manufactured imports (but not agricultural products) from Hungary by 1995. A less generous accord was reached with Czechoslovakia in October. A partial trade agreement had been signed by the EC and Romania in 1980, but Bucharest's commercial policies and execrable human rights record led Brussels to break off negotiations in 1989.

Such differentiation reflected political considerations that were seldom entirely absent from the Community's dealings with the East. The EC-CMEA accord was hailed in the West more as a symbol of intra-European rapprochement that might have a beneficial effect on human rights in Eastern Europe than as a commercial breakthrough. The East's recognition of West Berlin as an integral part of the European Community was perhaps a more tangible achievement, although this was soon overshadowed by the rapid movement toward German unification. On the economic side, the East Europeans redoubled their efforts to secure bilateral concessions, fearing for their access to the single market that the Community aims to forge by 1992. Their success will ultimately depend on their ability to produce competitive goods, and that in turn will require fundamental, structural reforms of their economies. The relationship is asymmetrical: the CMEA conducts more than one-third of its external trade with the Community but accounts for only 7 percent of the latter's trade. Indeed, the Community's trade with the CMEA, amounting annually to some $50 billion (excluding intra-German trade), half of which is with the Soviet Union, is no greater than its trade with Sweden.

As for the United States, less than one-half of 1 percent of its global trade is accounted for by the East European six. Assistant Secretary of State Rozanne L. Ridgway commented at a congressional hearing in October 1987 that "we don't do much business with Eastern Europe. [. . .] Our national policy . . . requires us to impose limits on that trade, at the same time as business and trade practices impose limits on the enthusiasm of many of our businessmen. So prospects for expanding trade are mixed, and likely to remain so."[108] Total turnover has hovered around $2.4 billion for several years. In 1989, American exports stood at $1.02 billion and imports at $1.35 billion. (The corresponding values for Yugoslavia were $501 million and $802 million, and for the Soviet Union, $4.2 billion and $702 million.) The trade balance was favorable only with respect to Bulgaria (thanks largely to corn sales) and Poland. Poland, Hungary, and Romania accounted for close to 80 percent of U.S. imports from the six, although Romania's exports were halved by the surrender of MFN.

The Reagan administration had pursued a selective policy of encouraging American exporters and investors. One option was wider East European participation in the programs of OPIC (Overseas Private Investment Corporation), a federal agency that insures U.S. investors against political risks such as expropriation. The extension of OPIC programs to Communist countries required approval by Congress, where human rights considerations and the reservations of organized labor inspired much diffidence. In 1989, Yugoslavia and China were eligible for these programs; the only other East European participant, Romania, had lost its eligibility in 1987 because of its oppressive labor policies. A State Department initiative to offer OPIC programs in Hungary was aborted in May 1988 when the House defeated the relevant amendment to

OPIC's reauthorization; the AFL-CIO had criticized Hungarian labor practices and objected to the export of U.S. jobs. OPIC president Craig Nalen expressed the more positive viewpoint, that "these seeds of capitalism [are] being planted to our advantage," and observed that the key question was whether American initiatives helped to "weaken the link between mother Russia and the satellites." [109]

Forty years of export controls, ideological animosity, socialist bureaucratic hindrances, and receptive alternate markets have ill prepared American businessmen for the emerging opportunities in Eastern Europe. Not a single U.S.-based company tendered for a share in the multimillion-dollar restructuring project financed by the World Bank in Hungary a few years ago. Yet the U.S. economy produces many of the goods needed by the East Europeans, notably in the agribusiness and energy sectors, in environmental technology, and in other high-tech spheres. The prospects for export growth depend therefore mostly on the East Europeans' ability to obtain hard currency, by trade and credits, and on the marketing skills of American business. In 1990, the Commerce Department and Cocom took major steps to decontrol all but the latest and most sensitive technologies, and the impact of Jackson-Vanik waned as democratizing regimes eliminated restrictions on travel and other human rights. In the spring of 1990, Washington extended permanent MFN status to Poland, Hungary, and Czechoslovakia. And as some of the East Europeans opened up their economies to foreign investment, American companies began to move in.

Prospects for Trade and Investment. Recognizing that their import needs far exceed their export possibilities, most of the East European countries have sought joint ventures and industrial cooperation with Western firms. They hoped that the infusion of foreign capital, technology, and managerial know-how would be a low-cost way of improving their competitiveness and access to world markets. In the 1970s, West Germany alone almost doubled, to over five hundred, its cooperation agreements with the East, mainly with Poland, Hungary, and Romania. Various models emerged, ranging from the Romanian "enclave system," in which all accounting, settlement, and valuation of inputs was done in foreign currency, to the Hungarian variant, in which accounting was done in both foreign and local currency. [110]

On the whole, the experience disappointed the expectations of all parties concerned. The laborious process of dealing with the East's byzantine bureaucracies frustrated Western partners, as did the problems of assuring a marketable quality of output. Western businessmen often encountered difficulty in securing basic economic and commercial statistics (or a local telephone directory) and were compelled to negotiate with government agencies rather than with end users of their product. They were also discouraged by the insistence of some of the hard-currency-strapped regimes on countertrade, whereby payment for Western imports was made with Eastern products; by the late 1980s some 40 percent of Western imports into Eastern Europe were covered by such "compensation trade."

Creaky transportation and telecommunications infrastructures were another deterrent; an attempt to make a telephone call in Warsaw or Budapest has sorely tested the endurance of many a visitor. But the single greatest hindrance to the establishment and success of joint ventures remained the lack of convertible currency in the CMEA, which prevents Western partners from reaching a regionwide market.

The East Europeans, in turn, found that their expectations of technological benefits and substantial revenues from hard currency export failed to materialize, partly because Western firms were prepared to transfer process technology (that is, how to produce and market goods) more readily than advanced product technology. Hungary's deputy trade minister Imre Dunai observed ruefully in April 1988 that the 135 joint ventures in operation had brought in less than $100 million and served mainly to replace imports; in 1987, the exports of these joint ventures to hard currency markets were $35 million less than their imports.[111]

Such deterrents to joint ventures are even more critical at a time when most Western economies themselves have unused production capacity and unemployment and when there are attractive opportunities for investment in newly industrializing countries.[112] Yet the East European hunger for foreign investment grows. Industrial restructuring needs capital and modern equipment, and even second-class imported technology can be put to profitable use, if only within the CMEA market. Hungary and Poland were the first to liberalize their regulations, allowing full foreign ownership and trying to reduce structural disincentives, and by early 1990 the others were beginning to follow suit.

The East European market's size and potential for development certainly offer scope for profitable trade and investment. It has a combined population of 140 million: 38.2 million in Poland, 23.3 million in Yugoslavia, 23.2 million in Romania, 16.6 million in East Germany, 15.6 million in Czechoslovakia, 10.6 million in Hungary, 9 million in Bulgaria, and 3 million in Albania. According to CIA estimates, the richest, East Germany, had in 1989 a per capita gross national product of $9,679, roughly half the West German level; the comparable figure for Czechoslovakia was $7,878; for Hungary, $6,108; for Bulgaria, $5,710; for Yugoslavia, $5,464; for Poland $4,565; and for Romania, $3,445. Such calculations, given the problems of defining domestic product and currency conversion, are at best approximate, and some estimates are even lower.[113]

For all their economic vicissitudes, the countries of Eastern Europe do enjoy some comparative advantages that should encourage foreign investment. Their labor costs are lower than Spain's and Portugal's, and the labor force (especially in East Germany, Czechoslovakia, and Hungary) possesses skills that could be easily upgraded. The levels of literacy and education are high. Proximity to the huge West European market minimizes transportation costs. The infrastructures, though obsolescent, are closer to Western than to third world standards. And the long-dormant seeds of local entrepreneurship are beginning to germinate. These advantages and the pent-up demand for infrastructure equipment and producer and consumer goods are beginning to lure Western investors as the reformist regimes legislate privatization and offer enterprises at bargain-basement prices and as the OECD governments grant new credits, investment guarantees, and trade benefits.

The prospects are best in Hungary, which was the first to sanction full foreign ownership; in East Germany, which is being taken over by West German finance and industry; and in Czechoslovakia. In Poland, despite the financial stabilization program, the chaotic state of the economy and political controversy over privatization (the relevant law was passed only in July 1990) remained a deterrent to substantial investment. The valuation of state-owned assets was a serious obstacle. Lech Walesa was delighted when the Polish-American heiress Barbara Piasecka-Johnson proposed to invest $100 million in the historic Lenin (renamed Gdansk) Shipyard, but the deal fell through when a Western accounting firm estimated that the shipyard was worth less than $10 million. Still, by the beginning of 1990 West Germany alone had 230 joint ventures operating in Poland.

Hungary, then, became the preferred target of foreign investors. In July 1988, the Michigan firm Guardian Industries entered into a $115 million joint venture to manufacture float glass. The following year, General Electric paid $150 million to buy a controlling interest in the Hungarian light bulb manufacturer Tungsram, which has annual sales of $300 million and exports 85 percent of its output. "We're trying to position ourselves for the decade ahead," commented General Electric's CEO, John F. Welch, Jr.; "It's a prudent risk at this point in history." [114] In 1990, General Motors committed over $100 million for a 67 percent interest in an automotive plant in western Hungary, and Ford also announced plans for an automotive parts plant. Citibank and Mc-Donald's are already installed in Budapest, and Playboy enterprises has launched a Hungarian version of its magazine.

Other foreign investment included the West German Tengelmann group's share in the Skala retail chain, the Hungarian-Japanese chemicals firm Polifoam, Suzuki Motor's plan to build a car plant, and the French computer group Bull International's association with the Hungarian electronics firm Videoton. The Western press barons Robert Maxwell and Rupert Murdoch and German publishers purchased major shareholdings in Hungarian newspapers. Even Washington's ambassador to Budapest, Mark Palmer, joined what he called a gold rush by abandoning diplomacy for the presidency of the Central European Development Corporation, an American-Canadian investment consortium. Whether or not joint ventures prove mutually profitable, they should contribute technology as well as production and marketing expertise and generate employment in the critical phase of economic restructuring.

The Hungarian experience foreshadows some of the pitfalls of foreign investment in Eastern Europe. Until the question of ownership is clarified, managers of state enterprises have less incentive to secure the best price from foreign bidders than to negotiate sweetheart deals for personal advantage; at least one dubious transaction, the purchase by a Western investment group of HungarHotels, had to be subsequently nullified in the courts. The West German Springer Group's acquisition of provincial newspapers nominally owned by the former ruling party also caused a furor and was rescinded. Intent on putting more than four hundred enterprises (worth an estimated $8 billion) on the auction block, the government belatedly established an agency in March 1990 to supervise foreign purchases and ensure arm's length transactions based on competitive bidding. Anticipate popular resentment at the sellout of the national patrimony to foreigners, particularly if Western standards of productivity impose massive layoffs. And the future role of the state in economic life, including ownership of resources and industries, will not be easily resolved in countries with a long history of paternalistic government, but a fascination with Western free-market theories.

Western Aid. By the end of the 1980s, as political and economic liberalism was making a dramatic comeback throughout the region, the old cold war strictures against trading with the enemy gave way to new and urgent questions: What should be the response of the United States and its OECD partners to the desperate need of these victims of socialism? Could they afford to let the reforms fail? The West was faced with the historic challenge of rehabilitating the economies of a free Eastern Europe. After forty years of modest results, economic leverage loomed as the optimal instrument of political interest.

Marx and Lenin, and more recently Khrushchev, confidently forecast the triumph of socialism over capitalism. Their heirs are finally acknowledging that the experiment has failed dismally. The resulting economic and social damage includes low productivity and technological backwardness, joined more recently by inflation, falling real incomes, and even a decline in life expectancy. By mismanaging and wasting human capital and other resources, socialism has indeed created a new third world in the heart of Europe. The verdict on socialist economics was implicit in the concluding document of the CSCE economic conference held in Bonn in April 1990: all participating states endorsed the principles of market economics and the need to enhance economic freedom and cooperation. The market had supplanted Marx as the new lodestar.

The cost of undoing this damage is high. The attempts to "restructure" the socialist economies, which aim essentially at reintroducing the laws of the market in the allocation of capital and labor, can bring no quick and painless relief. Few East European industrial or agricultural producers could at present survive open competition on the world market. And economic reform, if it is to have any chance of lasting success, will in the short term impose socially painful and divisive sacrifices.

An earlier generation of East Europeans was forced to accept prolonged sacrifice for the sake of eventual socialist plenty. The present generation faces the prospect of austerity for the distant, if more plausible, promise of market-generated abundance. The paternalism and egalitarianism of the socialist welfare state were not only economically ruinous but psychologically damaging. An opinion poll in Yugoslavia showed that 90 percent of respondents were not prepared to work as hard as the one million Yugoslavs employed in Western Europe for the sake of higher wages. The federal prime minister, Branko Mikulic, gave his interpretation of the results: "The conclusion of the poll is that two-thirds of the Yugoslav society is not ready to accept the market requirements of work, and therefore is not ready for reform." [115] (He was forced to resign six months later when parliament rejected an austerity program endorsed by the IMF.) It is scarcely surprising if the insecurities of the market have little appeal for the many who even by East European standards are at or below the poverty line.

The Swedish model of productive capitalism, comprehensive social benefits, and minimal unemployment is a popular alternative, but it is the product of unique circumstances and is in any case running out of steam. The West German notion of a "social market economy" is liberally evoked by the new East European governments, but the domestic and external factors that generated Germany's postwar "economic miracle" are also largely absent in the former Soviet sphere. The best of both worlds will remain a chimera, for there are no short cuts to the ideal state of social justice amidst material plenty. Although the disappointing performance of state socialism has momentarily galvanized support for liberal economics, prolonged hardship could easily induce demoralization and disillusionment.

For the West, one natural response is to gloat over the implosion of socialism and welcome the new opportunities for profitable business. But normal investment and commerce are an insufficient remedy for Eastern Europe's current crisis. Capital generally flows to areas of high return and low risk, and at present Eastern Europe hardly offers the most rewarding investment opportunities. Low labor costs have lured some Western companies to subcontract production in the East, but foreign investors have been more interested in selling to the East and earning hard currency profits than in developing Eastern export industries. Commercial lenders, burned by their earlier experience, are reluctant to reenter the East European market without IMF leadership and government guarantees. And commercial credits, even if efficiently allocated by the recipients, pale in comparison to their accumulated foreign debt and to the $500 billion of annual domestic investment in the Soviet bloc. Dependent on the Soviet Union for energy and raw materials and on the West for technology, and suffering unfavorable terms of trade in both sphere's, Eastern Europe would in this scenario remain a peripheral and backward region in the world economy.

There remain alternative, more politically charged, approaches to the conduct of economic relations with the East, inspired as much by considerations of ideological purpose as by security or economic interest. The most radically negative tendency, once found mainly in conservative American circles, was to have no truck or trade with Communists but to let them be hoist on their own petard. The view that their economic failure represented a net advantage for the free world was aired in the debates over Poland within the Carter and Reagan administrations. Nothing, therefore, ought to be done by the West to ease their economic misery. The greater that misery, the sooner they would be driven to abandon socialism. The security version of this point of view was that all trade, and particularly technology transfer, enhances the military potential of the Soviet bloc and therefore increases the threat to Western security.

After the East European revolutions of 1989, political instability arising from economic distress can no longer be regarded as a precursor of desirable reform but rather as a threat to the consolidation of reform. And indifference to the material hardships suffered by East Europeans, most of whom are ardently pro-Western, is more than ever morally and politically unjustifiable.

The most radical positive approach is to address the economic needs of the East Europeans with a massive program of economic assistance modeled on the Marshall Plan. The Italian industrialist Carlo De Benedetti's proposal to this effect in March 1988 was endorsed by former French president Valery Giscard d'Estaing and by *Le Monde*. A few other politicians and specialists, including the American Michael Mandelbaum, advanced variations on the theme, some with special reference to Poland. Secretary of State George Shultz's response at the time was categorical: a Marshall Plan for Eastern Europe should never be considered.[116]

Indeed, while evocation of the Marshall Plan's spirit may have been felicitous, circumstances qualified the analogy. That essentially American amalgam of generosity and enlightened self-interest was inspired by the perception of acute threat to the security of the United States and of the need to build a solid bulwark in Western Europe. The Europeans were to develop the modalities of the program, and they possessed the democratic institutions and market economies necessary to its success. Persuaded of the real and present menace posed by the Soviet Union and Communist ideology, Congress and the American people assumed the burden of massive outright aid. Today, even if assistance to the East were founded on sound economic and political calculations, the vast sums needed could not be appropriated. To be sure, the burden of aid can now be shared with America's affluent allies, but it is not likely to be comparable to the largess of the Marshall Plan.

Between the options of laissez-faire neglect and unrealistically generous aid there lies a more realistic, differentiated economic strategy for responding to the opportunities of the Gorbachev era. Specifically:

1. Only a fundamental reform of economic and political structures can bring the benefits of competition-driven growth and democratic legitimacy. Partial measures tend to create as many problems as they resolve and do not deserve Western subsidies.
2. The uncoordinated and competitive allocation of Western economic favors invites Eastern manipulation, damages allied relations, and undermines the political purpose of a differentiated strategy.
3. Where the necessary political and economic structural reforms are instituted, a concerted program of credits, trade preferences, debt relief, technical assistance, and training is eminently in the West's interest and within its means.
4. The rhetoric of reform must not cloud the West's judgment on the likelihood of success and on the balance of power. The scale of the Soviet Union's economic problems renders any conceivable Western aid wasteful and ineffectual; and the military power of even a reformed Soviet Union remains a threat to the rest of Europe. Aid can, on the other hand, invigorate the East European countries and draw them into a secure relationship with the West.

By the end of the 1980s, the United States and its allies were developing a strategy along these lines. The change in official attitudes, particularly in Washington, came slowly and grudgingly.

The East European countries, warned U.S. Deputy Assistant Secretary for Commerce Franklin J. Vargo in 1987, "will have to rely upon themselves to generate the productivity, technology and growth to support the economic needs of their peoples. Even with the best will in the world, the West cannot help but at the margin. Growth in exports to the West will be difficult to achieve. The West European markets, to which

Eastern Europe sells 90 percent of its hard currency exports, are not growing fast enough to provide the East Europeans with substantial export gains unless they can increase their market share."[117] Commerce Secretary William Verity reminded an East-West conference in Potsdam in June 1988 that "there is no short-cut to reform that can be bought by turning to the West for assistance. Fundamental to the poor economic performance of the Warsaw Pact nations is their inability to utilize technology, to innovate and change and to allocate capital to efficient uses. . . . These are massive systemic failings that can only be solved by changing the system itself." The East, therefore, "cannot look to the West for a bailout from its economic problems," and increased trade and investment "can and should accompany economic restructuring, but this commerce will follow changes—not lead them."[118] Armed with the sobering experience of the Polish economic crisis, Zbigniew Brzezinski recommended that assistance "should be based on clear indications that these countries are pursuing serious institutionalized economic and political reforms."[119]

Upon his return from an East European tour in early 1988, Deputy Secretary of State John Whitehead observed that "they are eager to move away from dependency on the Soviet Union—economically, politically and socially. To the extent that they want to move away from the Soviet Union, it is U.S. policy to welcome it."[120] Hungary, despite its heavy indebtedness, earned Washington's favor with its growing liberalism. High-level contacts multiplied, including a visit to the United States in July 1988 by General Secretary Karoly Grosz. Although U.S. exports to Hungary stagnated at a level under $100 million, imports rose from $172 million in 1985 to $305 million in 1987. The United States lobbied intensely to overcome the European Community's hostility to the admission of Hungary to GATT. The U.S. ambassador, Mark Palmer, and American experts and donors were instrumental in a joint venture to establish in Budapest the Soviet bloc's first school of business administration. But only in mid-1989, as Hungary joined Poland in firmly setting course toward democracy and economic liberalism, did a substantial American aid program materialize.

With respect to Poland, Washington remained steadfast in denying economic concessions to the Jaruzelski regime. The West's bias in favor of the private sector was evident in the first instances of economic aid. A private, nonprofit "Foundation for the Development of Polish Agriculture," backed by the Ford and Rockefeller Foundations, was established with Polish government approval in February 1988. Dedicated to helping Polish agriculture help itself, the Foundation arranged a $2.4 million loan from an Austrian bank to enable pig farmers to import high-quality pig feed; profits from the export of hams to the United States were expected to make the project self-sustaining and to fund agricultural research and development. The first international loan to Poland was granted in November 1988 by the World Bank: a $17.9 million credit to facilitate the export of frozen fruit and vegetables to Western Europe.

Initially, there was little Western consensus beyond agreement that Eastern Europe should not be treated as an undifferentiated bloc and that economic reforms in the region could not succeed without political change. Washington, and particularly Congress, was wary of the rush to finance *perestroika*. In June 1988, on the eve of the Toronto economic summit, the Senate unanimously passed a nonbinding resolution asking the president to "consult with allied leaders on the impact on Western security of tied and untied loans, trade credits, direct investment, lines of credit, joint ventures, government guarantees and other subsidies" to the Soviet bloc. Senator Bill Bradley repeated his earlier suggestion that "the flow of capital should be limited and proportionate to the degree of systemic reform."[121]

The Bush administration had hardly completed its initial foreign policy review when the roundtable accords in Warsaw impelled it to devise hurriedly a package of economic favors. The president recalled that when he visited Poland in September 1987, he had "told Chairman Jaruzelski and Lech Walesa that the American people and Government would respond quickly and imaginatively to significant internal reform of the kind that we now see."[122] The result was an eight-point package, disclosed in his Hamtramck speech on April 17, 1989, which included elimination of tariffs on selected Polish exports under the General System of Preferences (GSP), a concession normally extended only to underdeveloped countries.[123]

Since the president's offers were subject to congressional approval, he took pains to ward off potential criticism: "We will not act unconditionally. We will not offer unsound credits. We will not offer aid without requiring sound economic practices in return." One condition for the package, said his national security adviser, Brent Scowcroft, was IMF approval of Polish economic reforms aiming to expand the private sector. The European allies, stressed Bush, shared the view that "help from the West will come in concert with liberalization."

Indeed, the West promised little and demanded much. The declaration issuing from the NATO summit at the end of May warned that "it is essentially incumbent on the countries of the East to solve their problems by reforms from within":

We will seek expanded economic and trade relations with the Eastern countries on the basis of commercially sound terms, mutual interest and reciprocity. Such relations should also serve as incentives for real economic reform and thus ease the way for increased integration of Eastern countries into the international trading system.[124]

The European Community's foreign ministers drew up a policy toward Eastern Europe that followed the American strategy of differentiation. The Community formally suspended contacts with Romania but negotiated a favorable trade agreement with Poland. In early June, Prime Minister Thatcher offered Britain's support for an IMF economic revitalization program, for debt rescheduling, and for liberalization of the EC's trade quotas, as well as a five-year, $40 million (later increased to $80 million) "know-how fund" to provide Poland with advice and training in the mysteries of political pluralism and the market economy. A few weeks later, President Mitterrand visited Warsaw and declared that "clear-thinking and responsible men have shown they know how to organize free debate, free elections, and a profound transformation of public life in Poland."[125] He offered Poland the first Western credits since martial law ($25 million in short-term credits, and a further $80 million in credit guarantees when Poland and the IMF settled on an economic recovery program) and the rescheduling of $1.15 billion, more than one-third of Poland's debt to France.

After these cautious beginnings, the Western powers were driven by the dramatic acceleration of change in the second half of 1989 to devise a remarkably comprehensive economic strategy. Conversely, the growing radicalism of East European reformers was reinforced by the firm conditionality of the West's response. In preparation for the forthcoming economic summit, President Bush had written to the other leaders outlining Washington's program for Polish relief and inviting them to make a concerted commitment. The modest scale of the administration's proposed contribution owed to budgetary stringency, skepticism about the Poles' ability to administer it, and fear of arousing unrealistic expectations of American bounty. This prudence was not unwarranted, for when Bush arrived in Warsaw on July 9 the outlook was still for a Communist-dominated government despite the humiliation suffered by the party at the recent elections, and the Poles had yet to develop a credible economic reform program.

Warsaw was disappointed by the president's gifts—the Hamtramck package, specifying a $100 million grant for private enterprise, $15 million for pollution control, and $4 million for technical assistance and labor training. In recommending multilateral aid, rescheduling, and IMF and World Bank facilities, Bush was proposing to spend other people's money. Even Brent Scowcroft conceded that the American contribution was largely symbolic, "as much political and psychological as it is substantive." [126] At his next stop, in Budapest, the president delivered a scaled-down version of the Polish package: $25 million for a "Hungarian-American Enterprise Fund" and $5 million for the environment, along with the prospect of permanent MFN status and GSP preferences.

That the White House was content to let the West Europeans take the lead and assume the major part of the burden of a recovery program for the East was confirmed at the Paris economic summit of the G-7 group in mid-July. Soviet sensibilities, it was felt, might be ruffled by an ostensibly American-managed initiative. The solution, proposed by West Germany's Kohl, was to charge the EC Commission with the task of coordinating the response of OECD countries to the reform process in Poland and Hungary. The president of the Commission, Jacques Delors, was delighted at the implied extension of his mandate into the realm of foreign policy and promptly evoked "the spirit of a Marshall Plan for Eastern Europe." [127]

While in Warsaw a Solidarity government took office, in Washington the debate over the adequacy of the Bush initiative intensified. Complained a frustrated State Department expert, "Because we basically have no money, we are going to be prevented from responding effectively to the greatest opportunity to alter the map of Europe since 1945." [128] The administration did extend $108 million in emergency food aid to Poland, and it included in its request to Congress $200 million for a fund to stabilize Polish currency, contingent on Warsaw reaching an agreement with the IMF. Bush also announced the formation of a top-level presidential mission to examine Poland's economic plans and needs.

But Congress, which in the past had acted mainly to constrain positive economic leverage in Eastern Europe, was now galvanized by the democratic revolution rapidly engulfing the region. Aid for Eastern reform became a popular cause in both parties and on November 18, two days after hearing an impassioned appeal from Lech Walesa, Congress passed legislation providing $852 million for Poland and $86 million for Hungary, double the funding requested by the administration. The stated purpose of the "East European Democracy Act of 1989" was to "facilitate the transition from state-directed controls to a free market economy." The Illinois Democrat who steered the bill through the Senate, Paul Simon, termed it "a wager on Poland's experiment with democracy and an investment in our security."[129] It earmarked $240 million for the Polish enterprise fund and $60 million for the Hungarian, $125 million in food aid, federal guarantees for up to $200 million in loans to Polish importers of American products, and $10 million for Polish training programs, in addition to the $200 million stabilization fund. It also directed the administration to seek "a generous and early rescheduling program" for Poland's debt.

The bill was no Marshall Plan, but it represented a substantial contribution to the emerging multilateral rescue operation. A contemporaneous opinion poll suggested that the average American was not in a generous mood. Seventy-four percent of the respondents opposed spending the savings generated by troop withdrawals from Europe on aid, and 80 percent felt that the United States should not launch a second Marshall Plan for Eastern Europe.[130] Fortuitously, the beneficiaries of the original Marshall Plan were now rising to the challenge.

"We cannot allow Poland to fail," concluded a spokesman of the European Commission after rhetorically recounting the risks of pumping aid into that leaky ship.[131] The first meeting of OECD countries, convened by Delors in August, had addressed the question of emergency food aid for Poland. The second meeting, in late September, debated the Commission's "action plan" for reinforcement of Polish and Hungarian economic reform, focusing on agriculture, access to Western markets, foreign investment, professional training, and environmental protection. In late October, France announced a three-year, $700 million emergency assistance program for Poland, and a few weeks later Chancellor Kohl visited Warsaw to unveil a $2.2 billion package, mostly in the form of loan guarantees and insurance but including the write-off of $400 million in commercial loans and the conversion of another $254 million into zlotys for reinvestment in Poland.

The collapse of the Honecker regime prompted Bonn to dangle potentially even vaster assistance. As the country became unified—economically in July, politically in October 1990—the immense costs of conversion to market economics and Western standards were vividly revealed. Unifying the currencies involved the injection of $31 billion into the economy. An additional $29 billion was allocated to subsidize the East's pensions, housing, unemployment insurance, highways, and railways. To make the East's industries competitive would require over $500 billion in investment. Within a year of the revolution, the East's industrial output had fallen by 42 percent, and almost 2 million of the 8.8 million work force became unemployed. Another 500,000 civil servants were expected to lose their jobs as a consequence of unification, and unemployment was projected to reach 30 percent in 1991. These costs and estimates reflected some unique features of unification, but they also indicated the distance to be travelled before the rest of the region could come close to the economic levels of the industrialized West.

Though the Federal Republic was destined to be the biggest single source of aid, the events in East Germany and the consequent speculation about German unification aroused French apprehensions that Bonn's priorities might shift away from the new plans for Community integration. To reinforce the principle of concerted action, President Mitterrand (who was also serving as president of the Community in the second half of 1989) convened an impromptu EC summit on November 18; the agenda included emergency aid for the East European countries, their future relationship with the Community, and Mitterrand's proposal for a new development bank. "All participants shared one sentiment," reported Mitterrand at a midnight press conference, "and that was joy . . . because of the new march of Eastern Europe towards freedom." Chancellor Kohl, for his part, averred that "he who thinks that we should now withdraw from Europe and take care of German things betrays the reform movement in East Germany, Poland, Hungary, and maybe tomorrow in Czechoslovakia, as well as betraying *perestroika* in the Soviet Union." [132]

In early December, the regular EC summit endorsed a $1 billion aid package for Poland and Hungary as well as the creation of a European Bank for Reconstruction and Development and a foundation for training

East European managers. A few days later, the twenty-four OECD foreign ministers, meeting in Brussels, agreed on a $1 billion stabilization fund for Poland and extended the promise of assistance in the so-called Phare program to East Germany, Czechoslovakia, Bulgaria, and Yugoslavia "at the time they put in place the necessary political and economic reforms"; by the following February, all these and Romania as well had submitted formal requests for aid.[133] The Poles concurrently reached agreement with the IMF on a tough economic reform program, a step that cleared the way for a $723 million IMF credit as well as new World Bank projects and OECD bridging loans. In January 1990, Japan's Prime Minister Toshiki Kaifu announced in West Berlin a billion-dollar aid program for Poland and Hungary, including a contribution to the multilateral stabilization fund and export and investment guarantees. While the terms for the new development bank were being worked out, the European Investment Bank approved a loan of 1 billion ($1.2 billion) ecus loan for those two countries. In February, the Paris Club agreed to reschedule nearly one-quarter of the Polish debt and to extend a moratorium on repayments until March 1991, although no one was optimistic about Poland's ability to ever pay it off. And in July, the Phare program was extended to the other East European supplicants with the exception of Romania, whose democratic record was not judged satisfactory.

The OECD countries thus responded with uncommon speed and ingenuity to the pressing needs of the two leading reformers in the East, establishing mechanisms and precedents for eventual aid to their neighbors as well. The measures promised to avert immediate financial collapse and ease the stresses of conversion to market economics, but they could not guarantee the sustained modernization of Eastern Europe's industry and agriculture. That task will require, in addition to multifaceted domestic adaptation, greater foreign investment and increased access to world markets.

The European Bank for Reconstruction and Development (known as BERD by its French acronym) broke new ground in being the first financial institution created jointly by East and West (its founding members comprise the OECD states, the six East European countries, Yugoslavia, and the Soviet Union), and it promises to become a powerful agent of modernization. Mitterrand made no bones about the political purpose of the initiative—"to give the people of these countries the means they require to make liberty, democracy and pluralism a reality." [134] Washington's reservations were met by a Soviet undertaking not to borrow more than its capital contribution for a period of three years, and by the provision reserving 60 percent of the bank's loans for the private and cooperative sectors. The United States subscribed 10 percent of the bank's $12 billion capital base, the European Community 51 percent, and the Soviet Union 6 percent. The rest was contributed by the other OECD and Eastern countries.

The East's economic rehabilitation will also be contingent on its access to the global, and primarily to the West European, market. By May 1990, the Community had concluded trade and cooperation agreements with Czechoslovakia, East Germany, and Bulgaria offering concessions similar to those extended earlier to Poland and Hungary, and it was preparing to open offices in Warsaw and Budapest. Delors's Commission, meanwhile, set to the task of developing terms for association agreements that would provide them with even greater economic concessions.

The economic integration of the two Europes will not be easy. Recognition of the East's immense needs induced the Council of Europe in May 1990 to call for a $400 billion "Marshall Plan," but even more modest concessions can raise problems. Western Europe is not eager to absorb cheaper food or manufactures or surplus labor, nor to further extend its regional and social fund benefits. When in early 1990 the Commission unveiled a plan to raise by 18 percent the quota for steel imports from Eastern Europe, the Community's steel producers protested vigorously. Yet the East Europeans will need markets as well as loans, technical aid, and training programs if they are to overcome the legacy of forty years of state socialism. It could take a decade for most to become economically acceptable candidates for full membership in an expanded Community. That continental extension of Jean Monnet's vision deserves both persistence and sacrifice on the part of West Europeans and Americans.

Counsel is the cheapest form of aid, and there is great demand for it as the East Europeans set about to reconstructing a market economy from scratch. This is the only demand that the West can readily satisfy. The IMF has already delivered expert advice on macroeconomic policy, and the East Europeans are also seeking advice from, and membership in, the OECD, where only Yugoslavia currently enjoys associate status.

Secretary-General Jean-Claude Paye indicated that the conditions for membership in this club of industrialized countries are a market economy and pluralistic democracy (criteria that were not always applied in the past), but the East Europeans can tap the OECD's broad expertise even before formal adhesion. The United States offered an extra $1 million to the secretariat to develop a specialized East European unit.[135] And bilateral consultations, such as meetings between Hungarian and Polish delegations and the U.S. Securities and Exchange Commission, are multiplying.

As economic barriers fall, the politically sensitive issue of the role of Germany emerges. The Germans enjoy natural advantages in commerce with the East—proximity and familiarity as well as a powerful and export-oriented economy. Memories of the Third Reich leave a residue of animosity, particularly in Poland and Czechoslovakia, where past regimes made a conscious effort to diversify their commercial links with the West. Polish suspicions are fueled by an alleged West German preference for investing in the former German territories. Paradoxically, the non-German East Europeans also fear that the costs of unification might reduce their share of West German economic favors and investment. Indeed, as East Germany's prime minister, Lothar de Maiziere, queried when the deal on economic union was concluded in May 1990, "Which other country gets such a good starting position as we with this treaty?"[136]

"Eastern Europe will be primarily a German market" a Bonn expert confidently predicted.[137] There is, however, some legitimate ambivalence about the prospect that the East Europeans will simply trade Soviet for German economic domination. What is in question is not the merits of West Germany's democracy and economy but the political influence that would inevitably accompany the consolidation of a German economic sphere in Eastern Europe, where the mark is likely to become the key currency. Such influence, however benign, can unsettle small and vulnerable nations in the midst of reasserting their autonomy. And Germany's Western neighbors worry about the further strengthening of the continent's economic superpower.

The revival of a historical pattern of German preponderance in East-Central Europe may be mitigated by secular trends and compensatory policies. The dependence of the East Europeans on one proximate economic superpower may be diluted as they join a global economy characterized by international competition, a proliferation of multinational companies, and far-flung investment. Moreover, as the European Community advances toward a single market and a common foreign policy, its commercial and political relations with the several East European countries should come to reflect European rather than specifically German interests. But for this to occur, the other major West European powers, particularly France, will have to assume a more active role in defining foreign and commercial approaches toward Eastern Europe, and in promoting economic relations in the context of such policy. And the United States can exert similar compensatory leverage in its economic policies and encouragement of European unification.

The West's coordinated economic program to reinforce reform may be insufficient, and it might even be considered niggardly in comparison to the $14 billion "Marshall Plan" being developed by the United States and Japan for the Philippines, or indeed to American aid for Panama and Nicaragua. In the case of the most heavily indebted East European countries, Poland and Hungary, Western creditors will probably have to consider writing off much of the debt to save them from prolonged and politically destabilizing penury. Conditionality will not be easy to apply and calibrate vis-a-vis regimes that enthusiastically profess Western values. Nor will generosity be easy to sell to taxpayers as the novelty of a democratized Eastern Europe wears off.

The crisis that erupted in the Persian Gulf in August 1990 only aggravated the economic misery of the Eastern European countries. All of them readily enrolled in the UN embargo against Iraq and occupied Kuwait, thereby suspending lucrative contracts and the repayment of Iraqi debts. The precipitous rise in the price of oil promised to be even more damaging. With the cuts in Soviet oil deliveries and the necessity of paying for future Soviet supplies in hard currency, the East Europeans were facing a critical energy shortage and more unfavorable terms of trade. In the case of Czechoslovakia, oil imports would consume all of the country's hard currency earnings. The IMF estimated that the region's real GDP would fall by an average of 5.3 percent in 1990 and stagnate, at best, in 1991.[138] Even Czechoslovakia, which earlier had denied any need for substantial foreign aid, now clamored for relief.

At the same time, the East Europeans' claim on Western resources was diluted by the fraying of the consensus on economic policy toward the Soviet Union. In the summer of 1990, the European Community, led by West Germany and France, parted ways with the United States in urging coordinated aid to that country despite the chaotic state of its economy and economic reforms. Bonn went so far as to guarantee $3 billion in bank credits to the Soviet Union as part of the unification bargain. Despite this diversion, and the potential for squandering scarce resources, the West maintained its unity of purpose in regard to Eastern Europe: to encourage self-determination, democratization, and reintegration into a community of free nations. Forty years after Yalta, the West has not fully exorcised its partial responsibility for the dismal fate of the East Europeans. Consequently, there lingers a sense of moral obligation to help them recover, without, of course, jeopardizing Western security. That security is not enhanced by chronic economic crisis. A new Eastern Europe possessed of more pluralistic institutions and rational economic structures can be an asset to Western security and a profitable trading partner.

America's postwar experience with economic leverage in Europe offers mixed lessons. The security rationale for embargoes and sanctions notwithstanding, punitive measures had little positive impact on the pace of reform in the East. Unilateral sanctions, exemplified by Jackson-Vanik, had only a marginal effect on the policies of regimes that could afford to forgo American favors. They occasionally served a valid symbolic purpose but undermined allied solidarity in the process. Positive economic leverage was not much more successful, as demonstrated by the Polish experience of the 1970s.

The Marshall Plan, then, remains the shining example of economic leverage that worked. It rested on a common appraisal of problem and remedy. To be sure, the stimulus of an acute perception of threat is absent now, but nonetheless the United States can again play a critical part in the collective response to the challenge of liberalism that is sweeping Eastern Europe.

6

Security Structures

Т he contest for Europe has stood at the heart of the confrontation between East and West since World War II. Extension of Soviet hegemony over Poland and the rest of Eastern Europe accentuated the threat to the rest of the continent, and by 1947 Western strategists became preoccupied with the political and military security of free Europe. All other considerations were subordinated to bolstering Western Europe's military defenses and integrative institutions. While the people of Eastern Europe were nominally considered to be friendly captives of a hostile power, their countries were in the enemy camp. For all the rhetoric of liberation and covert attempts at destabilization, containment was therefore fundamentally a defensive strategy to safeguard and strengthen the West, to consolidate rather than challenge the division of Europe.

Forty years later, with the Soviet empire gripped by reformist ferment, and with an economically and politically confident Western Europe moving ever closer to unity, the stability of this standoff is being challenged by new geopolitical uncertainties. In the late 1940s, Stalin's insecurities and ambitions and the West's sense of vulnerability conspired to divide the continent. Now that division is eroding, in the Kremlin's domain and within the Soviet Union itself.

The success of containment imposes a reappraisal of the comparatively comfortable calculus of defense of the status quo. This involves military disengagement and political realignment on terms that safeguard the security and accommodate the aspirations of all. Having served ably as guarantor of Western Europe's security, the United States now faces the challenge of guiding and facilitating the process of East European reintegration, and of elaborating security policies for a new European era. A complex geopolitical transformation is under way.

Alliance Politics: Security and Stability. Soviet hegemony imposed military as well as ideological and economic subordination on the countries of Eastern Europe. The West had no choice but to regard the East Europeans as extensions of Soviet power, the forward bases of an overwhelmingly powerful military machine that ostensibly threatened the security of Western Europe. The "captive peoples" may have been reluctant partners, but their totalitarian regimes possessed the capability to marshal human and material resources in the service of Soviet security needs. By 1950, the proportion of their resources allocated to military purposes far outstripped that in the West, and five years later the Warsaw Treaty formally converted the existing network of bilateral mutual security linkages into a multilateral political and military alliance.

Like a mirror image of NATO, the Warsaw Pact presented itself as a purely defensive alliance, established to protect socialist states against the threat of German militarism and revanchism and the hostile forces of imperialism led by the United States. There were, in fact, fundamental asymmetries between the two alliances. Membership in the Warsaw Pact was less than voluntary, although the East European regimes shared Moscow's ideological outlook and owed their survival to Soviet patronage. Moreover, the Poles and Czechs in particular felt vulnerable to German irredentism and shared Russia's historical mistrust of Germany. The most obvious asymmetry lay in the military realm, where the massive numerical superiority of the Warsaw Pact forces and the offensive doctrine imputed by NATO analysts to the Soviet military command made the Communist claim of defensive necessity questionable.

The other asymmetry involved intra-alliance relations. The Warsaw Pact's smaller members were initially wholly subordinated to their patron. The Warsaw Treaty, like the North Atlantic Treaty, made no provision for unilateral abrogation except upon notice one year before the end of its twenty-year term. In the case of NATO there was no challenge to France's sovereign right to withdraw from the joint military command. In contrast, the legally constituted Hungarian government's renunciation of the treaty during the 1956 revolution was ignored and superseded by the forceful reimposition of a more compliant regime. Albania, beyond Moscow's reach, effectively suspended its membership in 1961. When a few years later the Romanians secured the withdrawal of allied Soviet forces, the Kremlin tacitly accepted their apostasy, for there were propaganda advantages in this display of limited voluntarism. But in Hungary in 1956, in Czechoslovakia in 1968, and in Poland in 1980–81, the Warsaw Pact's most critical function came into play: to preserve the unity of the "socialist commonwealth" at its strategic front line.

Soviet and party control was imposed over the East European military establishments in the early postwar years, and the Warsaw Pact provided for a joint military command. A fully integrated military alliance materialized only in the 1970s, with the advent of new command and control mechanisms, joint training exercises, and modernization of equipment. The prevailing Soviet doctrine, as displayed in the Pact's exercises, was essentially offensive and initially nonnuclear. The objective was to engage the enemy on its own territory.[1]

At the end of the 1970s, the dominant role of the Soviet Union was affirmed in a secret Warsaw Pact agreement (the "Statute of the Joint Armed Forces and Organs of Their Command in Wartime"), which provided that in time of war or anticipated war, control of the East European armed forces would be exercised exclusively by the Supreme High Command, in operational terms by the Soviet General Staff. These troops could be deployed without prior consultation of the governments concerned.[2] Thus, for all practical purposes, the East Europeans surrendered their sovereignty in time of crisis, but even at other times the size and equipment of their armed forces were determined in Moscow. The imposition of Soviet command and military doctrine went hand in hand with substantial burden sharing in the form of manpower and domestic defense expenditure (which remained proportionately higher than for NATO members) as well as contribution to the maintenance of Soviet forces stationed in Eastern Europe.

From the Western perspective, then, the Warsaw Pact presented a formidable threat to security. It enjoyed the geographical advantage of strategic depth, a concentration of elite Soviet forces backed by national armies in the GDR, Poland, and Czechoslovakia, a vast numerical advantage in tanks, artillery, and other armored vehicles, and a standardization of equipment beyond the capability of the more pluralistic NATO. Outmanned and outgunned, NATO adopted a forward defense strategy to contain the aggressor at German border and, in the "Follow-on Forces Attack" (FOFA) plan devised in the early 1980s, to hit rear echelons of the Warsaw Pact forces by tactical nuclear strikes.

The reliability of the Warsaw Pact's East European component was difficult to assess. The domestic political and socioeconomic circumstances of the Soviet Union's allies and their low level of military preparedness (except for the GDR) raised doubts as to their potential performance in war. Western analysts tended to regard the GDR and Bulgaria as the USSR's most reliable allies, and assumed that in central front operations, East German units would be integrated into the Soviet first echelon, while the Poles (apart from possible frontline action aimed at northern Germany or Denmark) and the Czechs would be relegated to the second echelon. The standard expectation was that East European military discipline would hold during an initial Warsaw Pact assault, but that if NATO succeeded in preventing a quick and decisive Soviet victory, the reliability of the minor allies would rapidly dissipate. While the loyalty of the East European officer corps was not to be underestimated, the bonds were more professional than political, and they lacked domestic roots and reinforcement. Thus, even before the revolutions of 1989, East European military reliability was not considered likely to withstand the stress of combat and the pull of nationalistic sentiments.[3]

Deputy Assistant Secretary of State William Luers reminded Congress in 1978 that "it would be folly for NATO to devise a strategy or a tactic in Europe that was based on the assumption that Eastern European forces would not be fully effective in their fighting capacity against NATO forces."[4] Consequently, "worst-case" calculations of manpower and materiel overestimated the Pact's military capability. The East Europeans' morale and political commitment were no doubt weakened by the prospect of devastation that FOFA brought to their territory. Like West Germany, the countries of the northern tier and Hungary realistically anticipated that they would be the battleground in any foreseeable military engagement and therefore had a higher stake in detente than their less exposed allies. Detente, by the same token, weakened the cohesion of the Warsaw Pact and the Soviet Union's leverage.

Collective Security. In the early years of the cold war, the West's concentration on alliance building and military deterrence precluded serious consideration of alternative approaches to European security. The Soviet Union and its allies represented a unified military threat, and the erection of the Atlantic alliance precluded tampering with the status quo of a divided Europe. The need to nurture stability within the two camps reinforced the stability of their separation.

Article 11 of the Warsaw Treaty specifies that "should a system of collective security be established in Europe, and a General European Treaty of Collective Security concluded for this purpose, for which the Contracting Parties will unswervingly strive, the present Treaty shall cease to be operative from the day the General European Treaty enters into force."[5] This provision reflected a concurrent Soviet diplomatic initiative to alter the political and military balance.

On February 10, 1954, at the Berlin conference of the four powers, Soviet Foreign Minister Molotov advanced a "Draft General European Treaty" for collective security that was linked to a proposal regarding Germany. That proposal anticipated neutralization and confederal arrangements leading eventually to "democratic" unification. In the interim, most occupation forces would be withdrawn, though they could be reintroduced if security was threatened. The collective security regime originally adumbrated by Molotov assigned only observer status to the United States, which was patently unacceptable to the Western powers, and the latter also rejected an amended proposal that allowed for American participation in a European security system. The West apprehended that Molotov's schemes were designed solely to impede West German participation in NATO and reduce the American commitment to Western Europe's defense. Western security was equated with an expanded NATO, and mistrust of Soviet political promises had since Yalta become an axiom in U.S. foreign policy.

Even after West Germany's accession to NATO had become a fait accompli, the Russians revived their idea of a European security conference at the 1955 Geneva summit and proposed a zone for limitation and inspection of armaments encompassing the two Germanys and neighboring states. This prompted the West to advance the so-called Eden plan for European security, which envisioned a unified Germany as well as a limited arms zone with a military balance and verification measures. Although the two proposals had points in common, the West's commitment to NATO and its terms for German unification precluded compromise. As the integration of West Germany into the NATO military structure proceeded, Khrushchev abandoned his European security initiatives and instead precipitated crises over Berlin.

The Helsinki Final Act and CBMs. The confidence-building measures proposed by the United States as the Eighteen Nation Disarmament Conference in December 1962 foreshadowed the terms of the Helsinki Final Act, but in the 1960s, the two alliances were preoccupied with their own problems—control over nuclear weapons and the balance of European and American contributions in NATO, polycentrism and the Prague Spring in the Warsaw Pact. In the United States, the lone voice of Zbigniew Brzezinski persisted in advocating new multilateral frameworks for addressing European security and attenuating the division of the continent. Two years after the enunciation of the Brezhnev Doctrine, he again urged the creation of some permanent consultative mechanism, "a joint NATO-Warsaw Pact commission or a European security commission, to monitor eventual security arrangements and perhaps even to initiate others."[6] As noted earlier (chapter 3), the Nixon administration saw little merit in reopening the question of European security while it pursued a multipolar balance of power and detente with the Soviet Union, and the United States approached the CSCE with greater skepticism than the other participants.

The Helsinki Final Act's contribution to security, to reducing tensions and enhancing the autonomy of the East European countries, was nominal at best. Reiteration of the principles of sovereign equality and inviolability of frontiers offered no greater guarantee of security than the UN Charter, although it was noteworthy that a Warsaw Pact member, Romania, argued successfully for inclusion of the right to neutrality and of the prohibition of intervention in states' internal affairs "regardless of their mutual relations." But the first tentative step was taken to reduce the feasibility of surprise attack in the "confidence-building measures" (CBMs) enumerated in Basket I.

The most important CBM was the obligatory notification, at least twenty-one days in advance, of major military maneuvers exceeding a total of 25,000 troops. In the case of the Soviet Union, this requirement was limited to a depth of 250 kilometers from its European borders. The invitation of observers and other CBMs addressing smaller-scale maneuvers and other military movements were discretionary. By the end of 1983, NATO had given due notification of twenty-seven major maneuvers, and the Warsaw Pact of eighteen. Against the background of the Solidarity crisis, notification was given of two large Warsaw Pact exercises in the region in July and September 1980, though observers were not invited. There was no adequate notification of the Zapad 81 exercise, sponsored by the Soviet Union and held in the Byelorussian and Baltic areas in September 1981.[7] Thus, the Helsinki CBMs were not fully respected and did not materially impede the Warsaw Pact from putting military pressure on Poland. The voluntary CBM of encouraging contact between military personnel led to visits by a delegation from the U.S. National Defense University to Hungary and Romania in March 1981 and by two U.S. naval vessels to Romania in June 1982.

In sum, this first attempt at confidence building marginally increased the predictability of major military activities by the two alliances but offered scant protection to East Europeans against the strictures of the Brezhnev Doctrine.

Proposals came from France in 1978 and from the Warsaw Pact in March 1979 for the expansion of CBMs in the context of a conference on disarmament in Europe (CDE). After its initial experience with the geographically limited MBFR (mutual and balanced force reduction) talks (see below), the United States questioned the utility of a CDE, but the Carter administration helped develop a NATO proposal and President Reagan assented in principle to a CDE as part of the CSCE process. The grandly named Conference on Confidence and Security-Building Measures and Disarmament in Europe was convened in Stockholm in January 1984. Circumstances were not propitious: Soviet-American arms negotiations in Geneva had broken down, and NATO, after much official and public debate, was deploying Cruise and Pershing missiles to counter the threat of the Soviet SS-20 devices.

Nonetheless, the agreement reached in Stockholm in September 1986 achieved some tangible results, probably the most important of which was the commitment by the participants to "refrain from the threat or use of force in their relations with any state, regardless of that state's political, social, economic or cultural system and irrespective of whether or not they maintain with that State relations of alliance." This article 14 of the agreement was pointedly highlighted by the Romanians, and indeed its formulation challenged the legitimacy of the Brezhnev Doctrine of limited sovereignty more explicitly than had the Final Act. Moreover, article 16 stressed that noncompliance "constitutes a violation of international law." The agreement's other provisions, for observation and challenge inspections, enhanced the stability of mutual deterrence but offered scant protection against Warsaw Pact police actions. At best, commented the U.S. delegate to the CDE, the agreement raised the political cost of foreign intervention.[8]

In any case, such international commitments did not necessarily supersede dogma, for as an authoritative Soviet theorist had written in 1968, "in the Marxist conception, the norms of law, including the norms governing relations among socialist countries, cannot be interpreted in a narrowly formal way, outside the general context of the class struggle in the present-day world."[9] "For us," observed Brezhnev to the Czechoslovak Politburo after the 1968 invasion, "the results of World War II are inviolable, and we will defend them even at the cost of risking a new war."[10] Nor did the Helsinki Final Act deter the Warsaw Pact's chief of staff, General Sergei Shtemenko, from reiterating that a principal function of the alliance was to offer "fraternal assistance" in defense of socialism.[11] CBMs and affirmations of inviolable sovereignty, therefore, would not constitute an effective deterrent until they took precedence over the ideological rationales asserted by the Kremlin.

Gorbachev Discards the Brezhnev Doctrine.   These rationales began to weaken under Gorbachev's "new thinking" in foreign policy. On the occasion of the Bolshevik Revolution's 70th anniversary, he declared:

The time of the Comintern and the Cominform, and even the time of binding international conferences, is past. But the international Communist movement continues to exist. All the parties are completely and irreversibly independent. We talked about this as far back as the 20th Congress. True, we did not free ourselves of old habits at once. However, now this is an immutable reality. In this sense, the 27th CPSU Congress was also a final and irrevocable landmark.[12]

Although Gorbachev never referred explicitly to the Brezhnev Doctrine, his repeated assurances clearly addressed the substance if not the Western label of that policy. The Soviet-Yugoslav declaration of March 1989 invoked the same principle, and at the Bucharest summit of the Warsaw Pact in July, Gorbachev affirmed that socialist pluralism had international as well as domestic validity: the several Communist parties were totally independent and free to accommodate national circumstances ("without outside interference," said the communique) and to learn from each other to produce "unity in diversity."[13] And in his speech to the Council of Europe he had stressed that the concept of a "common European home" ruled out the threat or use of force within as well as between alliances.

It is doubtful that Gorbachev fully anticipated the consequences of a more permissive policy toward Eastern Europe. He blamed the crisis in the system not on socialism but on mistakes by previous Soviet and East European party leaderships. The possibility that some ruling parties might voluntarily surrender the leading role prescribed by Lenin struck at a fundamental principle of Soviet socialism. Yet Moscow sanctioned that surrender by the Polish party in the summer of 1989, when one of Gorbachev's associates, Yevgeny Primakov, stated that "this is entirely a matter to be decided by Poland."[14]

Gorbachev's new look was fraught with uncertainty about the compatibility of the diverse objectives of Soviet security, regional economic revival, and a socialist pluralism that rapidly transgressed the ideological boundaries of Marxism-Leninism. It remained, moreover, at least partly contingent on Gorbachev's success in the domestic sphere. But after a few years of his reign, America's Kremlinologists were coming to believe that *perestroika* was, in Brzezinski's words, a "massive, monumental transformation."[15] By the autumn of 1989 the administration had overcome its skepticism, as Secretary of State Baker allowed that "it would be folly indeed to miss this opportunity" to respond to the dramatic changes in Soviet policy.[16]

A year earlier, Kissinger had advanced the suggestion that the West offer Moscow a pledge of nonintervention in Eastern Europe in exchange for a Soviet promise to allow liberalization to occur at its own pace.[17] But such a scheme smacked of a superpower spheres-of-influence approach, at odds with the pluralistic spirit of the Helsinki process. The United States could hardly afford to renege on its interest in Eastern Europe's emancipation at the very moment when the prospect of self-determination presented itself. In the event, the administration's cautious and deliberately low-keyed reaction to the East European revolutions served the same end, to reassure the Soviets that the United States was not intent on fomenting turbulence in their sphere. Gorbachev's most radical departure from established policy was the implicit view that

Soviet security was better served by a less hegemonic relationship with the East European buffer zone. Objectively, those countries had become unproductive assets—indebted to the West, heavy consumers of Soviet energy repaid with low-quality products, politically restive, and of questionable military value. His initial conception was not divestment but rather the creation of an economically more productive, more pluralistic, but still socialist community.

The rapid eclipse of Communist power in Eastern Europe came as a surprise that the Gorbachev regime accommodated by turning necessity into a virtue. Addressing the Soviet legislature on October 23, 1989, Foreign Minister Shevardnadze reflected on the "historic, qualitative changes" in Eastern Europe: "New, alternative forces are entering the political arena in some of these countries. No one is bringing them in. They arise because the people want them." The Kremlin, he asserted, was undisturbed, indeed sympathetic. For good measure, Shevardnadze conceded that the Soviet intervention in Afghanistan had "violated the norms of proper behavior" and Soviet law.[18] Respecting Eastern Europe, said his spokesman Gennadi Gerasimov, "we now have the Frank Sinatra doctrine. He has a song, 'I had [sic] it my way.' So every country decides on its own which road to take."[19]

The communique issuing from the Warsaw Pact foreign ministers' meeting in the Polish capital on October 27 (the first such meeting chaired by a non-Communist) termed as essential the "right of every nation to independent decision-making about its . . . road to social, political and economic development, without outside interference."[20] A few weeks later, Gerasimov spelled it out: "The Brezhnev Doctrine is dead."[21] And in December, with the irreconcilable Czechoslovak regime finally out of the way, the original Warsaw Pact invaders officially made amends for the 1968 intervention. That invasion, said the declaration introduced by Gorbachev, had "interrupted the process of democratic renewal"; it constituted "interference in the internal affairs of Czechoslovakia and must be condemned."[22] The popular mood in Moscow favored the surrender of empire, for a survey revealed that large majorities did not want the Soviet Union to impede an East European country's decision to leave the Warsaw Pact or the CMEA, or to adopt a market economy.[23] "It is clear," said U.S. Defense Secretary Dick Cheney, that the likelihood of all-out conflict between the United States and the Soviet Union, between NATO and the Warsaw Pact, is probably lower now than it has been at any time since the end of World War II."[24]

There were some dissenting voices. The conservative Yegor Ligachev questioned Gorbachev's notion that peaceful coexistence takes precedence over the international class struggle, and he as well as some Soviet generals grumbled ominously about the "collapse of the Socialist camp" in Eastern Europe. Characterizing past Soviet behavior toward the region as "violence to history, democracy, traditions . . . and common sense," Foreign Minister Shevardnadze retorted that Soviet security was better served by an Eastern Europe free of communism than one where the USSR maintained unpopular regimes by force.[25] The tendency to de-ideologize relations with Eastern Europe was apparently becoming dominant in Soviet policy.

Gorbachev's renunciation of the Brezhnev Doctrine and his evocation of a "common European home" invited Western diplomatic initiatives to enhance the East Europeans' autonomy and attenuate the division of the continent without destabilizing the existing framework of European security. Much of the requisite policy adjustment had to come from the Soviet Union, which, in Walt Rostow's words, "would have to decide to accept a balance of power rather than an hegemonic solution to its legitimate security interest in Eastern Europe; that is, a solution guaranteeing that no other major power dominates Eastern Europe, rather than Soviet domination of the region."[26] But the United States and its allies also faced the challenges of geopolitical transformation—of redefining the conditions of their military security, addressing the complex problem of Germany, and nurturing the reintegration of the Eastern countries into a democratic community.

Military Disengagement. The early militarization of containment provided a bulwark behind which Western Europe could rebuild its economic and political self-confidence. The Western alliance's strategies were driven principally by a chronic sense of military vulnerability, and only secondarily by political fears of Soviet-induced procommunism and neutralism. East of the iron curtain, the Warsaw Pact assured the Soviet Union's military as well as ideological security. Crises such as the Hungarian revolution demonstrated the tenuous popular legitimacy of Moscow's client regimes, and even as a degree of military stability was forged by the two alliances, there remained a glaring asymmetry in their members' fundamental political stability. Soviet military force was the essential guarantee of Communist rule in Eastern Europe, and the West had little expectation that this force could be dislodged without risk to its own safety, let alone to Soviet influence in the region.

The option of military disengagement in Europe enjoyed little currency in cold war Washington, though Eisenhower and Dulles toyed with it in September 1953 (see chapter 2). Four years later, Khrushchev evoked the possibility of a phased, mutual withdrawal, and Polish Foreign Minister Adam Rapacki proposed a nuclear-free zone in Central Europe. George Kennan, Walter Lippmann, and the British Labour leaders Hugh Gaitskell and Denis Healey among others urged the West to explore the option of negotiating the withdrawal of foreign forces from Germany and Eastern Europe as a condition of German unification and satellite self-determination. But in Washington the view prevailed that the Soviets would not willingly risk the political status quo in their sphere by removing the military cement of empire, and that without a favorable change, partial military disengagement would only weaken the American component of the West's defenses. The conventional wisdom was reflected in Dean Acheson's observation that "I cannot for the life of me see how the movement toward a greater degree of national identity in Eastern Europe is furthered by removing from the continent the only power capable of opposing the Soviet Union."[27]

In July 1957, the United States, Britain, France, and West Germany issued the "Berlin Declaration," proposing free unification of the two Germanys and security guarantees for the Soviet Union and its allies if the reunited Germany chose to join NATO. This purely token gesture was more noteworthy for the implicit relegation of Eastern Europe to a Soviet sphere than for its positive terms, which were not expected to be acceptable to the Soviet Union. The neutralized Germany and weakened NATO sought by the Russians were equally unacceptable to the West. Khrushchev intensified his drive to consolidate the status quo, calling in 1958 for a general German peace treaty guaranteeing the separate status of the Federal Republic, the GDR, and West Berlin, and when the West rejected this, he provoked a protracted crisis over Berlin. Amidst such tensions, the question of military disengagement lost all immediacy.

Although arms control figured on the agenda of detente diplomacy in the late 1960s, military disengagement was no longer a Soviet priority. Brezhnev's objective for detente in Europe was primarily political: to legitimate the East European status quo, above all by securing recognition of the GDR, and then to normalize relations with the West Europeans, above all with the Federal Republic, in order to obtain economic benefits and loosen the ties between the two pillars of NATO. Reciprocal military disengagement held less attraction for the Kremlin, which somewhat paradoxically feared that significant American retrenchment would stimulate expansion of West European, and especially Bundeswehr, resources; moreover, the Prague Spring had confirmed that a Soviet military presence was needed to maintain political order in Eastern Europe. Brezhnev's political design was served by the reversal of a twenty-year-old West German policy when, in 1969, Willy Brandt discarded the Hallstein Doctrine and moved to acknowledge the division of Germany. The long-sought European security conference, in the Kremlin's scheme, would symbolically seal the political status quo.

Instead, the impetus for conventional arms reduction talks now came from the West, and for reasons that had nothing to do with Eastern Europe. The Atlantic alliance was suffering from discord between the Americans and the others over the desirable pace of detente and over burden sharing. Senator Mike Mansfield had been introducing resolutions since 1966 calling for a substantial reduction in the U.S. military presence in Europe, and public as well as congressional support for such a unilateral initiative was growing. The Harmel report, approved by NATO in December 1967, added the task of furthering detente to the alliance's basic function of assuring deterrence. NATO began to study the option of mutual force reductions and conveyed a specific proposal to the Warsaw Pact in 1970. The Pact, meanwhile, stepped up its campaign for a European security conference, beginning with a "Declaration on Strengthening Peace and Security in Europe" issued in Bucharest in July 1966.

The MBFR Talks. For Kissinger, the main purpose of talks on MBFR was to undercut the political appeal of Senator Mansfield's proposal to halve the American military contingent in Europe. Fortuitously, at the 24th CPSU Congress in March 1971, Brezhnev came out in favor of such talks and, in Kissinger's rendition, "saved our whole European defense structure from Congressional savaging."[28] The complex linkage between Soviet aid for peace in Vietnam, the German treaties and the Berlin agreement, the CSCE, and MBFR bore fruit, and at their 1972 summit, Nixon and Brezhnev agreed on launching the two multilateral conferences.

The preparatory meetings for MBFR began at Vienna on January 31, 1973. The area covered by the talks was to be Central Europe, defined as the two Germanys, Czechoslovakia, and Poland. The Pentagon and other allies had wanted to include Hungary (which was keen to participate), but Kissinger apparently had already conceded its exclusion, and in any case NATO would not agree to the quid pro quo of including Italy.[29] Other issues that could not be resolved at the preparatory talks included the conflict over balanced, meaning asymmetrical, reductions that would take into account the superior numerical strength of the Warsaw Pact versus proportional, or equal, decreases.

The formal MBFR conference opened in October, and although a succession of proposals and counterproposals narrowed some of the gaps, it became mired in technicalities. When the Warsaw Pact in June 1976 finally presented the essential basic figures on troop numbers, these fell short by some 157,000 of the NATO estimates for ground forces. The Soviets explanation that the NATO estimates included servicemen whose tasks in the West were performed by nonuniformed personnel did not end the controversy, and differences persisted over national ceilings and inspection and verification measures. When in October 1979 Brezhnev announced the unilateral withdrawal of 20,000 Soviet troops and 1,000 tanks from the GDR, NATO was unable to verify the claim.[30]

The MBFR circus survived the shock of Afghanistan, and the Soviet Union did not walk out as it later would from the START and INF talks in 1983, but persistent disagreement over the data base turned it into a sterile diplomatic exercise. The Warsaw Pact was modernizing its forces, and NATO came to fear that "stabilization" could diminish its own defensive capabilities.[31] France had argued from the outset that meaningful disarmament negotiations had to encompass the continent, from the Atlantic to the Urals.

Nor was MBFR linked in Western strategy to political change in Eastern Europe, although the State Department's report to Congress on policy toward that region made passing reference to "serious pursuit" of the Vienna talks.[32] In the end, the Solidarity challenge had been crushed without Soviet armed intervention, but the threat of invasion remained the ultimate guarantee of the socialist commonwealth's integrity. The modest objectives of MBFR did not promise to materially weaken that threat.

Most of the East European regimes, not to speak of their subjects, were more eager than Brezhnev's Kremlin for detente and arms control. Honecker and Czech leader Gustav Husak perhaps derived some sense of security from the Soviet military presence, but the others preferred to follow a path to legitimacy and modernization less constrained by the military burden and other strictures imposed by the Soviet Union in the name of security. In Western ranks, too, impatience spread at the glacial progress of military detente. In 1982, an international commission chaired by Olof Palme issued a "Blueprint for Survival" calling for sweeping, all-European disarmament talks. A key adviser to West German Social Democratic chancellors, Egon Bahr, appended a proposal for the withdrawal of all foreign nuclear weapons, the securing of an approximate balance of NATO and Warsaw Pact conventional forces, and, in the interest of stability, for leaving the two alliance systems "with their obligations and guarantees" unaltered.[33] And NATO's maverick, France, continued to agitate for pan-European arms control talks. The restlessness and voluntarism of the allies caused political as well as diplomatic headaches in Washington, and when in July 1986 they reacted negatively to the punitive U.S. bombing raid on Libya, the Senate once again threatened to withdraw American forces from Europe.

Dissension within the alliances bore little promise of overcoming the political division of Europe. The East European regimes sought normalization of commercial and other links, not the surrender of socialism. Western governments were also leery of tampering with the political status quo. Their security depended on the substantial weight of the Bundeswehr (all the more if the United States reduced its commitment), and the recurring spectre of a unified and perhaps neutral Germany consternated the European allies. The defense and arms establishments also had an interest in the preservation of the status quo. Unless fundamental change came about in the Soviet system, which no one, East or West, expected, the continued division of Europe seemed to serve the dominant interests.

Gorbachev's Diplomatic Offensive. Gorbachev's advent upset the fundamental immobility of this calculus of stability and security. The Atlantic alliance's complacency was shaken by the Reagan-Gorbachev summit in Reykjavik in October 1986, which paved the way for the elimination of INF (land-based, intermediate-range) missiles and was followed by the Soviet leader's "double-zero" proposal to eliminate shorter-range nuclear missiles as well. In NATO's deterrence strategy, these weapons served to offset the Warsaw Pact's conventional superiority. Without them, the conventional imbalance demanded remedy through either Western conventional rearmament or negotiated, asymmetrical reductions.

Most Western analysts focused on the risks of a denuclearized confrontation, and one West German concluded in 1987 that "it currently seems unrealistic to design arms control schemes that would change fundamentally the existing international political-military order in Europe." [34] Others, including the former American diplomat William Luers, evoked the potential benefits for Eastern Europe's political autonomy of substantial reductions in regional nuclear and conventional forces, particularly those of the superpowers. [35] Brzezinski stepped up his advocacy of such reductions coupled with a Europeanization of the West's defenses, and he suggested a Central European tank-free zone that could lessen the military threat to peaceful political change in Eastern Europe. [36] The more orthodox strategists in Washington continued to disparage schemes that might send the wrong message to the European allies regarding the American perception of threat.

Gorbachev underscored the growing irrelevance of the stalled MBFR talks when on April 18, 1986 in East Berlin he invited negotiation on the reduction of tactical nuclear as well as conventional forces from the Atlantic to the Urals. The Warsaw Pact's Budapest appeal on June 11 elaborated on the offer, and in September at the UN Foreign Minister Shevardnadze asserted that "we would generally not want our troops to be present anywhere beyond our national borders." [37] The development of a Western response was hampered by divergent perspectives on the appropriate forum for such talks. France, as before, preferred the pan-European CDE format to an alliance-to-alliance conference, partly on the calculation that such a setting might allow the East Europeans to play a more independent role, although the Stockholm experience allowed little optimism in this respect. The U.S. preference for a restricted forum independent of the CSCE process was more representative of

NATO views, and the alliance's Brussels declaration of December 11 called for NATO-Warsaw Pact talks on "conventional stability" as well as the extension of CDE talks on confidence-building measures.

Nevertheless, the potential leverage in linking security to human rights militated in favor of the CSCE framework, and by June 1987 NATO had devised a compromise putting both sets of talks (what was then labeled the Conventional Stability Talks, or CST, involving NATO and the Warsaw Pact, and the broader CDE) in that context. Gorbachev's diplomatic offensive was winning converts not only in Europe but also in the United States, where Senator Sam Nunn proposed a 50 percent cut in U.S. and Soviet forces in Central Europe to reduce the chances of a "short-warning attack," and Senator Bill Bradley declared that "if reform continues in the Soviet Union I believe we can cut U.S. and Soviet conventional forces in Central Europe and indeed nuclear weapons, by more than anyone has been prepared to talk about until now." [38]

The issue of Western security necessarily overshadowed the uncertain calculations of political benefits in Eastern Europe, but as the most enthusiastic advocate of detente, West German Foreign Minister Hans-Dietrich Genscher, observed in February 1987, "If there is a chance that, after 40 years of confrontation, there would be a turning point in East-West relations, it would be a mistake of historic proportions to let it slip away because of habits of thought which expect only the worst for the Soviet Union." [39]

Indeed, NATO approached the new Atlantic-to-Urals talks with conditioned skepticism, aiming at stabilization (that is, the reduction of asymmetries, particularly in armored forces) rather than major cutbacks. [40] A Pentagon report on long-term strategy, entitled "Discriminate Deterrence" and presented to President Reagan in January 1988, anticipated that the Soviet Union would develop smaller but more effective military forces and advocated preparation for "discriminating nuclear responses" (notably by France and Britain) as well as a retaliatory and offensive conventional capability by NATO in keeping with the FOFA plan. This new version of flexible response did not alleviate the malaise within the alliance, which was already rent by an American-West German dispute over modernization of NATO's tactical nuclear arsenal; President Mitterrand remarked that if Soviet troops reached Bonn, it would be too late to use France's nuclear weapons. [41]

The Road to CFE. At its March 1988 meeting, the North Atlantic Council declared that since the Soviet Union had not relaxed its military effort and had deployed far greater military forces than were required for its defense, credible deterrence required an "appropriate mix of adequate and effective nuclear and conventional forces" and the continued presence of such American forces in Europe. The declaration sought "security and stability at lower levels of armaments" and "gradually to overcome the unnatural division of the European continent, which affects most directly the German people" and explicitly linked arms control to human rights.[42] In November, NATO released a report on the Warsaw Pact's conventional military advantage, which it appraised at 51,500 main battle tanks compared to NATO's 16,400, 8,250 combat aircraft vs. 4,000, and more than 3 million troops vs. NATO's 2.2 million.[43]

In the event, NATO's prudent and grudging response allowed its adversaries to monopolize the diplomatic limelight by escalating proposals and unilateral concessions. In May 1987, Poland's General Jaruzelski advanced a plan for gradual withdrawal of nuclear and conventional weapons from Denmark and Hungary as well as the MBFR zone. The following February, Czechoslovakia's Milos Jakes proposed a "zone of confidence" between the two alliances; in June 1988, the Poles reiterated the Jaruzelski Plan; and in July, a joint working group of the West German SPD and the East German SED advanced a similar proposal. Meanwhile, Soviet and American inspectors were busily supervising the removal and destruction of missiles (867 American and 1,836 Soviet devices, including those in East Germany and Czechoslovakia) and launchers covered by the INF agreement.

At the United Nations, on December 7, 1988, Gorbachev once again stole a march on NATO by announcing that the Soviet Union would over two years reduce its armed forces by 500,000 soldiers. Nearly half of this cut as well as elimination of 10,000 tanks, 8,500 guns, and 800 combat aircraft was to come in the area west of the Urals, involving specifically six armored divisions (50,000 soldiers and 5,000 tanks) in Czechoslovakia, East Germany, and Hungary. Although the proposed measures made only a small dent in Soviet military capability, they caused the resignation of the Soviet chief of staff, Marshal Sergei Akhromeyev, who had opposed unilateral cuts. It all added up to less than 10 percent of the formidable Soviet presence in the area.[44]

All of the lesser Warsaw Pact members except Romania promptly followed suit, each announcing cuts of around ten thousand in troop strength and in defense budgets ranging from 4 percent in Poland to 17 percent in Hungary. From NATO's defensive perspective, the roughly 6 percent reduction of the Warsaw Pact's combined strength in Eastern Europe (1,677,100 Soviet and indigenous troops) did not go far toward eliminating the imbalance, particularly regarding armor. The International Institute for Strategic Studies nevertheless concluded that the Soviet unilateral withdrawals, when completed, would rule out the possibility of a surprise attack.[45]

Trimming defense budgets made sense for the faltering Soviet and East European economies, as did the recasting of their military establishments in a leaner and modernized mold. But even the modest beginnings of Soviet withdrawal were welcomed by the more reformist regimes and by populations that realistically regarded the Soviets as occupiers and regional policemen rather than as defenders. At least in Hungary, the leadership openly anticipated the eventual complete withdrawal of Soviet troops. "The presence of Soviet troops," said a party official in September 1988, "is not a fundamental condition of our external and internal security." And party chairman Reszo Nyers reported after a visit with Gorbachev that "we came to an agreement in principle that the troops reductions must be continued, and that, depending on the international situation, this process might be carried out to the very end."[46]

The CSCE review conference in Vienna came to an end on January 19, 1989. Foreign Minister Shevardnadze, belaboring the metaphor, commented that it had "shaken up the Iron Curtain, weakened its rusty supports, made new breaches in it and hastened its corrosion."[47] A few days later the MBFR talks received their epitaph, making way for the opening on March 9 of the new, twenty-three-nation "negotiations on conventional armed forces in Europe," or CFE, NATO having surrendered its "stability" leitmotif. NATO's opening position focused on main battle tanks, armored personnel carriers, and artillery, calling for equal ceilings that would require cuts of over 50 percent by the Warsaw Pact and 10 percent by the West as well as national and geographical sublimits. The Soviet counterproposal envisaged larger cuts and included missiles, combat aircraft, and personnel. At Strasbourg in July, Gorbachev was at his cajoling best in calling for reductions in all categories of weapons without damage to the West's principle of minimum deterrence.[48]

These preliminary skirmishes exacerbated a split within NATO over the scope of CFE, for Bonn openly favored the inclusion of tactical nuclear weapons to forestall the politically unpopular replacement of the obsolescent Lance missile. The United States as well as France and Britain feared that a mutual ban on short-range, land-based missiles (of which the Soviet Union possessed far more than NATO) would make the defense of Europe largely dependent on the credibility of the American strategic nuclear deterrent as long as there remained a conventional imbalance. Defense Secretary Cheney denounced the option as a "dangerous trap," and another U.S. official disparaged Bonn's eagerness as "grandstanding by a panic-stricken government."[49] The chairman of the House Armed Services Committee, Les Aspin, warned that Washington might withdraw its troops if Bonn refused to allow such weapons to be based in West Germany, but he also urged NATO to be more flexible in its options on conventional force cuts.[50] The pressure was on the Bush administration to resolve the NATO dispute and regain the initiative in the realm of military detente.

On May 29, 1989, at the NATO summit in Brussels, President Bush expanded the alliance's negotiating position to include land-based combat aircraft and helicopters (a Warsaw Pact demand) and a 20 percent reduction in U.S. manpower in Europe (by 30,000) to 275,000, a level to be matched by a Soviet cut of some 325,000 troops in Eastern Europe, with the proviso that the withdrawn forces were to be demobilized. He added an "open skies" proposal (recalling President Eisenhower's 1955 initiative) for unrestricted surveillance and verification of agreed arms control measures, as well as an accelerated schedule for the CFE talks allowing the reductions to be implemented by 1992 or 1993. Bonn's concerns were appeased by an agreement to initiate talks on partial reduction of short-range missiles (but not another zero, stressed Bush) as soon as the CFE talks had produced agreement on conventional forces. The question of a successor to the 88 aging Lance launchers in West Germany was sidestepped, and there was no question of totally denuclearizing NATO. On balance, the Bush administration chose wisely and prudently in giving priority to conventional reductions at the expense of START and other nuclear negotiations.

There remained numerous technical hurdles in the path of CFE, involving precise definitions of the affected arms and aircraft, regional ceilings, and the "prepositioning" of arms for reinforcement. But both the United States and the Soviet Union were displaying unprecedented negotiating flexibility and optimism that the balance of terror in Europe could be dramatically reduced without endangering their security interests.

The Warsaw Pact Implodes. As the Soviet-cultivated image of a threatening NATO faded, so did the cohesion of the Warsaw Pact. It was further undermined by the divergence in attitudes toward political and economic reform, which only widened with the advent of *perestroika*. At the July 1989 summit of the Warsaw Pact in Bucharest, Gorbachev declared that "there is a new spirit within the Warsaw Treaty, with moves toward independent solutions of national problems," and back in Moscow he told a television audience that "the Pact probably will transform itself from a military-political [alliance] to a political-military one." The Pact's appeal for the simultaneous disbandment of the two alliances, beginning with their military organizations, had been frequently iterated in the past, but now the manifestations of "socialist pluralism" enhanced its credibility.[51]

Momentarily, a faultline lay between the rapid moves toward political reform of Poland and Hungary and the immobilism of the other East European regimes. When a Solidarity-led coalition government was in the making in Poland, for example, Ceausescu reportedly proposed that the Warsaw Pact intervene to defend socialism in Poland.[52] In contrast, the Budapest parliament in September condemned Hungary's part in the 1968 invasion of Czechoslovakia. Alliance solidarity was further strained by Hungarian allegations that Romania posed a military threat (because of the dispute over the mistreatment of the Hungarian minority) and by the crisis involving East German refugees in Hungary. Yet by the end of 1989, all of the participants in the suppression of the Prague Spring, including the Soviet Union, had expressed their regrets, and all the interim governments of Eastern Europe professed a commonality of purpose that had little to do with the original functions of the Warsaw Pact.

As far back as the 1960s Romania had developed a more autonomous defense policy than other Pact members, and some twenty years later national military doctrines began to reemerge in the other East European countries as they sought to recover their freedom of action. Reformers continued to pay lip service to the sanctity of the Warsaw Treaty while displaying clearly independent tendencies. The new Polish foreign minister, Krzysztof Skubiszewski, declared that while abiding by existing "international obligations" he would pursue a "practical" foreign policy, and a government spokesman opined that "we want a Europe of states that are sovereign in international politics and independent in internal policy."[53]

Driven by economic necessity and encouraged by Moscow's permissiveness, Hungary's caretaker government announced a series of unilateral military cutbacks, the establishment of a demilitarized "zone of security, confidence-building and cooperation" along its borders with Austria and Yugoslavia, and the suspension of party control over the armed forces. Hungary, said General Laszlo Borsits at the CFE talks, "no longer gives priority to military power."[54]

There were other signs of progress in military detente. In November 1989, Hungary and Belgium agreed on a program of closer contacts between their military establishments. A proposal for such bilateral, confidence-building military relations was advanced at the CFE talks by France and Hungary in December, the first joint initiative by members of the two alliances. In January 1990, NATO and Warsaw Pact chiefs of staff met in Vienna for a three-week "military doctrine seminar," while Canada and Hungary conducted a trial exercise in aerial inspection in anticipation of the conference in Ottawa on President Bush's open skies initiative to supplement CFE verification measures.

At the end of 1989 Budapest took the even bolder step of requesting withdrawal of the remaining 50,000 Soviet troops in Hungary. Reporting on the initial talks with his Soviet counterpart, Prime Minister Miklos Nemeth said, "We agreed that the stationing of Soviet troops is the result of fully outdated political and military concepts and there is no political or military reason to have them here."[55] Similar negotiations were initiated by the new Czechoslovakian government for the withdrawal of the 75,000–strong Soviet contingent. Poland's Walesa had also called for the removal of the more than 50,000 Soviet troops in his country.

In early 1990, Moscow reached formal agreement with Prague and Budapest to remove its troops by June 1991, and the evacuation promptly began. The Soviet Union also started unilaterally to pull some units out of Poland, and it closed down the Pact's operational headquarters at Legnica. Out of concern with the German problem, the Mazowiecki government initially resisted domestic pressures to follow Czechoslovakia's and Hungary's lead. In September, after the agreements on German unification and arms control, it was the Polish Senate's turn to urge full Soviet evacuation and Poland's withdrawal from the military structure of the Warsaw Pact.

The emergence of non-Communist governments in Eastern Europe also affected the institutional structure and political cohesion of the Warsaw Pact. The Pact's nonmilitary controlling body, the Political Consultative Committee, had been composed of the Communist parties general secretaries. With those parties' monopoly power eliminated, it would be composed of heads of state or heads of government.[56] In addition, Moscow's military control, enshrined in the 1980 secret "statute," was circumscribed by Polish, Hungarian, and Czechoslovakian initiatives to make the operational use of national military forces subject to parliamentary approval.

The democratization of the Warsaw Pact imposed a fundamental review of the two alliances' military doctrines. In the forecast of an American analyst, "Soviet military planners will write their Eastern allies out of their operational plans, while Western planners will no longer automatically count them on the opposite side of the strategic balance."[57] Defense Secretary Cheney noted that "you may be able to make different assumptions about the extent to which those governments might join with the Soviet Government" in a hypothetical conflict.[58]

For Eastern Europe, escape from Marxism-Leninism bore an additional and crucial dimension: the recovery of national sovereignty. In legal theory sovereignty is absolute; in international politics, it is subject to a multitude of constraints. But democratic self-determination led East Europeans into a realm of speculation that only a few years ago would have been dismissed as dangerous fantasy. A long-term scenario outlined by the Hungarian socialist reformer and academic Attila Agh reflected the aspirations of many, perhaps most, East Europeans. The first, "Danish" step envisaged by Agh would be a qualification to Hungary's Warsaw Pact membership permanently excluding the stationing of nuclear weapons on national territory. In the second, "Greek" or "Romanian" stage, Hungary would reduce its participation in Warsaw Pact exercises while the Soviet Union repatriated its military contingent. The third,

"French" stage would involve the removal of remaining Soviet troops and Hungary's withdrawal from at least the military dimension of the Warsaw Pact. In the fourth, "Finnish" step, Hungary would conclude a mutual security agreement with the Soviet Union that allowed the former to pursue a foreign policy of "dynamic stability." The fifth, "Austrian" step would be the proclamation and international recognition of Hungary's neutrality. Hungary could then explore the feasibility of adhering to the European Community.[59]

In fact, the Democratic Forum-led coalition government formed in Budapest after the March/April 1990 elections adopted these ojectives and shortened the timetable. The new foreign minister, Geza Jeszenszky, had earlier proclaimed that Hungary would remain a member of the Warsaw Pact "as long as necessary, but not one day longer."[60] At the Warsaw Pact summit held in Moscow in June, the Hungarians indicated they would no longer participate in joint maneuvers and gave notice of their intention to withdraw by 1991.

That summit reflected the sweeping change in Eastern Europe; of the leaders who had attended the previous meeting eleven months earlier, only Gorbachev remained. The final communique declared that the concept of "the enemy," and therefore the military alliance itself, had become obsolete. The Pact would dismantle its joint command and other military structures and seek a new mission as a political organization dedicated to cooperation with the rest of Europe.[61] Responding to a Soviet suggestion for a nonagression treaty between the two alliances, a concurrent NATO meeting welcomed the possibility of cooperation in the redefinition of European security.

CFE and the "Peace Dividend." The East European revolution raised the pressure, in Congress and in such allied capitals as Bonn, for more radical troop reductions and cuts in defense spending. Europe absorbed around half of the U.S. $300 billion defense budget, and the lure of a "peace dividend" was proving irresistible. Lower troop-level targets could also facilitate Soviet accession to East European requests for evacuation and indirectly strengthen Gorbachev's hand at a time when *perestroika* was beset with economic troubles and ethnic strife.

By early 1990, National Security Adviser Brent Scowcroft was hinting that "lower numbers in consultation with the allies could certainly be contemplated."[62] The Soviet Union was beginning to withdraw its troops from Czechoslovakia, Hungary, and even Poland, the East Europeans were trimming defense budgets, and as the momentum of German unification accelerated, defections shrunk the GDR People's Army to half of its former strength. The Warsaw Pact's military capability was eroding rapidly. As a senior administration official observed before President Bush's State of the Union address, "It appeared that, in the area of arms control, specifically conventional arms control in Europe, events were running ahead of the [CFE] negotiations." [63] In that address, the president proposed that the CFE talks now aim at a ceiling of 195,000 Soviet and American troops in Central Europe (instead of 275,000 in non-Soviet Europe). The administration was adamant that the resulting level of 225,000 U.S. forces in Europe (including 30,000 American troops outside the central zone) would remain a nonnegotiable minimum. After securing Washington's pledge that the contingent outside Central Europe would not be increased, Moscow endorsed the Bush proposal. Throughout the spring of 1990 the CFE talks remained bogged down over the definition of tanks and armored vehicles and cuts in combat aircraft. Within the Warsaw Pact, the Soviet Union and its now independent-minded allies haggled over their respective shares of the armor allowed by an eventual CFE agreement. Hungary threatened to block any CFE agreement that failed to provide inspection rights between members of the same group. Meanwhile, the example set by the Soviet Union's unilateral withdrawals encouraged NATO's members to reap the popular peace dividend by planning cuts in military budgets and in their military commitment to NATO.

Safeguarding the alliance while reassuring Moscow and satisfying domestic budget cutters was no easy task. The NATO summit at London in July declared that the alliance "must reach out to the countries of the East which were our adversaries in the Cold War and extend to them the hand of friendship." [64] It offered to sign a joint declaration of non-aggression and invited the Warsaw Pact members to establish diplomatic liaison with NATO headquarters in Brussels. At the same time, the summit recast NATO's conventional and nuclear strategy. Abandoning "forward defense," it envisaged a smaller NATO force deployed in light screening units along the border between the about-to-be-reunited Germanys and heavier, multinational groups in the rear. The discord over nuclear arms was once again papered over with a "last resort" formula that preserved the principle of flexible response, and with the offer to negotiate the mutual removal of short-range nuclear weapons with the Soviet Union once CFE talks had run their course. At that time, said NATO, manpower ceilings for the nonsuperpower members of the CFE could also be negotiated.

After the Gorbachev-Kohl deal on unification, which was probably facilitated by NATO's conciliatory tack, the peace dividend momentum gathered speed. Britain and France declared that they would halve their forces in Germany. In September, the Pentagon announced plans for major cuts in the number of U.S. bases in Germany and elsewhere and the withdrawal of 40,000 troops from Western Europe over the next twelve months. The earlier CFE targets on conventional troop levels were fading in significance as the separate agreements on German unification and between Moscow and its allies raised the prospect of a total evacuation of Soviet forces by 1994.

A CFE accord took shape in early October with the agreement to limit each alliance's aircraft, tanks (20,000), armored personnel carriers (30,000), and artillery (20,000), and to institute a comprehensive verification system. The Soviet Union had to bear the lion's share of removing or scrapping such weaponry. This accord, signed by the two alliances in Paris on the occasion of the CSCE summit, represented a giant step toward a Europe free from the threat of major war.

For the West, the fear of a Soviet surprise attack was effectively dispelled, making the peace dividend safely attainable. For the East Europeans, the military disengagement mandated by the CFE promised greater diplomatic elbowroom in their quest for a secure niche in the common European house. Stalin's axiom that the victors would impose their social systems as far as their armies reached was once again confirmed, in reverse, as Soviet force and ideology receded from the region. But Eastern Europe is bound to remain a key to calculations of Soviet— or Russian—security. Therefore, paradoxically, consolidation of political autonomy in individual East European countries may be contingent on voluntary constraints on that autonomy. It may be in the West's interest to dissuade democratic forces from exploiting their freedom to sever all security links with the Soviet Union. The nationalistic euphoria of the moment will not easily heed such prudential advice.

Both the Soviet Union and the West evidently hope that the disintegration of alliances will work to their favor. Gorbachev's professed Europeanism and his radical disarmament proposals are at least partly calculated to loosen the bonds of the Atlantic alliance and induce neutralism, particularly among Germans. These goals can serve not only Soviet security but also renewed Russian ambitions toward predominance in Europe. NATO, for its part, anticipates that the powerful forces of nationalism and liberalism in Eastern Europe, and the immense problems of *perestroika* at home, will undermine the Soviet Union's offensive capability.

Meanwhile, the outline of a stable structure for European security grew more elusive as the prospect of German unification began to acquire substance in early 1990. Gorbachev condoned the rapid movement toward economic and social union but remained adamant that the new Germany could not be a member of NATO. Germany became the key problem for both alliances in the erection of a new "architecture" for Europe.

German Centrality. The West's preoccupation with the Soviet-Communist menace after World War II overshadowed the fact that Europe's decline and division resulted to a great extent from the historical ambitions of the Germans. For centuries the latter exerted a modernizing influence in Eastern Europe. Diligent German farmers settled throughout the region. German and Austrian business and finance spearheaded economic development. The urban culture of such great cities as Prague and Budapest acquired a pronounced Germanic flavor. But as the Habsburgs' grip weakened, the Bismarckian impulse of *Drang nach Osten* ("drive toward the East") turned a comparatively benign influence into a quest for domination. The first Russo-German war begat not only the apotheosis of national self-determination in Eastern Europe but also the triumph of Lenin's Bolsheviks. Thus, German imperialism served inadvertently as the midwife for an even greater threat to liberal democracy, and the lands between remained the most vulnerable to both threats.

The Nazi poison seeped into a region that Hitler was determined to dominate, and the second Russo-German war brought devastation and the expansion of Soviet power and ideology into the heart of Europe. The East Europeans lost more than their autonomy and material assets. Among the human costs were the extermination of much of their Jewish population and the expulsion of millions of ethnic Germans, most of whom had fatefully transferred their fealty to the thousand-year Reich. Defeated Germany lost not only Hitler's territorial acquisitions but also vast tracts of land that were assigned to Poland and the Soviet Union. In seeking to erase all vestiges of nazism and to cripple Germany's economic and military potential, the victors seemed intent on a peace even more punitive than that imposed at Versailles.

Germany was the country in the middle of the emerging East-West confrontation, and by late 1946 Washington's concern at Soviet hostility and obduracy was turning the Western occupied zones into the frontline of defense against communism. Stalin wanted to dominate all of Germany, and by controlling the heartland to extend unchallengeable influence over the entire continent. Any punitive intent on the part of the Western Allies was soon overshadowed by new priorities—economic reconstruction of a Western Europe that included the Federal Republic and the latter's military integration into a defensive perimeter. As an American historian speculated at the time, "The ghost of Hitler must have laughed ghoulishly to see the West building up Germany against Communist Russia." [65] West Germany lay at the vital center of the policy of containment. Its consolidation could not be jeopardized by serious consideration of Soviet schemes for neutralization, demilitarization, and unification even if such a formula appealed to at least a minority of Germans.

The United States found a staunch ally in Konrad Adenauer, who came to symbolize his country's conversion to democracy and firmly anchored Germany in the West. Franco-German reconciliation, European integration, and the American guarantee of West Germany's security became the vital components of his foreign policy. Adenauer simply refused to concede any legitimacy to division and the Soviet occupation zone. The Federal Republic, as its Basic Law stated, was the lawful representative of the entire German nation, and the sole acceptable alternative to the status quo was absorption of the eastern zone through self-determination into a liberal democratic Germany. Until then, the Hallstein Doctrine would preclude diplomatic relations with third parties who chose to recognize the German Democratic Republic.

The Western allies became committed to this precondition for a peace treaty, ostensibly on the grounds that only firm advocacy of maximalist goals could eventually bring the Soviet Union to compromise. Realistically, neither Adenauer nor his allies anticipated such a change of heart. But inflexibility on the principle of unification was Bonn's price for enlisting in the defense of the West. In October 1954, the lasting bargain was struck. The occupation regime was superseded by a quasi-sovereign Federal Republic that would make a substantial contribution to NATO's military strength. The three Western powers, in turn, committed themselves to peaceful unification through democratic self-determination, acknowledged that Bonn was the sole international representative of the whole German nation (agreeing thereby not to recognize the GDR), and affirmed that Germany's inner and outer boundaries were provisional until a final peace settlement.[66]

This pact suited the immediate security interests of all parties. NATO, in Lord Ismay's witticism, served to keep the Russians out, the Americans in, and the Germans down. Washington had no qualms about applying the principle of national self-determination to all Germans, and if the prospect of a united Germany aroused little enthusiasm in Paris and London, it was mercifully remote and hypothetical. By making detente hostage to German interests and improbable Soviet accommodation of those interests, the agreement in effect allowed Bonn to set the limits to Western approaches toward not only the GDR but the rest of Eastern Europe as well. Bonn's rigid posture only deepened the cold war as Khrushchev sought to legitimate the GDR with ultimatums over Berlin. But as long as it regarded the Soviet bloc as a monolithic threat, the West could afford this self-imposed constraint on its freedom of action.

Ostpolitik. The divergence between Bonn's national outlook and the other allies' broader perspective on policies toward the East became more apparent in the 1960s. The "policy of movement" adopted by West Germany in the early years of the decade aimed to expand commercial contacts with the East without surrender of the Hallstein Doctrine. It brought modest economic results but no political gains, and both the American and the Gaullist approaches to detente were hampered by Bonn's political inflexibility. The new *Ostpolitik* adumbrated by the Brandt-Kiesinger grand coalition and pursued with vigor by Chancellor Brandt after 1969 overturned existing doctrine. Bonn in a spate of treaties normalized relations with the East, accepting the territorial status quo and the existence of two German states "in one nation." Unification was no longer the precondition but the ultimate goal of detente, to be patiently pursued by a strategy of *Wandel durch Annaherung,* change through rapprochement. The West German foot thus shifted from the brake to the accelerator of detente, creating a new set of problems for the Atlantic alliance.[67]

For the United States, West Germany's strength and location at NATO's front line made it the key European ally, notwithstanding the sentimental special relationship with Britain. The centrality of the Federal Republic in Washington's European policies was succinctly formulated by Dean Acheson: "A major—often the major—consideration should be their effect on the German people and the German government."[68] In the zero-sum game of the cold war, Bonn's Hallstein Doctrine and its quiet nurturing of economic relations with the GDR could be condoned as harmless manifestations of national sentiment. In the more complex circumstances of detente, the divergence in Western interests and tactics became harder to ignore.

That divergence manifested itself both in the broad context of East-West relations and in the specific sphere of policy toward Eastern Europe. By the late 1970s Bonn had become the most persistent promoter of political and military detente. At the same time, both *Ostpolitik* and *Deutschlandpolitik* (policy toward the GDR) departed from the logic and practice of the policy of differentiation pursued by the United States. The functionalist premise of *Ostpolitik* was that the expansion of commercial relations would bring immediate and mutual economic benefits and over time induce political liberalization in the East. It would rebuild Germany's markets in the region, appease historical animosities, loosen the East Europeans' dependence on the Soviet Union, and weave a web of interdependence that served West Germany's economic as well as security interests. Since the Soviet Union and the GDR in particular were suspicious of Western tactics to divide the Warsaw Pact, attempts at differentiation were considered by Bonn to be counterproductive, and *Ostpolitik* therefore stood for a strategy of "synchronization"—the pursuit of normal relations unencumbered by political conditions and implicitly attuned to Soviet sensibilities.[69]

The comparative political neutrality of *Ostpolitik* could be regarded as an expedient rationalization for the unrestricted economic penetration of Eastern Europe. It also may have reflected an understandable inhibition on the part of Bonn to assume the role of human rights crusader. To their credit, the West Germans gave humanitarian aid generously, and their religious organizations actively supported the impoverished churches in the East. But Bonn scrupulously avoided linking economic favors to broader human rights considerations and political reform. In the first half of the 1980s, for instance, its turnover with neo-Stalinist Czechoslovakia, reformist Hungary, and martial-law Poland all hovered in the narrow band of $1.6–2 billion. Only when *perestroika* seemed to sanction reform and pluralism did Bonn venture to apply some differentiation, notably with some major credits for Hungary in 1988–89.

To be sure, America's other European allies were equally reluctant to adopt a policy of economic differentiation even if some of them, notably France, gave more public attention to human rights issues than did the Germans. But West Germany had by far the greatest potential economic leverage, accounting for close to 40 percent of the industrialized world's trade with Eastern Europe (the American share being 4 percent, Italy's 9 percent, and France's 7 percent).[70] Effective leverage depends on willingness to deny as well as extend economic favors, and as West Germany increased its stake in East-West trade, it could argue that it would bear the brunt of the cost of any Western sanctions. Moreover, tariffs and barriers to agricultural imports are set collectively in the European Community, limiting the scope of individual countries for political manipulation of their external commerce. Nevertheless West Germany, like the others, retained numerous facilities for differentiation, including loans, credit insurance, regulation of joint ventures and barter deals, and other nontariff barriers.

America's pursuit of economic differentiation was thus undermined principally by the West Germans' alternative approach to the East. They (along with the other Europeans) participated only grudgingly in Cocom and resisted American attempts to impose economic sanctions, notably in the Afghanistani and Polish crises. The political effectiveness of differentiation and sanctions was open to question, but in any event Bonn's cooperation was essential to a meaningful Western strategy, and *Ostpolitik* diluted such a strategy. The architects of *Ostpolitik* were not comfortable with either the human rights crusade launched by Jimmy Carter or Ronald Reagan's obsession with the "evil empire." Sensitive to Soviet displeasure, Chancellors Brandt and Schmidt both urged Washington to wind down the Radio Free Europe/Radio Liberty operation in Munich. The West, warned Foreign Minister Genscher at a conference at Potsdam in June 1988, "should not entertain any thoughts of employing its undoubted economic and technological strength as a lever vis-a-vis our eastern neighbors."[71] If these policy divergences caused some irritation in Washington, they were accommodated with a remarkable absence of public discord. Washington was not about to jeopardize NATO solidarity on basic security issues and fuel neutralist sentiments in West Germany by openly criticizing Bonn's *Ostpolitik*.

Inter-German Relations. The Federal Republic's *Deutschlandpolitik* was an equally anomalous element in the Western approach to Eastern Europe. From the beginning, the allies treated East Germany (apart from Berlin) as Bonn's exclusive preserve. They followed West Germany's lead in diplomatic ostracism of the GDR, then in its recognition. The United States, even after it established relations with the GDR in 1974, maintained a low profile and subordinated its policies to Bonn's wishes. This tacit acceptance of Bonn's primacy rested on the Federal Republic's claim to represent all Germans and dedication to eventual unification.

In the cold war, the strictures of the Hallstein Doctrine only reinforced a consensual Western policy to isolate the Soviet bloc. But from its inception the Federal Republic strove to preserve economic links with the eastern zone, ostensibly for humanitarian reasons as well as to underscore the principle of national unity and to give the East Germans a marginal alternative to total economic dependence on the Soviet bloc. As early as October 1949 the two Germanys agreed to special commercial relations, which in the Federal Republic were administered by an "Inter-Zonal Trade Trustee," officially an organ of West German industrial and trading organizations. No duties were levied in the exchange of goods, and East German purchases were free of value-added tax. The GDR's special status was accommodated in a protocol to the Rome Treaty establishing the European Economic Community, giving it indirect access to that market. Nor did the normalization of state relations between the Federal Republic and the GDR in 1972 alter the privileged nature of their mutual trade.

By the mid-1950s inter-German turnover accounted for 11 percent of the GDR's foreign trade. It grew by 75 percent between 1955 and 1960, and quadrupled in the 1970s, before falling to around 6 percent of the GDR's total foreign trade (and to only 1.5 percent of West Germany's) in the 1980s. But the Federal Republic remained its third-largest trading partner (after the Soviet Union and Czechoslovakia) and its principal source of Western technology. That technology, in turn, strengthened the GDR's export capability, not least in the direction of the Soviet Union.

The Rome protocol did not grant the GDR duty-free access to the rest of the Community, but in practice some East German goods did filter into other EC countries. Inter-German trade was cleared in special units of account that inflated the value of the East German mark. The credits that financed the GDR's bilateral deficit in goods and services, known as the "swing," originally came from private West German institutions. In 1967, five-year federal export credits were extended, and by the late 1980s the annual (interest-free) swing credit stood at DM 850 million. When in the early 1980s the East European debt crisis scared off Western lenders, West German banks provided some DM 2 billion to bolster the GDR's creditworthiness.

In addition to these trade and credit facilities, the GDR received from West Germany a plethora of other financial contributions estimated to amount to more than DM 2.5 billion a year.[72] In the aggregate, these benefits and transfers added roughly 4 percent to the national product of the German Democratic Republic. Bonn's disarming rationale for this economic bounty was that it helped to stabilize inter-German relations, ease the lot of East Germans, and secure humanitarian concessions from the GDR. The latter consistently rejected any notion of linkage between politics and economics, and indeed the pattern of development in inter-German trade showed little correlation with changes in political relations. In the early 1980s, West German loans apparently induced the GDR to ease some emigration and travel restrictions, although the Kremlin set a limit to inter-German detente by vetoing Honecker's proposed visit to Chancellor Kohl in September 1984. But after taking the historic step of recognizing the GDR, Bonn did not adopt Washington's criteria for differentiation and never made its massive economic subsidy conditional on political or economic liberalization.

Deutschlandpolitik thus represented a perverse form of differentiation favoring one of the most orthodox and repressive regimes in Eastern Europe. To the extent that it sought stability, it stabilized authoritarian rule and socialist economics. To the extent that it facilitated human contacts, family reunification, and emigration, the policy responded to nationalistic sentiments and served unexceptionable humanitarian ends, but it also relieved domestic pressure on the Honecker regime. The special inner-German relationship was cultivated in official visits to the

GDR by Brandt in 1970 and Schmidt in 1981, in Honecker's delayed return visit in September 1987, and in Kohl's casual private visit to Dresden in May 1988. The historic Honecker trip to Bonn led Jeane Kirkpatrick to observe (rather prematurely) that "the spectre of a reunited Germany is again haunting Europe."[73] What it did reflect was the somewhat fanciful West German notion that a separate and deeper detente could be nurtured with the Honecker regime.

Yet that regime remained steadfast in its policy of *Abgrenzung,* or political demarcation, as resistant as the Czech and the Romanian regimes to the spread of *perestroika.* Before the Gorbachev era opened, it had also served as Moscow's principal East European surrogate in the third world, providing military assistance and secret police training in places such as Angola and Ethiopia. Its intelligence services were the KGB's most assiduous collaborators. Clearly, no rational Western policy would have identified the GDR as a candidate for preferential treatment. Indeed, in the months before the unexpected revolution in East Berlin, even Bonn was becoming disenchanted with the results of the twenty-year-old policy of "small steps" of *Wandel durch Annaherung,* which had intensified economic relations without inducing the Honecker regime to reform.

Having accepted the principle of primary West German responsibility for relations with the GDR, Washington had little choice but to condone the anomalous outcome. When in late 1986 Richard Perle, then an assistant secretary of defense, ventured the opinion that Bonn should spend less on subsidizing the GDR and more on NATO, he was roundly condemned by all shades of the West German political spectrum.[74] The notion that West Germany possessed distinctive national interests gained popularity as an America personified by Ronald Reagan and a European unification that seemed to stagnate in the early 1980s lost some of their appeal to Germans. If *Ostpolitik* and *Deutschlandpolitik* did not visibly promote political change in the East, they at least served mutual economic interests and put relations on a businesslike basis. This unprovocative and pragmatic approach, in Bonn's belief, would induce a stable environment in which political liberalization could materialize at the pace chosen by the Soviet Union and its client regimes.

German Nationalism and National Interest.   In Western perceptions, the Federal Republic's image as dutiful ally long overshadowed its most basic and enduring interest, the cause of the German nation and of German minorities marooned in the socialist world. Bonn concentrated its active concern about human rights on those Germans spread across the East. By paying a substantial per capita ransom, it bought the release of not only East German dissidents but tens of thousands of ethnic Germans from Ceausescu's Romania, earning that impoverished country over DM 1 billion in the 1980s. In its economic diplomacy with the Soviet Union it bargained for the emigration rights of ethnic Germans. And East German visitors to the Federal Republic were offered "welcome money" and travel concessions. All ethnic German emigrants automatically received citizenship and material assistance, including pensions, in the Federal Republic at a time when most other refugees from socialism encountered a closed door in Western countries (including West Germany) unless they could prove to have been victims of active political persecution. In 1989 alone, a record 720,909 Germans from all over Eastern Europe and the Soviet Union found haven in the Federal Republic, 343,854 of them from the GDR.[75]

When in 1989 concerted Western aid for reformist Poland came on the agenda, the main stumbling block in Polish-West German negotiations was the status of that country's German minority, which the Warsaw government chose not to recognize. The West Germans' humanitarian interest in the fate of their conationals was understandable, but the practical effect was yet another invidious divergence in Western policy towards Eastern Europe, with West German notions of differentiation working against those of its allies. If Bonn was tacitly allowed by its allies to adopt a comparatively voluntaristic policy toward Eastern Europe, in pursuing the goal of German unification it could not avoid contending with the vital interests of other large and small European powers and the United States. As long as the political division of Europe seemed immovable, the Western allies could afford to pay lip service to the principle of democratic unification without worrying about its strategic implications.

The "German question" remained dormant, apart from the occasional alarum when a Soviet probe met with undercurrents of German nationalism and neutralism. But West German democracy was firmly anchored in the West, and the Kremlin's periodic ploys stiffened NATO solidarity instead of seducing the Germans into another Rapallo. Pan-German sentiments did not disappear, but the prevailing view, notably among the political elite, was that unification would only come about in the distant future through European reconciliation and integration and not by some bilateral inter-German negotiation. It seemed inconceivable that the Soviet Union would give up its German garrison-state. And while the German treaties of the early 1970s and international recognition of the GDR made the absence of a formal peace treaty as well as the residual rights of the former occupying powers somewhat irrelevant (except with respect to Berlin), all parties assumed that unification depended on the consent of at least those powers.

Before the East European revolutions of 1989 precipitated a fundamental reevaluation of the political and strategic balance in Europe, then, West Germany's approaches to the East were already distinctive. Bonn nurtured such paradoxes as a constitutional commitment to unification with a formally recognized separate sovereign state, and preferential treatment of a neo-Stalinist regime. Yet another paradox lay in the success of the West Germans in exploiting their subordinate and divided postwar status to secure a privileged relationship with the GDR and the rest of the Eastern bloc.

Professions of "new thinking" in Soviet foreign policy coincided with, and reinforced, a modest renascence in nationalist feelings among West Germans, and by the end of the 1980s the German question had come to life again. Reflecting on the division of Germany, Valentin Falin, a key Gorbachev adviser, allowed that if the two Germanys "one day decide to become militarily neutral, that will create a new situation in Europe, and then we'll talk about it."[76] Reform and the relaxation of Soviet hegemony were, according to Deputy Secretary of State Lawrence Eagleburger, putting that question "back on the international agenda."[77] Those processes promised to weaken the Warsaw Pact's military capability, and it was clearly in the Soviet Union's interest to play on West German fears of becoming a nuclear battlefield and hopes for unification in order to divide NATO. There was ample opportunity as the dispute over Cruise and Pershing missiles produced massive peace demonstrations; the SPD displayed remarkable ideological relativism in its accord with the East German SED party on a nuclear-free zone; and Foreign Minister Genscher stood consistently at the forefront of detente advocacy. The new short-range missiles proposed by the Americans, Genscher reminded the Bundestag in April 1989, would be able to hit "the other part of our fatherland."[78] The Gorbymania sweeping West Germany was reflected in a 1988 poll, which found that only 24 percent of West Germans regarded the Soviet Union as a military threat.[79] Perceptions of national interest were leading West Germany toward an ever more distinctive foreign policy.

West Germany's leaders never suspended their public advocacy of eventual unification. "The German question," declared Chancellor Kohl at a party conference in June 1988, "is open and remains open. The CDU will never accept this injustice."[80] Kohl registered this desire on his visits to Moscow in July 1983 and October 1988 and in his meetings with Gorbachev in Bonn in June 1989. "This division is unnatural," he told Gorbachev in 1988; "The cohesion of the Germans is a historical and human reality which politics cannot ignore." The Soviet leader retorted that altering the status quo would be "an unpredictable and even dangerous business."[81] As a leading analyst of German affairs noted, "Moscow wants to leave the German question open in such a manner so as to maximize Soviet influence in both East and West Germany."[82] Germany was divided because Europe was divided, and as the military and ideological confrontation receded, the debate over the prospects of unity inevitably intensified.[83]

Bonn's dilemmas in attempting to reconcile its evolving *Ostpolitik* and *Deutschlandpolitik* paled in comparison with the problems of the East Berlin regime. The GDR began in the mid-1970s to style itself the "socialist German nation-state" and to conjure up the existence of a separate national identity with evocations of Bismarck and Frederick the Great. The futility of such mythmaking was tacitly conceded when in 1989 the SED's top ideologist, Otto Reinhold, explained why East Germany could not afford to follow the lead of the Soviet Union, Poland, and Hungary in reform: the only justification for a separate state was ideological, and the GDR "is conceivable only as an anti-fascist and socialist alternative to the Federal Republic." He asked rhetorically, "What kind of right to exist would a capitalist GDR have alongside a capitalist Federal Republic?"[84] This was, indeed, a compelling rationale for *Abgrenzung* and the uncompromising stance of the East Berlin regime.

Yet forty years of socialism did not persuade East Germans of its superiority. The GDR's economy was the most efficient in the Soviet sphere, but productivity and real income remained far below the levels in the Federal Republic, and West German television brought daily reminders of this chronic disparity. The flood of refugees from the GDR in the fall of 1989, through Hungary and the Federal Republic's embassies in Prague and Warsaw, only confirmed the tenuous nature of its legitimacy, compelling Honecker to restrict travel to those countries as well. He was adamant that "normal, good neighborly relations between the GDR and the FRG can be formed only when the euphoria about a 'united Germany' is put aside," and his successor, Egon Krenz, did not tarry in denouncing Bonn's refusal to recognize East German citizenship.[85] But the peaceful demonstrations in Leipzig, East Berlin, and Dresden following Gorbachev's October visit indicated that the virus of *perestroika* and liberalism was spreading even in the tightly controlled GDR.

Kohl's Drive for Unity.   Bonn wasted no time in exploiting the fissures in the Warsaw Pact to destabilize the Honecker regime. On August 25, as thousands of East Germans streamed into Hungary hoping to find a door to the West, Chancellor Kohl met Hungarian Premier Miklos Nemeth, who told him that in the absence of Soviet objections and despite Honecker's protests Hungary would open its frontier. There was at least an implicit linkage between this gesture and the granting of a $279 million West German loan to Hungary; on a visit to Budapest in November, Genscher expressed Bonn's gratitude and support for Hungary's quest for association with the European Community.[86]

When in November the Berlin Wall was first opened, Kohl interrupted his Warsaw visit to return to Bonn, where the Bundestag deputies greeted the news with an emotional chorus of "Deutschland uber Alles." "We are prepared," he declared, "to offer far-reaching help if genuine and thorough-going political and economic reforms take root."[87] Krenz, the interim East German party leader, continued to insist that unification was not on the agenda, while the reformist prime minister, Hans Modrow, raised the prospect of closer relations based on bilateral treaties. As East German demonstrators began to openly call for unification, Kohl on November 28 unveiled a plan for "confederal structures," including joint committees that after free elections in the East would develop common economic, environmental, and other policies, and for associate membership for East Germany in the European Community.

The West German Social Democrats endorsed the Kohl plan, although they laid stress on linking the processes of German and European unification and on explicit guarantees of the Polish border. In an address to their congress, the writer Gunter Grass voiced some reservations about the pursuit of pan-German unity:

Despite all our protestations, even well-intentioned ones, we Germans would once again be feared. For our neighbors would gaze at us with justifiable mistrust and from ever-increasing distance, which would very quickly give rise to a renewed sense of isolation and with it the dangerous self-pitying mentality that sees itself as "surrounded by enemies." A reunited Germany would be a colossus, bedeviled by complexes and blocking its own path and the path to European unity. On the other hand, a confederation of the two German states, and their declared renunciation of a unified state, would benefit European union, especially because, like the new German self-conception, it too will be a confederation.[88]

Such prudential advice was scarcely heard amidst the nationalistic euphoria over the crumbling Wall. Opinion polls showed that large majorities of Germans East and West yearned for unification.

The principle that Germans should be in charge of resolving the problem of unification lay behind Kohl's failure to discuss the confederation program with his allies or with the East, where Bonn's independent spirit caused much uneasiness. While allowing for the peaceful development of intra-German relations, Gorbachev was still insistent that "no harm come to the GDR. It is our strategic ally and a member of the Warsaw Treaty. It is necessary to proceed from the postwar realities— the existence of the two sovereign German states, members of the United Nations. Departure from this threatens . . . destabilization in Europe."[89] He pleaded for Mitterrand's support, reportedly warning that "the same day the reunification of Germany is announced, a general will be sitting in my armchair."[90]

The communique issuing from the European summit in Strasbourg on December 9, 1989 incorporated Kohl's call for "unity through free self-determination" with the proviso that this should occur "in full respect of the relevant agreements and treaties and of all the principles defined by the Helsinki Final Act." Eastern Europe's borders, declared Mitterrand, are unchangeable; altering one would be "contagious," and he had "never asked my partners to restore the French empire of 1805."[91] And the four powers' ambassadors held a rare meeting in Berlin—"to remind the Germans who's in charge," as a French official put it.[92]

German unification continued to enjoy solid official and public support in the United States. That goal found clear favor with proportionately more Americans than Europeans, and comparatively few Americans were worried by the prospect of a unified Germany becoming the dominant power in Europe. One poll indicated that 46 percent believed unification would benefit the United States, and 25 percent the Soviet Union.[93] The rapid pace of revolution in the East forced the Bush administration to react deftly. In early November, when Gorbachev wrote to Bush endorsing the changes in East Germany and urging prudence, Secretary of State Baker still opined that it was "premature to jump, to make the great leap, and it is a big leap, from the right to free travel on part of East Germans, to the question of reunification."[94] But the administration soon confirmed that the Federal Republic was its favored ally and jumped on the bandwagon of unification. The following month, President Bush outlined in Brussels his preferred conditions: free elections in both East and West Germany, respect for the Helsinki Final Act's stipulation that Europe's postwar boundaries can be changed only by peaceful negotiation, and Germany's continuing adhesion to NATO and the European Community. Consultation with Bonn's allies and Eastern neighbors, declared Secretary of State Baker in West Berlin a week later, was essential to this peaceful and gradual process.[95]

Amidst these qualifying declarations, the viability of East Germany was rapidly ebbing. In the new year, emigrants continued to flood into the Federal Republic at a rate of over two thousand a day. Social turmoil and a growing labor shortage were undermining the economy, prompting Kohl to plead with the East Germans to stay and work at home for a better future. Meanwhile, tangible signs of de facto intra-German integration multiplied, including a major grant from Bonn for environmental cleanup projects, and West German companies were champing at the bit to move into the new market with investments and joint ventures. And unification became a prominent slogan of East German demonstrators.

By the end of January East German party leader Gregor Gysi was conceding that "this process can no longer be stopped," and Gorbachev himself accommodated the inevitable when after conferring with the harassed Prime Minister Modrow he insisted that all the Helsinki participants had to be included in the discussion of German unification. The SPD's Egon Bahr exulted: "There are no longer any differences between our and the Soviet General Secretary's views. It is no longer a question of if, but when how and what form a unified German state might take."[96] Back in East Berlin, Modrow unveiled a plan for a "united fatherland": The two Germanys would first develop mechanisms for economic integration, then joint institutions in a militarily neutral confederation. The final stage would be the creation of a "unified German state in the form of a German federation through elections in both parts of the confederation, the convening of a single parliament which would decide on a single constitution and a single government, with its seat in Berlin." All this would be sealed by a peace treaty with the wartime allies.[97]

Modrow's plan evoked Stalin's proposals of the early 1950s, and Chancellor Kohl promptly rejected the provision for neutrality as well as Foreign Minister Shevardnadze's concurrent proposal that Europeans, Americans, and Canadians all vote or conduct "wide parliamentary discussions" on the issue of unification. But the domestic political appeal of unification soon led Kohl to force the pace, pointing to the impending economic collapse of East Germany and calling for talks on a currency union. Soon after the March elections, in which the triumph of the Christian Democrats owed much to Kohl's bribe of an equal exchange rate, the terms were settled for economic and monetary union effective July 2, 1990. The two German governments agreed on the quick route to unity via Article 23 of the Federal Republic's constitution (which allowed the individual East German states to accede to the Federal Republic) and on the desirability of early pan-German elections, reflecting Kohl's hope that his party would benefit from having been the architect of unification.

Two Plus Four Make One. The Western allies had tacitly given the Germans free rein to prepare for unity, the only proviso being that the new state should remain in NATO. Neither Washington nor Bonn wished to have unification negotiated in the CSCE and made hostage to the consensus of that comprehensive but unwieldy forum. Yet, as a senior administration official affirmed, "there was the realization that the pace of events was creating the reality that German unification was not just an idea whose time had come, but a reality that was upon us."[98] Bonn and the State Department therefore devised the "two-plus-four" formula for negotiating the terms of a unification that all regarded as inevitable. The two Germanys would develop the domestic terms of unification, leaving the four principal wartime allies to exercise their legal rights by addressing the broader security aspects. The other allies and CSCE participants, according to this scenario, would ratify the results at the Helsinki summit tentatively scheduled for late 1990.

At the open skies conference in Ottawa in February, Foreign Minister Shevardnadze gave the Soviet Union's assent to the proposed framework. But if unification was inevitable, so was the revival of apprehensions among Germany's neighbors. While the two-plus-four formula served Bonn's sense of urgency, it offended the excluded NATO allies, particularly Italy and Belgium. The four powers responded with the promise of formal consultations, and eventually of a special NATO meeting on the question. The Poles were furious; Prime Minister Mazowiecki protested that "our security matters cannot be settled by proxy for us." The State Department contented itself with observing that Poland did not have the same legal standing as the four powers, but thanks largely to French pressure on Bonn, Polish sensibilities were soothed by an invitation to Warsaw to participate in the discussions on Germany's eastern borders.[99]

At their Camp David meeting a few days later, Bush and Kohl dismissed the options of neutralism and of the French model and confirmed the necessity of continuing full German membership in NATO. The United States, declared the president, welcomed the movement toward unification and regarded Europe's borders, including the German-Polish frontier, as inviolable. Kohl stuck to his position that the latter principle would have to be ratified by a freely elected, all-German government. "U.S. military forces should remain stationed in a united Germany and elsewhere in Europe, as a continuing guarantor of stability," said Bush; "The enemy is unpredictability."[100]

It was sign of the times that the emphasis on America's military contribution to stability was widely interpreted as a reassurance to Germany's neighbors. German reunification, reflected former CIA director Richard Helms in an article in the *Washington Post*, "has become a kind of runaway freight train that nobody—East or West—seems able to contain. And that doesn't bode well for the future."[101]

The only apprehension that really counted was that of the Soviet Union, and Gorbachev remained adamant through his summit meeting with Bush in June that Germany could not remain a full member of NATO. While the Soviet people and most of their leaders had accepted with good grace the loss of the rest of Eastern Europe, the German issue struck a raw nerve, reviving historic anxieties as well as concern at the potential loss of influence in Central Europe. One opinion poll indicated that the majority of Soviets approved of unification but opposed German membership in NATO.[102] The Kremlin insisted that a CFE treaty limit Germany's armed forces and proposed variously that the country be nonaligned, neutralized, a member of *both* alliances, or, at the very least, suspend (as France had done) its military participation in the alliance; European security, argued the Soviets, should be guaranteed by a new regime built on the CSCE that would supersede both NATO and the Warsaw Pact.

The gap between East and West over Germany's status could not be easily bridged. Secretary of State Baker had endorsed Genscher's February suggestion that the eastern part of a united Germany be demilitarized, as well as a later compromise formula allowing Soviet forces to remain there temporarily. Bonn expressed readiness to pay the cost of Soviet forces in the former GDR and to fulfill East Germany's commercial contracts with the Soviet Union, and it dangled before Moscow the lure of substantial economic benefits. But the Western allies, including Kohl, were as adamant as Gorbachev on the issue of alliance membership. The impasse nevertheless revealed a malaise within both alliances. In the Warsaw Pact, Czechoslovakia, Hungary, and Poland broke ranks in openly endorsing German membership in NATO as the best guarantee of stability. And in the West, ambivalence about the emergence of a dominant Germany was mixed with uncertainty about the future role of NATO and the United States. Although Moscow seemed prepared to let social and economic union proceed while the military status remained unresolved, the Germans were impatient to secure full sovereignty.

The German question thus reimposed itself with dramatic suddenness on the international agenda. For much of their history the Germanic people had lived in several separate states, but a half century after the end of the Second World War no one openly disputed their right to self-determination and unification. Warned a senior official in Bonn six months before the fall of the Wall, "If anyone, after the end of the division of Europe, should insist that Germany must not be unified and that Germans, uniquely, should be denied the right to self-determination, then they would be threatening seriously Germany's anchorage in the West."[103] Sensitive to foreign criticism of Bonn's haste in seeking national unity and of the restrictive two-plus-four formula, Genscher assured a meeting of European Community foreign ministers in Dublin on February 20, 1990, that "nothing will happen behind the backs of the four powers and nothing will happen behind the backs of our European partners."[104]

The *New York Times* editorialized on November 19, 1989, that "neither Europeans, Russians, Americans, nor indeed German leaders themselves are ready or eager to see a Fourth Reich," and it subsequently adopted an apprehensive tone about the pace of unification, but most Americans remained sanguine about the prospect. The same could not be said for all of Germany's neighbors. The late French author Francois Mauriac's aphorism, "*J'aime tellement l'Allemagne que je prefere qu'il y en ait deux*" (I love Germany so much that I prefer two of them), was quoted frequently after the opening of the Berlin Wall. The West German embassy in Paris reported on the skepticism of the French "political class" as former foreign minister Jean Francois-Poncet publicly fretted about the "economic and political hegemony of a nation of 80 million inhabitants becoming the industrial colossus of Europe."[105] Early surveys indicated that the majority of Frenchmen favored unification while remaining worried about the economic weight of an enlarged Germany.[106] By autumn, with unification a reality, a poll showed that only 37 percent of the French were pleased.

The predominant concern in governing circles was that West Germany, in Jacques Delors's words, "would be tempted by a destiny other than the construction of Europe."[107] And one big Germany, fretted the *Economist,* "could out-argue and out-manoeuvre the mere Britains and Frances and Italys on any issue where its interests differed from theirs."[108] Willy Brandt used to observe disparagingly that "the German question is a French question." Mitterrand insisted that he was not afraid of reunification, but the strategic balance and political stability of the emerging Europe is bound to be tested by the reaffirmation of pan-German interests and the weight of a self-confident Germany.[109]

In parts of Eastern Europe, the prospect of unification revived old fears. Poles are the most sensitive; a plurality of those surveyed in January 1990 opposed unification, and a majority expressed fear about Germany seeking territorial expansion.[110] Arguing in favor of German membership in NATO, Foreign Minister Krzystof Kubiszewski observed at a Warsaw Pact meeting that neutrality could "foster tendencies that might lead Germany to be a great power on its own."[111] Bonn's prevarication regarding the Oder-Neisse frontier only fueled these apprehensions.

Polish treaties with the GDR in 1950 and the Federal Republic in 1970 confirmed that boundary, but West German leaders, seeking to appease right-wing irredentists and the domestic lobby of postwar refugees (some 13 million Germans were expelled from the Sudetenland and the territories transferred to Poland), occasionally invoked the lack of a peace treaty to qualify these commitments. Kohl on his visit to Warsaw and in his November 1989 program for unification skirted the issue, and he commented rather disingenuously (considering the sweeping claims of the Basic Law) that, while the 1970 treaty bound West Germany and Poland, as West German chancellor he was "not authorized to make declarations on behalf of [all] Germany."[112] He subsequently made border guarantees conditional on agreement by Warsaw to renounce war reparations claims and to grant recognition and rights to its German minority. The Polish government thereupon threatened to deliver a bill for the labor of the million Poles forced to work in Nazi Germany. The discord prompted the Kremlin as well as Bonn's allies, including President Bush, to affirm the permanence of the Oder-Neisse frontier. Fearing for the progress of unification, the two German parliaments in June formally recognized the frontier.

Concern in Germany's other vulnerable neighbor, Czechoslovakia, has been more muted. President Havel paid his first foreign visits to the two Germanys, declaring diplomatically that "as long as it remains peaceful and democratic, it can be as large as it wants." But his earlier suggestion that Czechoslovaks apologize for the postwar expulsion of the Germans drew the ire of many of his compatriots, and Prague's historic fears inspired its insistence that a united Germany remain subject to the constraints of NATO membership.[113] The Hungarians, for their part, basked in the goodwill generated in Bonn by their earlier action on refugees and enthusiastically endorsed unification.

Some East Europeans fear German irredentism, others Germany's growing economic and political influence, but their more immediate and pragmatic concern is that Bonn will concentrate its economic aid on East Germany at their expense. The fear of irredentism may be appeased by appropriate international guarantees and the progressive unification of a liberal democratic Europe; the sense of vulnerability to ostensibly benign forms of influence is likely to endure. Although the diminuation of Franco-German enmity sets a promising precedent, that reconciliation came about only when the French recovered their economic self-confidence and acquired, thanks to de Gaulle, the vision of a European mission. Germany's East European neighbors are too small and weak to shed their ambivalence about a future in the shadow of that powerful country.

In the face of such Eastern and Western apprehensions, Bonn took some pains to assure its neighbors and allies that it remained steadfast in its commitment to NATO and European unity and conscious of the interests of others in its pursuit of unification. "It would be anti-historical and implausible to assert that it is a matter for the Germans alone whether and how they freely determine their fate and whether they follow their path with or against their neighbors," said Kohl soothingly in accepting an honorary doctorate from the Catholic University of Lublin.[114] But the architects of a new Europe will have no easy time drawing up a blueprint that accommodates the reemerging national interests and historical animosities.

The stability of the process of reconstruction might have been aided, and the apprehensions of Germany's neighbors forestalled, had Bonn responded to the East German revolution by abrogating its constitutional commitment to unification, recognizing the sovereignty of the emerging democratic East German state and treating its citizens like all others to stop the hemorrhage of its population. The United States as well as the other allies could, in turn, have indicated that unification was not a primary objective but a residual option on the road to a united, secure, and democratic Europe. But the powerful nationalistic passions inspired by the fall of the Wall and the realization on both sides that without that shelter the East German economy might collapse drove the leaders of the two Germanys to present the world with a fait accompli. Fears about Gorbachev's future also impelled Kohl to "bring the hay into the barn before the storm."

Backed by West Germany's political and economic power, de facto unification left even Gorbachev with little option but to endorse the principle while fighting a rearguard action on the issue of alliances. And no one in the West was prepared to compromise even temporarily on the principle of self-determination. The need to accommodate the Germans caused Delors to advise the European Parliament that East Germany was a special case and could join the European Community by virtue of the Community's commitment to German unification. Among Western leaders, only Prime Minister Thatcher openly expressed reservations about automatically taking in "a state that had been either Communist or Nazi since the 1930s."[115] Thus, paradoxically, the Germans, who bear heavy responsibility for the East Europeans' absorption into a Soviet empire in the aftermath of Hitler's war, successfully imposed the primacy of their national interests in the reconstruction of Europe.

The historic deal that effectively ended the Second World War was forged by Kohl and Gorbachev at the latter's holiday retreat in Stavropol on July 16. United Germany could remain in NATO. Its armed forces would be reduced to 370,000 (the West German Bundeswehr alone had some 480,000) and could be deployed in the Eastern region (made out of bounds to other NATO forces) after the last Soviet troops had left in 1994. Until then, Germany would pay for maintenance of the Soviet garrison and contribute (in an amount later set at $8.8 billion) to the cost of resettling the troops in the Soviet Union. And as a further bribe, Kohl offered $3 billion in government-guaranteed credits to help Moscow repay its debt to Germany. Germany renounced atomic, chemical, and biological weapons, and a nonaggression pledge and bilateral treaty on economic cooperation were also part of what Foreign Minister Genscher termed the Final Settlement. The day after the Stavropol breakthrough (christened Stavrapallo by historically minded skeptics), a two-plus-four meeting in Paris satisfied Poland with Germany's promise to make all the necessary legal provisions for unqualified recognition of the Oder-Neisse frontier.

On September 12, the six foreign ministers ceremonially signed the two-plus-four treaty in Moscow, and on October 3, Germany's unification was consummated. In Berlin, which at East German insistence was to become the new capital, the original allied powers gave up their occupation rights; American, British, and French troops would remain as guests until the Soviets departed. "In the future, only peace will emanate from German soil," declared Kohl. "We will resolutely continue to strive for European unification with the same determination with which we worked toward German unity."[116]

If there was general satisfaction with the terms of this settlement, the same could not be said for the process that led to it. President Bush's notion that the United States and Germany were destined to be "partners in leadership" was belied by Kohl's voluntaristic diplomacy. In his single-minded pursuit of a compromise with Gorbachev, the West German chancellor had failed to consult his allies, and Secretary of State Baker, for one, was less than pleased. To be sure, the terms were broadly consistent with Washington's prescriptions, but bilateral agreement on troop levels and denuclearization and the implicit economic bribe went beyond the West's coordinated strategy. Bonn's unilateralism aroused apprehensions in other allied capitals as well. British distaste for a German-dominated Europe was exposed in the impolitic remarks of Nicholas Ridley, one of Mrs. Thatcher's ministers.[117] And when President Mitterrand met Kohl at Munich in September, his caustic reference to rivalries and misunderstandings in the new Europe implied a cooling in Franco-German relations. The centrality of Germany in the continental balance of power had been reaffirmed, but historical memories as well as new economic realities made for uneasiness as Europeans and North Americans set to the task of devising a new architecture for the post-cold-war era.

Europeanism and Regionalism.   As Gorbachev relaxed the strictures of Pax Sovietica in Eastern Europe, the possibilities of geopolitical transformation and realignment began to excite the imagination. After concentrating for decades on the possibilities of nurturing evolutionary change, the West was driven to devise an effective strategy for consolidating politically and economically the East European revolutions and reworking European security arrangements.

The maintenance of Europe's stability and security as the Soviet empire recedes will be no easy task, for once again, as in the aftermath of the First World War, there will reemerge a collection of weak states diverse in their political and economic development, divided by ethnic feuds, and jealous of their new autonomy. While seeking closer association with the West, they will have to accommodate Russia's enduring influence and security interests. In this diversified and pluralistic setting, there will be a greater need than ever for a steady and concerted Western approach.

When in September 1989 Deputy Secretary of State Eagleburger warned of a "tendency for the member states of the NATO Alliance to compete in expanding their relations with the East," the East European revolution was incomplete and the Western responses were yet to be fully formulated. But his observation that the West Europeans had "the principal political stake in making the transition to a new and undivided Europe a peaceful and orderly one" reflected the Bush administration's pragmatic disposition to pass the torch to the allies.[118] In the 1960s, Kissinger had similarly voiced a preference for leaving the frustrating problem of Eastern Europe to the West Europeans, and in the mid-1980s, Brzezinski argued for the latter to assume a greater share of the burden with respect to military security as well.

As American policy moved beyond containment, Western Europe's considerable assets and its proximity to East Europe seemed to justify such a transfer of responsibility away from the United States. And as the salience of Eastern Europe in American policy waned, the necessity grew for reformulating European policy to encompass the East. But the West Europeans did not share common interests or a uniform strategy toward the East. The Germans were the most deeply involved commercially and disposed to assert special interests and competence, and indeed the notion of a German-led *Mitteleuropa* resurfaced in debates among West German intellectuals and politicians. Chancellor Kohl tried to embed the concept in the spirit of Europeanness:

Because of our geographic situation and because of our history, we Germans are obligated to maintain good relations with West and East. For us Germans there are many historical ties to the East. We share a deep understanding of the cultural unity of Europe, in all its variety and with all its differences. We consider our neighbors in Central and Eastern Europe—not only in this cultural sense— as parts of Europe.[119]

As they turn westward, East Europeans pragmatically welcome the material benefits of German economic influence, but Germany's closest neighbors, Poland and Czechoslovakia, if not others, fear excessive dependence. Germany as the predominant regional power holds little appeal for them. Most East Europeans identify neither with a German *Mitteleuropa* nor with a Russian-oriented Eastern Europe but simply with Europe.[120]

Attempts to conjure up a distinctive Central Europe excluding the Germans appear even more unrealistic and anachronistic in the age of European integration and a global economy, and at a time when communications technology is inducing a homogenization of cultural and political values. Nostalgia for an embellished Habsburg era and a sense of vulnerability in the new pluralistic, market environment may however momentarily lend force to a quest for new regional linkages.

The "East Europe" stretching from the Baltic to the Black Sea was a geopolitical fabrication, not a natural agglomeration of strategic and economic interests. The integration imposed through the Warsaw Pact and CMEA scarcely reduced the cultural diversity and the economic disparities within the region. Historical interests and cleavages resurfaced in the wake of the 1989 revolutions. Poland, Czechoslovakia, Hungary, Slovenia, and Croatia were busy reorienting themselves westward, and democratization was proceeding more smoothly there than in the Balkans. The problem of ethnic minorities soon reemerged in Hungary's relations with its neighbors, and in Polish-German relations as well. Divisive ethnic nationalism strained federal Czechoslovakia and Yugoslavia as well as unitary Romania.

Ideas for multilateral cooperation have proliferated. In early January 1990, Brzezinski suggested that Poland and Czechoslovakia join forces in a confederation to fill the vacuum of power between Germany and the Soviet Union, recycling the similar scheme of the Polish government-in-exile during the war. Neither Prague nor Warsaw warmed to the idea. The Poles did look worthward to Baltic cooperation, especially with secessionist Lithuania. Czechoslovakia's Havel convened a summit meeting with Poland and Hungary at Bratislava in April to coordinate the three countries' return to Europe, but the initiative led nowhere. Italy was instrumental in converting the earlier Alpine-Adria Working Group into a "Pentagonal" association including Austria, Czechoslovakia, Hungary, and Yugoslavia. At its meeting in August at Venice, the group developed ambitious plans for cooperation in such functional spheres as transport and the environment, but the East European members made clear that their overriding interest lay in joining the European Community. Budapest also raised the possibility of "Tisza-Carpathian" cooperation linking eastern Hungary with eastern Slovakia, sub-Carpathian Ukraine, and Serbia's Vojvodina province, regions that not coincidentally all have Hungarian minorities. And Bulgaria, Romania, Yugoslavia, and Turkey have also talked of closer cooperation.

Some of these regional linkages may deepen and serve useful ends, but they will neither assume the functions of the Warsaw Pact and CMEA nor serve as an alternative to association with the European Community. Given the region's diversity, the goal of Community membership will not be reached by collective effort, and the East Europeans are realistically concentrating on bilateral diplomacy to approach it. Inevitably, the solidarity born out of rejection of Soviet hegemony is rapidly giving way to discrete definitions of national interest.

If East Europeans have mixed feelings about the prospect of a German-led *Mitteleuropa*, the other West Europeans are equally cool to the idea. Only France has persisted in pursuing continental interests, a prominent one being to bind Germany economically and militarily into a European community. This interest also inspired the agreement in early 1988 on closer Franco-German military cooperation, including the formation of a mixed Franco-German brigade stationed in the Federal Republic. The Gaullist campaign to reinforce autonomy in Eastern Europe tried to bypass Moscow but failed to pay dividends, and France's subsequent championing of human rights in the East was marred by its premature hosting of Jaruzelski and Honecker. Nor was the active pursuit of human rights and cultural relations matched in the economic sphere, for, de Gaulle's legacy of industrial modernization notwithstanding, France remained a minor player in East-West trade.

And yet, despite its modest and inconsistently applied policies in the past, France remained the most promising generator of a concerted West European policy towards Eastern Europe. Bonn was hampered by its special interests and image problems. Prime Minister Thatcher was an eloquent advocate of liberalization in the East, but Britain's grudging approach to a deepening of the Community's political and economic integration undermined its credibility as an agent of deeper as well as broader European unification. The notion that France could Europeanize *Ostpolitik* by infusing it with a new political drive and vision had some advocates at the Quai d'Orsay. Dominique Moisi, associate director of the French Institute of International Relations, commented that France is "the only truly political entity that could play a decisive role in the construction of a politically unified Europe, provided [it] surmounts its economic weakness"; ideally, he added, a European *Ostpolitik* should "combine Germany's pragmatism with France's antitotalitarian criticism," meaning, presumably, German money and French political purpose.[121]

The revolutions in the East only accentuated the need for a pan-European strategy. Gorbachev's notion of a "common European home" with room for the Soviet Union evoked de Gaulle's vision of a revitalized

Europe from the Atlantic to the Urals; it also invited leadership that transcends frontiers and historical animosities and is respectful of democratic values and the requisites of the balance of power. Europe is nervous about the prospect of German leadership, even though Germans are hardly bereft of political wisdom. France is a minor nuclear power and has recovered its economic self-confidence. A certain complementarity of interests and assets make the two nations ideal partners in the enterprise of reuniting Europe. Franco-German collaboration in the development of a Community policy towards the East can both serve French security interests and mitigate the apprehensions that German unilateralism can arouse in both East and West.

"The rapprochement of the two Europes constitutes for us, Europeans, the great task of this end of the century *(la grande affaire de cette fin de siecle)*," announced President Mitterrand in 1988.[122] The postwar reconciliation of French and Germans, facilitated by new supranational institutions, was already a signal accomplishment. The most obvious framework for promoting a continental vision remains the European Community, and Eastern Europe could provide the stimulus for realizing the long-cherished vision of a common Community foreign policy.

A salutary precedent was set when the Organization for Economic Cooperation and Development assigned the task of coordinating aid for Poland and Hungary to the Commission. Jacques Delors, the Commission president, approached the task with a keen sense of historic mission. President Mitterrand rose to the challenge with eloquent speeches linking European unity and the reintegration of the East Europeans. His efforts to harmonize West European responses, especially the European development bank initiative, were partly calculated to constrain and Europeanize Bonn's economic penetration of the East. Mitterrand's urgency also came from concern that Bonn would lose its ardor for European unity as it concentrated on the rehabilitation of the former East Germany and pursued other new opportunities in the East.

Indeed, there soon appeared in the European Community a divergence between "deepeners" and "wideners," between those (mainly France, Italy, and the Commission) who wanted rapid progress towards economic and monetary union, and common security and foreign policies, and others more willing to relax the pace of integration in order to facilitate expansion. The latter tendency was displayed by West Germany's Genscher in October 1989, and although Bonn subsequently

reaffirmed its Community loyalties it became understandably preoccupied with East Germany. The Community, argued Delors, "must not
only strengthen itself but also maintain the hopes of others." His strategy was to maintain the momentum of federalization, to build a strong
and united Community that could forge a mutually beneficial relationship with neutral neighbors. He hoped that the creation of a "European
Economic Space," a new structured relationship under discussion with
the European Free Trade Association, could be extended to include the
East Europeans.[123] Mitterrand, for his part, tried to ride both horses,
unveiling in March 1990 a visionary but elusive scheme for pan-European "confederation" and the next month joining Kohl in proposing a
political union of the Twelve by 1993, with common foreign and security policies.

Finlandization and Beyond. The United States and Western Europe
must gird and coordinate their policies at a time when the temptation is
great to passively relish their ideological victory over Marxism-Leninism. The Soviet socialist paradigm has registered what Brzezinski called
the "grand failure" of the century.[124] The new paradigm is liberalism.
The necessary radical changes in East European structures and attitudes
are bound to create social stress and may yet be displaced by regression
to authoritarianism, especially in the Soviet Union. But the wave of
reform has left its mark, just as fifty years of socialism have left the East
Europeans impoverished, insecure, and unprepared for the hard road
back without Western help.

Eastern Europe's future depends not only on its own resourcefulness
but also on the evolution of Soviet policy and the readiness of a united
West to offer the appropriate inducements and reassurances. The hoary
concept of Finlandization has been evoked more often as a threat to
Western solidarity than as an escape for the East Europeans from the
Soviet embrace. Its applicability to much of Eastern Europe was questionable, since in terms of Soviet security Finland's peripheral location is
hardly comparable to the strategic importance of Poland, Czechoslovakia, or East Germany. And while Finland prospered, it had to pay
political tribute to the Soviet Union in refusing to accept Marshall Plan
aid, exercising considerable self-censorship (notably on the subject of
Soviet-Communist attempts at subversion and blackmail), and refraining
from official condemnation of the Soviet invasions of Hungary, Czecho-

slovakia, and Afghanistan. Still, if Gorbachev's version of detente is allowed to mature, the East Europeans will inevitably claim the Yalta promise of which, so far, Finland has been the sole beneficiary. Finland, in turn, may find its sovereignty less qualified and may serve again as a test case of Soviet permissiveness. Significantly, on a visit to Helsinki in October 1989, Gorbachev depicted Finland's neutrality as a positive feature rather than as a concession by the Soviet Union.

The suitability of the Austrian model of self-imposed neutrality as a road to the European Community is about to be tested. The Vienna State Treaty of 1955 prohibits economic and political union with Germany, but the concurrently adopted neutrality law does not explicitly preclude broader international, nonmilitary commitments. As Austria prepared to submit its application for membership, the Soviet attitude was that such a step was inconsistent with permanent neutrality. Membership would bind Austria to follow "all decisions taken in the framework of the Community," observed the Soviet spokesman Gennadi Gerasimov, and "the majority of the members of the Community are also members of NATO or of the Western European Union."[125]

Neutrality presents problems for the Community as well at a time when the coordination of foreign and security policies mandated by the Single European Act gets under way. If neutrality prevents Austria from accepting security obligations and joining the Community, there remain other mechanisms for closer association, but for its Eastern neighbors the road to European integration is bound to be even longer and more difficult. Their greatest fear, that the single market scheduled for 1992 will only accentuate the isolation of their faltering economies, can be assuaged by bilateral trade concessions and aid programs. The Community has already sent the appropriate differentiating signals in its trade negotiations, favoring the more democratic East European countries. But an emerging paradox of European reunification is that the more rapid the progress toward political integration of the Twelve, the greater the hurdles for East Europeans to Community membership. Conversely, attempts to accommodate the special geopolitical circumstances of the East may impede such progress. One happy circumstance is strong popular support in the West for eventual adherence of the East Europeans to the Community; a survey in January 1990 showed large majorities in France and Britain (as well as in the United States and Poland) in favor of that prospect.[126]

Further integration of the existing Community should not be made hostage to the uncertainties of change in the East. The Warsaw Pact is becoming a looser and less militarized association, but it is premature to bank on its early dissolution and the codified neutrality of any of its members. The Community, for its part, can accommodate a nonaligned Ireland but presumably not members who also belong to the Warsaw Pact or who are formally neutral in a politically sensitive zone. The more realistic scenario is for some East European countries to win sufficient latitude in their foreign relations to obtain a form of association with EFTA and the Community that is not incompatible with Soviet security interests.

Indeed, after Moscow accepted membership of a united Germany in NATO, the option of neutrality lost much of its appeal, and attention focused on complementary, pan-European security regimes. When Henry Kissinger proposed, in a lecture at Prague on June 20, 1990, the creation of a neutral belt consisting of Poland, Czechoslovakia, and Hungary (in addition to Austria), the immediate reaction was that Czechoslovakia had no interest in serving as a new buffer zone. The emerging attitude of the countries concerned was represented in Hungarian Foreign Minister Geza Jeszenszky's reflection the following month that "if the Cold War is hopefully and happily really over and the Soviet Union and the West no longer regard each other as enemies, then it no longer makes sense to declare oneself neutral." [127]

Whatever new structure of security may emerge, it is imperative for the Community to forge a consensus, to signal to the East Europeans the terms of association they will have to satisfy and assure them that they will receive equal and uniform consideration. Such a blueprint will help focus the policies of reformist regimes. The United States can help formulate the criteria for a concerted Western approach, not least in the sphere of military security. The Bush administration recognizes that the revolutions in the East and military disengagement magnify the importance of constructing a politically cohesive Europe possessed of military as well as economic self-confidence. The president noted that a unified European community of nations could be "a magnet that draws the forces of reform forward in Eastern Europe." [128]

America and the Architecture of Europe. America's East European dilemmas are rapidly merging into the general problem of the future of

Europe. As Washington weaves together the various strands of its European policies, its interests dictate a secure and unified Europe. That means not only expansion and intensification of institutional relations with the Community but also a reassessment of the actual and desirable balance of power and interests among its members.

The progress of military disengagement in Central Europe and German unification raises new security problems. In the era of containment, West Germany occupied a central role in Washington's European policy by virtue of its economic and military assets and strategic importance, and the Bush administration has only reconfirmed this priority. "The United States and the Federal Republic have always been firm friends and allies," declared President Bush at Mainz in May 1989; "But today we share an added role—partners in leadership." [129] Yet as the Warsaw Pact disintegrates and the Soviet threat recedes, stability becomes less dependent on German military ballast. Since leadership is to be shared, the United States would be well advised to broaden its focus from Bonn (and London) to include Paris, Brussels, and Rome, in the interest of European unity and security.

The uncertain future of the USSR complicates the task of the architects of a new Europe. The USSR is in the early stages of structural disintegration, and at least in the short term it is likely to experience more turbulence than stability. As the East Europeans began to consolidate democracy, the world's attention turned to the secessionist tendencies at work in the Baltic region and several other republics and the revival of Russian nationalism. These forces, along with deepening economic crisis, put in question not only the prospects of democratization and marketization but the very survival of the Soviet state. The West's cautious reaction to Lithuania's declaration of independence reflected the dilemmas of policy toward a superpower in agony.

The deepening crisis of *perestroika* might precipitate unfavorable changes in Soviet leadership and policy, but by now most Soviets regard Eastern Europe as irretrievably lost. To be sure, the Soviet chief of staff, General Mikhail Moiseyev, openly criticized Gorbachev's proposed party platform in February 1990 for failing to address the serious political situation in the region.[130] Ligachev later lamented that "the positions of imperialism have strengthened incredibly." A conservative counterrevolution in the Soviet Union would probably not have the capacity to restore the status quo ante simultaneously in that country and in Eastern

Europe. Yet even if a momentarily self-absorbed Soviet Union allows the rest of Europe to peacefully come together, Russian nationalism and the military arsenal of a superpower cannot be factored out of the new architecture of Europe.

For the present, as Charles Gati observed in his splendid analysis of *The Bloc that Failed,* the Soviet Union has "nothing of significance to contribute to the region's emerging order."[131] Its will to apply military or commercial leverage is sapped by ideological and economic disarray. But Gorbachev cannot erase Russia's historic interest in a sphere of influence in Eastern Europe, and Soviet military power as well as the region's dependence on Soviet natural resources remain potent sources of influence. Nor is he likely to condone unilateral liquidation of the Warsaw Pact or the network of bilateral security treaties with his neighbors. The alternative of an "East-Central European Union" (modeled on the Western European Union), a trial balloon floated by Hungary's Prime Minister Jozsef Antall in August 1990, will hardly appeal to Moscow if it excludes the Soviet Union. Only if the Soviet Union imploded would such regional alternatives be feasible, and in that event the extension of a Western-based security system to Eastern Europe would become preferable.

Therefore, as the West looks beyond the CFE round of military disengagement, it will have to consider the costs and benefits of redefining European security, including NATO, the rock on which it has built its entire postwar security strategy. A radical rethinking of that strategy will depend primarily on the consolidation of liberal reform in the Soviet Union. If one accepts the conventional wisdom that the ideological and economic contest has been won, the remaining danger to the West is purely military. If, in turn, the Soviet Union's assertions of "defensive sufficiency" are translated into significant demilitarization of the Central European theater, then the reintegration of the East European countries into a free community is worth the price of symmetrical reduction in NATO's military dimension and of a further institutionalization of the CSCE as a mechanism for mediating disputes. Whether or not there ever was a danger of Western Europe's Finlandization, or of its subjection to nefarious Soviet influence, the success of containment has deprived it of any credibility.

If the German problem is addressed with due sensitivity to the interests of other Europeans, then the well-founded as well as anachronistic apprehensions in both camps could be laid to rest. The real prospect now is for the Finlandization of Eastern Europe, where it will signify transitional accommodation of the Soviet Union's lingering sense of insecurity. Henry Kissinger asked,

In the long run, aren't arrangements in Finland more useful to Soviet security than those in Eastern Europe? Is it possible to devise arrangements that would give the Soviets security guarantees (widely defined) while permitting the peoples of Eastern Europe to choose their own political future? Under such a system, it would be possible to conceive a drastic reduction of all outside forces in Europe —including those of the U.S.—that might revolutionize present concepts of security.[132]

As Kissinger the historian knows full well, security guarantees depend on the will and means to back them up, and such precedents as the prewar Locarno agreements offer little ground for optimism. What the West can promise is not to exploit Eastern Europe's emancipation for military advantage, and to do its share in devising a new security regime for Europe that would respect the spirit of the Final Act and the right to independence and voluntary association of all European countries.

The outlines of this new regime emerged at the Paris summit of the CSCE in November 1990. The replacement of the two alliances by an invigorated CSCE was Gorbachev's preferred scenario, one that drew some support from the Germans as well as the new Czechoslovak government, which proposed the creation of a "European Security Commission." Washington was loath to consider any scheme that threatened the integrity of NATO, and with good reason, for the CSCE has no more military divisions than the Pope and operates on the principle of unanimity, hardly the basis for effective collective security. The Bush administration nevertheless went along with the concept of institutionalizing the CSCE, partly to give the new East European democracies a say in security matters and to avoid isolation of the Soviet Union. The "Charter of Paris for a new Europe," signed at the CSCE summit, provided for a small secretariat to be located in Prague, a Conflict Prevention Center in Vienna, a Warsaw office to collect data on (and eventually monitor) elections, and a parliamentary Assembly of Europe to be attached to the Council of Europe. The secretariat will help prepare annual ministerial meetings. The Conflict Prevention Center was charged with supervising a confidence-building exchange of military information, and some, notably the Germans, anticipated that it might eventually play a mediating role in disputes between CSCE participants.

The CSCE has served the cause of human rights and military disengagement well, and it can play an expanded role in the new architecture of security. But a solid architecture needs well-laid foundations, and in the foreseeable future no single security regime can address all the conceivable threats to peace and stability in Europe. The Soviet Union, even as it tries to reinvent itself amid mounting disintegrative pressures and economic travails, remains a military superpower. An expanded and powerful Germany may become more assertive in pursuit of its national interests, including economic penetration of the East. Democracy and autonomy offer no guarantee of neighborly consensus in Eastern Europe, where nationalism and prolonged economic distress could spark off violent confrontations; nor is regional peace likely to be assured by a moribund Warsaw Pact. At best, East European tensions might be held in check by the mediating functions of a revamped CSCE and Council of Europe. At worst, the fractious East Europeans will become pawns in a new German-Soviet contest for influence.

A sober assessment of risks inspired George Kennan's prudential recommendation in early 1990 for a three-year moratorium on basic changes in the two alliance structures.[133] The Warsaw Pact is the more imperiled of the two, but it may linger on as a consultative body. There is little doubt either in the West or in Eastern Europe (apart from the Soviet Union) that NATO, with a solid American presence, remains the essential component of a stable balance of power on the continent. The task therefore is to adapt that alliance to the ongoing processes of military disengagement, West European unification, and East European realignment. As Soviet forces withdraw and the East Europeans become friends instead of the enemy's outposts, NATO's forward defense strategy becomes politically untenable. Shevardnadze's surprise announcement at the CSCE Copenhagen meeting in June that the Soviet Union would make additional cuts in its tactical nuclear arsenal in Central Europe only reinforced the disposition of Washington and its allies to negotiate the removal of land-based nuclear weapons, in effect to denuclearize Germany. That would leave NATO with the option of deploying extended-range, tactical air-to-surface missiles, and the problem of where to base them if Germany is de-nuclearized.

Another NATO dilemma lies in the realm of conventional forces. Europeans and Americans are keen to reap the peace dividend as the Soviet threat recedes, but what is the configuration and size of conventional forces adequate to meet the remaining threat? In his commencement address at Oklahoma State University in May, President Bush declared that the United States was "not going to allow Europe to become safe for conventional war" and that "militarily significant U.S. forces must remain on the other side of the Atlantic for as long as our allies want and need them."[134] But most of those troops are in the Federal Republic, where popular support for their maintenance waxes and wanes unpredictably.[135] One proposed palliative, originating in Bonn, is to restructure NATO into multinational army corps that would require fewer American troops and be more palatable to West Germans. NATO's conventional troop strength could probably be reduced substantially in the form of professional armies as an alternative to large conscript armies. While such calculations may appear alarmist at a time of Soviet "new thinking" and domestic turmoil, they take into account the unaltered reality of Soviet military preponderance on the continent and the unpredictability of a superpower wrestling with its historic purpose and identity.

While Western Europe has the potential to develop an adequate conventional deterrent force if the Americans leave, their departure would undermine the credibility of the protection offered by the U.S.-based strategic nuclear force. A credible West European nuclear deterrent, in turn, would require a problematic expansion and coordination of French and British capability. In the long run, the European Community should assume primary responsibility for defense and regional security even as it draws the East Europeans into the fold. In the interim, mutual force reductions and treaty guarantees do not obviate the necessity of preserving the only democratic guardian of European security, NATO, and the tangible assurance of America's strategic umbrella.

Having won Gorbachev's verbal concession that it (along with Canada) has a place in the "common European home," the United States must remain engaged in the task of reforming the political structure of Europe. For fifty years, America's strategy and approaches shared the premise that Soviet socialism and hegemony in Eastern Europe suppressed national desires for self-determination. The United States could not guarantee early realization of that goal but remained committed to undoing the political division of Europe. As containment reaps its reward, new challenges face Washington in the complexity of Europe's politics. A multidimensional strategy to advance America's interests is gradually emerging. A policy review in the summer of 1989 concluded that progress toward deeper European Community integration should be encouraged, coupled with a battle against EC protectionism in GATT and other forums. Washington has tried to forge new links with the Brussels Commission and to reinforce the latter's Atlanticism, notably by having it coordinate the OECD's aid to Eastern Europe. While the United States is destined to be an onlooker in the process of broader European integration, its interests also dictate that it promote both orderly expansion of the Community to include the East Europeans and pan-European, confederal aspirations that may best be advanced through the Council of Europe. Though eager to reap its peace dividend, Washington remains committed to the preservation of NATO and a military presence on the continent. It has at the same time accepted the CSCE as an embryonic security regime for Europe. As active participant of engaged advocate, America retains a vested interest in the drafting of the new architecture necessitated by containment's success.

Washington's global interests are many, only one of which is Eastern Europe. Yet arguably Europe remains at the core of America's strategic and political interests, and the democratization and reintegration of Eastern Europe would represent the crucial victory in a war that has been waged for half a century. Enlightened self-interest as well as the sense of moral mission that has distinguished America's international outlook demand that the effort be sustained especially now, when the dominant tendencies in Eastern Europe appear so favorable.

In short, this is no time for precipitous military withdrawal and political disengagement from the affairs of Europe. The temptations to pass the buck to the West Europeans, to be niggardly in material aid for the East Europeans, and to end America's military presence on the continent must all be resisted. The United States can exert its considerable influence to see to it that Atlanticism and Europeanization are complementary and mutually reinforcing tendencies in stabilizing the process of transformation. America's unique consistency of purpose, its material wealth, and its military power have been essential assets in the protracted struggle for Europe. The United States must remain actively engaged as stabilizer and guarantor for the foreseeable future.

Notes

Chapter 1

1. Quoted in Alan Palmer, *The Lands Between* (London: Weidenfeld and Nicolson, 1970), p. 251.
2. U.S. Congress, Senate, Committee on Foreign Relations, and Department of State, *A Decade of American Foreign Policy: Basic Documents, 1941–1949* (Washington, D.C., 1950), p. 481.
3. More extensive treatments of America's wartime policies regarding Eastern Europe can be found in Lynn Etheridge Davis, *The Cold War Begins: Soviet-American Conflict over Eastern Europe* (Princeton, N.J.: Princeton University Press, 1974); Geir Lundestad, *The American Non-policy towards Eastern Europe, 1943–1947* (New York: Humanities Press, 1975); Bennett Kovrig, *The Myth of Liberation: East-Central Europe in U.S. Diplomacy and Politics since 1941* (Baltimore: Johns Hopkins University Press, 1973); Richard C. Lukas, *The Strange Allies: The United States and Poland, 1941–1945* (Knoxville: University of Tennessee Press, 1978); Michael M. Boll, *Cold War in Balkans: American Foreign Policy and the Emergence of Communist Bulgaria, 1943–1947* (Lexington: University Press of Kentucky, 1984).
4. Milovan Djilas, *Conversations with Stalin* (New York: Harcourt, Brace & World, 1962), p. 114.
5. See Vojtech Mastny, *Russia's Road to the Cold War* (New York: Columbia University Press, 1979), pp. 60–80.
6. Mastny, *Russia's Road*, p. 224.

7. U.S. Department of State, *Foreign Relations of the United States: Diplomatic Papers* (hereafter cited as FRUS), 1941, vol. 1 (Washington, D.C., 1958), pp. 368–69.

8. Memorandum from Secretary of State Hull to President Roosevelt, February 4, 1942, FRUS 1942, Vol. 3, p. 510.

9. William C. Bullitt, "How We Won the War and Lost the Peace," *Life,* August 30, 1948, p. 94; and see Kovrig, *Myth of Liberation,* pp. 7–8.

10. John Colville, *The Fringes of Power: Downing Street Diaries, 1939–1955* (London: Hodder and Stoughton, 1985), p. 658; see also p. 674.

11. Bradley F. Smith, *The Shadow Warriors: O.S.S. and the Origins of the C.I.A.* (New York: Basic Books, 1983), pp. 237, 243, 351–52; see also Lev Bezymensky, "General Donovan's Balkan Plan," *International Affairs* (Moscow), no. 8 (August 1987): 116–26.

12. U.S.S.R., Ministry of Foreign Affairs, *Correspondence between the Chairman of the Council of Ministers of the U.S.S.R. and the Presidents of the U.S.A. and the Prime Ministers of Great Britain during the Great Patriotic War of 1941–1945* (Moscow, 1957), vol. 2, pp. 206–7; see also Mastny, *Russia's Road,* pp. 77–78, 83–84.

13. Elliot Roosevelt, *As He Saw It* (New York: Duell, Sloan & Pearce, 1946), p. 184.

14. Cordell Hull, *The Memoirs of Cordell Hull* (New York: Hodder & Stoughton, 1948), p. 1442.

15. George F. Kennan, *Memoirs, 1925–1950* (Boston: Little, Brown, 1967), p. 211.

16. Kennan, *Memoirs,* pp. 222–23.

17. Julian Amery quoted in Nicholas Bethell, *The Great Betrayal* (London: Hodder & Stoughton, 1984), p. 22.

18. See FRUS 1945, *The Conferences at Malta and Yalta,* 1955 pp. 217–25.

19. FRUS 1944, vol. 4, pp. 1025–26.

20. FRUS, *Malta and Yalta,* p. 103.

21. FRUS, *Malta and Yalta,* p. 235.

22. Charles E. Bohlen, *Witness to History, 1929–1969* (New York: Norton, 1973), pp. 175–77.

23. U.S. Department of State, *Postwar Foreign Policy Preparation, 1939–1945* (Washington, D.C., 1949), pp. 372–73, 655–57; Edward R. Stettinius, Jr., *Roosevelt and the Russians: The Yalta Conference* (Garden City, N.Y.: Doubleday, 1950), pp. 68, 87.

24. Winston S. Churchill, *The Second World War: Triumph and Tragedy* (Boston: Houghton Mifflin, 1953), p. 393.

25. FRUS, *Malta and Yalta,* pp. 973–74.

26. James F. Byrnes, *Speaking Frankly* (New York: Harper, 1947), p. 32.

27. W. Averell Harriman and Elie Abel, *Special Envoy to Churchill and Stalin, 1941–1946* (New York: Random House, 1975), pp. 412–13.

28. World Peace Foundation, *Documents on American Foreign Relations, 1944–1945* (Princeton, N.J.: Princeton University Press, 1947), pp. 24–25.

29. Walter Millis, ed., *The Forrestal Diaries* (New York: Viking, 1951), p. 40.
30. Harry S. Truman, *Memoirs: Years of Decisions* (Garden City, N.Y.: Doubleday, 1955), p. 15.
31. Memorandum of conversation by Charles Bohlen, April 20, 1945, FRUS 1945, vol. 5, p. 232.
32. See Kovrig, *Myth of Liberation,* pp. 41–43.
33. Kennan, *Memoirs,* p. 212.
34. John Lewis Gaddis, *The United States and the Origins of the Cold War, 1941–1947* (New York: Columbia University Press, 1972), pp. 259–61.
35. Department of State *Bulletin,* August 4, 1946, pp. 229–32.
36. FRUS 1946, vol. 6, p. 216; see also Byrnes, *Speaking Frankly,* pp. 143–44.
37. See Thomas G. Paterson, *Soviet-American Confrontation: Postwar Reconstruction and the Origins of the Cold War* (Baltimore: Johns Hopkins University Press, 1973), pp. 101–2, and Walter Ullmann, *The United States in Prague, 1945–1948* (Boulder, Colo.: East European Quarterly, 1978), pp. 39–47.
38. Truman, *Years of Decisions,* p. 245.
39. Edgar Snow, quoted in Mastny, *Russia's Road,* p. 357.
40. Wiliam D. Leahy, *I Was There* (New York: McGraw-Hill, 1950), p. 485.
41. Gaddis, *United States and the Origins of the Cold War,* p. 241.
42. See Kennan to Byrnes, March 6, 1946, FRUS 1946, vol. 5, pp. 516–20.
43. W. W. Rostow, *The Division of Europe after World War II: 1946* (Austin: University of Texas Press, 1982), pp. 60, 87, and passim.
44. Department of State *Bulletin,* September 15, 1946, pp. 496–501.
45. Gaddis, *United States and the Origins of the Cold War,* p. 315.
46. Kennan to Byrnes, February 22, 1946, FRUS 1946, vol. 6, pp. 696–709.
47. *Vital Speeches of the Day,* vol. 12, March 15, 1946, pp. 329–32.
48. Gaddis, *United States and the Origins of the Cold War,* pp. 321–22.
49. Smith to secretary of state, May 31, 1946, FRUS 1946, vol. 6, p. 758.
50. Joint Chiefs of Staff, JIS, "Capabilities and Intentions of the U.S.S.R. in the Post-War Period," July 9, 1946, p. 167.
51. Daniel Yergin, *Shattered Peace* (Boston: Houghton Mifflin, 1977), p. 255.
52. Truman, *Years of Decisions,* p. 552.
53. Department of State *Bulletin,* December 23, 1945, p. 1020.
54. FRUS 1946, vol. 6, pp. 272–73.
55. See Stephen D. Kertesz, *Between Russia and the West: Hungary and the Illusions of Peacemaking, 1945–1947* (Notre Dame, Ind.: University of Notre Dame Press, 1984), and Bennett Kovrig, "Peacemaking after World War II: The End of the Myth of National Self-Determination," in Stephen Borsody, ed., *The Hungarians: A Divided Nation* (New Haven: Yale C.I.A.S., 1988), pp. 69–88.
56. World Peace Foundation, *Documents on American Foreign Relations, 1947* (Princeton, N.J.: Princeton University Press, 1949), p. 2.
57. Lundestad, *American Non-policy,* p. 342.

58. Harriman to secretary of state, November 22, 1945, FRUS 1945, vol. 5, p. 191.
59. Paterson, *Soviet-American Confrontation,* pp. 101–2.
60. For the contending views on this question, see Robert A. Pollard, *Economic Security and the Origins of the Cold War, 1945–1950* (New York: Columbia University Press, 1985), and Joyce and Gabriel Kolko, *The Limits of Power: The World and United States Foreign Policy, 1945–1954* (New York: Harper and Row, 1972).
61. Gaddis, *United States and the Origins of the Cold War,* pp. 322–23. On the stages of Communist takeover, see Charles Gati, *Hungary and the Soviet Bloc* (Durham, N.C.: Duke University Press, 1986), Part 1.
62. George F. Kennan, "The Sources of Soviet Conduct," *Foreign Affairs,* vol. 25, no. 4 (July 1947): 566–82.
63. Dean Acheson, *Present at the Creation* (New York: Norton, 1969), p. 225.
64. See Kennan, *Memoirs,* pp. 333–42.
65. JCS 1769/1, Joint Strategic Survey Committee, "United States Assistance to Other Countries from the Standpoint of National Security," April 29, 1947, FRUS 1947, vol. 1, pp. 738–50.
66. Josef Korbel, *The Communist Subversion of Czechoslovakia, 1938–1948* (Princeton, N.J.: Princeton University Press, 1959), p. 182.
67. NSC Action 17, December 17, 1947; Paterson, *Soviet-American Confrontation,* p. 102.
68. Walter Laqueur, *A World of Secrets: The Uses and Limits of Intelligence* (New York: Basic Books, 1985), p. 113.
69. See Eugenio Reale, *Avec Jacques Duclos: Au banc des accuses a la reunion constitutive du Kominform a Szklarska Poreba (22–27 septembre 1947)* (Paris: Plon, 1958).
70. Kennan, *Memoirs,* p. 403.
71. Jean Edward Smith, "The View from USFET: General Clay's and Washington's Interpretations of Soviet Intentions in Germany, 1945–1948," in Hans A. Schmidt, ed., *US Occupation in Europe after World War II* (Lawrence: Regents Press of Kansas, 1978), p. 75.
72. Harry S. Truman, *Memoirs: Years of Trial and Hope* (Garden City, N.Y.: Doubleday, 1956), p. 174.
73. Kennan, *Memoirs,* pp. 421–24, 443–44; Acheson, *Present at the Creation,* p. 291.
74. See Kovrig, *Myth of Liberation,* pp. 83–86.
75. NSC 7, "The Position of the United States with Respect to Soviet-Directed World Communism," March 30, 1948.
76. NSC 20/1, "U.S. Objectives with Respect to Russia," August 18, 1948.
77. NSC 20/4, "U.S. Objectives with Respect to the USSR to Counter Soviet Threats to U.S. Security," November 23, 1948.
78. NSC 58/2, "United States Policy Toward the Soviet Satellite States in Eastern Europe," December 8, 1949.
79. Joint Chiefs of Staff, Joint Intelligence Committee, "Most Likely Period for

Initiation of Hostilities between the U.S.S.R. and the Western Powers,"
August 22, 1950.

80. NSC 73, "The Position and Actions of the United States with Respect to
Possible Further Soviet Moves in the Light of the Korean Situation," July 1,
1950.

81. Stewart Stephen, *Operation Splinter Factor* (Philadelphia: Lippincott, 1974),
pp. 162–64; Karel Kaplan, *Dans les archives du comité central: Trente ans
de secrets du bloc soviétique* (Paris: Albin Michel, 1978), pp. 167–68.

82. John Lewis Gaddis, "Containment and the Logic of Strategy," *The National
Interest,* no. 10 (Winter 1987/8): 32.

83. NSC 68/2, "United States Objectives and Programs for National Security,"
September 30, 1950 (these are the conclusions of NSC 68, April 14, 1950,
as approved in NSC Action 30, September 29, 1950).

84. NSC 71/1, "State Department Report on the Rearmament of Western Germany," July 3, 1950.

85. For Stalin's note, see Department of State *Bulletin,* April 7, 1952, pp. 551–
52. On the Soviet-East German aspects, see Jean Edward Smith, *Germany
beyond the Wall* (Boston: Little, Brown, 1969), p. 218; Adam B. Ulam,
Expansion & Coexistence: The History of Soviet Foreign Policy, 1917–67
(New York: Praeger, 1968), pp. 506–38; and Ann L. Phillips, *Soviet Policy
toward East Germany Reconsidered: The Postwar Decade* (Westport, Conn.:
Greenwood Press, 1986). The West German historian Werner Maser reports
that at the time of Stalin's initiative, the Russians made an extraordinary
overture to Rudolf Hess, who was held in Berlin's Spandau prison: he was
invited to endorse the East German version of socialism and resume his
political career in order to rally the support of former Nazis throughout
Germany (Reuter's, September 4, 1987; Associated Press, September 5,
1987).

86. Acheson, *Present at the Creation,* p. 630.

87. Memorandum of conversation with French Ambassador Bonnet et al., June
12, 1952, *Official Conversations and Meetings of Dean Acheson* (1949–
1953), University Publications of America, 1980 (microfilm).

88. U.S. Department of State, Office of Intelligence Research, "Extent and
Stability of Soviet Control over European Satellites," August 3, 1951.

89. The NSC's "Reappraisal of United States Objectives and Strategy for National Security" (NSC 135/3, September 25, 1952) argued that "where
operations can be conducted on terms which may result in a relative de-
crease in Soviet power without involving unacceptable risks, the United
States should pursue and as practicable intensify positive political, economic, propaganda, and para-military operations against the Soviet bloc,
particularly those operations designed to weaken Kremlin control over the
satellites and the military potential of the Soviet system. However, we
should not overestimate the effectiveness of the activities we can pursue
within the Soviet orbit, and should proceed with a careful weighing of the
risks against the possible gains in pressing upon what the Kremlin probably

regards as its vital interests." At best, the West might be able to "sap the morale of the satellite leaders and encourage rifts," thereby increasing the Kremlin's preoccupation with internal security. Meanwhile, Western economic warfare could "help to deprive the Soviet orbit of needed resources and retard the development of [its] military potential."

90. Laqueur, *World of Secrets*, p. 358 note 10.
91. NSC 18, "State Department Report on the Attitude of this Government toward Events in Yugoslavia," July 6, 1948.
92. NSC 18/2, "Economic Relations between the United States and Yugoslavia," February 17, 1949. See also Beatrice Heuser, *Western "Containment" Policies in the Cold War: The Yugoslav Case, 1948–53* (London: Routledge, 1989), pp. 88–91.
93. John Ranelagh, *The Agency: The Rise and Decline of the CIA* (New York: Simon and Schuster, 1986), p. 140.
94. See Bela K. Kiraly, "The Aborted Soviet Military Plans against Tito's Yugoslavia," in Wayne S. Vucinich, ed., *At the Brink of War and Peace: The Tito-Stalin Split in a Historic Perspective* (New York: Columbia University Press, 1982), pp. 237–88.
95. NSC 18/3, "United States Policy toward the Conflict between the USSR and Yugoslavia," November 10, 1949.
96. Bethell, *Great Betrayal*, p. 119.
97. NSC 73/1, "The Position and Actions of the United States with Respect to Possible Further Soviet Moves in the Light of the Korean Situation," July 29, 1950. See also Heuser, *Western "Containment" Policies*, pp. 149–54.
98. NSC 18/6, "The Position of the United States with Respect to Yugoslavia," March 7, 1951; Heuser, *Western "Containment" Policies*, pp. 168–70.
99. Department of State *Bulletin*, June 12, 1949, pp. 756–58.
100. *New York Times*, March 17, 1950.
101. NSC 10/2, "Office of Special Operations," June 18, 1948.
102. See NSC 68/3, "United States Objectives and Programs for National Security," December 8, 1950; Ranelagh, *The Agency*, pp. 219–20; and NSC 86/1 (recommendations still classified).
103. *New York Times*, May 3 and November 25, 1951.
104. Cord Meyer, *Facing Reality: From World Federalism to the CIA* (New York: Harper & Row, 1980), p. 111.
105. JCS 1735/84, Joint Intelligence Committee, "Psychological Warfare Planning in Support of Joint Outline Emergency War Plan," September 11, 1951.
106. NSC 74, "A Plan for National Psychological Warfare," July 10, 1950.
107. Stephen, *Operation Splinter Factor*, p. 9.
108. *Ibid.*, pp. 97–101.
109. See Kaplan, *Archives*, pp. 140–58.
110. John Prados, *Presidents' Secret Wars: CIA and Pentagon Covert Operations from World War II through to Iranscam* (New York: Quill/Morrow, 1986), pp. 89, 222–23, 235.

111. Bethell, *Great Betrayal*, pp. 35–39.
112. *Ibid.*, p. 118.
113. Prados, *Presidents' Secret Wars*, p. 46.
114. JCS 1654/4 cited in Bethell, *Great Betrayal*, p. 113.
115. Bethell, *Great Betrayal*, pp. 116–18.
116. For more detail see Kovrig, *Myth of Liberation*, chapter 3.
117. U.S. Congress, Congressional Record, 82nd Cong., 1st sess., 1951, pp. A7975–7, "Penetration Program against Communism," extension of remarks made by the Hon. Alexander Wiley in the Senate on January 2, 1951.
118. U.S. Congress, House, Committee on Foreign Affairs, *The Mutual Security Program: Hearings*, 82nd Cong., 1st sess., 1951, pp. 1106–9.
119. Paul H. Nitze, *U.S. Foreign Policy, 1945–1955* (Washington, D.C.: Foreign Policy Association, 1956), p. 48.
120. James Burnham, *Containment or Liberation* (New York: John Day, 1953), pp. 138, 223. See also William Henry Chamberlin, *Beyond Containment* (Chicago: Regnery, 1953).
121. John Foster Dulles, "A Policy of Boldness," *Life*, May 19, 1952, pp. 146–60.
122. Council on Foreign Relations, *Documents on American Foreign Relations, 1952* (New York: Harper, 1953), pp. 80–83.
123. *New York Times*, August 26, 1952.
124. *New York Times*, August 28, 1952.
125. *New York Times*, October 5, 1952.
126. Louis L. Gerson, *The Hyphenate in Recent American Politics and Diplomacy* (Lawrence: Unviersity Press of Kansas, 1964), pp. 198–99; Athan G. Theoharis, *The Yalta Myths: An Issue in U.S. Politics, 1945– 1955* (Columbia: University of Missouri Press, 1970), pp. 149, 238–43; and Robert A. Divine, *Foreign Policy and U.S. Presidential Elections, 1952– 1960* (New York: New Viewpoints, 1974), pp. 54–55, 84.

Chapter 2

1. Council on Foreign Relations, *Documents on American Foreign Relations, 1953* (New York: Harper, 1954), p. 20.
2. Emmet John Hughes, *The Ordeal of Power* (New York: Atheneum, 1963), p. 207.
3. Department of State Bulletin, February 9, 1953, pp. 212–16.
4. U.S. Congress, House, Committee on Foreign Affairs, *Hearings on House Joint Resolution 200: Joining with the President of the United States in a Declaration regarding the Subjugation of Free Peoples by the Soviet Union*, 83rd Cong., 1st sess., 1953, pp. 3–22.
5. Account of telephone conversation with Congressman Walter Judd, March 28, 1953, Dulles Papers, Princeton University.

6. Hughes, *Ordeal of Power*, p. 101.
7. Walter Laqueur, *A World of Secrets: The Uses and Limits of Intelligence* (New York: Basic Books, 1985), p. 117.
8. John Colville, *The Fringes of Power: Downing Street Diaries, 1939–1955* (London: Hodder and Stoughton, 1985), p. 650.
9. Leonard Mosley, *Dulles: A Biography of Eleanor, Allen, and John Foster Dulles and Their Family Network* (New York: Dial Press/James Wade, 1978), p. 331.
10. Hughes, *Ordeal of Power*, pp. 103–4.
11. Robert A. Divine, *Eisenhower and the Cold War* (New York: Oxford University Press, 1981), p. 108.
12. *New York Times*, April 19, 1953.
13. Colville, *Fringes of Power*, p. 672.
14. Department of State, Office of Intelligence Research, "New Elements in West German Foreign Policy," July 3, 1953.
15. Department of State, Office of Intelligence Research, "Problems and Policies of a Reunited Germany," July 12, 1955.
16. John Lewis Gaddis, *Strategies of Containment: A Critical Appraisal of Postwar American National Security Policy* (New York: Oxford University Press, 1982), p. 190.
17. Colville, *Fringes of Power*, pp. 679–80, 683.
18. Colville, *Fringes of Power*, pp. 692–702.
19. Charles E. Bohlen, *Witness to History, 1929–1969* (New York: Norton, 1973), p. 371.
20. *New York Times*, May 19, 1955.
21. U.S. Congress, Senate, *Executive Sessions of the Senate Foreign Relations Committee* (historical series), Vol. 8, 84th Cong., 2d sess., 1956, p. 23.
22. Gaddis, *Strategies of Containment*, pp. 145–46.
23. Gaddis, *Strategies of Containment*, pp. 155, 160–61.
24. Quoted in Eugene Davidson, *The Death and Life of Germany* (New York: Knopf, 1959), p. 332–33.
25. Thomas Powers, *The Man Who Kept the Secrets: Richard Helms & the CIA* (New York: Knopf, 1979), p. 46.
26. Record of Dulles telephone conversation, June 17, 1953, *Minutes of Telephone Conversations of John Foster Dulles and of Christian Herter*, University Publications of America (microfilm).
27. James B. Conant, *My Several Lives* (New York: Harper & Row, 1970), p. 601.
28. Pierre Nord and Jacques Bergier, *L'actuelle guerre secrete* (Paris: Encyclopedie Planete, 1967), p. 161.
29. On the morning of June 17, Dulles had advised Eisenhower to avoid answering questions about "our stimulating this." Record of Dulles telephone conversations with Eisenhower, June 17, 1953, and with Frank Wisner, June 12, 1954.
30. Joint Chiefs of Staff, JCS 1735/200, "National Psychological Program with

Respect to Germany," August 31, 1953 (original draft dated February 20, 1953).

31. Edmond Taylor, "RIAS: The Story of an American Psywar Outpost," in William E. Daugherty, ed., *A Psychological Warfare Casebook* (Baltimore: Johns Hopkins University Press, 1958), pp. 145–50; Davidson, *Death and Life of Germany*, p. 334.

32. See Melvin Croan, "East Germany: Lesson in Survival," *Problems of Communism*, no. 11, 1962, p. 8; Stefan Brant, *The East German Rising* (London: Thames & Hudson, 1955), pp. 168–74; Arnulf Baring, *Der 17. Juni 1953* (Bonn: Deutsche Bundesverlag, 1958), p. 68; and *New York Times*, March 16, 1963.

33. Colville, *Fringes of Power*, p. 672.

34. Minutes of cabinet meeting, July 10, 1953, *Minutes and Documents of the Cabinet Meetings of President Eisenhower (1953–1961)*, University Publications of America (microfilm).

35. Hughes, *Ordeal of Power*, p. 147; U.S. Congress, Senate, Committee on Foreign Relations, *Documents on Germany, 1944–1959*, 86th Cong., 1st sess., 1959, pp. 110–12.

36. C. L. Sulzberger, *A Long Row of Candles: Memoirs & Diaries (1934–1954)* (New York: Macmillan, 1969), pp. 914–15.

37. *Documents on American Foreign Relations, 1953*, p. 40.

38. Joseph Barber, ed., *Diplomacy and the Communist Challenge: A Report on the Views of Leading Citizens in Twenty-five Cities,* (New York: Council on Foreign Relations, 1954), pp. 8, 37.

39. Louis L. Gerson, *The Hyphenate in Recent American Politics and Diplomacy* (Lawrence: University Press of Kansas, 1964), p. 213.

40. JCS 1735/170, "Report by the Joint Strategic Plans Committee to the Joint Chiefs of Staff on Implementation of Section 101(a)(1) of the Mutual Security Act of 1951 (Kersten Amendment)," February 24, 1953.

41. NSC/143, "Proposal for a Volunteer Freedom Corps," February 14, 1953.

42. NSC/143/2, "A Volunteer Freedom Corps," May 20, 1953.

43. NSC Action 2348, December 28, 1960.

44. NSC, Operations Coordinating Board, "Progress Report on United States Policy on Soviet and Satellite Defectors (NSC/86/1)," April 18, 1956.

45. Department of State *Bulletin*, April 13, 1953, pp. 539–41.

46. S. Kracauer and P. L. Berkman, *Satellite Mentality* (New York: Praeger, 1956), p. 153; U.S. Department of State, *Program Test of Voice of America's New York and Munich Output in Hungarian*, prepared by the Institute of Communications Research, Inc., Washington, D.C., 1953.

47. Cord Meyer, *Facing Reality: From World Federalism to the CIA* (New York: Harper & Row, 1980), pp. 114, 117–18.

48. See, for instance, Dulles's letter to Henry Ford II, March 25, 1954, Dulles Papers.

49. NSC Actions 817, 826.

50. NSC 158, "United States Objectives and Actions to Exploit the Unrest in

the Satellite States," July 29, 1953. The "National Psychological Program with Respect to Germany" (JCS 1735/200, August 31, 1953) set out the following tasks: (a) To stimulate popular suspicion of Soviet intentions with respect to Germany; (b) To persuade Soviet-orbit peoples that a unified Germany integrated into a European Community is a guarantee against the revived German drive to the East; (c) To convince Soviet-orbit peoples that the weakening of Soviet power in East Germany is a necessary prerequisite to their own liberation; (d) To sustain the resistance of Soviet-orbit peoples toward the day when their active participation in their own liberation will be required.

51. NSC 174, "United States Policy toward the Soviet Satellites in Eastern Europe," December 11, 1953. In assessing the East European situation, the NSC found that "known underground groups capable of armed resistance . . . are now generally inactive"; that "the ability of the USSR to exercise effective control over, and exploit the resources of, the European satellites has not been appreciably reduced, and is not likely to be, as long as the USSR maintains adequate military forces in the area"; that the death of Stalin had created "new problems which may lend themselves to exploitation"; and that "it does not appear likely that a non-Soviet regime on the Tito model will emerge in any of the satellites under existing circumstances." The proposed courses of action included encouragement of passive resistance and continuing review of the possibility of detaching Albania from the Soviet bloc.

52. NSC, Operations Coordinating Board, "Progress Report on United States Policy toward the Soviet Satellites in Eastern Europe (NSC 174)," July 16, 1954.

53. Robert T. Holt and Robert W. Van De Welde, *Strategic Psychological Operations and American Foreign Policy* (Chicago: University of Chicago Press, 1960), pp. 208–23.

54. Robert T. Holt, *Radio Free Europe* (Minneapolis: University of Minnesota Press, 1958), p. 162.

55. Powers, *Man Who Kept the Secrets*, pp. 45–47.

56. Gaddis, *Strategies of Containment*, p. 158; John Ranelagh, *The Agency: The Rise and Decline of the CIA* (New York: Simon & Schuster, 1986), p. 279.

57. *Der Tagesspiegel* (West Berlin), March 26, 1954.

58. Minutes of cabinet meeting, March 27, 1953.

59. Department of State, Office of Intelligence Research, "East-West Trade Activities of the Council of Europe," September 12, 1955.

60. NSC 5501, "Basic National Security Policy," January 6, 1955.

61. NSC 5412/1, "Covert Operations," March 12, 1955.

62. Papers on Geneva Conference goals, July 7, 1955, Dulles Papers.

63. Richard Goold-Adams, *A Time of Power* (London: Weidenfeld & Nicolson, 1962), p. 206; *Executive Sessions of the Senate Foreign Relations Committee* (1956), p. 17.

64. Memorandum of June 18, 1955, Dulles Papers; *New York Times,* June 30, 1955.
65. Harold Macmillan, *Tides of Fortune, 1945–1955* (London: Macmillan, 1969), p. 615.
66. NSC, Operations Coordinating Board, "Progress Report on United States Policy toward the Soviet Satellites in Eastern Europe (NSC 174)," February 29, 1956.
67. *New York Times,* August 25, 1955.
68. NSC, Operations Coordinating Board, "Progress Report on United States Policy Relating to East Germany (NSC 174)," May 17, 1956.
69. *New York Times,* April 25, 1956.
70. Ranelagh, *The Agency,* p. 286.
71. Ray Cline, *Secrets, Spies, and Scholars* (New York: Acropolis, 1976), p. 164; William Colby, *Honorable Men: My Life in the CIA* (New York: Simon and Schuster, 1978), p. 133; Powers, *Man Who Kept the Secrets,* p. 80.
72. *Executive Sessions of the Senate Foreign Relations Committee* (1956), pp. 375–77, 510.
73. Laqueur, *World of Secrets,* p. 359.
74. NSC Action 1530, March 22, 1956.
75. Dulles telephone coversation, April 30, 1956.
76. *Executive Sessions of the Senate Foreign Relations Committee* (1956), p. 503.
77. Meyer, *Facing Reality,* p. 119.
78. William R. Corson, *The Armies of Ignorance: The Rise of the American Intelligence Empire* (New York: Dial Press/James Wade, 1977), p. 367; Ranelagh, *The Agency,* p. 287; *New York Times,* November 30, 1976.
79. Holt and Van De Welde, *Strategic Psychological Operations and American Foreign Policy,* pp. 230–32.
80. *New York Herald Tribune,* February 18, 1956.
81. Robert A. Divine, *Foreign Policy and U.S. Presidential Elections, 1952–1960* (New York: New Viewpoints, 1974), pp. 94ff, 128; Gerson, *Hyphenate in Recent American Politics and Diplomacy,* pp. 217–9; New York Times, August 16, 1956.
82. Dulles telephone conversation, June 28, 1956.
83. *New York Times,* June 29, 1956.
84. Council on Foreign Relations, *Documents on American Foreign Relations, 1956* (New York: Harper, 1957), p. 212; U.S. Congress, *Congressional Record,* 84th Cong., 2d sess., 1956, 102: pp. 11339, 11355–67.
85. Dulles telephone conversation, June 28, 1956.
86. Stewart Stephen, *Operation Splinter Factor* (Philadelphia: Lippincott, 1974), p. 213.
87. Department of State, Office of Intelligence Research, "Independent Courses of Action of the Polish Regime since Gomulka's Return to Power," April 11, 1957.

88. Dulles telephone conversation, July 10, 1956.
89. Dulles telephone conversations with Lodge and Yarrow, October 22, 1956.
90. Ranelagh, *The Agency*, p. 304.
91. NSC 5616, "U.S. Policy toward Developments in Poland and Hungary," October 31, 1956.
92. *Nowa Kultura*, December 2, 1956, quoted in Melvin J. Lasky, ed., *The Hungarian Revolution: A White Book* (New York: Praeger, 1957), p. 159.
93. See Nikita Khrushchev, *K[h]rushchev Remembers* (Boston: Little, Brown, 1970), pp. 416–29, and Oleg Penkovskiy, *The Penkovskiy Papers* (Garden City, N.Y.: Doubleday, 1965), p. 212.
94. Veljko Micunovic, *Moscow Diary* (Garden City, N.Y. Doubleday, 1980), p. 127.
95. Paul E. Zinner, ed., *National Communism and Popular Revolt in Eastern Europe* (New York: Columbia University Press, 1956), pp. 462–64.
96. Micunovic, *Moscow Diary*, p. 140.
97. Robert D. Murphy, *Diplomat among Warriors* (Garden City, N.Y.: Doubleday, 1964), p. 428. The American minister to Hungary, Christian Ravndal, who had returned home shortly before the outbreak, allowed that he had "expected something of this sort around the end of the year" (*New York Herald Tribune*, October 25, 1956).
98. Laqueur, *World of Secrets*, p. 123; Meyer, *Facing Reality*, p. 127; Herman Finer, *Dulles over Suez* (Chicago: Quadrangle, 1964), p. 343.
99. Dwight D. Eisenhower, *Waging Peace* (Garden City, N.Y.: Doubleday, 1964), p. 63.
100. Brian McCauley, "Hungary and Suez, 1956: The Limits of Soviet and American Power," in Bela K. Kiraly et al., eds., *The First War between Socialist States: The Hungarian Revolution of 1956 and Its Impact* (New York: Brooklyn College Press, 1984), p. 297.
101. *Documents on American Foreign Relations, 1956*, pp. 255–56; Murphy, *Diplomat among Warriors*, p. 429; C. L. Sulzberger, *The Last of the Giants* (New York: Macmillan, 1970), p. 336.
102. Dulles telephone conversation, October 24, 1956.
103. Dulles telephone conversations with Lodge and Eisenhower, 25 October 1956.
104. Eisenhower, *Waging Peace*, pp. 67–8.
105. NSC Actions 1623, 1628, 26 October 1956.
106. Dulles telephone conversation, 26 October 1956.
107. *Documents on American Foreign Relations, 1956*, pp. 45–6.
108. Murphy, *Diplomat among Warriors*, p. 428.
109. Finer, *Dulles over Suez*, p. 349.
110. Finer, *Dulles over Suez*, p. 353.
111. Dulles telephone conversation, 29 October 1956; Bohlen, *Witness to History*, p. 413.
112. Dulles telephone conversation, 29 October 1956.

113. Dulles telephone conversation with Shanley, 29 October 1956; New York Times, 1 November 1956.
114. Corson also alleges that the CIA had infiltrated Red Sox/Red Cap groups into Hungary, Czechoslovakia, and Romania to foment revolt (*Rise of the American Intelligence Empire*, p. 369).
115. Colby, *Honorable Men*, pp. 134–5; cf. E.H. Cookridge, *Gehlen: Spy of the Century* (New York: Random House, 1972), pp. 304–5.
116. Colby, *Honorable Men*, p. 135.
117. Colby, *Honorable Men*, p. 135; Powers, *Man Who Kept the Secrets*, pp. 74–5; Ranelagh, *The Agency*, p. 307.
118. Meyer, *Facing Reality*, pp. 128–30.
119. Holt, *Radio Free Europe*, p.194.
120. Allan A. Michie, *Voices through the Iron Curtain: The Radio Free Europe Story* (New York: Dodd, Mead, 1963), pp. 265–6; United Nations, *Report of the Special Committee on the Problem of Hungary* (New York, 1957), p. 18.
121. Dulles telephone conversations with Allen Dulles, 29 October 1956, and with Eisenhower, 30 October 1956.
122. Eisenhower, *Waging Peace*, p. 59; Hughes, *Ordeal of Power*, p. 220.
123. *Documents on American Foreign Relations, 1956*, p. 50.
124. McCauley in Kiraly, *First War*, p. 304.
125. Eisenhower, *Waging Peace*, p. 82.
126. Ranelagh, *The Agency*, pp. 305–6; Murphy, *Diplomat among Warriors*, p. 430.
127. Ranelagh, *The Agency*, p. 306.
128. Eisenhower, *Waging Peace*, p. 88.
129. Roscoe Drummond and Gaston Coblentz, *Duel at the Brink* (London: Doubleday, 1961), pp. 176–7.
130. NSC 5616, U.S. Policy toward Developments in Poland and Hungary, 31 October 1956.
131. McCauley in Kiraly, *First War*, pp. 304–5.
132. Bohlen, *Witness to History*, p. 417.
133. McCauley in Kiraly, *First War*, p. 306; Edmond Taylor, "The Lessons of Hungary," *The Reporter*, 27 December 1956, pp. 18, 21.
134. Dulles telephone conversation, 2 November 1956; McCauley in Kiraly, *First War*, pp. 307–8.
135. Message from Budapest, 4 November 1956, White House Office, Office of the Staff Secretary: Records, 1953–61, Dwight D. Eisenhower Library, Abilene, Kansas.
136. United States Information Agency, *Hungary: American Statements and Actions* (London, n.d.), pp. 32, 34; Hughes, *Ordeal of Power*, p. 223; Eisenhower, *Waging Peace*, p. 95; Philip Deane in *The Scotsman*, 7 November 1956.
137. Dulles telephone conversation, October 29, 1956.

138. Joseph P. Lash, *Dag Hammarskjold* (London: Cassell, 1962), p. 93. For a detailed analysis of action and inaction at the UN, see Gordon Gaskill, "Timetable of a Failure," *The Virginia Quarterly Review,* Vol. 34, No. 2 (Spring 1958), pp. 162–90.
139. Dulles telephone conversation, 2 November 1956.
140. Eisenhower, *Waging Peace,* p. 89.
141. United Nations, Security Council, *Official Records,* 753rd meeting (November 3, 1956), p. 17.
142. See note 122.
143. U.S. Congress, House, Committee on Foreign Affairs, *Report of the Special Study Mission to Europe on Policy toward the Satellite Nations,* 85th Cong., 1sst. sess., 4 June 1957, pp. 4, 7.

Chapter 3

1. U.S. Congress, House, *Report of the Special Study Mission,* pp. 6–7, 14–16.
2. Edward Weintal and Charles Bartlett, *Facing the Brink* (New York: Scribner's, 1967), pp. 210–11.
3. William R. Corson, *The Armies of Ignorance: The Rise of the American Intelligence Empire* (New York: Dial Press/James Wade, 1977), pp. 370–72.
4. NSC 5707/8, "Basic National Security Policy," June 3, 1957.
5. White House Leadership Meeting, January 1, 1957, "General Presentation to Congressional Leaders," Dulles Papers, Princeton University; Council on Foreign Relations, *Documents on American Foreign Relations, 1957* (New York: Harper, 1958), p. 41.
6. *New York Times,* May 11, 1957.
7. Department of State *Bulletin,* January 27, 1958, pp. 122–27; Arnold Wolfers, ed., *Alliance Policy in the Cold War* (Baltimore: The Johns Hopkins University, Press, 1959), pp. 156–57.
8. Z. A. Kruszewski, "The Polish-American Congress, East-West Issues, and the Formulation of American Foreign Policy," in Mohammad E. Ahrari, ed., *Ethnic Groups in U.S. Foreign Policy* (Westport, Conn.: Greenwood Press, 1987), pp. 91–92.
9. *New York Times,* June 18, 1958.
10. "Report on the Changing Situation in Hungary," *Congressional Record,* 88th Congress, 1st sess., May 15, 1963, p. 8646.
11. Assembly of Captive European Nations, *Resolutions,Reports, Organization,* 9th sess., New York, 1962–63, p. 116.
12. Walter A. Laqueur, *World of Secrets: The Other Uses and Limits of Intelligence* (New York: Basic Books, 1985), p. 130.
13. Zbigniew Brzezinski and William E. Griffith, "Peaceful Engagement in Eastern Europe," *Foreign Affairs,* 39, no. 4 (Spring 1961): 642–54.

14. John Lewis Gaddis, *Strategies of Containment: A Critical Appraisal of Postwar American National Security Policy* (New York Oxford University Press, 1982), p. 209.
15. *New York Times,* January 31, 1961.
16. *New York Times,* October 15, 1962.
17. Department of State *Bulletin,* October 28, 1963, pp. 656–57.
18. Joseph F. Harrington, "Romanian-American Relations during the Kennedy Administration," *East European Quarterly,* 18, no. 2 (June 1984): 224–25.
19. See Harrington, "Romanian-American Relations during the Kennedy Administration," and Joseph F. Harrington and Bruce Courtney, "Romanian-American Relations during the Johnson Administration," *East European Quarterly,* 22, no. 2 (June 1988): 213–29.
20. Department of State *Bulletin,* March 16, 1964, pp. 390–6.
21. Department of State *Bulletin,* June 15, 1964, p. 923.
22. Zbigniew Brzezinski, *Power and Principle: Memoirs of the National Security Adviser, 1977–1981* (New York: Farrar, Straus & Giroux, 1983), p. 76.
23. Department of State *Bulletin,* March 13, 1967, pp. 418–19.
24. Zbigniew Brzezinski, "The Framework of East-West Reconciliation," *Foreign Affairs,* 46, no. 2 (January 1968):, 256–75.
25. Department of State *Bulletin,* October 2, 1967, p. 434.
26. Honore M. Catudal, *Kennedy and the Berlin Wall Crisis: A Case Study in U.S. Decision Making* (Berlin: Berlin Verlag, 1980), p. 175.
27. Catudal, *Kennedy and the Berlin Wall Crisis,* pp. 217–18.
28. *Neues Deutschland* (East Berlin), June 16, 1961.
29. Catudal, *Kennedy and the Berlin Wall Crisis,* pp. 242, 249–50.
30. Robin A. Remington, *Winter in Prague* (Cambridge, Mass.: MIT Press, 1969), p. 225.
31. Zdenek Mlynar, *Night Frost in Prague: The End of Humane Socialism* (London: Hurst, 1980), p. 157.
32. *New York Times,* September 21, 1968; see Viktor Suvorov, *The Liberators* (London: Hamish Hamilton, 1981), pp. 153–57.
33. Thomas M. Cynkin, *Soviet and American Signalling in the Polish Crisis* (London: Macmillan, 1988), pp. 17ff.
34. *New York Times,* May 2, 1968.
35. Department of State *Bulletin,* June 10, 1968, p. 741.
36. *New York Times,* July, 20, 23 1968.
37. Cynkin, *Soviet and American Signalling,* p. 32.
38. John C. Campbell, "Czechoslovakia: American Choices, Past and Future," *Canadian Slavonic Papers,* 11, no. 1 (1969): pp. 13–14.
39. Lyndon Baines Johnson, *The Vantage Point: Perspectives of the Presidency, 1963–1969* (New York: Holt, Rinehart & Winston, 1971), p. 486.
40. E. H. Cookridge, *Gehlen: Spy of the Century* (New York: Random House, 1972), p. 361; Laqueur, *World of Secrets,* pp. 134, 357 note 61.
41. Johnson, *Vantage Point,* 487–88.

42. Laqueur, *World of Secrets*, p. 134. See also Karen Dawisha, *The Kremlin and the Prague Spring* (Berkeley: University of California Press, 1984), and Jiri Valenta, *Soviet Intervention in Czechoslovakia, 1968: Anatomy of a Decision* (Baltimore: Johns Hopkins University Press, 1979).
43. Brzezinski, *Power and Principle*, p. 465. See also the views of the Polish Colonel Ryszard J. Kuklinski in *Orbis*, Winter 1988, pp. 6, 8.
44. Department of State *Bulletin*, 23 September 1968; "The Imperial Relationship: A Conversation with Zbigniew Brzezinski," *Freedom at Issue*, no. 98 (September-October 1987): 21.
45. *New York Times*, September 18, 1968.
46. Department of State *Bulletin*, October 7, 1968, pp. 350–51.
47. *New York Times*, August 22, 1968.
48. Josef Korbel, *Detente in Europe: Real or Imaginary?* (Princeton, N. J.: Princeton University Press, 1972), p. 91; *Pravda*, September 26, November 13, 1968.
49. Henry A. Kissinger, *American Foreign Policy*, 3d. ed., (New York: Norton, 1977), pp. 76–77.
50. Brzezinski, *Power and Principle*, p. 150.
51. "U.S. Foreign Policy for the 1970s: A New Strategy for Peace," a report to the Congress by Richard Nixon, president of the United States, Washington, D.C., February 18, 1970, pp. 138–39.
52. "U.S. Foreign Policy for the 1970s: The Emerging Structure of Peace," a report to the Congress by Richard Nixon, president of the United States, Washington, D.C., February 9, 1972, pp. 49–51.
53. Statement delivered to the Senate Foreign Relations Committee, September 19, 1974; see Kissinger, *American Foreign Policy*, pp. 171–72.
54. *New York Times*, October 13, 1974.
55. Henry Kissinger, *White House Years* (Boston: Little, Brown, 1979), p. 1265.
56. Raymond L. Garthoff, "Eastern Europe in the Context of U.S.-Soviet Relations," in Sarah Meiklejohn Terry, ed., *Soviet Policy in Eastern Europe* (New Haven: Yale University Press, 1984), p. 322.
57. Department of State *Bulletin*, April 30, 1973, pp. 533–38.
58. Department of State *Bulletin*, August 25, 1969, p. 169. See also Rowland Evans, Jr., and Robert D. Novak, *Nixon in the White House: The Frustration of Power* (New York: Random House, 1971), pp. 98–100, and Raymond L. Garthoff, *Detente and Confrontation: American-Soviet Relations from Nixon to Reagan* (Washington, D.C.: Brookings Institution, 1985), p. 73.
59. Garthoff, *Detente and Confrontation*, pp. 218–19, 221, 227–28.
60. See Kissinger, *White House Years*, pp. 408–12, 529–34, and Henry Kissinger, *Years of Upheaval* (Boston: Little, Brown, 1982), pp. 143–48, 154–59.
61. See Ernest D. Plock, *The Basic Treaty and the Evolution of East-West German Relations* (Boulder, Colo.: Westview Press, 1986), pp. 68–79.
62. On the background of the European security conference, see Bennett Kovrig,

"European Security in East-West Relations: History of a Diplomatic Encounter," in Robert Spencer, ed., *Canada and the Conference on Security and Co-operation in Europe* (Toronto: Center for International Studies, 1984), pp. 3–19.

63. Department of State *Bulletin*, 26 June 1972, pp. 898–99.
64. Helmut Sonnenfeldt, quoted in *Time*, August 4, 1975, p. 22.
65. *Time*, December 16, 1974, p. 58.
66. *New York Times*, April 6, 1976; Rowland Evans and Robert Novak column in *Washington Post*, March 22, 1976; U.S. Congress, House, Subcommittee on International Security and Scientific Affairs of the House Committee on International Relations, *United States National Security Policy Vis-a-Vis Eastern Europe (The "Sonnenfeldt Doctrine")*, 94th Cong., 2d sess., 1976, p. 2.
67. *New York Times*, June 26, 1976.
68. *New York Times*, October 7, 1976; and see William G. Hyland, *Mortal Rivals: Superpower Relations from Nixon to Reagan* (New York: Random House, 1987), pp. 177–79.
69. *Time*, October 25, 1976, pp. 10–11.
70. *New York Times*, October 17, 1976.
71. Brzezinski, *Power and Principle*, pp. 149–50.
72. Presidential Directive 21 was signed by Carter on September 13, 1977. See Brzezinski, *Power and Principle*, pp. 53, 296–97, and *Time*, June 12, 1978, p. 19.
73. Brzezinski, *Power and Principle*, pp. 297, 300, 53; *New York Times*, May 11, 1977.
74. U.S. Congress, House, Committee on International Relations, Subcommittee on Europe and the Middle East, *Hearings on U.S. Policy toward Eastern Europe*, 95th Cong., 2d sess., September 7 and 12, 1978, pp. 41–46; U.S. Congress, House, Committee on International Relations, Subcommittee on Europe and the Middle East, *Hearings*, 96th Cong., 1st sess., July 12, 1979, p. 12.
75. *Time*, June 12, 1978, p. 19.
76. *Los Angeles Times*, October 14, 1987. See also Vladimir Socor, "The Limits of National Independence in the Soviet Bloc: Rumania's Foreign Policy Reconsidered," *Orbis*, Fall 1976, pp. 707–32; and Ion Mihai Pacepa, *Red Horizons* (Washington, D.C.: Regnery Gateway, 1987).
77. Brzezinski, *Power and Principle*, p. 299. See also U.S. Congress, House of Representatives, Committee on International Relations, Subcommittee on Europe and the Middle East, *The Holy Crown of St Stephen and United States-Hungarian Relations*, hearings, 95th Cong., 1st sess., November 9, 1977.
78. See Laurence Silberman, "Yugoslavia's 'Old' Communism," *Foreign Policy*, (Spring 1977): 3–27.
79. See U.S. Congress, *Hearings on U.S. Policy toward Eastern Europe*, pp. 47–49, 55.

80. Department of State, "U.S. Policy and Eastern Europe," *Current Policy* 139, Washington, D.C., 1980, p. 4.
81. Brzezinski, *Power and Principle*, pp. 297–99. The State Department had counseled against a meeting with Cardinal Wyszynski for fear of provoking the government, but Brzezinski and Rosalynn Carter nevertheless paid him an unannounced visit carrying a message of good wishes from the president.
82. Brzezinski, *Power and Principle*, p. 464.
83. *New York Times*, August 23, 1980.
84. Brzezinski, *Power and Principle*, p. 464.
85. Kuklinski in *Orbis*, Winter 1988, pp. 14–15.
86. Zbigniew Brzezinski, "White House Diary, 1980," *Orbis*, Winter 1988, pp. 35–37; *Pravda*, December 4, 1980; *New York Times*, December 5, 1980.
87. *New York Times*, November 29, December 4, 1980.
88. *Pravda*, December 6, 1980.
89. Brzezinski, "White House Diary," pp. 38, 41; Kuklinski in *Orbis*, Winter 1988, p. 16.
90. Kuklinski in *Orbis*, Winter 1988, pp. 16–17; Brzezinski, "White House Diary," pp. 41–44.
91. Brzezinski, "White House Diary," pp. 44–45.
92. *Ibid.*
93. *New York Times*, December 3, 1980.
94. Cynkin, *Soviet and American Signalling*, pp. 74–75; *New York Times*, December 13, 1980.
95. Brzezinski, "White House Diary," pp. 47–48; *Pravda*, December 14, 1980.
96. Brzezinski, *Power and Principle*, p. 528; see also Kuklinski in *Orbis*, Winter 1988, p. 18.
97. *New York Times*, January 17, 1981.
98. See Lincoln Gordon, "Interests and Policies in Eastern Europe: The View from Washington," in Gordon et al., *Eroding Empire: Western Relations with Eastern Europe* (Washington, D.C.: Brookings Institution, 1987), pp. 121–22.
99. Department of State *Bulletin*, February 1981, p. "H"; Alexander Haig, *Caveat: Realism, Reagan, and Foreign Policy* (New York: Macmillan, 1984), p. 239.
100. *Pravda*, March 5, 1981.
101. *Pravda*, April 26, 1981.
102. Kuklinski in *Orbis*, Winter 1988, pp. 20–24.
103. Haig, *Caveat*, pp. 241, 247.
104. *New York Times*, February, 2, 11, 12, 1981.
105. *New York Times*, April 5, 6, 1981.
106. *New York Times*, April 9, May, 6, 1981.
107. *New York Times*, March 27, 1981.
108. *Pravda*, June 12, 1981.

109. *New York Times,* June 13, 17 1981.
110. *New York Times,* September 19, 1981.
111. *Pravda,* September 20, 1981.
112. Department of State *Bulletin,* November 1981, pp. 19, 52.
113. *New York Times,* October 25, 1981.
114. Kuklinski in *Orbis,* Winter 1988, p. 25.
115. *New York Times,* December 7, 1981.
116. Gordon et al., *Eroding Empire,* pp. 124–25; Cynkin, *Soviet and American Signalling,* pp. 201, 250 note 8.
117. *New York Times,* December 14, 1981.
118. See Gordon et al., *Eroding Empire,* p. 125 note 72, and *Newsweek,* October 10, 1983, p. 43.
119. Department of State *Bulletin,* January 1982, p. 42.
120. Bob Woodward, *Veil: The Secret Wars of the CIA, 1981–1987* (New York: Simon and Schuster, 1987), pp. 177–78.
121. See "The Imperial Relationship: A Conversation with Zbigniew Brzezinski," pp. 21–22.
122. Haig, *Caveat,* p. 250.
123. Department of State, "American Foreign Policy: Current Documents, 1981," Washington, D.C., pp. 623–24.
124. Department of State *Bulletin,* September 1982, p. 31.
125. Michael Mandelbaum, "The United States and Eastern Europe: A Window of Opportunity," p. 384, and Dominique Moisi, "French Policy toward Central and Eastern Europe," p. 361, in William F. Griffith, ed., *Central and Eastern Europe: The Opening Curtain?* (Boulder, Colo.: Westview Press, 1989).
126. Woodward, *Veil,* p. 375.
127. See Charles Gati, "Polish Futures, Western Options," *Foreign Affairs,* 61, no. 2 (Winter 1982–83): 305.
128. Garthoff, "Eastern Europe in the Context of U.S. Soviet Relations," p. 338.
129. David B. Funderburk, *Pinstripes and Reds* (Washington, D.C.: Selous Foundation Press, 1987), pp. 33–34, 52–54.
130. *New York Times,* June 9, 1982.
131. Department of State *Bulletin,* April 1985, p. 46.
132. *Ibid.,* November 1983, pp. 19–22.
133. Mikhail Gorbachev, *Perestroika: New Thinking for Our Country and the World* (New York: Perennial Library/Harper & Row, 1987), p. 151.
134. For instance, Gennady Gerasimov, quoted by Reuter, September 4, 1987. See also Karen Dawisha, *Eastern Europe, Gorbachev, and Reform: The Great Challenge* (Cambridge: Cambridge University Press, 1988), chapter 7.
135. "East-West Relations and Eastern Europe (An American-Soviet Dialogue)," *Problems of Communism,* 37, no. 3–4 (May-August 1988): 55–70; *Los Angeles Times,* July 10, 1988; Gorbachev, *Perestroika,* p. 149.
136. *Der Spiegel,* 1988, pp. 119–20; Charles Gati, "Eastern Europe on Its Own," *Foreign Affairs,* 68, no. 1 (Fall 1989): 106.

137. *New York Times,* November 23, 1987.
138. *The Independent* (London), February 4, 1988.
139. *New York Times,* June 13, 1987; Department of State *Bulletin,* October 1987, pp. 36–37; *New York Times,* August 27, 29, 1987.
140. White House, "National Security Strategy of the United States," Washington, D.C., January 1988), p. 27.
141. Department of State *Bulletin,* April 1988, pp. 66–68.
142. *New York Times,* February 28, 1988.
143. Department of State *Bulletin,* May 1988, p. 54.
144. *Washington Post,* May 11, 1988.
145. *New York Times,* June 9, 1988.
146. United States Information Service, July 28, 1988.
147. Kruszewski, "Polish-American Congress," pp. 93–94.
148. *Washington Post,* October 7, 1987.
149. Warsaw television, September 28, 1987.
150. *New York Times* and *Washington Post,* September 28, 1987.
151. RFE/RL Central News, October 8, 1987.
152. Reuter, May 5, 1988; *New York Times,* May 8, 1988.
153. Reuter, July 28, 1988.
154. USIS (Ottawa), "U.S.-Soviet Relations: A New Policy for the 1990s," May 12, 1989.
155. USIS, May 31, 1989.
156. *New York Times,* April 18, 1989.
157. *Financial Times* (London), April 25, 1989.
158. *New York Times,* July 6, 7, 1989.
159. *New York Times,* July 14, August 26, 1989.
160. *New York Times,* July 10, 1989.
161. *New York Times,* July 11, 1989.
162. USIS, January 18, 1990.
163. Reuter, December 26, 1989.
164. *Globe and Mail* (Toronto), November 23, 1989.

Chapter 4

1. See Clifford Orwin and Thomas Pangle, "The Philosophical Foundation of Human Rights," in Marc F. Plattner, ed., *Human Rights in Our Time* (Boulder, Colo.: Westview Press, 1984), pp. 1–22.
2. See Roger Pilon, "The Idea of Human Rights," *The National Interest,* no. 5 (Fall 1986): 99–101.
3. See Maurice Cranston, *What Are Human Rights?* (New York: Taplinger, 1973).
4. U.S. Congress, Commission on Security and Cooperation in Europe (hereafter cited as Helsinki Commission), *Hearings on Implementation of the Helsinki Accords, The International Covenants on Human Rights: Pros-*

pects on U.S. Ratification, 100th Cong., 2d sess., March 29, 1988, p. 12; see also Schifter's statement at the Ottawa CSCE meeting, June 4, 1985, in Vojtech Mastny, *Helsinki, Human Rights, and European Security: Analysis and Documentation* (Durham, N.C.: Duke University Press, 1986), pp. 287–89.

5. Geir Lundestad, *The American Non-policy towards Eastern Europe, 1943–1947* (New York: Humanities Press, 1975), p. 342.
6. Department of State *Bulletin*, June 12, 1949, pp. 756–58.
7. *New York Times*, February 25, 1950.
8. *New York Times*, January 10, 1952.
9. John Foster Dulles, "A Policy of Boldness," *Life*, May 19, 1952, pp. 154, 157.
10. Council on Foreign Relations, *Documents on American Foreign Relations, 1956* (New York: Harper, 1957), pp. 57–58.
11. U.S. Congress, Senate, Joint Resolution 111, 86th Cong., 1st. sess.; Richard M. Nixon, *Six Crises* (Garden City, N.Y.: Doubleday, 1962), pp. 251–52.
12. See Zbigniew Brzezinski and William E. Griffith, "Peaceful Engagement in Eastern Europe," *Foreign Affairs* 39, no.4 (Spring 1961).
13. Department of State *Bulletin*, July 2, 1962, p. 25.
14. Edward Weintal and Charles Bartlett, *Facing the Brink* (New York: Scribner's, 1967) p. 164.
15. Department of State *Bulletin*, December 23, 1968, pp. 647–48.
16. Quoted in Joshua Muravchik, *The Uncertain Crusade: Jimmy Carter and the Dilemmas of Human Rights Policy* (Lanham, Md.: Hamilton Press, 1986), p. xviii.
17. See Henry Kissinger, *White House Years* (Boston: Little, Brown, 1979, pp. 412–16.
18. John J. Maresca, *To Helsinki: The Conference on Security and Cooperation in Europe, 1973–1975* (Durham, N.C.: Duke University Press, 1985), pp. ix, xi, xii.
19. Luigi Vittorio Ferraris, ed., *Report on a Negotiation: Helsinki-Geneva-Helsinki, 1972–1975* (Alphen: Sijthoff & Noordhoff, 1979), p. 16.
20. Maresca, *To Helsinki*, p. 36.
21. James Ring Adams, "From Helsinki to Madrid," in Plattner, *Human Rights in Our Time*, p. 107.
22. Ferraris, *Report on a Negotiation*, p. 135.
23. Maresca, *To Helsinki*, p. 52.
24. Ferraris, *Report on a Negotiation*, p. 300.
25. Ibid., p. 436.
26. Gerald R. Ford, *A Time to Heal* (New York: Berkeley Books, 1980), p. 287.
27. *New York Times*, October 7, 1976.
28. James F. Brown, quoted in Sig Mickelson, *America's Other Voice: The Story of Radio Free Europe and Radio Liberty* (New York: Praeger, 1983), p. 120.

29. Cord Meyer, *Facing Reality: From World Federalism to the CIA* (New York: Harper & Row, 1980), p. 133.
30. Mickelson, *America's Other Voice*, p. 156n1, 2.
31. Meyer, *Facing Reality*, p. 136.
32. Jan Sizoo and Rudolf Th. Jurrjens, *CSCE Decision-making: The Madrid Experience* (The Hague: Nijhoff, 1984), pp. 180–81.
33. An amendment to the Foreign Assistance Act of 1961, introduced in 1974 as a sense of Congress resolution and made binding in 1978 as Section 502, prohibited security assistance to governments that engage in a "consistent pattern of gross violations of internationally recognized human rights" unless the president certified extraordinary circumstances. The Harkin amendment (section 116 of the same act) prohibited economic assistance on the same grounds "unless such assistance will directly benefit needy people." Section 701 of the International Financial Assistance Act of 1977 advised the executive to steer multilateral banks away from granting assistance to human rights violators. See David P. Forsythe, "Congress and Human Rights in U.S. Foreign Policy: The Fate of General Legislation," *Human Rights Quarterly* 9, no. 3 (1987): 382–404; and for a listing of pertinent U.S. legislation, appendix D in David D. Newsom, ed., *The Diplomacy of Human Rights* (Lanham, Md.: University Press of America, 1986), pp. 223–35.
34. Mastny, *Helsinki, Human Rights, and European Security*, p. 115.
35. Ibid., pp. 116
36. Department of State *Bulletin*, June 1978, p. 1.
37. Muravchik, *Uncertain Crusade*, p. 14.
38. Brzezinski, *Power and Principle*, pp. 128, 149.
39. Brzezinski, *Power and Principle*, p. 156.
40. Muravchik, *Uncertain Crusade*, p. 57.
41. United States Information Service, April 30, 1977; Muravchik, *Uncertain Crusade*, p. 89.
42. Muravchik, *Uncertain Crusade*, p. 105.
43. Brzezinski, *Power and Principle*, p. 128.
44. Jeane Kirkpatrick, "Dictatorships and Double Standards," *Commentary*, Vol. 68, No. 5 (November 1979): 34–45.
45. Muravchik, *Uncertain Crusade*, p. 145.
46. Richard Schifter, "Human Rights and U.S. Foreign Policy," Department of State *Bulletin*, August 1987, p. 76.
47. For a list of human rights nongovernmental organizations, see appendix E in Newsom, *Diplomacy of Human Rights*, pp. 237–39.
48. Brzezinski, *Power and Principle*, p. 297.
49. *Helsinki, What Next?* (Berlin: Panorama DDR, 1977), pp. 21–24, 56–60.
50. *New York Times*, March 20, 1978.
51. Mastny, *Helsinki, Human Rights, and European Security*, pp. 185
52. *New York Times*, November 5, 1981.

53. Tamar Jacoby, "The Reagan Turnaround on Human Rights," *Foreign Affairs* 64, no. 5 (Summer 1986): 1075.
54. *New York Times,* June 1, 1986.
55. Lynne A. Davidson, "Romania, CSCE and the Most-Favored-Nation Process, 1982–84," in Newsom, *Diplomacy of Human Rights,* p. 190.
56. Forsythe, "Congress and Human Rights in U.S. Foreign Policy," pp. 401–2.
57. See Davidson, "Romania, CSCE and the Most-Favored-Nation Process," pp. 194–96.
58. Assistant Secretary J. Edward Fox protested in a letter to Congressman Dante Fascell, chairman of the Committee on Foreign Affairs, on April 8, 1987 that the Dornan resolution (H. Res. 56) conveyed the impression that "a serious human rights issue is being used by the United States to promote nationalistic and territorial concerns and that the United States wishes to redraw the borders of Eastern Europe."
59. Helsinki Commission, *Hearings,* May 5, 1987, pp. 5, 7.
60. David B. Funderburk, *Pinstripes and Reds* (Washinton, D.C.: Selous Foundation Press, 1987), pp. 79, 103, 34, 85–86, 189, 196.
61. Helsinki Commission, *Hearings,* June 25, 1985, p. 49.
62. RFE/RL Central News, September 9, 1987.
63. Ion Pacepa claims that Israel also paid ransom, but covertly (*New York Times,* October 14, 1987).
64. *Washington Post,* May 6, 1990.
65. Jacoby, "The Reagan Turnaround on Human Rights," p. 1083.
66. See, for instance, Helsinki Commission, *Fulfilling Our Promises: The United States and the Helsinki Final Act,* November 1979.
67. See H. Gordon Skilling, "CSCE in Madrid," *Problems of Communism,* 30, (July-August 1981) 6–7.
68. Max M. Kampelman, *Three Years at the East-West Divide* (New York: Freedom House, 1983), p. 8.
69. Ibid. p. 77.
70. Mastny, *Helsinki, Human Rights, and European Security,* p. 27.
71. Ibid. pp. 352–69. For the U.S. ambassador's assessment, see Kampelman, *Three Years at the East-West Divide,* pp. 113–21.
72. Helsinki Commission, *The Helsinki Process and East West Relations: Progress in Perspective,* March 1985.
73. Helsinki Commission, *Hearings,* October 3, 1985, p. 30.
74. Helsinki Commission, *The Helsinki Process,* pp. 113–20.
75. Helsinki Commission, *Hearings,* October 3, 1985, p. 76.
76. Public Law 99–79.
77. Mastny, *Helsinki, Human Rights, and European Security,* pp. 285, 290, 303.
78. Helsinki Commission, *Hearings,* June 25, 1985, pp. 179, 182.
79. Mastny, *Helsinki, Human Rights, and European Security,* p. 317.

80. Michael Novak, "Ordinary People," *The National Interest,* no. 5 (Fall 1986): p. 77.
81. Helsinki Commission, *Hearings,* March 18–June 18, 1986, p. 246.
82. *Moscow News,* June 5, 1988.
83. Helsinki Commission, *Hearings,* November 4, 1986, p. 19.
84. *New York Times,* January 5, 1989.
85. *Financial Times,* January 18, 1989.
86. Reuters, January 16, 1989.
87. *New York Times,* January 18, 1989.
88. *New York Times,* January 17, 1989.
89. Agerpres (Romania), December 31, 1988.
90. See Jonathan Eyal, "The London Information Forum and Future Trends in East European Attitudes toward International Radio Broadcasts," *Radio Free Europe Research,* Munich, June 27, 1989.
91. United States Information Service, December 21, 1989.
92. *Times Literary Supplement* (London), February 19–25, 1988, p. 199.
93. *Karima* (Budapest), November 26, 1987.
94. *Magyar Hirlap,* April 18, 1988.
95. *The Economist,* August 30, 1986.
96. *Wall Street Journal,* June 8, 1989.
97. *RFE/RL Daily Report,* May 6, 1989.
98. *Nepszabadsag,* March 10, 1989.
99. *RFE/RL Daily Report,* May 8, 1989.
100. Timothy Garton Ash, "Refolution [sic] in Hungary and Poland," *The New York Review,* August 17, 1989, p. 10.
101. *Magyar Nemzet,* June 7, 1989.
102. *Washington Post,* August 17, 1989.
103. *Financial Times,* March 30, 1989; *Nepszabadsag,* March 10, 1989.
104. *Gazeta Wyborcza,* June 1, 1989.
105. *RFE/RL Daily Report,* September 14, 1989.
106. *The Economist,* January 27, 1990, p. 48.
107. *Neues Deutschland,* June 15, 1988.
108. *New York Times,* February 18, 1989.
109. *Financial Times,* January 19, 1989.
110. Reuter, September 7, 1987.
111. Reuter, June 26, 1988.
112. *Toronto Star,* December 10, 1989.
113. Reuter, January 30, 1990.
114. Associated Press, February 24, 1988.
115. *Globe and Mail* (Toronto), January 24, 1990.
116. Radio Bucharest, November 28, 1988.
117. *Nepszabadsag,* March 15, 1989.
118. *The New York Review,* April 27, 1989, p. 9.
119. Associated Press, January 19, 1990.
120. Reuter, November 24, 1989.

121. National Endowment for Democracy, Annual Report, 1988.
122. USIS, November 16, 1989.
123. *New York Times,* May 13, 1990.
124. *RFE/RL Daily Report,* February 7, 1990.

Chapter 5

1. Philip Hanson, *Western Economic Statecraft in East-West Relations* (London: Royal Institute of International Affairs/Routledge & Kegan Paul, 1988), p. 3.
2. Department of State, Office of Intelligence Research, "East-West Trade Continues to Decline," October 21, 1952.
3. U.S. Department of State, *Foreign Relations of the United States: Diplomatic Papers,* 1949, Vol. 5 (Washington, D.C.) p. 363.
4. Department of State, Office of Intelligence Research, "Prospects for Encouraging Defection of Eastern European Orbit Countries by Economic Means," July 28, 1950.
5. Department of State, Office of Intelligence Research, "Vulnerability of the Soviet Bloc to Existing and Tightened Western Economic Controls," January 26, 1951.
6. NSC 91/1, "East-West Trade," November 17, 1950.
7. Richard J. Ellings, *Embargoes and World Power: Lessons for American Foreign Policy* (Boulder, Colo.: Westview Press, 1985), p. 81.
8. Ibid., pp. 87–89.
9. Public Law 91–184, section 23.
10. Department of Defense, Office of the Director of Defense Research and Engineering, "An Analysis of Export Control of U.S. Technology—A DOD Perspective," February 2, 1976; see also J.F. Bucy, "Technology Transfer and East-West Trade," *International Security 5,* no. 3 (Winter 1980/81): 132ff.
11. Public Law 96–72.
12. Gordon B. Smith, ed., *The Politics of East-West Trade* (Boulder, Colo.: Westview Press, 1984), p. 10.
13. *Fortune,* May 30, 1983, p. 112.
14. Hans Jacobsen, "U.S. Export Control and Export Administration Legislation," in Reinhard Rode and Hans Jacobsen, eds., *Economic Warfare or Detente: An Assessment of East-West Relations in the 1980s* (Boulder, Colo.: Westview Press, 1985), p. 223n17.
15. Ibid., pp. 217–18.
16. National Academy of Sciences/National Academy of Engineering/Institute of Medicine, Committee on Science, Engineering, and Public Policy, Panel on the Impact of National Security Controls on International Technology, *Balancing the National Interest: U.S. National Security Controls and Global*

Economic Competition (Washington, D.C.:National Academy Press, 1987), pp. 177, 264–75 (hereafter cited as the Allen Report).

17. Allen Report, pp. 168–73.
18. North Atlantic Assembly, Sub-Committee on Advanced Technology and Technology Transfer, Draft interim report, September 1987, p. 15.
19. *Financial Times*, August 17, 1987; *Wall Street Journal*, September 28, 1987.
20. *Wall Street Journal*, January 22, 1988.
21. Reuter, January 29, 1988.
22. *Wall Street Journal*, February 23, 1988. See also Linda Melvern, Nick Anning, and David Hebditch,*Techno-Bandits: How the Soviets Are Stealing America's High-Tech Future* (Boston: Houghton Mifflin, 1984).
23. *The Sunday Times* (London), January 24, 1988.
24. Reuter, September 22, 1987; North Atlantic Assembly, Draft interim report, pp. 6–9.
25. Associated Press, October 20, 1987; North Atlantic Assembly, Draft interim report, p. 5; Associated Press, November 4, 1987; *Washington Times*, October 21, 1987.
26. Reuter, September 22, 1987.
27. North Atlantic Assembly, Draft interim report, p. 9.
28. *Washington Post*, February 28, 1988.
29. *New York Times*, July 20, 1989.
30. Reuter, June 8, 1990.
31. Thane Gustafson, quoted in Hanson, *Western Economic Statecraft*, p. 30.
32. Department of Defense, *Soviet Military Power: An Assessment of the Threat, 1988* (Washington, D.C., GPO, 1988), p. 149.
33. Peter Wiles, quoted in Hanson, *Western Economic Statecraft*, p. 9.
34. NSC progress reports on the implementation of NSC 18/2 (Economic Relations between the United States and Yugoslavia) and NSC 18/4 (United States Policy toward the Conflict between the USSR and Yugoslavia), April 11, 1949, August 19, 1949, February 1, 1950, October 16, 1950.
35. Stephen C. Markovich, "American Foreign Aid and Yugoslav Foreign Policy," in Peter J. Potichnyj and Jane P. Shapiro, eds., *From Cold War to Detente* (New York: Praeger, 1976), pp. 79–80, 82–85.
36. Department of State *Bulletin*, October 29, 1956, pp. 664–65.
37. NSC Action Memorandums 132 and 212, January 15, and December 14, 1962.
38. Council on Foreign Relations, *Documents on American Foreign Relations 1956* (New York: Harper, 1957), pp. 45–46.
39. Joseph F. Harrington, "Romanian-American Relations during the Kennedy Administration," *East European Quarterly* 18, no. 2, June 1984: pp. 224–25.
40. Department of State *Bulletin*, February 23, 1963, pp. 303–5.
41. Department of State *Bulletin*, June 15, 1964, p. 923; *New York Times*, January 5, 1965.

42. Department of State, *Report to the President of the Special Committee on U.S. Trade Relations with East European Countries and the Soviet Union,* presented at the White House on April 29, 1965 (Washington, D.C., 1966).
43. Department of State *Bulletin,* May 30, 1966, pp. 839–40, 843–44.
44. Department of State *Bulletin,* March 25, 1968, p. 422.
45. Department of State *Bulletin,* September 9, 1968, p. 262.
46. Samuel Pisar, *Coexistence and Commerce: Guidelines for Transactions between East and West* (New York: McGraw-Hill, 1970), p. 70.
47. Henry Kissinger, *White House Years* (Boston: Little, Brown, 1979), p. 154.
48. *New York Times,* October 13, 1974.
49. Department of State *Bulletin,* April 30, 1973, pp. 533–8.
50. United States Information Service, April 10, 1975.
51. Ellings, *Embargoes and World Power,* p. 93.
52. See Reinhard Rode, "The United States," in Rode and Jacobsen, *Economic Warfare or Detente,* pp. 189–90.
53. See Ion Mihai Pacepa, "The Defector's Story," *The Washingtonian,* December 1985, pp. 171–82, and David B. Funderburk, *Pinstripes and Reds* (Washington, D.C.: Selous Foundation Press, 1987), pp. 34, 161–62.
54. Wlodzimierz Siwinski, "Why Poland Lost its Creditworthiness," in Paul Marer and Wlodzimierz Siwinski, eds., *Creditworthiness and Reform in Poland: Western and Polish Perspectives* (Bloomington: Indiana University Press, 1988), p. 25.
55. Siwinski, "Why Poland Lost its Creditworthiness," p. 26.
56. Ibid., pp. 27–28.
57. Gabriel Eichler, "A Banker's Perspective on Poland's Debt Problem," in Marer and Siwinski, *Creditworthiness and Reform in Poland,* p. 202.
58. Jerry F. Hough, *The Polish Crisis: American Policy Options* (Washington, D.C.: Brookings Institution, 1982), p. 11.
59. Hough, *The Polish Crisis,* p. 16.
60. Zbigniew Brzezinski, "U.S. Policy toward Poland in a Global Perspective," in Marer and Siwinski, *Creditworthiness and Reform in Poland,* p. 321.
61. Richard Portes, "East Europe's Debt to the West: Interdependence is a Two-Way Street," *Foreign Affairs* 55, no. 4 (July 1977): 768.
62. Stansfield Turner, *Secrecy and Democracy: The CIA in Transition* (Boston: Houghton Mifflin, 1985), p. 119.
63. *Financial Times,* August 13, 1980.
64. Alexander Haig, *Caveat: Realism, Reagan, and Foreign Policy* (New York: Macmillan, 1984), pp. 81, 111.
65. See Thomas M. Cynkin, *Soviet and American Signalling in the Polish Crisis* (London: Macmillan, 1988), pp. 218–23.
66. *New York Times,* April 26, 1981.
67. See Gary C. Hufbauer and Jeffrey J. Schott, *Economic Sanctions Reconsidered: History and Current Policy* (Washington, D.C.: Institute for International Economics, 1985), pp. 655–66, 683–712.

68. Lincoln Gordon, *Eroding Empire: Western Relations with Eastern Europe* (Washington, D.C.: Brookings Institution, 1987), pp. 97–98.

69. See *Wall Street Journal,* February 26, 1982.

70. *New York Times,* October 10, 1986.

71. Janos Kornai, *A hiany* (Budapest: Kozgazdasagi es jogi, 1982).

72. Associated Press, November 4, 1988.

73. *The Economist,* April 23, 1988, p. 79.

74. For a superb analysis of the economic and other aspects of Hungary's peripheral status, see Andrew C. Janos, *The Politics of Backwardness in Hungary, 1825–1945* (Princeton N.J.: Princeton University Press, 1982).

75. Jan Winiecki, *The Distorted World of Soviet-Type Economies* (Pittsburgh: University of Pittsburgh Press, 1988), p. 205; see also Neven Sesardic and Domenico Settembrini, *Marxian Utopia?* (London: Centre for Research into Communist Economies, 1985).

76. Reuter, October 6, 1988.

77. *Globe and Mail* (Toronto), November 18, 1989.

78. *New York Times,* November 19, 1989.

79. *Die Welt,* April 24, 1989.

80. Reuter, August 26, 1989.

81. *New York Times,* December 12, 1989. A Polish economist argued that the only solution was to buy out the top layer of the Communist-appointed bureaucracy (Jan Winiecki, *Gorbachev's Way Out?* [London: Centre for Research into Communist Economies, 1988]).

82. See *The Costs and Benefits of the Soviet Empire, 1981–83* (Santa Monica, Calif.: Rand Corporation, August 1986).

83. *Globe and Mail* (Toronto), February 19, 1990.

84. *Washington Post,* February 28, 1988.

85. Vlad Sobell, "The Reshaping of the CMEA's Scientific Program," *RFE Research,* (Munich) August 23, 1988.

86. Associated Press, January 6, 1990.

87. *Financial Times,* March 12, 1990.

88. See *The Economist,* December 16, 1989, pp. 68–69.

89. *Globe and Mail* (Toronto), January 10, 1990.

90. *New York Times,* December 20, 1987.

91. *Financial Times,* November 11, 1987.

92. Associated Press, March 23, 1988.

93. Austrian Institute for Economic Research report, cited by Reuter, March 16, 1988.

94. Organization for Economic Cooperation and Development, *Financial Market Trends,* Paris, February 1989.

95. See *PlanEcon Report,* 4, nos. 12–13 (March 30, 1988).

96. *Financial Times,* August 6, 1988.

97. *Financial Times,* August 3, 1988.

98. *The Economist,* March 10, 1990, p. 116.

99. *International Herald Tribune,* March 4, 1988.

100. *Wall Street Journal,* February 17, 1988.
101. Valerie J. Assetto, *The Soviet Bloc in the IMF and the IBRD* (Boulder, Colo.: Westview Press, 1988), pp. 43–45, 50.
102. Ibid., p. 191.
103. Ibid., pp. 139–59.
104. Ibid., p. 32.
105. See Paul Marer, "Centrally Planned Economies in the IMF, the World Bank, and the GATT," in Joseph C. Brada, Ed A. Hewitt, and Thomas A. Wolf, eds., *Economic Adjustment and Reform in Eastern Europe and the Soviet Union* (Durham N.C.: Duke University Press, 1988), pp, 242–45.
106. See Robert M. Cutler, "Harmonizing EEC-CMEA Relations: Never the Twain Shall Meet?" *International Affairs* 63, no. 2 (Spring 1987): 259–70.
107. Reuter, June 24, 1988.
108. United States Information Service, October 29, 1987.
109. *Washington Times,* July 21, 1988.
110. Paul Marer and Eugeniusz Tabaczynski, *Polish-U.S. Industrial Cooperation in the 1980s* (Bloomington: Indiana University Press, 1981), pp. 21–22.
111. Radio Budapest, April 9, 1988.
112. See Klaus Bolz, "Industrial Cooperation," in Rode and Jacobsen, *Economic Warfare of Detente,* pp. 63–71.
113. See *The Economist,* March 10, 1990, p. 71.
114. *Business Week,* November 17, 1989, p. 61.
115. Associated Press, July 21, 1988.
116. Associated Press, May 22, 1988; RFE/RL Central News, June 16, 1988.
117. *Financial Times* "East European Markets" (special section), October 2, 1987.
118. RFE/RL Central News, June 11, 1988.
119. United States Information Service, June 16, 1988.
120. United Press International, February 13, 1988.
121. *Financial Times,* June 20, 1988; *New York Times,* October 15, 1987.
122. *New York Times,* April 18, 1989.
123. Other proposals were OPIC guarantees to stimulate American investment in Poland; a program associating the Commerce Department, the Small Business Administration, and business organizations in the promotion of contacts with Poland's private sector; an administration initiative to explore new exchanges, training, and educational programs in support of the private sector; encouragement of debt-for-equity trades to alleviate Poland's commercial debt burden; favorable rescheduling arrangements of Poland's government debt through the Paris Club; support for new IMF and World Bank loans; and consideration of loans to the Polish private sector by the International Finance Corporation, a World Bank subsidiary that aids private enterprise in developing countries.
124. *The Independent* (London), May 31, 1989.

125. *RFE/RL Daily Report,* June 16, 1989.
126. *New York Times,* July 11, 1989.
127. *Globe and Mail* (Toronto), July 18, 1989.
128. *New York Times,* August 26, 1989.
129. *New York Times,* November 19, 1989.
130. Business Week/Harris poll conducted November 13–14, 1989, *Business Week,* November 27, 1989, p. 70.
131. *Toronto Star,* October 15, 1989.
132. *Globe and Mail* (Toronto), November 20, 1989.
133. Reuter, December 14, 1989.
134. Reuter, January 16, 1990.
135. *The Economist,* March 3, 1990, p. 66.
136. Associated Press, May 19, 1990.
137. Meinhard Miegel, director of the Institute for Economics and Social Policy, quoted in the *New York Times,* July 2, 1990.
138. *The Economist,* September 22, 1990, p.73.

Chapter 6

1. See Joseph C. Douglass, *Soviet Military Strategy in Europe* (New York: Pergamon, 1980).
2. Zbigniew Brzezinski, "Peaceful Change in a Divided Europe," in Uwe Nerlich and James A. Thomson, eds., *Conventional Arms Control and the Security of Europe* (Boulder, Colo.: Westview Press, 1988), pp. 19–20.
3. See Daniel Nelson, *Alliance Behavior in the Warsaw Pact* (Boulder, Colo.: Westview Press, 1986), pp. 62, 66–68; Daniel Nelson, ed., *Soviet Allies: The Warsaw Pact and the Issue of Reliability* (Boulder, Colo.: Westview Press, 1984), p. 266 and chapters on individual countries; and Jeffrey Simon and Trond Gilberg, eds., *Security Implications of Nationalism in Eastern Europe* (Boulder, Colo.: Westview Press, 1986), pp. 202–12.
4. U.S. Congress, House, Committee on International Relations, Subcomittee on Europe and the Middle East, *Hearings on U.S. Policy toward Eastern Europe,* 95th Cong., 2d sess., September 7 and 12, 1978, p. 46.
5. Robert H. McNeal, ed., *International Relations among Communists* (Englewood Cliffs, N.J.: Prentice-Hall, 1967), p. 83.
6. Zbigniew Brzezinski, "America and Europe," *Foreign Affairs,* 49, no. 1 (October 1970): pp. 11–30. See also Brzezinski, "The Framework of East-West Reconciliation," *Foreign Affairs* 46, no. 2 (January 1968): 256–75, and Brzezinski, *Alternative to Partition: For a Broader Conception of America's Role in Europe* (New York: McGraw-Hill, 1965).
7. Helsinki Commission, *The Helsinki Process,* 1985, pp. 19, 29.
8. Robert Barry, quoted in Vladimir Kusin, "Brezhnev Doctrine Rejected in the Stockholm Agreement?" *RFE Research,* September 29, 1986, p. 3. The Stockholm Agreement extended the coverage of major CBMs on Soviet

territory to the Urals; required earlier notification (42 days) of "military activities," lowering the threshold to 13,000 troops, 300 tanks,200 missions by aircraft or helicopters, or 3,000 troops in an amphibious landing or parachute drop; specified notification by annual calendar of exercises by more than 40,000 troops; and made mandatory the invitation of two observers from each signatory to military activities involving more than 17,000 troops or 5,000 in an amphibious landing or parachute drop. States suspecting non compliance could also request mandatory inspections on short notice. Inspections were limited by quota, members of an alliance could resort to "challenge inspections" against each other, and military "alerts" were exempted from the notification requirement. See John Borawski, *From the Atlantic to the Urals: Negotiating Arms Control at the Stockholm Conference* (New York: Pergamon, 1988), p. 111 and passim.

9. S. Kovalev, *Pravda*, September 26, 1968.
10. Zdenek Mlynar, *Night Frost in Prague: The End of Humane Socialism* (London: Hurst, 1980), p. 241.
11. *New York Times*, May 8, 1976.
12. *Pravda*, November 3, 1987. The reappraisal of alliance relations had begun the previous year, when the Soviet Politburo issued a relevant memorandum and a CMEA summit was convened in Moscow. See Ronald Asmus, "Evolution of Soviet-East European Relations under Mikhail Gorbachev," *RFE Research*, September 29, 1989, p. 2.
13. Tass, July 7, 8, 1989.
14. *New York Times*, August 16, 1989.
15. *Washington Post*, May 8, 1989. See also Seweryn Bialer, "'New Thinking' and Soviet Foreign Policy," *Survival* 30, no. 4 (July/August 1988): 291–309; Robert Legvold, "The Revolution in Soviet Foreign Policy," *Foreign Affairs*, Vol. 68, No. 1 (Fall 1989): 82–98; Charles Gati, "Gorbachev and Eastern Europe," *Foreign Affairs* 65, no. 5 (Summer 1987): 958–75; Stephen M. Meyer, "The Sources and Prospects of Gorbachev's New Political Thinking on Security," *International Security*, 13, no. 2 (Fall 1988), 124–63; and Thomas M. Cynkin, "*Glasnost, perestroika,* and Eastern Europe," *Survival* 30, no. 4 (July/August 1988): pp. 310–31.
16. *New York Times*, October 24, 1989.
17. *Sunday Star* (Toronto), April 2, 1989.
18. *New York Times*, October 24, 1989.
19. Reuter, October 16, 1989.
20. Associated Press, October 28, 1989.
21. *New York Times*, November 12, 1989.
22. *New York Times*, December 5, 1989.
23. *Moscow News*, January 1990, no. 2.
24. Reuter, November 20, 1989.
25. *Ogonek*, no. 11, 1990, quoted in *RFE/RL Daily Report*, March 22, 1990.
26. W. W. Rostow, "On Ending the Cold War," *Foreign Affairs*, 65, no. 4 (Spring 1987): 848.

27. Dean Acheson, "The Illusion of Disengagement," *Foreign Affairs* 36, no. 3 (1958): p. 378. See also Bennett Kovrig, *The Myth of Liberation: East-Central Europe in U.S. Diplomacy and Politics since 1941* (Baltimore: Johns Hopkins University Press, 1973) pp. 227–28.

28. Henry Kissinger, *White House Years* (Boston: Little, Brown, 1979), p. 949, and see also pp. 399–402, 947–48.

29. Raymond L. Garthoff, *Detente and Confrontation: American-Soviet Relations from Nixon to Reagan* (Washington, D.C.: Brookings Institution, 1985), p. 481n19.

30. On the early phase of MBFR, see John G. Keliher, *The Negotiations on Mutual and Balanced Force Reductions: The Search for Arms Control in Central Europe* (New York: Pergamon, 1980).

31. A German analyst reflected that "the entire Western effort at Vienna since 1973 could be viewed as a protracted disengagement from that trap inch by inch" (Lothar Ruehl, *MBFR: Lessons and Problems* [London: International Institute of Strategic Studies, 1982], pp. 33–34).

32. U.S. Congress, *Hearings on U.S. Policy toward Eastern Europe*, p. 39. See also Jonathan Dean, *Watershed in Europe: Dismantling the East-West Military Confrontation* (Lexington, Mass.: Lexington Books/D.C. Heath, 1987), pp. 267–69.

33. Independent Commission on Disarmament and Security Issues, *Common Security: A Blueprint for Survival* (New York: Simon and Schuster, 1982), pp. 182–83.

34. Joachim Krause, *Prospects for Conventional Arms Control in Europe* (Boulder, Colo.: Westview Press/Institute for East-West Security Studies, 1988), p. 26.

35. William H. Luers, "The U.S. and Eastern Europe," *Foreign Affairs*, 65, no. 5 (Summer 1987): p. 991.

36. Zbigniew Brzezinski, *Game Plan: How to Conduct the U.S.-Soviet Contest* (Boston: Atlantic Monthly Press, 1986), pp. 105–8, and Brzezinski, "Peaceful Change in a Divided Europe," pp. 21–22. The case for Europeanization was also argued eloquently by David Calleo in *Beyond American Hegemony: The Future of the Western Alliance* (New York: Basic Books, 1988).

37. *New York Times,* September 24, 1986.

38. *Washington Post,* April 25, 1987; Senator Bill Bradley's press release, August 27, 1987.

39. Speech at Davos, Switzerland, February 1, 1987, quoted in John Borawski, "Toward Conventional Stability in Europe?" *Washington Quarterly,* 10, no. 4 (Autumn 1987): 28.

40. See Jonathan Dean, "Will Negotiated Force Reductions Build Down the NATO-Warsaw Pact Confrontation?" *Washington Quarterly* 11, no. 2 (Spring 1988): 73, and David S. Yost, "Beyond MBFR: The Atlantic to Urals Gambit," *Orbis* 31, no. 1 (Spring 1987): pp. 99–134.

41. *International Herald Tribune,* January 13, 1988.

42. NATO communique, Brussels, March 3, 1988.
43. NATO, *Conventional Forces in Europe: The Facts,* Brussels, November 1988. A smaller imbalance was reported by the International Institute of Strategic Studies (*The Military Balance 1988–89* [London, 1988]), while the Warsaw Pact on January 30, 1989, released statistics widely differing from those of NATO (*The Economist,* February 4, 1989, p. 45).
44. Before the withdrawals, the Soviet Union had 562,000 troops stationed in Eastern Europe: 380,000 in the GDR, 80,000 in Czechoslovakia, 62,000 in Hungary, and 40,000 in Poland. The concurrent reorganization of Soviet forces complicated precise calculation of the net reductions that could be expected by 1991; see the estimates in Douglas Clarke, "Warsaw Pact Arms Cuts in Europe," *RFE Research,* February 22, 1989.
45. International Institute of Strategic Studies, *The Military Balance 1989–90* (London, 1989).
46. Csaba Tabajdi in *Magyar Hirlap,* September 27, 1988; Radio Budapest, July 26, 1989.
47. Associated Press, January 20, 1989.
48. *New York Times,* July 7, 1989.
49. *New York Times,* April 25, 1989.
50. *Washington Post,* May 8, 1989.
51. Reuter, July 8, 10, 1989.
52. Associated Press, October 3, 1989.
53. *The Economist,* September 16, 1989, p. 50; *Globe and Mail,* (Toronto), October 21, 1989.
54. Associated Press, January 20, 1990.
55. Reuter, January 24, 1990.
56. Tass, January 21, 1990.
57. Douglas C. Clarke, "What Future for the Warsaw Pact?" Radio Free Europe, *Report on Eastern Europe,* vol. 1, no. 3., (January 19, 1990): 39.
58. *New York Times,* November 12, 1989.
59. Vlad Sobell, "Austria, Hungary, and the Question of Neutrality," *RFE Research,* August 14, 1989, p. 31.
60. *RFE/RL Daily Report,* November 9, 1989.
61. *New York Times,* June 8, 1990.
62. *Financial Times,* January 8, 1990.
63. *Globe and Mail* (Toronto), February 1, 1990.
64. *New York Times,* July 7, 1990.
65. Thomas Bailey, *America Faces Russia* (New York: Columbia University Press, 1950), p. 327, quoted in Alan A. Platt, "The Setting of U.S. Foreign Policy toward the Federal Republic of Germany," in Uwe Nerlich and James A. Thomson, eds., *The Soviet Problem in American-German Relations* (New York: Crane Russak, 1985), p. 65.
66. Josef Joffe, "The View from Bonn: The Tacit Alliance," in Lincoln Gordon, *Eroding Empire: Western Relations with Eastern Europe* (Washington, D.C.: Brookings Institution, 1987), pp. 139–40.

67. See Angela Stent, *From Embargo to Ostpolitik* (New York: Cambridge University Press, 1981).
68. Quoted in Platt, "The Setting of U.S. Foreign Policy," p. 75.
69. See Joffe, "The View from Bonn," pp. 163–64.
70. These 1985 statistics are tabulated in Gordon, *Eroding Empire*, pp. 332–33.
71. *New York Times,* July 18, 1988.
72. For 1989, it was estimated that the GDR would earn DM 525 million in transit taxes for road traffic to West Berlin, DM 450 million from compulsory currency exchange for visitors, DM 200 million for postal services, over DM 400 million for "humanitarian services" (including ransom for political prisoners, some 2,500 in 1985 alone), and another DM 2–3 billion from sundry private remittances, bringing the total hard currency transfer close to DM 5 billion, or some $2.6 billion (*The Economist,* 7 October 1989, p. 56). See also Joffe, "The View from Bonn," p. 157; Michael Kaser, "The Economic Dimension," in Edwina Moreton, ed., *Germany between East and West* (Cambridge: Cambridge University Press, 1987), pp. 128–33; and Lawrence L. Whetten, *Germany's Ostpolitik: Relations between the Federal Republic and the Warsaw Pact Countries* (London: Oxford University Press, 1971), p. 132.
73. *Washington Post,* September 14, 1987.
74. *Der Spiegel,* December 22, 1986, pp. 28–29.
75. Reuter, January 6, 1990.
76. *The Independent* (London), May 13, 1989.
77. United States Information Service, September 15, 1989.
78. *The Economist,* May 27, 1989, p. 47.
79. Reuter, January 12, 1988.
80. Reuter, June 13, 1988.
81. *New York Times,* October 29, 1988.
82. Angela E. Stent, "East German Quest for Legitimacy," *Problems of Communism* 35, no. 2 (March-April 1986): 85.
83. See the review article by Joyce Marie Mushaben, "A Search for Identity: The 'German Question' in Atlantic Alliance Relations," *World Politics* 40, no. 3 (April 1988): 403–7.
84. Barbara Donovan, "Reform and the Existence of the GDR," *RFE Research,* August 25, 1989, pp. 1–2.
85. *Pravda,* October 5, 1989; Associated Press, October 21, 1989.
86. Jim Hoagland, "Europe's Destiny," *Foreign Affairs* 69, no. 1 (Spring 1990): 40.
87. Associated Press, November 9, 1989.
88. *New York Times,* January 7, 1990.
89. *New York Times,* December 12, 1989.
90. Quoted in *The Economist,* May 12, 1990, p. 49.
91. *The Economist,* December 16, 1989, p. 51.

92. *New York Times,* December 12, 1989.
93. *The Economist,* January 27, 1990, p. 49. The survey found 61 percent of Americans in favor and 13 percent opposed, with only 29 percent expressing concern about a German-dominated Europe. Another poll found 71 percent of Americans favoring unification (*Business Week,* November 27, 1989, p. 70).
94. *New York Times,* November 12, 1989; *Globe and Mail* (Toronto), November 14, 1989.
95. *New York Times,* December 12, 1989.
96. *Globe and Mail,* January 31, 1990; Reuter, February 1, 1990.
97. Reuter, February 1, 2, 1990.
98. *Globe and Mail* (Toronto), February 15, 1990.
99. Associated Press, February 15, 1990.
100. *New York Times,* February 26, 1990.
101. *Washington Post,* February 25, 1990.
102. *RFE/RL Daily Report,* April 23, 1990.
103. *Toronto Star,* June 4, 1989.
104. Associated Press, February 21, 1990.
105. *Financial Times,* January 5, 1990; *New York Times,* November 15, 1989.
106. *The Economist,* January 27, 1990, p. 49, and October 6, 1990, p. 53.
107. *Time,* November 6, 1989, p. 27.
108. *The Economist,* November 11, 1989, p. 14.
109. Quoted by Andre Fontaine in *Le Monde,* October 12, 1989; *New York Times,* November 110, 1989.
110. *The Economist,* January 27, 1990, p. 49. A poll taken in February found 64 percent of Poles opposed to unification (*The Independent* (London), February 19, 1990).
111. *Globe and Mail* (Toronto), March 19, 1990.
112. Reuter, November 9, 1989. See Jan B. de Weydenthal, "The Politics of the Oder-Neisse Line," *RFE Research,* December 15, 1989.
113. Associated Press, January 3, 1990; *New York Times,* January 6, 1990; Radio Free Europe, *Report on Eastern Europe,* September 14, 1990, p. 15.
114. Reuter, November 14, 1989.
115. Reuter, January 18, 1990; *Toronto Star,* March 11, 1990.
116. Associate Press, October 4, 1990
117. See Dominic Lawson, "Saying the Unsayable about the Germans," *The Spectator* (London), July 14, 1990, pp. 8–10.
118. United States Information Service, September 15, 1989.
119. Quoted in Gebhard Schweigler, "The Domestic Setting of West German Foreign Policy," in Nerlich and Thomson, *The Soviet Problem in American-German Relations,* p. 44.
120. For the debate on these issues, see George Schopflin and Nancy Wood, eds., *In Search of Central Europe* (London: Polity Press, 1989), and the special issue of *Daedalus* 119, no. 1 (Winter 1990), especially the contri-

butions of Timothy Garton Ash, "Mitteleuropa?" Tony Judt, "The Rediscovery of Central Europe," and Jacques Rupnik, "Central Europe or Mitteleuropa?"

121. Dominique Moisi, "French Policy toward Central and Eastern Europe," in William F. Griffith, ed., *Central and Eastern Europe: The Opening Curtain* (Boulder, Colo.: Westview Press, 1989), pp. 364–65. See also Pierre Hassner, "The View from Paris," in Gordon, *Eroding Empire*, pp. 188–231, and Alfred Grosser, "Pour une 'Ostpolitik' franco-allemande," *Le Monde,* October 22, 1987.

122. Quoted in Timothy Garton Ash, "Tuning the Violins," *The Spectator,* December 10, 1988, p. 18.

123. *Financial Times,* October 16, 1989; *The Economist,* October 14, 1989, p. 55.

124. See Zbigniew Brzezinski, *The Grand Failure: The Birth and Death of Communism in the Twentieth Century* (New York: Scribner's, 1989).

125. *Financial Times,* May 18, 1988.

126. *The Economist,* January 27, 1990, p. 49.

127. Radio Free Europe, *Report on Eastern Europe,* September 14, 1990, p. 14, and July 27, 1990, p. 18.

128. *Globe and Mail* (Toronto), December 11, 1989.

129. United States Information Service, June 1, 1989.

130. *Krasnaya Zvezda,* February 10, 1990, quoted in *RFE/RL Daily Report,* February 12, 1990; *Globe and Mail* (Toronto), June 21, 1990.

131. Charles Gati, *The Bloc that Failed: Soviet-East European Relations in Transition* (Bloomington: Indiana University Press, 1990), p. 192.

132. *Newsweek,* September 19, 1988, pp. 34, 37.

133. United States Information Service, January 18, 1990.

134. *Washington Post,* May 5, 1990.

135. In April 1990, a majority of West Germans favored American withdrawal (Associated Press, April 12, 1990). In June, 25 percent favored withdrawal, 28 percent continued stationing, and a further 39 percent mixed NATO units (*The Economist,* June 30, 1990, p. 46).

Bibliography

The following is a list of secondary sources referred to in the endnotes. Published and unpublished official documents, Radio Free Europe Research Reports, and daily press sources are not included.

Acheson, Dean. *Present at the Creations.* New York: Norton, 1969.
———. "The Illusion of Disengagement." *Foreign Affairs,* Vol. 36, No. 3 (1958).
Ahrari, Mohammad E., ed. *Ethnic Groups in U.S. Foreign Policy.* New York: Greenwood, 1987.
Ash, Timothy Garton. "Refolution [sic] in Hungary and Poland." *The New York Review,* 17 August 1989.
Assetto, Valerie J. *The Soviet Bloc in the IMF and the IBRD.* Boulder: Westview, 1988.
Baring, Arnulf. *Der 17. Juni 1953.* Bonn: Deutsche Bundesverlag, 1958.
Bethell, Nicholas. *The Great Betrayal.* London: Hodder & Stoughton, 1984.
Bezymensky, Lev. "General Donovan's Balkan Plan." *International Affairs* (Moscow), No. 8, August 1987.
Bialer, Seweryn. " 'New Thinking' in Soviet Foreign Policy." *Foreign Affairs,* Vol. 68, No. 1 (Fall 1989).
Bohlen, Charles E. *Witness to History, 1929–1969.* New York: Norton, 1973.
Boll, Michael M. *Cold War in the Balkans: American Foreign Policy and the Emergence of Communist Bulgaria, 1943–1947.* Lexington: University Press of Kentucky, 1984.

Borawski, John. *From the Atlantic to the Urals: Negotiating Arms Control at the Stockholm Confrence.* New York: Pergamon, 1988.

Borsody, Stephen, ed. *The Hungarians: A Divided Nation.* New Haven: Yale C.I.A.S., 1988.

Brada, Joseph C., et al, eds. *Economic Adjustment and Reform in Eastern Europe and Soviet Union.* Durham: Duke University Press, 1988.

Brant, Stefan. *The East German Rising.* London: Thames & Hudson, 1955.

Brzezinski, Zbigniew. *Alternative to Partition: For a Broader Conception of America's Role in Europe.* New York: McGraw-Hill, 1965.

———. *Game Plan: How to Conduct the U.S.-Soviet Contest.* Boston: Atlantic Monthly Press, 1986.

———. *The Grand Failure: The Birth and Death of Communism in the Twentieth Century.* New York: Scribners, 1989.

———. *Power and Principle: Memoirs of the National Security Adviser, 1977–1981.* New York: Farrar, Straus, Giroux, 1983.

———. "America and Europe." *Foreign Affairs,* Vol. 49, No. 1 (October 1970).

———. "The Framework of East-West Reconciliation. *Foreign Affairs,* Vol. 46, No. 2 (January 1968).

———. "White House Diary, 1980." *Orbis,* Winter 1988.

Brzezinski, Zbigniew, and William E. Griffith. "Peaceful Engagement in Eastern Europe." *Foreign Affairs,* Vol. 39, No. 4 (1961).

Bucy, J.F. "Technology Transfer and East-West Trade. *International Security,* Vol. 5, No. 3 (Winter 1980–81).

Bullitt, William C. "How We Won the War and Lost the Peace." *Life,* 30 August 1948.

Burnham, James. *Containment or Liberation.* New York: John Day, 1953.

Byrnes, James F. *Speaking Frankly.* New York: Harper , 1947.

Calleo, David P. *Beyond American Hegemony: The Future of the Western Alliance.* New York: Basic Books, 1988.

Campbell, John C. "Czechoslovakia: American Choices, Past and Future. *Canadian Slavonic Papers,* Vol. 11, No. 1 (1969).

Catudal, Honore M. *Kennedy and the Berlin Wall Crisis: A Case Study in U.S. Decision Making.* Berlin: Berlin Verlag, 1980.

Chamberlin, William Henry. *Beyond Containment.* Chicago: Regnery, 1953.

Churchill, Winston S. *The Second World War: Triumph and Tradegy.* Boston: Houghton Mifflin, 1953.

Cline, Ray. *Secrets, Spies, and Scholars.* New York: Acropolis, 1976.

Colby, William. *Honorable Men: My Life in the CIA.* New York: Simon and Schuster, 1978.

Colville, John. *The Fringes of Power: Downing Street Diaries, 1939–1955.* London: Hodder and Stoughton, 1985.

Conant, James B. *My Several Lives.* New York: Harper & Row, 1970.

Cookridge, E. H. *Gehlen: Spy of the Century.* New York: Random House, 1972.

Corson, William R. *The Armies of Ignorance: The Rise of the American Intelligence Empire.* New York: Dial/James Wade, 1977.

Cranston, Maurice. *What Are Human Rights?* New York: Taplinger, 1973.

Croan, Melvin. "East Germany: Lesson in Survival." *Problems of Communism,* No. 11, 1962.

Cutler, Robert M. "Harmonizing the EEC-CMEA Relations: Never the Twain Shall Meet?" *International Affairs,* Vol. 63, No. 2 (Spring 1987).

Cynkin, Thomas M. *Soviet and American Signalling in the Polish Crisis.* London: Macmillan, 1988.

———. "*Glasnost, perestroika,* and Eastern Europe." *Survival,* Vol. 30, No. 4 (July/August 1988).

Daugherty, William E., ed. *A Psychological Warfare Casebook.* Baltimore: Johns Hopkins Press, 1958.

Davidson, Eugene. *The Death and Life of Germany.* New York: Knopf, 1959.

Davis, Lynn Etheridge. *The Cold War Begins: Soviet-American Conflict over Eastern Europe.* Princeton: Princeton University Press, 1974.

Dawisha, Karen. *Eastern Europe, Gorbachev, and Reform: The Great Challenge.* Cambridge: Cambridge University Press, 1988.

———. *The Kremlin and the Prague Spring.* Berkeley: University of California Press, 1984.

Dean, Jonathan. *Watershed in Europe: Dismantling the East-West Military Confrontation.* Lexington, Mass.: Lexington Books/Heath, 1987.

———. "Will Negotiated Force Reductions Build Down the NATO-Warsaw Pact Confrontation?" *The Washington Quarterly,* Vol. 11, No. 2 (Spring 1988).

Divine, Robert A. *Eisenhower and the Cold War.* New York: Oxford University Press, 1981.

———. *Foreign Policy and U.S. Presidential Elections, 1952–1960.* New York: New Viewpoints, 1974.

Djilas, Milovan. *Conversations with Stalin.* New York: Harcourt, Brace & World, 1962.

Douglass, Joseph C. *Soviet Military Strategy in Europe.* New York: Pergamon, 1980.

Drummond, Roscoe, and Gaston Coblentz. *Duel at the Brink.* London: Doubleday, 1961.

Dulles, John Foster. "A Policy of Boldness." *Life,* 19 May 1952.

Eisenhower, Dwight D. *Waging Peace.* Garden City, N.Y.: Doubleday, 1964.

Ellings, Richard J. *Embargoes and World Power: Lessons for American Foreign Policy.* Boulder: Westview, 1985.

Evans, Rowland, Jr., and Robert D. Novak. *Nixon in the White House: The Frustration of Power.* New York: Random House, 1971.

Ferraris, Luigi Vittorio, ed. *Report on a Negotiation: Helsinki-Geneva-Helsinki, 1972–1975.* Alphen: Sijthoff & Nordhoff, 1979.

Finer, Herman. *Dulles over Suez.* Chicago: Quadrangle, 1964.

Ford, Gerald F. *A Time to Heal.* New York: Berkeley, 1980.

Forsythe, David P. "Congress and Human Rights in U.S. Foreign Policy: The Fate of General Legislation." *Human Rights Quarterly,* Vol. 9, No. 3 (1987).

Funderburk, David B. *Pinstripes and Reds.* Washington, D.C.: Selous Foundation Press, 1987.

Gaddis, John Lewis. *Strategies of Containment: A Critical Appraisal of Postwar American National Security Policy.* New York: Oxford University Press, 1982

————. *The United States and the Origins of the Cold War, 1941–1947.* New York: Columbia University Press, 1972.

————. "Containment and the Logic of Strategy." *The National Interest,* No. 10, Winter 1987/8.

Garrett, Stephen A. *From Potsdam to Poland: American Policy toward Eastern Europe.* New York: Praeger, 1986.

Garson, Robert A. "American Foreign Policy and the Limits of Power: Eastern Europe 1946–1950." *Journal of Contemporary History,* Vol. 21, No. 3, (July 1986).

Garthoff, Raymond L. *Detente and Confrontation: American-Soviet Relations from Nixon to Reagan.* Washington, D.C.: Brookings Institution, 1985.

Gaskill, Gordon. "Timetable of a Failure." *The Virginia Quarterly Review,* Vol. 34, No. 2 (Spring 1958).

Gati, Charles. *The Bloc that Failed: Soviet-East European Relations in Transition.* Bloomington: Indiana University Press, 1990.

————. *Hungary and the Soviet Bloc.* Durham: Duke University Press, 1986.

————. "Eastern Europe on Its Own." *Foreign Affairs,* Vol. 68, No. 1 (Fall 1989).

————. "Gorbachev and Eastern Europe." *Foreign Affairs,* Vol. 65, No. 5 (Summer 1987).

————. "Polish Futures, Western Options." *Foreign Affairs,* Vol. 61, No. 2 (Winter 1982–83).

Gerson, Louis L. *The Hyphenate in Recent American Politics and Diplomacy.* Lawrence: University Press of Kansas, 1964.

Goold-Adams, Richard. *A Time of Power.* London: Weidenfeld & Nicolson, 1962.

Gorbachev, Mikhail. *Perestroika: New Thinking for Our Country and the World.* New York: Perennial Library/Harper & Row, 1987.

Gordon, Lincoln, et al. *Eroding Empire: Western Relations with Eastern Europe.* Washington, D.C.: Brookings Institution, 1987.

Griffith, William F., ed. *Central and Eastern Europe: The Opening Curtain?* Boulder: Westview, 1989.

Haig, Alexander. *Caveat: Realism, Reagan, and Foreign Policy.* New York: Macmillan, 1984.

Hanson, Philip. *Western Economic Statecraft in East-West Relations.* London: R.I.I.A./Routledge & Kegan Paul, 1988.

Harriman, W. Averell, and Elie Abel. *Special Envoy to Churchill and Stalin, 1941–1946*. New York: Random House, 1975.

Harrington, Joseph F. "Romanian-American Relations during the Kennedy Administration." *East European Quarterly,* Vol. 18, No. 2 (June 1984).

———, and Bruce Courtney. "Romanian-American Relations during the Johnson Administration." *East European Quarterly,* Vol. 22, No. 2 (June 1988).

Heuser, Beatrice. *Western "Containment" Policies in the Cold War: The Yugoslav Case, 1948–53.* London: Routledge, 1989.

Hoagland, Jim. "Europe's Destiny." *Foreign Affairs,* Vol. 69, No 1 (1990).

Holt, Robert T. *Radio Free Europe.* Minneapolis: University of Minnesota Press, 1958.

———, and Robert W. Van De Welde. *Strategic Psychological Operations and American Foreign Policy.* Chicago: University of Chicago Press, 1960.

Hough, Jerry F. *The Polish Crisis: American Policy Options.* Washington, D.C.: Brookings Institution, 1982.

Hufbauer, Gary C., and Jeffrey J. Schott. *Economic Sanctions Reconsidered: History and Current Policy.* Washington, D.C.: Institute for International Economics, 1985.

Hughes, Emmet John. *The Ordeal of Power.* New York: Atheneum, 1963.

Hull, Cordell. *The Memoirs of Cordell Hull.* New York: Hodder & Stoughton, 1948.

Hyland, William G. *Mortal Rivals: Superpower Relations from Nixon to Reagan.* New York: Random House, 1987.

Independent Commission on Disarmament and Security Issues. *Common Security: A Blueprint for Survival.* New York: Simon and Schuster, 1982.

International Institute of Strategic Studies. *The Military Balance, 1989–90.* London: I.I.S.S., 1989).

Jacoby, Tamar. "The Reagan Turnaround on Human Rights." *Foreign Affairs,* Vol. 64, No. 5 (Summer 1986).

Janos, Andrew C. *The Politics of Backwardness in Hungary, 1825–1945.* Princeton: Princeton University Press, 1982.

Johnson, Lyndon Baines. *The Vantage Point: Perspectives of the Presidency, 1963–1969.* New York: Holt, Rinehart & Winston, 1971.

Kampelman, Max M. *Three Years at the East-West Divide.* New York: Freedom House, 1983.

Kaplan, Karel. *Dans les archives du comite central: Trente ans de secrets du Bloc sovietique.* Paris: Albin Michel, 1978.

Keliher, John G. *The Negotiations on Mutual and Balanced Force Reductions: The Search for Arms Control in Central Europe.* New York: Pergamon, 1980.

Kennan, George F. *Memoirs, 1925–1950.* Boston: Little, Brown, 1967.

———. "The Sources of Soviet Conduct." *Foreign Affairs,* Vol. 25, No. 4 (July 1947).

Kertesz, Stephen D. *Between Russia and the West: Hungary and the Illusions of* ✓
Peacemaking, 1945–1947. Notre Dame: Notre Dame University Press,
1984.

Khrushchev, Nikita. *K[h]rushchev Remembers*, ed. by Strobe Talbott. Boston:
Little, Brown, 1970.

Kiraly, Bela K., et al, eds. *The First War between Socialist States: The Hungarian
Revolution of 1956 and Its Impact.* New York: Brooklyn College Press,
1984.

Kirkpatrick, Jeane. "Dictatorships and Double Standards." *Commentary*, Vol.
68, No. 5 (November 1979).

Kissinger, Henry A. *American Foreign Policy.* New York: Norton, 3rd. edn.,
1977.

———. *White House Years.* Boston: Little, Brown, 1979.

———. *Years of Upheaval.* Boston: Little, Brown, 1982.

Kolko, Joyce and Gabriel. *The Limits of Power: The World and United States
Foreign Policy, 1945–1954.* New York: Harper and Row, 1972.

Korbel, Josef. *The Communist Subversion of Czechoslovakia, 1938–1948.*
Princeton: Princeton University Press, 1959.

———. *Detente in Europe: Real or Imaginary?* Princeton: Princeton University
Press, 1972.

Kornai, Janos. *A hiany.* Budapest: Kozgazdasagi es jogi, 1982.

———. *The Road to a Free Economy.* New York: Norton, 1990. ✓

Kovrig, Bennett. *The Myth of Liberation: East-Central Europe in U.S. Diplo-*
macy and Politics since 1941. Baltimore: Johns Hopkins University Press,
1973.

Kracauer, S., and P. L. Berkman. *Satellite Mentality.* New York: Praeger,
1956.

Krause, Joachim. *Prospects for Conventional Arms Control in Europe.* Boulder:
Westview/Institute for East-West Security Studies, 1988.

Laqueur, Walter. *A World of Secrets: The Uses and Limits of Intelligence.* New
York: Basic Books, 1985.

Lash, Joseph P. *Dag Hammarskjold.* London: Cassell, 1962.

Lasky, Melvyn J., ed. *The Hungarian Revolution: A White Book.* New York,
Praeger, 1957.

Leahy, William D. *I Was There.* New York: McGraw-Hill, 1950.

Luers, William H. "The U.S. and Eastern Europe." *Foreign Affairs*, Vol. 65, No.
5 (Summer 1987).

Lukas, Richard C. *The Strange Allies: The United States and Poland, 1941–
1945.* Knoxville: University of Tennessee Press, 1978.

Lundestad, Geir. *The American Non-policy towards Eastern Europe, 1943–
1947.* New York: Humanities Press, 1975.

Macmillan, Harold. *Tides of Fortune, 1945–1955.* London: Macmillan, 1969.

Marer, Paul, and Wlodzimierz Siwinski, eds. *Creditworthiness and Reform in
Poland: Western and Polish Perspectives.* Bloomington: Indiana University
Press, 1988.

Marer, Paul, and Eugeniusz Tabaczynski. *Polish-U.S. Industrial Cooperation in the 1980s.* Bloomington: Indiana University Press, 1981.

Maresca, John J. *To Helsinki: The Conference on Security and Cooperation in Europe, 1973–1975.* Durham: Duke University Press, 1985.

Mastny, Vojtech. *Helsinki, Human Rights, and European Security: Analysis and Documentation.* Durham: Duke University Press, 1986.

———. *Russia's Road to the Cold War.* New York: Columbia University Press, 1979.

McNeal, Robert H., ed. *International Relations among Communists.* Englewood Cliffs, N.J.: Prentice-Hall, 1967.

Melvern, Linda, et al. *Techno-bandits.* Boston: Houghton Mifflin, 1984.

Meyer, Cord. *Facing Reality: From World Federalism to the CIA.* New York: Harper & Row, 1980.

Meyer, Stephen M. "The Sources and Prospects of Gorbachev's New Political Thinking on Security." *International Security,* Vol. 13, No. 2 (Fall 1988).

Michie, Allan A. *Voices through the Iron Curtain: The Radio Free Europe Story.* New York: Dodd, Mead, 1963.

Mickelson, Sig. *America's Other Voice: The Story of Radio Free Europe and Radio Liberty.* New York: Praeger, 1983.

Micunovic, Veljko. *Moscow Diary.* Garden City, N.Y.: Doubleday, 1980.

Millis, Walter, ed. *The Forrestal Diaries.* New York: Viking, 1951.

Mlynar, Zdenek. *Night Frost in Prague: The End of Humane Socialism.* London: Hurst, 1980.

Moreton, Edwina, ed. *Germany between East and West.* Cambridge: Cambridge University Press, 1987.

Mosley, Leonard. *Dulles: A Biography of Eleanor, Allen, and John Foster Dulles and Their Family Network.* New York: Dial/James Wade, 1978.

Muravchik, Joshua. *The Uncertain Crusade: Jimmy Carter and the Dilemmas of Human Rights Policy.* Lanham: Hamilton Press, 1986.

Murphy, Robert D. *Diplomat among Warriors.* Garden City, N.Y.: Doubleday, 1964.

Mushaben, Joyce Marie. "A Search for Identity: The 'German Question' in Atlantic Alliance Relations." *World Politics,* Vol. 40, No. 3 (April 1988).

Nelson, Daniel. *Alliance Behavior in the Warsaw Pact.* Boulder: Westview, 1986.

———, ed. *Soviet Allies: The Warsaw Pact and the Issue of Reliability.* Boulder: Westview, 1984.

Nerlich, Uwe, and James A. Thomson, eds. *Conventional Arms Control and the Security of Europe.* Boulder: Westview, 1988.

———. *The Soviet Problem in American-German Relations.* New York: Crane Russak, 1985.

Newsom, David D., ed. *The Diplomacy of Human Rights.* Lanham: University Press of America, 1986.

Nitze, Paul H. *U.S. Foreign Policy, 1945–1955.* Washington: Foreign Policy Association, 1956.

Nord, Pierre and Jacques Bergier. *L'actuelle guerre secrete.* Paris: Encyclopedie Planete, 1967.

Novak, Michael. "Ordinary People." *The National Interest,* Fall 1986.

Pacepa, Ion Mihai. *Red Horizons.* Washington, D.C.: Regnery Gateway, 1987.

Palmer, Alan. *The Lands Between: A History of East-Central Europe since the Congress of Vienna.* London: Weidenfeld and Nicolson, 1970.

Paterson, Thomas G. *Soviet-American Confrontation: Postwar Reconstruction and the Origins of the Cold War.* Baltimore: Johns Hopkins University Press, 1973.

Penkovskiy, Oleg. *The Penkovskiy Papers.* Garden City, N.Y.: Doubleday, 1980.

Phillips, Ann L. *Soviet Policy toward East Germany Reconsidered: The Postwar Decade.* New York: Greenwood, 1986.

Pilon, Roger. "The Idea of Human Rights." *The National Interest,* Fall 1986.

Pisar, Samuel. *Coexistence and Commerce: Guidelines for Transactions between East and West.* New York: McGraw-Hill, 1970.

Plattner, Marc F., ed. *Human Rights in Our Time.* Boulder: Westview, 1984.

Plock, Ernest D. *The Basic Treaty and the Evolution of East-West German Relations.* Boulder: Westview, 1986.

Pollard, Robert A. *Economic Security and the Origins of the Cold War, 1945– 1950.* New York: Columbia University Press, 1985.

Portes, Richard. "East Europe's Debt to the West: Interdependence is a Two-way Street." *Foreign Affairs,* Vol. 55, No. 4(July 1977).

Potichnyj, Peter, and Jane P. Shapiro, eds. *From Cold War to Detente.* New York: Praeger, 1976.

Powers, Thomas. *The Man Who Kept the Secrets: Richard Helms and the CIA.* (New York: Knopf, 1979.

Prados, John. *Presidents' Secret Wars: CIA and Pentagon Covert Operations from World War II through to Iranscam.* New York: Quill/Morrow, 1986.

Ranelagh, John. *The Agency: The Rise and Decline of the CIA.* New York: Simon and Schuster, 1986.

Reale, Eugenio. *Avec Jacques Duclos: Au banc des accuses a la reunion constitutive du Kominform a Szklarska Poreba (22–27 septembre 1947).* Paris: Plon, 1958.

Remington, Robin A. *Winter in Prague.* Cambridge, Mass.: MIT Press, 1969.

Rode, Reinhard, and Hanns-D. Jacobsen, eds. *Economic Warfare or Detente: An Assessment of East-West Relations in the 1980s.* Boulder: Westview, 1985.

Roosevelt, Elliot. *As He Saw It.* New York: Duell, Sloan & Pearce, 1946.

Rostow, W. W. *The Division of Europe after World War II: 1946.* Austin: University of Texas Press, 1982.

———. "On Ending the Cold War." *Foreign Affairs,* Vol. 65, No. 4 (Spring 1987).

Ruehl, Lothar. *MBFR: Lessons and Problems.* London: International Institute of Strategic Studies, 1982.

Schmidt, Hans A., ed. *US Occupation in Europe after World War II*. Lawrence: Regents Press of Kansas, 1978.

Schopflin, George, and Nancy Wood, eds. *In Search of Central Europe*. London: Polity Press, 1989.

Sesardic, Neven, and Domenico Settembrini. *Marxian Utopia?* London: Centre for Research into Communist Economies, 1985.

Silberman, Laurence. "Yugoslavia's 'Old' Communism." *Foreign Policy*, Spring 1977.

Simon, Jeffrey, and Trond Gilberg, eds. *Security Implications of Nationalism in Eastern Europe*. Boulder: Westview, 1986.

Sizoo, Jan, and Rudolf Th. Jurrjens. *CSCE Decision-making: The Madrid Experience*. The Hague: Nijhoff, 1984.

Skilling, H. Gordon. "CSCE at Madrid." *Problems of Communism*, Vol. 30, July-August 1981.

Smith, Bradley F. *The Shadow Warriors: O.S.S. and the Origins of the C.I.A.* New York: Basic Books, 1983.

Smith, Gordon B. *The Politics of East-West Trade*. Boulder: Westview, 1984.

Smith, Jean Edward. *Germany beyond the Wall*. Boston: Little, Brown, 1969.

Spencer, Robert, ed. *Canada and the Conference on Security and Co-operation in Europe*. Toronto: Center for International Studies, 1984.

Stent, Angela. *From Embargo to Ostpolitik*. New York: Cambridge University Press, 1981.

———. "East German Quest for Legitimacy." *Problems of Communism*, March-April 1986.

Stephen, Stewart. *Operation Splinter Factor*. Philadelphia: Lippincott, 1974.

Stettinius, Edward R., Jr. *Roosevelt and the Russians: The Yalta Conference*. Garden City, N.Y.: Doubleday, 1950.

Sulzberger, C. L. *A Long Row of Candles: Memoirs & Diaries, (1934–1954)*. New York: Macmillan, 1969.

———. *The Last of the Giants*. New York: Macmillan, 1970.

Suvorov, Viktor. *The Liberators*. London: Hamish Hamilton, 1981.

Taylor, Edmond. "The Lessons of Hungary." *The Reporter*, 27 December 1956.

Terry, Sarah Meiklejohn, ed. *Soviet Policy in Eastern Europe*. New Haven: Yale University Press, 1984.

Theoharis, Athan G. *The Yalta Myths: An Issue in U.S. Politics, 1945–1955*. Columbia: University of Missouri Press, 1970.

Truman, Harry S. *Memoirs: Years of Decisions*. Garden City, N.Y.: Doubleday, 1955.

———. *Memoirs: Years of Trial and Hope*. Garden City, N.Y.: Doubleday, 1956.

Turner, Stansfield. *Secrecy and Democracy: The CIA in Transition*. Boston: Houghton Mifflin, 1985.

Ulam, Adam B. *Expansion & Coexistence: The History of Soviet Foreign Policy, 1917–67*. New York: Praeger, 1968.

Ullmann, Walter. *The United States in Prague, 1945–1948*. Boulder: East European Quarterly, 1978.

Valenta, Jiri. *Soviet Intervention in Czechoslovakia, 1968: Anatomy of a Decision*. Baltimore: Johns Hopkins University Press, 1979.

Vucinich, Wayne S., ed. *At the Brink of War and Peace: The Tito-Stalin Split in a Historic Perspective*. New York: Columbia University Press, 1982.

Weintal, Edward, and Charles Bartlett. *Facing the Brink*. New York: Scribner's, 1967.

Whetten, Lawrence L. *Germany's Ostpolitik: Relations between the Federal Republic and the Warsaw Pact Countries*. London: Oxford University Press, 1971.

Winiecki, Jan. *The Distorted World of Soviet-type Economies*. Pittsburgh: Pittsburgh University Press, 1988.

———. *Gorbachev's Way Out?* London: Centre for Research into Communist Economies, 1988.

Wolfers, Arnold, ed. *Alliance Policy in the Cold War*. Baltimore: Johns Hopkins Press, 1959.

Woodward, Bob. *Veil: The Secret Wars of the CIA, 1981–1987*. New York: Simon and Schuster, 1987.

Yergin, Daniel. *Shattered Peace*. New York: Houghton Mifflin, 1977.

Yost, David S. "Beyond MBFR: The Atlantic to Urals Gambit." *Orbis*, Vol. 31, No.1 (Spring 1987).

Zinner, Paul E., ed. *National Communism and Popular Revolt in Eastern Europe*. New York: Columbia University Press, 1956.

Index

188⁵